TWO ROADS TO
WAR

TWO ROADS TO WAR

WAR

The French and British Air Arms
from Versailles to Dunkirk

ROBIN HIGHAM

NAVAL INSTITUTE PRESS
ANNAPOLIS, MARYLAND

Naval Institute Press
291 Wood Road
Annapolis, MD 21402

Library of Congress Cataloging-in-Publication Data
Higham, Robin D. S.
  Two roads to war : the French and British air arms from Versailles to Dunkirk / Robin Higham.
     p. cm.
  Includes bibliographical references and index.
  ISBN 978-1-61251-058-3 (hbk. : alk. paper) — ISBN 978-1-61251-085-9 (e-book) 1. World War, 1939-1945—Aerial operations, French. 2. World War, 1939-1945—Campaigns—France. 3. Air power—France—History—20th century. 4. World War, 1939-1945—Aerial operations, British. 5. Britain, Battle of, Great Britain, 1940. 6. Air power—Great Britain—History—20th century. I. Title. II. Title: French and British air arms from Versailles to Dunkirk.
  D788.H54 2012
  940.54'4941--dc23
                              2011051954

20 19 18 17 16 15 14 13 12   9 8 7 6 5 4 3 2 1
First printing

The publisher wishes to express its gratitude to Andrew Thomas, Tony Holmes, and Peter B. Mersky for their assistance in obtaining the photographs used on the cover of this volume and the author's forthcoming *Unflinching Zeal: The Air Battles over France and Britain, May–October 1940*.

To Barbara, for sixty years of happiness,
companionship, support, and faith.

CONTENTS

TABLES

ABBREVIATIONS

AA	antiaircraft (Br.); for French, *see* DCA
AASF	Advanced Air Striking Force (Br.)
ACBEF	Air Component of the British Expeditionary Force
ADGB	Air Defence of Great Britain
AHB	Air Historical Branch (Br.)
AIR	Air Ministry and RAF Records (Br.)
AMSO	air member for supply and organization (Br.)
AMSR	air member for supply and research (Br.)
AOC	air officer commanding (Br.)
AOC-in-C	air officer commanding in chief (Br.)
BAFF	British Air Forces France, 1940
BCR	bomber-combat-reconnaissance aircraft (Fr.)
BEF	British Expeditionary Force
C_3	command, control, and communications (Br.)
CAS	chief of the Air Staff (Br.)
CGPF	Confédération Générale du Patronat Français; general confederation of French *patronats* (Fr.)
CGT	Confédération Générale du Travail; general confederation of labor (Fr.)
CH	Chain Home [RDF stations] (Br.)
CID	Committee of Imperial Defence (Br.)
CIGS	chief of the Imperial General Staff (Br.)
CSA	Conseil Supérieur de l'Air: supreme air council (Fr.)
CSDN	Conseil Supérieur de la Défense Nationale; superior council of national defense (Fr.)
CSG	Conseil Supérieur de la Guerre; superior council of war (Fr.)
CSSAD	Committee for the Scientific Survey of Air Defence (Br.)
DAT	Défense Aérienne du Territoire; air defense of the territory (Fr.)
DCA	*défense contre avions*; defense against aircraft (Fr.); for British, *see* AA

DCAS	deputy chief of the Air Staff (Br.)
EKW	Eidgenössische Konstruktions Werkstätte; Swiss federal construction works
FAA	Fleet Air Arm (Br.)
GQG	Grand Quartier-Général: army field HQ (Fr.)
GQGA	the HQ of the Armée de l'Air in wartime (Fr.)
GSAF	état-majeur de l'Armée de l'Air; general staff air force (Fr.)
HDAF	Home Defence Air Force (Br.)
HQ	headquarters
IFF	identification, friend or foe (Br.)
MT	motor transport (Br.)
NCO	noncommissioned officer (Br.); *sous-officier* (Fr.)
ORC	Operational Requirements Committee (Br.)
POL	petrol (gasoline), oil, and lubricants (Br.)
PSOC	Principal Supply Officers Committee (Br.)
RAE	Royal Aircraft Establishment (Br.)
RAF	Royal Air Force (Br.)
RAFVR	Royal Air Force Volunteer Reserve (Br.)
RDF	radio direction finding, known after 1943 as radar
RFC	Royal Flying Corps (Br.)
RNAS	Royal Naval Air Service (Br.)
R/T	radio telephone (Br.)
SBAC	Society of British Aircraft Constructors (Br.)
SD	secret document [ex., *SD98*] (Br.)
SGA	Société Générale d'Aéronautique; general aeronautical society (Fr.)
SHAA	Service Historique de l'Armée de l'Air: air force historical service (Fr.)
SPAD	Société Pour l'Aviation et ses Dérivés; company for aviation and its derivatives (Fr.)
WA	Western Air (Br.)
WIS	wireless intelligence screen
ZOAE	Zone d'Opérations Est; air zone of operations east (Fr.)
ZOAN	Zone d'Opérations Nord; air zone of operations north (Fr.)
ZOANE	Zone d'Opérations Nord-Est; air zone of operations northeast (Fr.)
ZOAS	Zone d'Opérations Sud; air zone of operations south (Fr.)

PREFACE

Two Roads to War is not about the defeat of France per se, but rather about how the air side of the two victorious allies of 1918, with the world's two largest air services, suffered such different fates during May–September 1940. In one sense this is a narrow presentation focusing on the badly neglected tale of the Arme Aéronautique (French air arm) of the Armée de Terre (French army)—after 1933, the Armée de l'Air (French air force). Within that framework this work briefly examines much of the French structure, including the geographic, social, political, economic, and technological base on which the aeronautical edifice was erected, as well as those who controlled its destiny, its enemies, the legacies of the Great War (World War I), and defense policies.[1]

Yet this history is not restricted to the French side. It also crosses the English Channel to compare what happened in Paris with the background and actions in London. Airpower should have been an important part of the defense of France during 1940, as it once had been in 1918, but it was not. That is what this book is about. It uses the British side of the story in a sense as a control to illustrate what could have been possible, not to denigrate the French. Hopefully, what I have to say herein will provide new insights and a middle ground.

The two major historiographical controversies of the interwar years—appeasement and the fall of France—are both peripheral to this book. In both debates the analysis has been cyclical as new generations view the two topics.

Comparative Studies

The historians of modern France, especially those in Gaul, have not exercised due diligence in seeking explanations of the catastrophe, the calamity, the defeat of 1940. There is no question that it was a military defeat, and for that the military undoubtedly deserves the blame, but that only explains the immediate cause.

France was a democracy and so the rulers of the Troisième République (third republic) have to shoulder at least their fair share of the burden because they, as the superior authority, did not prepare France for war or develop a viable alternative. Briefly during January–June 1932 there was a French defense minister, Édouard Daladier, who became defense minister from 1936 almost to the end of the war in June 1940, who was a veteran of World War I, as were others. But it was Daladier's responsibility to see that the armed forces, notably the Armée de Terre and the Armée de l'Air, had doctrines and the wherewithal that meshed and met the basic needs of French defense. That quarrelsome uncertainty affected the development and production of weapons, notably of tanks and aircraft, and the best modern conception of their use in Gallic circumstances.

Gen. Maurice Gamelin was only in favor of tanks as support for the infantry, not as de Gaulle envisaged them as an arm like the cavalry. He had even less use for aircraft, and his basic strategy of meeting the Germans far forward in Belgium with the Dyle/Breda plan so as not to fight on French soil was fundamentally flawed, even when seen as parrying the initial German thrust; that thrust, of course, came as a surprise, and he had no reserves to counter it. But as this work shows, Gamelin was a wet blanket where the Armée de l'Air was concerned, and the accession to the Boulevard Victor of Guy La Chambre, a Gamelin man from the Ministère de la Guerre (ministry of war) who favored Armée de Terre cooperation in all its forms, was retrograde and too late.

In that era of the Technological Revolution in aviation, a lack of doctrine stunted the evolution of modern aircraft. The result was that the Armée de l'Air in May 1940 did not have fighters equal to the German Me-109, and had few modern bombers and the engines to power them, certainly none equal in quality and quantity to the Do-17, the He-111, the Ju-88, and the Stuka. In addition, most of the Armée de l'Air's reconnaissance and observation machines were equal to the Luftwaffe's Hs-126. Neither did the Armée de l'Air have the necessary air and ground crew, nor antiaircraft (DCA, *défense contre avions*), the French flak. For those failings the chief of État-Majeur de l'Armée de l'Air (GSAF; general staff air force) must be blamed. These people lacked the training, the vision, and the skills to solve the problems.

The historiographic debate about the fall of France emerged immediately from 1940. Marshal Philippe Pétain, as the head of the Vichy regime, blamed the rulers of the Troisième République for leading the country down the path to ruin, and later added that France was being punished for the moral failure of the rotten République.[2] The Riom *procès* of 1942 tried unsuccessfully to pin the blame on the leadership; and then, too, Professor Marc Bloch, who had served in the Armée de Terre during 1914–1918 war and again in 1939–1940, stressed the loss of faith of the upper classes in the greatness of France after the Front Populaire (Socialist popular front) election success of 1936.[3] He thus had traced the decline to Fascism and defeatism. Even before Marc Bloch's manuscript, *Strange Defeat,* written in 1940 and published in 1946, foreign-policy journalist André Géraud under the pseudonym Pertinax had written *Les Fossoyeurs* (later translated as *The Gravediggers of France*), which accused the leadership of the 1930s of gross incompetence.[4]

After World War II, decadence (*la décadence*) was widely accepted by a whole spectrum of French politicians as a way of discrediting their rivals. Ignoring their own guilt, the Communists accused the regimes of being corrupt as well as decadent. From another quarter, the Gaullists excoriated the Troisième République as powerless. They argued that France had lacked a "man on horseback" like de Gaulle.[5] The historian Paul Renouvin and his adherents, Jean-Baptiste Duroselle and Maurice Baumont, cast the net wider, fishing in international waters where they found intense forces (*forces profondes*) to show, among other influences, that of domestic politics on foreign policy. Also, the short-lived cabinets and politicians' desire for personal aggrandizement left them little time for dynamic initiatives in diplomacy. The politicians had lost sight of the public interest in their handling of events of the 1930s.

In 1979 the well-known work by Duroselle, *La Décadence, 1932–1939,* totally limned the Troisième République as cowardly, weak, and degenerate.[6] Earlier, in 1969, American reporter William L. Shirer in *The Collapse of the Third Republic* had emphasized the failure of the Paris leadership due to its

weakness, which included personal ambition and the ambition of the leaders' mistresses, as well as a different agenda by the vengeful Gen. Maxime
Weygand, who was part of the Vichy regime.[7] In addition, Shirer noted the
ineffective, manipulative General Gamelin, the devious politicians Pierre
Laval and his puppet Philippe Pétain, as well as Paul Reynaud's controlling
mistress, Countess Hélène de Portes.

Recent historians Talbot Imlay, Anthony Adamthwaite, and Nicole
Jordan have accepted both the decadence view and the weakness of the pre-
1940 Parisian leadership, while the Canadian Robert B. Young averred in his
In Command of France that the defeat of 1940 was a military responsibility,
for the politicians had done their best in the climate of the day.[8] Young has
been followed by both French- and English-speaking authors such as Jean-
Pierre Azema, Jean-Louis Crémieux-Brilhac, Martin Alexander, Eugenia
Kiesling, and Martin Thomas, who believe that France's international weakness was due to the impact of the Great Depression and its delaying of
Rearmament, and so no blame can be laid on the leadership for a failure to
stand up to Hitler but rather must fall on decadence.

There is evidence in recent years that in spite of opposition the dynamic
man on horseback, de Gaulle, is historically both alive and well, and that
historians of France, still mostly the English-speaking, are beginning to
once again reassess 1940.[9] Robert Gilda, an Oxford don, in his opening
statements for *Marianne in Chains*, explains how he found that the French
had still not come to grips with the many diverse facets of their history.[10]
They still clung to ideological and political interpretations that colored their
debates. The secrets needing to be revealed to enable the people to come to a
restful solution still lay in the departmental, municipal, and church archives
and still were protected on the grounds that 1940 was yet too close for "*la
France profonde*" to be fully exposed.[11] And those views continue to afflict
modern Francophiles.

However, the argument presented herein returns to a middle continental ground on which the leadership of both the Armée de Terre and the
Armée de l'Air are held responsible for the defeat of 1940. Together, with
both the political leadership and the turmoil in the aircraft industry in particular, and with the arrogance of the *patronats* (the wealthy capitalist French

class), the comparison and contrast is made with insular Great Britain to show that, generally, in the same circumstances viable solutions were possible. This work explains, then, why the courses adopted by the British led to victory in the summer of 1940 Battle of Britain. And this book is limited to the narrow, neglected—certainly in France—story of the air arms. Thus it is not concerned solely with explaining the defeat of the Armée de l'Air, except to note that the lack of doctrine, confusion in command, late start, and dearth of resources made the Armée de l'Air virtually impotent due to causes that stretched back before the 1920s. On the other hand, the question as to whether appeasement was the right policy for Britain is not the issue here. The point is that Neville Chamberlain saw the Royal Air Force (RAF) as the least expensive national defense, and thus ensured the supply of money needed for RAF Expansion, whereas across the English Channel (in French, the Manche) the Armée de l'Air was short of funding until 1938, in part because both a policy and a manufacturing infrastructure first had to be built and aircraft and engines designed and tested, and in part because of inflation.

Part of the background to understanding the state of mind in 1940 has to be the recognition that the interwar years saw a fundamental change in the context in which war and peace were waged, and stabilized the new doctrines in armored warfare, grand-strategic and tactical bombing, submarine warfare, carrier aircraft, and the development of radar (then known as radio direction finding, or RDF). All of these progressive actions impacted the budgets and mores of the armed forces, though the trends were different in each country. Historians Millett, Murray, and Watman in 1986 suggested questions to be posed in order to reach some elucidation, but thought that the answers for 1940 were more opaque, even if more complex.[12] For one thing, General Gamelin, in charge of the French military, had always thought the subject of armor needed more study, and thus the Armée de Terre reached no conclusions. The École Supérieure de Guerre (high war school), which should have taken a broad approach, instead formed and articulated doctrine based on the study of a few 1918 battles of World War I.

Murray and Watman in 1986 had studied military effectiveness and noted that it was achieved through the conversion of military resources to fighting power, including physical and political assets. Victory was the outcome of battle and the result of organizational activity—political, strategic, operational, and tactical—taking into account the limits of the present. Thus victory requires the military to have the cooperation of the political élite once the services have specified what is needed to parry any threats, for to do so they must have the backing of the middle, the skilled, and the upper classes, as well as plans. Conversely, the political leadership has to ensure that grand-strategic goals are in harmony with the forces available. It must be kept in mind, however, that neither France nor Britain had an effective military in 1940.

Two Roads to War is also about planning uncertainties and managing technological change; because they are a matter of national security and grand strategy, the story has to start at the top in an attempt to find out why the Armée de l'Air did not and could not meet its obligations. This work continues the themes of Robin Higham and Stephen J. Harris' *Why Air Forces Fail*, and makes a detailed comparison of the Armée de l'Air with the RAF. The latter body went its own way from 1918 to 1940, though it emerged from the same World War I as did the Armée de l'Air across the Channel.[13] The roots of the answers as to why go back a long way.

Although it is common for comparative studies of enemies to appear, very little attention has been devoted to allies. *Two Roads to War* attempts to delineate as fairly as possible, in spite of the paucity of French records and secondary works, the two paths that took the allies of 1918 back to war together again in 1940. This is not a broad approach, but rather one focusing on the air arms because in the interwar years of 1918–1940 they moved from being ancillary forces to center stage. In fact, both Hitler and Chamberlain from different positions saw air forces as important, swift, and economical. Yet airpower cannot be built overnight, and therefore it is the approach by the French and by the British to that creative process that is the main theme of this book.

One of the contrasts and comparisons between the Armée de l'Air and the RAF was that the French force was always peripheral, whereas the British force was central. This situation is critical to the analysis presented herein. The dominant Armée de Terre expected the Armée de l'Air to be its

handmaiden; in Britain, however, army cooperation was low on the independent RAF's priorities, and in the war the Air Component of the British
Expeditionary Force (ACBEF) was quite inadequate. In France, the whole
question of ground support was debated and was divisive and unsettling
militarily, whereas in Britain it was simply regarded as inferior to bombing
the enemy's industrial will to make war.

Although the causes of the defeat of France in 1940 have been debated
ever since, historians have paid zero attention to the role and place of the
Armée de l'Air in that defeat. Granted, it could not have affected the war's
outcome much, yet this lack of historiographical attention has no doubt
been due to the fact that very few historians either have been trained in or
have had an interest in the technological air service. Historians of France
have been much more comfortable arguing about politics and the Armée
de Terre, yet the story of the timing and development of the Armée de l'Air,
its doctrine, and its equipment, personnel, and budgets allows a real insight
into what ailed France before 10 May 1940.

Two Roads to War takes the debate about France in 1940 back to the
basics—at least in the military, aviation, and technological worlds. It answers
in a microcosmic way the question, Why did France fall? and reveals how
the Troisième République acted in a field in which it should have been first,
not a runner-up.

Much of *Two Roads to War* has as an undercurrent the response to
the challenge of modernization in the leading-edge field of aviation. Yet
much of the political decision-making—and then that at the top by military
men—was made by Victorians born roughly between 1860 and 1885. The
switch to the next generation—those born after 1885—did not come until
about 1940, though in the air force staffs the younger generation's influence
was apparent earlier.[14]

Technological decisions and defense policy are part of this work—how
they were made and are made in a political, social, and economic context,
very much as Elizabeth Kier conveyed in *Imagining War*, that they are formulated by the military in their cultural context.[15] Thus the issues between
owner/managers and labor over shop-floor practices, and the introduction
of women into the process, are of concern. In this field, as in others, the

differences between the French and British milieu reinforce what is noticeable about national character—those intellectual and operational traits that today might be deemed politically incorrect stereotypes. Also to be considered are class attitudes at the time in the interwar years because both Gallic and Anglo-Saxon societies were stratified. Decision-making depended on the national prejudices of personalities and on their experiences, as much as on the machinery of government and industry.

Increasingly, logistics in most armed forces ranks low. Note that in the German forces, neither in the Wehrmacht nor the Luftwaffe was logistics regarded as a staff post. Yet a staff officer needed to assume that there were sufficient resources, careful coordination, and adequate supplies combat-loaded. Secrecy was preserved and at least tactical surprise achieved, with the *schwerpunkt* (focus, or emphasis) carefully chosen to produce victory for a clearly defined air purpose.

At the root of the Armée de l'Air's problems was lack of funding—credits. Although Fridenson and Lecuir have shown that the Armée de l'Air did receive a steadily increasing allocation of francs from 1936, the increase was vitiated by inflation.[16] The nationalization of the aircraft industry wasted funds, bifurcated design and manufacturing, and resulted in failure to concentrate all efforts to develop and test both engines and aircraft, as well as ancillary needs such as radio. The Morane-Saulnier MS 406, the principal Armée de l'Air fighter in 1939, had not been wrung out in testing, for instance, while the accounting of production was thoroughly misleading. Aircraft "on charge" were nowhere near ready for war.

But the heart of the matter lay in French financing, a weakness that went back to Louis XIV and the Marine Nationale (the French national navy, often called the Royale), which in the late seventeenth century was sacrificed to pay the bills of the Armée de Terre. The lack of a clear role for the Armée de l'Air meant that it did not have a somewhat suitable block of credits until 1938, when at last production began to roll. Certainly by 1940 French aircraft production in terms of pure numbers was close to the German, but the matériel was inadequate. The trouble with French finances was not that France was a poor country with too few people aspiring still to be a great power, but that its finances were shackled until 1937 to the gold standard. And this, as Braudel would note in *The Identity of France* (*L'Identité de la France*), was related to the fact that far more than Britain, France was a nation of shopkeepers and lacked entrepreneurs—risk-takers.[17] Gaul lacked the positive view of a permanent national debt that existed in London.

Paul Reynaud did finally understand this in 1938, but it was too late. Those who argue that France had the arms and the manpower to stop the Germans in 1940, and then to adopt the preferred long-war grand strategy, have not done their sums. A long war would have been very expensive, especially with France vulnerable to German air power. But, of course, the answer to how to fund a war cannot be known, except perhaps by computer simulation.

The immediate cause of France's defeat was military, but the intermediate and far more complex cause was grand-strategic, with all the ramifications that implies. And that is what this book attempts to explain, using Britain as a foil or control.

In the summer of 1939, the RAF carried out the last prewar exercises with 33,000 men, 1,300 aircraft, 100 antiaircraft (AA) guns, 600 searchlights, and 100 barrage balloons. As a result, two scientists from Bawdsey were assigned to the Stanmore Research Section of Fighter Command headquarters (HQ); in 1941 Stanmore was redesignated the Operational Research Section.[18]

Until 15 March 1940 the work had been limited to the effectiveness of the air defense system. After that date the Operational Research Section had to help Dowding manage the 110 squadrons in France. On 14 May Dowding learned that Prime Minister Churchill wanted to send ten more squadrons to the battle in France. Dowding asked to attend the Cabinet meeting. In two hours his Operational Research people came up with the graph showing that the impact of losses at double the replacement rate would become unacceptable. Churchill understood.

Operational Research made two important contributions to the outcome of the Battle of Britain: it perfected RDF, and it stopped the attrition of Hurricanes in France and of irreplaceable pilots.[19]

In their collection of essays, *The Fog of Peace and War Planning*, Talbot Imlay and Monica Duffy Toft offer seven lessons to keep in mind:

1. Effective war planning requires as many inputs as possible.

2. The short- and long-term perspectives have to be balanced in planning.

3. Bets have to be hedged, especially in times of technological change.

4. There must be flexibility in identifying friends and foes.

5. Formal allied planning requires effective preparation.

6. The balance of power within an alliance may undermine planning.

7. Effective military and strategic planning requires flexibility.[20]

How did the GSAF in Paris match up to these requirements? And how did the Air Council in London match up?[21]

Of necessity in the aviation field, I have written for three audiences: my fellow scholars, aviation professionals, and history buffs. Critics of my chronologies that often move back and forth in time need to understand that I believe that the historian's job is to clarify, a task often necessitating flashbacks. This also guides my penchant for following themes—herein, of countries—from start to breaking point, then relating another issue until these various strands can be brought together later in the work.

—*Robin Higham*
Manhattan, Kansas
July 2010

INTRODUCTION
France to 1940

From 1903 to the present, as Rod Kedward noted in *France and the French*, conflicting portraits of the French have been advanced. They are seen as obsessed and passionate about ideas, but are dominated by conflict. Definitions hold sway for a few years, are abandoned, and then reinvented. French creativity has an identifiable quality, yet categories of "Frenchness" have originated that were both exclusive and excluding, establishing new boundaries in a struggle in which the battle for and against is prized. The French believe they have a distinctive history, culture, and society, of which after World War I there were many different examples, as Fernand Braudel in his two volumes of *The Identity of France* so well delineated. French history is painted both on a wide canvas and in separate panels (categories) of experience. These panels are filled with a rich and complex social and cultural scene unphased by passing politicians and events, though occasionally, as with World War I or the turmoil of the mid-1930s, shadowed by them. Regarding the memory of the Franco-Prussian War, while official bodies searched for reasons, the public splurged on the commemorative in spite of outright official opposition due to concerns about the stability of the République.[1]

The twentieth century to 1940 was stalemate and equilibrium followed by the strains of modernization that broke the Troisième République, the parliamentary democracy that had managed to survive since 1870. From 1936 on there was a technological, economic, and human shift, but the

1

legacy of World War I lasted through the dark Vichy days of 1940–1944. Complacency and ambivalence were prevalent in the interwar years, powered by activists creating history out of unity, diversity, and difference. Yet Marianne—the personification of France—remained to 1931 a major actor on the stage, though there were still pluralities of the histories of France. In the post-1918 era, the Troisième République stood for reason and universalism, and some thought that France alone upheld the highest values of truth and had a civilizing role to play in the world. But from before 1914 on, the new forces of nationalism and patriotism had arisen to challenge that view.

Gen. Philippe Pétain emerged from World War I as a benevolent leader who cared for the welfare and lives of his men—he had handled the mutinies of 1917 as strikes and gave up continuous costly offensives, and so was regarded in the years to 1944 as a genuine hero. The danger of revolution in the back of the minds of the general staff was avoided. The very determined Clemenceau as *premier* (prime minister) was backed by President Raymond Poincairé from Verdun, and military and industrial reorganization had produced the masses of artillery and aircraft needed for victory. With Marshal Ferdinand Foch as generalissimo, Clemenceau regularly visited the front. Morale and the Armée de Terre survived the German March 1918 offensive, and the Armistice was signed on 11 November 1918.[2]

World War I had devastated the *patrie's* (homeland's) ten northeastern *départments,* and 11,000 schools, town halls, and churches were destroyed, together with 350,000 houses, 2.5 million hectares (6,177,500 acres) of agricultural land, 65,000 kilometers (40,389 miles) of roads, 1,800 kilometers (1,118 miles) of canals, and 5,000 kilometers (3,106 miles) of railways. The losses of French workers through invasion, in percentages, included

- 41 percent of the miners;
- 11 percent of the quarrymen;
- 13.4 percent of the food industry workers;
- 29.4 percent of the textile workers;
- 52.7 percent of the metallurgical industry workers;
- 14 percent of the ordinary metalworking industry workers; and
- 18 percent of the lime, brick, pottery, and glassmaking industry workers.[3]

Of the 1.4 million identifiable dead, 40 percent of these involuntary victims were at state expense transferred to their home graves. The birth rate, 1914–1918, fell by 1.4 million, to be added to the casualties on the home front and an additional 200,000 who died of influenza during 1918–1919—a total loss of 3 million. A quarter of the infantry sent to the front were killed. On top of these numbers, 3 million were wounded, including 300,000 who were permanently disfigured. This *génération du feu* (the generation that had been through the fire) was considered to have inalienable rights and the *mutilés de guerre* (war wounded) had reserved seats on public transport. The infantry became the men of both myth and history. Not surprisingly, when barely twenty years later the next generation of infantrymen (known in French as the *poilus*, or hairy ones) were sent to war, they were soon averred to be apathetic and to have low morale.

World War I had once again, as in the days of Louis XIV, made Paris the center of the country. There stereotypes developed of war profiteers, lazy workers, and, in rural areas, rapacious farmers—images that lingered. What happened to industry was epitomized by Louis Renault, autocrat, automaker, technocrat, entrepreneur, and partner with labor. Private industry excluded the state and avoided revolution, and there was after 1918 a return to family values and gender roles. The Parlement (parliament) in France strengthened male roles, banned abortion and contraception, and stressed duty to the nation. But blaming women for not marrying and procreating did not square with the loss of so many men.

No sooner had the war ended than the *union sacrée* (the wartime bonding of labor and capital) of 1914 dissolved, as labor vociferously sought benefits and the *patronats* reverted to laissez-faire. A vocal class war erupted. Socialism received a boost from Lenin's 1919 proclamation of the Comintern, and France, which from 1894 to 1917 had been in a Russian alliance, now saw a rapid rise of urban Communists, raising fears of another 1871 commune. In May 1920 Léon Blum persuaded 67 percent of the Socialists to join the Comintern.[4]

In foreign and domestic policy the important issue was whether to make Germany pay to restore France or whether to come to a new Franco-German rapprochement. The *bleu-horizon* (veterans) group in Parlement sought reparations in memory of the blue-clad *poilus*. The attitude was one of civic, not military, pride. But Aristide Briand's attempts to reduce reparations failed and French and Belgian troops occupied the Ruhr in 1923, while Britain abstained. The failure of the occupation and rapid inflation (Table 1) led to the Dawes Plan of 1924. Édouard Herriot formed a new government on a platform of peace and disarmament and led to Briand's recognition of the Soviet Union and Germany, and to the pacific Locarno peace treaties of 1925 guaranteeing frontiers and arbitration, followed three years later by the Kellogg–Briand Pact outlawing war. There was a feeling of peace and security. But Britain's preference for imperial trade scuttled Briand's last proposal—for European economic union—as did the rise of German nationalism.

France in 1929 had archaic economic and social organizations. The country still had illusions of its status as a great power and its social harmony (though actually a blocked society), as well as the political sense of triumph over the trials of war. And yet France had a feeble executive—a shifting Parlement with parties lacking discipline and consistency that prevented governments from vigorously attacking the new problems.[5] In the early 1930s, because of inexact statistics, the government regarded the unemployment caused by its monetary policy as of secondary importance. Moreover, many of the unemployed were women, whom the men thought belonged at home. The employers sought to use Laval's deflationary policies to rid

TABLE 1. The Franc vs. the British Pound—Inflation

DATE	FRANCE	GREAT BRITAIN
July 1914	100	100
July 1915	123	132
July 1916	142	161
July 1917	184	202
July 1918	244	218
July 1919	261	217
July 1920	373	262

Source: Fontaine, *French Industry During the War*, 417.

themselves of social insurance and family allowances. Unemployment was a great strike-breaker, as employers more and more gained the upper hand.[6]

In the post-1918 world, the French enjoyed the complacency of believing that it was French political ideals and social structure that had brought victory, although they also believed that there needed to be political and social change. The clash of these two led to unrest over the questions of reform and modernization. Nevertheless, most of the fabric of French society was preserved or created in the 1920s. The war had shifted the French population from more than half on the land to more than half urban by 1931, but the rural areas remained distinctively French. The peasants condemned the urban industrial culture, politics, and society. Jeanne d'Arc (Joan of Arc) of Lorraine, which was again French, was canonized in 1920. In the villages there was a perpetual conflict between the school teacher and the priest, between democracy and hierarchy. Outside Brittany there was a low birth rate and abandoned buildings. In spite of the work of the Ministère de l'Agriculture (ministry of agriculture), Paris tended to neglect the plight of the peasants because of the remembrance of high wartime food prices. The Chambre des Députés (chamber of deputies) was fiscally conservative and balked at support for the peasantry. Parlement saw a monolithic rural France and not the fractured and regional reality.

During the war France had attracted a large immigration, yet once the struggle ended the colonists were shipped home. Some—notably the Belgians, Italians, and Spaniards—however, stayed on. Postwar the Confédération Générale du Travail (CGT; general confederation of labor) sought to keep the differential in wages. Xenophobic outbursts occurred whenever the economy dropped, but employers reinvited lower-paid foreign workers, which stirred immigration's social, political, and cultural dynamics. By 1931 at least 1 million Italians were working in France, but Algerians and Africans, as well as other Muslims, were regarded with suspicion and had difficulty gaining employment.

Mechanical engineering had really begun to take hold after 1900 and was accelerated by wartime demand, as were the chemical and cement industries, which grew with the needs of postwar reconstruction. As a result, French industrial growth exceeded that of Germany and the United

States by 1930. The eight-hour law of 1919 was converted to three shifts to achieve round-the-clock production. The war also accelerated the move from the less-than-ten-worker factory to a larger one, in which labor and modernization soon clashed, for assembly lines still could be manned by inexpensive unskilled people. The CGT thus rationalized the use of technology, together with shorter hours and higher pay. Yet companies such as the Renault automotive works increasingly were seen as divided between skilled French and unskilled foreign workers. Strikes declined after 1920 as the unions lost members and reformers and revolutionaries competed for workers' loyalty. Still, on the whole, the Political Center controlled until the 1950s. Catholics, especially in Alsace-Lorraine, remained strong, and anti-clerical sentiment was muted.

Investors were not happy, however, as between 1925 and 1926 the franc declined from 100 to 235 to the English pound. During 1928, while Poincaré still ruled, on the military side General Pétain had decided the lesson of World War I was defense and so dedicated a permanent line of fortifications in place of the 1914–1918 field fortifications—the infamous trenches. The defense minister, André Maginot, himself a wounded veteran, saw the Maginot Line begun in 1927, the concrete fortifications—tank obstacles and artillery defenses—along the borders with Germany. The next year changes began with the enactment of the Social Security Law, funded by both employers and workers, and a program of 200,000 new apartments for the many urban workers who lived in the suburbs.

By the end of the 1920s when Poincaré retired, the Troisième République was securely established, but democracy was still a work in progress—women had yet to achieve equality. The élites, meanwhile, set out in their automobiles to discover France using the new Michelin guides, as town maps began to be posted.

Britain to 1940

World War I cost Britain, including Ireland, roughly 1 million military and civilian killed and twice that many wounded.[7] The debt was ten times what it had been in 1914, and after the war the British faced continuing expenses of health care, job training, and placement for ex-servicemen. The war had seen the creation of the Ministry of Health in Britain as military physicals revealed the poor state of the men due to inadequate nutrition, sickness, and working conditions—but one of the social reforms boldly demanded by the working classes. The 1914–1918 war had consumed the nation's mercantile wealth, especially in loss of shipping, overseas markets, and investments in a generally disorganized world in which New York had become the principal financial center instead of London, and dollar debts were a primary concern.[8]

In Ireland, and in distant India, Egypt, and Palestine, there were nearly intolerable problems related to race and peace settlements. At the same time, the self-governing Dominions of Canada, Union of South Africa, Commonwealth of Australia, and Commonwealth of New Zealand sought more autonomy and a new nationalism, and articulated a reluctance to be committed again to any European war or even—as in the 1922 Chanak crisis at the Dardanelles, where the British and French were challenged by Turkish troops—to war with the new Turkey.[9] In 1923 the Imperial Conference recognized the right of the dominions to make treaties with former powers. In 1926 they were declared coequal, and in 1931 the empire became the commonwealth.

The "khaki election" of 14 December 1918—a balloting influenced by either wartime or postwar attitudes, for which all men over twenty-one and women over thirty were able to vote—brought an overwhelming victory to the coalition under Lloyd George, prime minister since 1916. (It was in 1928 that women were finally equally enfranchised with men, to vote at twenty-one.) The 1918 election platform had promised punishment of the German war criminals from the just-ended conflict, full payment by the defeated powers for the costs of that war, and prevention of the dumping of foreign goods in Britain. These promises, however, greatly hampered Lloyd George's freedom of action at the Peace of Versailles in 1919.

In the meantime, the Government of Ireland Act had separated the south, Eire, from British Northern Ireland. And young economist John Maynard Keynes wrote that there were economic consequences of Versailles, including the ruination of British shipbuilding by reparations in the form of German liners and cheaper-built cargo ships. The blight therefrom on the northeast shipyards lasted into World War II. The switchover

from war to peacetime industrial production and the return to domestic-
ity of women still did not provide enough jobs for returning ex-servicemen, many of whom were young and had never worked long enough to
have a skilled trade. The result was growing unemployment, especially in
coal, iron, steel, and exports. By 1921 about 1 million were unemployed and
receiving welfare (the dole), which the Emergency Unemployment Act of
March 1921 had boosted to twenty shillings a week for men and eighteen
for women. The miners struck starting in March, when government control
of the mines ended and the idea of nationalization was rejected, and ending
in 1 July when the government's offer of subsidy and increased wages was
accepted. What also had hurt the miners was the strategic shift of the Royal
Navy and the shipping industry to Middle Eastern and American oil fuel,
replacing hard Welsh coal as the world-standard steaming fuel.

In early 1921 the Unionists withdrew support from the Welshman
Lloyd George, who was succeeded by Unionist (now Conservative) Bonar
Law; in November Law had won a majority of seats in the Commons. As
the Liberals split between those supporting former Prime Ministers Herbert
Asquith and Lloyd George, the Labour Party, with 142 seats, became for the
first time His Majesty's Loyal Opposition. Bonar Law resigned for reasons of
ill health and was succeeded by Stanley Baldwin in May 1923. Unfortunately,
Baldwin misjudged and in late December called a fresh general election,
which the Conservatives lost badly. Thus, in early 1924 the first Labour
government took office under Ramsay MacDonald, with former workers
elevated to Cabinet status.

Great Britain recognized the Soviet Union de jure in February and nego-
tiated a commercial treaty that included an agreement to loan the Soviets
money when the Tsarist debts had been paid off. This was followed by a
fresh election in October, which the Conservatives won handily, owing to
the revelation of the Zinoviev letter, which supported the United Kingdom's
Comintern (Communist) Third International, instructing British subjects
to provoke a revolution. But Communism was not strong enough in Britain
for the letter to create the atmosphere needed to spark that revolution.

The second Baldwin government at once denounced the treaties with
the Soviet Union and refused to sign the Geneva protocol, which MacDonald

had sponsored but which the dominions had opposed, for it defined as an aggressor any nation unwilling to submit to arbitration; the dominions believed the risks to mutual assistance too great for their isolated lands.

Early in 1926 a commission reported against the continuation of the coal subsidy. British miners went on strike on 1 May. Two days later a general strike showed sympathy for four days. About 2.5 million of the 6 million trade union members in the country went out, but order, transport, and essential services were maintained by volunteers from the upper classes, many of them ex-officers. The Trades Union Council called off the strike on 12 May with the understanding that negotiations on wages and hours would be continued. The miners stayed out until 19 November, when they surrendered unconditionally.

In May 1929 the statutory five-years' election was held and Labour emerged with 288 seats to the Conservative party's 260. One of MacDonald's first acts was to renew relations with the Soviet Union. Earlier, in 1922, the Conservative-led government had made notable cuts in the budget, affecting public programs. Sir Eric Geddes was chair of the committee for national expenditures, and his cuts became known as the "Geddes Axe." Subsequently, in 1931, a group of financial experts—the May Committee— reported a prospective deficit of £100,000 and recommended a cut, among others, in welfare. The Cabinet split, the majority siding with Labour, of whom there were then more than 2 million unemployed. The split caused the resignation of Prime Minister MacDonald and the subsequent formation of a National Coalition government. The Labour Party expelled its members who had joined the National Coalition group, but they in turn formed the National Labour group. Shortly thereafter Britain was forced to abandon the gold standard, and the pound dropped to 72 percent of its value against the dollar.

Labor

It is against this background that the developments of the late 1930s must be seen. The aircraft industry in France was by 1936 ripe for an explosion. It was in the throes of modernization technically, which also impacted the attitudes of the owners, the workers, and the state. The *patronats*, the reputed two hundred families that owned a solid share of industry, especially the larger ones, represented by the Comité des Forges (committee of the ironworks proprietors, a group of steel industry leaders) were stubborn, detached, wealthy, and strongly opposed to confrontation or negotiation with labor. Just as the stronger governments ruled by decrees, so too did the *patronats* order their factories by fiat. Some of them pushed scientific management—rationalization, which brought conflict with skilled workers, whose piece rates were to be changed and whose complex skills were divided, so that semiskilled and even much less expensive unskilled labor would perform the simplified tasks. Less-skilled workers could be women, as they had been in World War I, paid below the rates paid to men. This dilution of labor, as it was called, differed on either side of the Channel due both to national attitudes and to the existing relations between employers and employees.

Paradoxically, although French employers refused to talk to their workers, they were in a patronizing way aware of their activities in the factories, but also spied on them at home, amply assisted by the local *gendarmes* (police officers), who kept a close watch on Leftist and Syndicalist attitudes.[10] There was no equivalent to this standoff in Britain. There the unions had been negotiating with the owners since 1900 and had the parliamentary Labour Party to represent them. In addition, the wartime welfare work closed down by 1920, whereas in France women were trained in the École des Surintendantes d'Usine (school of factory superintendents) in Paris to be factory superintendents—social workers of sorts—a concept that spread out rapidly across France in the interwar years.

During World War I modern methods of scientific management, or rationalization, were imported to France from the United States and were known either as Taylorism or Fordism, named for their founders, Frederick Winslow Taylor and Henry Ford. After 1914 large brightly lit factories were built, with a continuous flow from raw materials to finished goods, especially in the areas of automotive and electrical supplies. This was in sharp contrast to the common ill-lit *ateliers* (workshops) where the majority of French employees toiled. The impact of Fordism was most immediate and greatest on the Parisian metalworking establishments, which had to install automatic or semiautomatic machinery. For the owners the goal was to lower labor costs and to curtail the freedom of skilled workers, as well as payment of wages by results and the tightening of shop-floor discipline. The new factories enjoyed economies of scale, the larger being more efficient.

In Britain, the change to U.S.-style production was less noticeable as the Home markets consumed smaller batches of goods. Skilled workers resisted any move to greater production flows, and as long as the crafts-based system yielded profits, employers also were not eager to change. In France, however, an incentive to Fordism was the shortage of skilled labor that had been evident from the 1890s to World War II. Thus both employer-run and municipal-run technical schools were the path to advancement. Lacking the shop-floor stewards, who in Britain could persuade management to change, the French worker was helpless to make their case.

World War I had shocked the French into using the philosophy of Taylorism to increase production, and also had encouraged the employment of women. The loss of the industrial northeast put additional pressure on the Paris region and shifted work from the arsenals to private industry. War production had been dominated by the Comité des Forges in conjunction with the Ministère de la Guerre and later of the Ministère de l'Armement (ministry of armaments). The workers had no voice, but the seed for the movement for nationalization of production was planted at that time. The Comité used its power to concentrate production in the larger firms, while for self-protection the smaller establishments had to group together. Citroen, the motorcar company, built an enormous twelve-hectare factory—equal to 120,000 square meters, or 29.65 acres—near the Eiffel Tower, and soon 21 percent of its employees were women.

From August 1915 on, Albert Thomas, the Socialist-appointed under-secretary for artillery, had used his power to control labor and put pressure on the Comité to improve the lot of workers. In addition, he set up the Conseil de Contrôle de Travail (labor control board) to mediate between Armée de Terre and its delegated soldiers, and the workers and their employers. Thomas and his staff soon began moving skilled men away from the newly divided tasks that semiskilled labor could handle. In December 1916 he headed the recently established Ministère de l'Armement and began to plan for a "new France," a country that would emerge from the war much more efficient and paying higher wages, which would allow workers greater purchasing power. At that point, even the workers saw the labor-saving devices as a boon.

During the war the unions had collapsed, in part because agitators could easily be sent to the battlefield. Taylorism with its interlocking departments was never really accepted, however, in spite of the mechanized advances such as the use of conveyer belts to facilitate movement of materials within the factory. But employers were brutal in cutting pay rates and demanding faster and increased production as well as longer hours. To protect the women against these changes, to guard motherhood, in 1916 Thomas created the Conseil du Travail de Femme (committee on women's work) and in 1917 he imposed minimum wages that narrowed the gap between the sexes.

In contrast, in Britain the war strengthened the unions and the shop stewards through which skilled men could protect their interests. A 1914 general strike was called off, union men joined the armed forces, and domestic divisions evaporated. Volunteering left the factories short of workers, and so the government stepped in. His Majesty's Treasury conference of 19 March 1915 gave the state great powers, and negotiations about any supply became tripartite, with labor and the state considering issues of wages and the organization of work. The two sides retained a decisive influence throughout the war, which benefited both men and women, and as far as owners were concerned, skilled workers were less expensive than new machinery.

The standing importance of the craft trades in Britain had no counterpart in France. In Britain the major issue regarding workers was dilution, the fragmentation of skill. At the same time, however, the skilled were recognized as invaluable, and thus rationalization kept them at the upper echelon. As war production expanded, skilled artisans were needed for extensive retooling tasks and to place industry on a war footing—a fact most employers recognized. The Treasury Agreement put through by Lloyd George as chancellor of the exchequer was binding, ensured dilution during the war, and forbade strikes: issues were to be settled by arbitration. At Lloyd George's invitation, the Transport and General Workers Union, as well as the other workers' unions, were silent signers on 19 March 1915. That June the Ministry of Munitions under Lloyd George came into being with two hundred staff recruited from business who allocated resources and controlled both the arsenals and the two hundred–plus factories built by the government and subsequently operating in 1918. These were pioneers in standardization and mass-production techniques, and were heavily staffed by women.

By the end of the war, more than eight thousand firms were using more than 2 million workers. Factory inspections ensured generally the best use of space and labor. The British Ministry of Munitions gradually obtained far more control over the shape and education of war production than ever did the French. All of this helped the British avoid the sharp drop in morale that occurred in France when war weariness set in and rumors were into war profiteering. Yet on both sides of the Channel, manufacturers were forced to the division of tasks so that less-skilled workers could be used, while at the same time owners were mechanizing. And in both countries the increased employment of women lowered costs and raised output.

In France, at Verdun in 1916 and after, men were retained only if the physical demands of the job demanded their strength. By early 1918, 100,000 women were in the Parisian metal trades. At that same time in Britain, 597,000 women were at work. As the men were withdrawn, rationalization moved in apace, in the name of efficiency. In Britain, inspectors were middle-class women, and new methods were demonstrated by female instructors, all helping to move women to higher levels of increased pay and greater self-esteem. By 1917 government contracts in shell-filling called for at least 80 percent of production to be by women, thus providing a pool of highly skilled women for the postwar era, whose lower cost threatened men's positions.

The period from 1918 to about 1934 was one of recovery from the enormous physical, economic, and psychological impact of World War I. France in ways fared better than Great Britain because of the necessity to spend in order to rebuild the northeast and to care for the veterans. Investments rose until late 1929, and a succession of international connections culminated in the 1928 Kellogg–Briand Pact outlawing war. But underlying these developments was fear—of Germany as again an aggressor, much as in 1870 and 1914, and of unemployment, and a declining confidence in the future of France, together with an unwillingness to pay for defense and to invest in the modernization of French industry.

Across the Channel economic conditions were no better and unemployment was more persistent. However, a strong pride in the British nation and its Empire still existed. Britain's new way was onward. And in spite of the impact of the Versailles settlement, sectors of the economy were making the shift to modernization and the employment of women. More particularly, the aircraft industry was advancing and the Air Ministry parceled out contracts among sixteen airframe and four engine firms (known as the Ring), and so kept an eye on the future in which modernization went hand in hand with the Technological Revolution.

PART I

LEGACIES OF WORLD WAR I

BRITAIN AND FRANCE

Introduction

The explanation for the phenomena of 1940 is rooted in the history of traditional enemies forced again into an alliance by the emergence of Germany, first victorious over France in 1871. To this must be added France's near defeat (or Pyrrhic victory) at Verdun in 1916 and French postwar hopes for peace, concern over great power status, and a defensive *mentalité* personified by the Maginot Line. Beneath or behind all this was the structure of French politics and a habit of talking, but not of acting.

Two important questions remain: Why was France defeated in those forty-six days of May–June 1940? And why have historians of France not looked deeply into the origins and nature of the Armée de l'Air? In their studies of the defeat of 1940, they give the air service scarcely a few paragraphs. Yet are both questions symbolic of myths?

Since June 1940 the French either have acknowledged that France was in a very difficult time in the 1930s and into 1940, or have attempted to protect the "Gallic lost cause." In 1940 and afterwards in the 1942 Vichy Riom *procès*, where Marshal Pétain and Guy La Chambre sought to prove the responsibility for the French defeat by the Germans, and in memoirs and official histories, French officialdom tried to make the case that the defeat of 1940 was inevitable, fated by the rottenness of French society, by the activities of the Front Populaire, by the military, and by superior German manpower and weapons. This Vichyist pretense was challenged after the war by Charles de Gaulle and others, who laid the blame upon the government (i.e., the politicians) for a willingness to make war with the purely defensive strategy of the 1918 generals who believed they had won in the trenches and would win with the Maginot Line, and eventually be able to take the offensive through Belgium against a spent enemy.

Grand Strategy

Grand strategy is a national policy that is politically, diplomatically, economically, socially, and militarily related to potential enemies, much less so to possible allies. The armed forces tailor themselves to meet grand-strategic conditions with the monies allocated, which is almost never what is deemed necessary. In France after 1918 grand strategy was the province of the Centre des Hautes Études Militaires (center for high military studies). The École de Guerre (war college) withered under the great marshals like the aging Pétain, and became engrossed in minutiae of divisional handling and running of set-piece battles. In the French system up to June 1940, the emphasis was still on the power of reasoning and on an academic approach to study, whereas in the British Army the emphasis was to integrate the academic and the actual with the application of knowledge and judgment to war conditions.

In Britain the crisis over the fate of the RAF was fought out during 1917–1927 at a time of declining international tensions that led to the 1925 Locarno peace treaties. In France the critical years, 1932–1940, coincided with the rise of new domestic and international tensions. I. B. Holley Jr. long ago suggested that institutional structure shaped technological and doctrinal change. He was correct, at least for the 1920s and 1930s, as this book shows.[1]

In many ways the story here is of the histories of peoples of very differing geographic, linguistic, and national temperaments, between the turbulent legacies of glory and defeat; and of Bonapartism, monarchism, and republicanism, and the smug stability of Victorian splendid insular isolation and the glories of the Empire. By 1939 the French had come volubly to doubt their moral self-confidence, while north of the Channel the attitude was one of moral certitude with a stiff upper lip. Both countries had a fear of another Western Front.

The Background

The nineteenth century background is important because all of the leaders in the French and British air services were born in that Victorian time and had experienced victories in the Great War, as World War I was called until 1939. Marshal Pétain, the defender of Verdun in 1916, was a senior counselor all through the interwar years and on beyond the 1940 Armistice into the Vichy period (1940–1944).

The air services were fledglings in 1914, their organization in France tied strongly to the army, but in Britain split between the rival naval and military wings of the Royal Flying Corps (RFC) created in 1911. By the outbreak of World War I, the naval wing had become the progressive Royal Naval Air Service (RNAS), which by 1918 was a well-acknowledged part of the fleet. The RFC was the British Army's air arm, its organization chart established in 1915. But competition in procurement coupled with the needs of the air defense of Britain itself led to the creation by Act of Parliament in late 1917 of a single air service, the Royal Air Force (RAF), under the Air Ministry.

By the end of the war, Britain was in possession of a well-integrated air defense network whose main components consisted of an early-warning system linking the Observer Corps posts and sound locators by telephone lines to a central London Air Defence Area control room; a command structure that maintained a series of plots of reported enemy raiders and directed fighters to their targets by wireless (radio); and a protective screen deploying balloon barrages, searchlights, antiaircraft (AA) guns, and fighter squadrons.[2]

During World War I the French economy was increasingly controlled by the British through joint commissions regulating imports and shipping, among other areas. This caused a quiet resentment in Gaul, while it added to John Bull's confidence and disdain for the French, especially when the British Expeditionary Force (BEF) believed it bore the brunt of the war because of the 1917 French mutinies.

It was ironic that between 1904 and 1914 France had regained its optimism and believed that the next war would be short and that the élan of the *offensive à outrance* (offensive to excess) would carry the day. World War I deflated that confidence. Only in 1939 did optimism return with the thought that France could prevent a short war by parrying the opening German offensive and delaying the final victorious blow for several years until German resources had been worn down and France could go on the offensive and claim victory. In 1914 victory took four years (204 weeks); in 1940 defeat came in 6 weeks.

German Gothas bombed Paris starting on 30 January 1918; 36 French citizens died and 190 were injured. The bombing caused fear, boosted sales of injury insurance, and raised questions as to whether householders had to shelter outsiders during raids, of which there had been twenty-one by 11 March. The special German gun aimed at Paris also lobbed shells into the city.

Certainly, the French were much concerned about management, size, and efficiency of industry from 1916 to 1917, when the engineers took control of war production. But postwar the aircraft firms remained small, cautious, family affairs with few government orders until 1934; though stimulated and supported by civil aviation, the latter's numbers were minimal. Perhaps the real difference across the Channel was that the British parlayed the 1931 Schneider Trophy win into the Spitfire by 1936—a fighter that stayed in the front line throughout World War II. In 1940 the French were only just getting their equivalent, the underarmed D-520.[3]

One reason for the failure of the French government to appreciate modern war was the way in which the Conseil Supérieur de la Guerre (CSG; superior council of war), founded in 1872, gradually expelled the civilians and became dominated in 1911–1912 by Gen. Joseph Joffre. In 1906 the Conseil Supérieur de la Défense Nationale (CSDN; superior council of national defense) was created to be the apex of Paris' planning for war. It met only four times from 1906 to 1908, however, and not again until 1911, when the schedule was changed to semiannually. Apparently the CSDN never considered the financial side of war planning, which has been called "incoherent." However, the private Banque de France filled the void and bolstered its gold reserves: it saw trouble ahead. It also advanced large sums to the government in 1911 at a time when Joffre told the prime minister that France had only a 70 percent chance of victory in a war with Germany.

The Consequences of World War I, 1914–1918

After the successful defense at Verdun in 1916 France was victorious in static trench warfare and began to move forward. From 1918 France was wedded to those concepts. Across the Channel the British abhorred the very idea of another continental commitment while still dealing with the painful economic aftermath of World War I. Thanks to the program of official histories and to the short link between the 1914–1918 and 1939–1945 wars, the former histories were, if read, a blueprint for the latter. Britain started to gear up for a new war in 1934 after the collapse of the World Disarmament Conference at Geneva, the 1931 Japanese threat in the Far East, and the emergence of Germany once again as the enemy in place of the longtime foe, France.[4]

In World War I the army staffs provided the overall guidance for the aviation or aeronautical substaffs, and officers, especially senior officers, went back and forth between the ground and air staffs. Both in London and in Paris these staffs were primarily concerned with the procurement of the people and production to enable policy and plans to be carried out.

Once at war, wastage, consumption, and logistics in general—as well as manpower concerns—created enormous, disruptive, monolithic machines that exhausted both laissez-faire management and manpower. Only gradually did countries come to realize that they had to have a planned economy. It was the initial failure to realize and implement such an economy that led to the Russian Revolution of 1917, to Walter Rathenau in Germany, to mutinies in France, and to the War Cabinet clique in Britain.

New ministries came into being to deal with munitions and weapons. Aviation made quantum leaps in airframes, engines, and strategy and tactics. By the end of the war in 1918, the air element had become both an ancillary of sound strategy and a handmaiden of the surface forces, with independent bombing raids well behind the lines.[5] But imperfect knowledge between politicians and generals, as Carl von Clausewitz noted, led to trouble when powers were not well defined. Titles and duties expanded haphazardly.[6]

Relationships were always tense in World War I due to the stalemate in the field and to the strong personalities who emerged in France, as well as to the problems defining the limits of power between politicians and the more technically minded military. In Parlement the Chambre des Députés had lost power due to political scandals. Georges Clemenceau defended Marshal Foch in June 1918 when the Germans almost broke through again to Paris, and there followed a mutual pruning of the Haut Commandement (High Command). Later, when it came to peace, the Foreign Office told the marshal that he could handle armistice negotiations, but peace terms were the province of the government.

The war cost France mortally, 5 million casualties, and in 1935, according to Cyril Falls, it was "divided, scared, and spiritless."[7] Historians Stanley Hoffman and Marc Bloch agreed.[8] A nation needed a good history—conditions in which an able civilian government maintained national interests by effective diplomacy closely supported by a military that was willing to stay in its proper place, noted J. C. King. The government had to know the ends desired and the cost, and the military had to have the means to achieve those ends, which required great material resources, vast reserves of manpower, room to maneuver, and strong allies.[9]

France after 1918 forgot the *union sacrée* and blamed the generals for not foreseeing a modern war and for not finding a solution to it, thereby causing France unaffordable casualties; this pessimistic view lingered throughout the twentieth century. The optimists have revived Plan XVII—used by the French general staff as it went to war in 1914 with Germany—and offensive-mindedness.[10] French analysis of military history has been conditioned by politics. In the interwar years the Left supported the defensive and allocated the offensive to the militarists and the Right. The British Army was quite apolitically secure; its role and purpose could be criticized. In France such questions coalesced with those of political loyalty. Yet France survived World War I and the failure of Plan XVII, so why did it collapse in 1940? For these reasons:

1. The Troisième République of 1914 was much stronger and more patriotic than that of 1939–1940, which teetered on the brink of disintegration.

2. In 1914 French popular morale was more resilient due to the patri-
    otic fillip versus the National Revival; in 1940 the middle class had
    lost faith and the unions appeared to see low productivity and lack
    of patriotism as a positive good.

3. The army of 1914 was much better than the army of 1940 and had a
    better Haut Commandement.

4. In 1914 the French believed the war would be short and thus morale
    rose after August 1914, whereas in 1940 they thought the war
    would be long and thus morale declined. In the 1930s Gen. Maurice
    Gamelin faced the problem that Col. Charles de Gaulle's and Paul
    Reynaud's ideas of a mechanized army required professionalization,
    which would infuriate the political center.[11]

Gamelin had graduated from the École Spéciale Militaire de Saint-Cyr
(special military school of Saint-Cyr), the leading French military academy,
and was promoted to brigadier general during World War I. He became the
army chief of staff in 1931, president of the CSG and army inspector in 1935,
and chief of staff of CSDN in 1938. Paul Reynaud was the finance minister during 1930, colonies minister from 1931 to 1932, justice minister from
1932 to 1938, and again finance minister from 1938 to 1940.

In 1914 the strategy of the offensive divided French people the least. It
also served to help the Armée de Terre overcome its deficiencies and get it out
from under the Capt. Alfred Dreyfus affair of the late 1890s and early 1900s,
which involved that French officer's false conviction of treason, accused of
spying for the Germans. Yet the army's problem was less one of doctrine than
one of inefficiency, as Michael Howard has said. Wasn't the Armée de Terre of
1914 called upon to make a strategic offensive that beggared—was beyond—
its capabilities? The French government had refused to allow an offensive
into Belgium to meet the Germans, as this would undo the 1839 neutrality
treaty and thus forfeit Belgian and British aid.[12] In 1940 the Gamelin forward
plan led to one-third of his force being cut off in the northeast.

Both in 1914 and in 1940 the Armée de Terre was forced to work in
a hostile political environment and to coordinate the fight with allies that
were far from committed to going to the wall for France, and deal as well
with bureaucratic infighting, a Haut Commandement that reigned but did

not work, poor training, poor leadership, and deficiencies of matériel. Both in 1914 and in 1940 the German plan of attack caught the Armée de Terre unprepared. In 1940 the Germans had a greater ability to exploit their initial victories. In both 1914 and 1940 the French were very vulnerable to confusion and subsequent demoralization.

Emerging from the gallant, grim, deadly 1916 battle of Verdun, with its thousands and thousands of dead and wounded, was the idea that air assets should not be wasted in penny packets assigned to the infantry and artillery supporting the Armée de Terre, but instead should be concentrated to obtain air superiority over the decisive battlefield, using their flexibility to cover those on the ground and to prevent the enemy from observing for his guns. The Germans had concentrated 180 aircraft and their artillery, depriving the French of aerial observation by either balloon or aircraft, but the French responded by mobilizing fifteen fighter squadrons with new aircraft and thus regained air superiority. The French were no longer blind at Verdun and the Germans lost the battle. By 1918 this concentration had become the famous Duval Air Division with its centralized resources, which the American airman Billy Mitchell adapted and used in his summer 1918 Meuse-Argonne offensive ground-support activities.

The surprising part of World War I was that in spite of the loss during 1914–1915 of 30 percent of French industrial capacity in the northeast, on top of the iron ore and coal taken in Alsace-Lorraine in 1871, the country was still able to provide the masses of shells, guns, bullets, rifles, and machine guns to win the war, despite the fact that in four years the 5 million French casualties equaled the workforce employed in 1914. Both the British and the French aircraft industries were revolutionized on the production side during the 1914–1918 war.

Yet the management of the political economy had a certain weakness. In France 67 percent of the adult males were in the Armée de Terre and the budget rose from 5 billion francs in 1914 to 190 billion in 1918. But taxes paid for only 20 percent of the cost. According to Gerd Hardach, the French mobilization Plan XVII of 1912 made no mention of industrial mobilization.[13] One result was that when 5.6 million men were called up, only 34 percent of the 12.6 million active males remained in the population for industrial work. However, by 1917 the shortage was not as acute, for raw materials had become less available. Progressively adopting American Taylorism—Frederick Taylor's "scientific management" principles—France showed a tremendous potential for economic growth and adapted quickly to arms production. Throughout the war, says Hardach, France was the largest Allied arms producer with imported coal, coke, iron, and steel, and profited from large war orders.[14]

The French were forced to accept British help, which the latter insisted be regulated by commissions that controlled wheat, coal, credit, and shipping. On the French side, the commerce and industry minister used international procedures to allocate resources to individual firms, thus restricting their autonomy and flexibility, especially versus their rivals. But the system enabled production and profits to be maintained without higher prices and wages. In all this, according to John F. Godfrey and Richard F. Kuisel, World War I shifted the goals from stability to modernization and the rise of economic management (the planned economy) while catastrophically undermining traditional beliefs in the old methods.[15] This led to a new pyramid of power erected not by bluebloods but by men with lubricants in their veins who could build up each stage and who used cost accounting and other such intelligent tools to inform the top so that proper directions could be sent down to run the edifice. And Charles S. Maier has shown that this empowered a middle-class community that provided corporate controls that eclipsed the bureaucracy. At the same time, the war enabled the growth of the state's power to handle the political economy.[16] After 1914, however, France lacked the three essentials of a great nation—capital for credit, transportation, and production.

As Godfrey noted in his *Capitalism at War*, the French political system affected the relations of bureaucracy and industry in the 1914–1918 war because of how it functioned. The outcome was that policy was enshrined in law and gave the government the means to control industry in wartime.[17] This was an important legacy to the interwar years. Policies were made by the Cabinet and became law either by ministerial decrees or through the process of the Parlement, possible because that body was in session eight months of the year. But because the legislative process was slow and ministerial tenures short, a minister who did not remain at his position through several cabinets and with the strong backing of his colleagues was unlikely to see his goals accomplished. When he did remain in office for some time, he then gained control over his senior permanent civil servants. As he had not recruited and trained them, though, he needed his own personal staff or cabinet.

The government could only succeed in its policies if it was persuasive and powerful, and if the matters were urgent. Parlement's control was exercised through procedural maneuvering, the moving of amendments, repeated debates upon general government policies—with the risks of a vote of no confidence—and the daily questioning of ministers. The Chambre des Députés and the Sénat (the French Senate) elected their own presidents who were not members of the Cabinet, and thus they set their own orders of business, which made for reduced governmental effectiveness. Debates and projects were more important than progress toward an objective, even victory in war. The Sénat's strategy was to delay until the government fell, generally in about six months.

More seriously, governments were controlled by commissions in the Parlement. These were grandstanding committees that had evolved during the Troisième République, one for each ministry. Each commission was made up after 1916 of forty-four members and acted in the name of the whole Chambre des Députés or of the Sénat. They were permanent, whereas the cabinets were not, and they were critical to the passage of legislation. The Comité du Budget (budget commission of the Chambre) and the Comité des Finances (finance commission of the Sénat) were in privileged positions; they had the right from 1914 to make on-the-spot inspections of war matériel.

On 2 August 1914 President Raymond Poincaré declared that a state of siege existed in the eighty-six metropolitan and three African départementes; the laws of 1849 and 1879 came into force, curbing civil liberties and authorizing the army to requisition anything it needed. At the same time, there were no provisions for civilian needs nor for the roles of Parlement, of ministers, and of the military handling of supply firms and labor, nor for who should allocate priority matériel. The Ministère de la Guerre had assumed a short war and overlooked the impact of total mobilization on the economy. From 4 August when Parlement ratified the state of siege and removed itself from the war, the government ruled by executive decree à la Louis XIV.

Early in August 1914, even before the declaration of war, the labor minister in Paris lifted the overtime restrictions for industries involved in national defense to maintain and increase production. Shortly, women and adolescents were added to the workforce; 89 of the 114 inspectors of factories were called up, and 19 retired. The military took control of the war matériel producers. No similar plans, however, seem to have been laid or to have been considered for 1939.[18]

But very quickly a shortage of munitions highlighted the years of neglect of industrial preparation needed for war. Skilled hands had to be retrieved from the army, but at the same time the immediate loss of northeast France hampered recovery. Moreover, the bureaucrats were inexperienced in modern war and lacked the talents needed, and the flight of the government to Bordeaux, as in 1870, bifurcated leadership. But France did grasp the task and reorganized the economy to meet the challenges of war: consortia were created in the various areas of supply, military and civilian, and new offices emerged to handle fresh responsibilities. In 1917 Premier Clemenceau, with his iron determination to win the war, ended legislative control of the executive. He placed in key bureaucratic positions hardworking, efficient, and responsible executives, many of whom were businesspeople and technocrats.

In February 1918 the government obtained total decree authority to cover production, distribution, and sale of products for human and animal consumption. Policies subsequently evolved to meet specific crises. But deprived of its industrial and raw materials in the northeast, France had to seek credit, production, and transportation from abroad. The country had to import wheat, coal, and sugar, and it had to pay for them. Necessity caused the creation of interallied purchasing and shipping commissions and parallel organizations within France. And the British increasingly demanded that the French make the same sacrifices and accept the same limitations as their British counterparts, thus forcing the almost complete regulation of the French economy.

Each time the British were asked to make up French deficiencies, they demanded greater French internal controls. In January 1916 London created the Shipping Control Committee reporting directly to the Cabinet. Earlier, in mid-1915, on any day there were some two hundred ships lying idle in French ports. The press was not amused. The solution was regulation of the French railways to make more goods (freight) trains available to clear the harbors. That summer was not a good one for French harvests and was followed by unrestricted U-boat warfare, which forced the French to impose import controls. When at the end of 1916 Lloyd George became prime minister in London, Britain really applied the pressure. By the end of 1917 London and Paris had combined their purchasing and distribution systems as well as licensing, which in 1918 included the United States. The Inter-Allied Food Council was set up in 1917. The last stage was the creation in 1918 of the Inter-Allied Munitions Council.

On top of the crushing manpower casualties and the pressing nature of what was really a Pyrrhic victory, the French smarted from the affront to their great power status of this evidence that they could not run their own economy but had to submit to the mercantile sense and dominance of the British. Godfrey shows how the Allies protected the living standards of their populations and at the same time equipped their armies for victory—with a political economy of war.[19]

France, 1914–1918

In France, the tensions between the front (the *grand quartier général*, or GQG; French army field HQ) and Paris led throughout the war to appointments and political dismissals in both places. The GQG Service Aéronautique attempted to meet the unanticipated needs of the front and of the reserves. Industry received contracts for both aircraft and engines, but efficient production was hampered by lack of blueprints, rising labor and material costs, and so on, as well as the calling up of skilled labor. Also creating havoc was the habit of the front to send pilots directly to factories to commandeer needed replacement machines.

Deliveries in late 1914 were half those promised and lacked accountability. Divisions between GQG and Paris broke into the open in July 1915 and caused changes in leadership. Three months later, a statistical office was established, together with an inspector general at the front to keep tabs on matériel there. In Paris the directorates were reorganized and reported to the newly created undersecretary of state for the twelfth directorate (supply). However, these changes did not solve the need for interchangeability of parts, probably not really possible at the time of rapid technological change. All of this had led to a politically inspired stalemate by May 1916.

One of the tensions was between the introduction of reliable engines and the development of those of higher horsepower for new designs, which was also a tension between quantity and quality. By 1917 French aviation was going on the offensive with Pétain of Verdun in command. He advocated seizing local air superiority, as over Verdun, while allowing forces to protect observation aircraft. In July he complained that only 55 percent of the 1,292 planes manufactured had reached the front and that these lacked manuals, were short of spares and some even of engines, while others had poorly installed guns, or no fuel tanks or radiators—complaints that also antedated 1940.

After the Briand Cabinet fell early in 1917, the new under-secretary, an air observer, moved to unify and centralize his organization. Parts were subcontracted to expand production and the labor force rose from the 12,000 in 1914 to some 90,000 in 1917, but there were still thirty-seven different types of aircraft on order. A proposal to produce four thousand aircraft by October 1918 was approved, but foundered for shortage of workers. Moreover, Division Commander Duval needed four hundred pilots a month rather than the two hundred he was getting in 1917. (Part of the problem was accident attrition at 50 percent per month.)

On 15 November 1917 Georges Clemenceau became prime minister and at once decreed action. Already 75 percent of French aircraft and engine production in September was of modern types, and production for all of 1917 was 14,915 aircraft and 23,092 engines.

By 1918 the number of types of aircraft in production had been reduced to thirteen, and casualties had been reduced to 1,324 in combat and 1,003 from accidents annually. During May to October accidents were 75 percent of combat casualties (though GQG estimated them at 33 percent). However, new designs took twelve months to produce and a further three months to introduce to squadrons.

In 1918 finally came the technological management of production with Albert Caquot of balloon fame put in charge of the S.T.Aé. (Section Technique de l'Aéronautique; technical section for aeronautics). He quickly discovered and cured the fault in the 220-horsepower Hispano-Suiza engine, which failed the ten-hour endurance test, soon raising it to one hundred hours. As Bernard Gonon has noted, the 300-horsepower Renault by 1918 was achieving two hundred hours and the weight per horsepower had dropped from 1914's 4.8 pounds to 1.6 pounds.[20] French understanding of engines was well advanced of the British by 1919.[21] In 1918 alone French engine-makers delivered 44,563 engines versus the British total of 41,000 for four years of World War I. By the 1918 Armistice, French manufacturers were delivering an engine every ten minutes, twenty-four hours a day, and a complete airplane every fifteen minutes.[22]

Labor underwent a severe transformation during the war. By November 1918 the 185,000 workers were 23 percent women. The American Taylorism had been pressed, but the shop floor had resisted for the time-and-motion studies deskilled jobs, and so the government stepped in with subsidies and the few *patronats* profited. The solutions discussed in 1914–1915 were still unsettled in 1939. The war disintegrated the trade union movements, but there were also strikes and turnover: Renault during 1914–1918 hired 135,925 workers to maintain a force of 22,500 in 1918.[23]

While the British suffered seven times the strikes with forty-nine times the workers out, as Laura Lee Downs pointed out in *Manufacturing Inequality*, British owners and workers talked with each other and kept verbatim notes, whereas the French could not deal face to face, as Stanley Hoffman noted in 1959.[24] In November 1918 the Arme Aéronautique had 336 squadrons with 6,417 pilots, 1,682 observers, and 80,000 ground-services personnel, but overall had lost 77 percent of the aircraft on strength, including rebuilds.

Britain, 1914–1918

World War I saw 3 million people involved in the arms industries and another 850,000 officers and men killed by 1918, with the loss of junior officers being three times that of soldiers.[25] And, noted A. J. P. Taylor, there was still a legacy of 1.5 million wounded and gassed, which caused wide moral disaffection. Britain had also lost 40 percent of its merchant fleet.[26]

Owing to the way the British aircraft industry was started, its path was different from that across the Channel, yet not always more advanced.[27] The RNAS was technically progressive, whereas the RFC Military Wing sought to standardize. The Royal Aircraft Factory at Farnborough designed both airframes and engines, while the RNAS gave Rolls-Royce a German Mercedes automobile and told the company to develop an aeroengine.

The 1914 months of the war saw only 193 aircraft delivered, 99 of which were licensed French designs.[28] But in October the British War Office opened design and production to the trade and soon sent engine fitters and airframe riggers to be trained.

While in 1915 Brig. Gen. Hugh Trenchard succeeded to the post of adviser to the commander of the BEF, the RFC was run from the War Office by Gen. David Henderson and Sefton Brancker. But both the RFC and the RNAS, as John H. Morrow notes, were hampered by their failure prewar to see the need for air arms, and their consequent need to create infrastructures.[29] Moreover, the RFC insisted it needed officer pilots, resulting in a collection of individuals who regarded air combat as sport and suffered 50 percent casualties.

Although the RNAS had to transfer Home Air Defence to the RFC on 16 February 1916, it did think grand-strategically, began a night-bombing campaign in Belgium, and initiated plans for an Anglo-French bombing campaign against Germany. Meanwhile, public fears and political attacks characterized the German zeppelin raids as an air menace about to ruin the country. This combined with demands for 20,000 planes, reprisal raids, and support for a single air ministry. Though the War Office and the Admiralty competed in the marketplace, in 1915 some thirty-four companies supplied 1,680 machines.

To overcome shortages the War Office shifted from competitive bids to cost-plus contracts, while advancing 20 percent for materials and paying another 60 percent when the aircraft was approved by the Aeronautical Inspection Department and successfully tested, after which the balance was paid. In the case of engines, 30 percent were French supplied. This led to all British requests being filtered by the French government, which then took control of its own aircraft industry. All told, only 1,721 were delivered.

For 1916, the RFC concentrated on getting a brigade wing for each division. Formation flying was ordered to combat the Fokkers, the "V" (vic) of three being created as escorts for the venerable BE-2Cs. RFC losses in the winter of 1916 were only 31 to the enemy, 33 from deterioration in the open, and 134 to accidents. The latter created a conflict between the offensive-minded RFC in France and HQ London, which saw the need for more than fifteen hours of training before combat. By 1917 there were twenty-five new training establishments in Britain versus eleven a year earlier. Because Hugh Dowding, in 1940 the victorious leader of RAF Fighter Command, asked that squadrons with high casualties be relieved, he was sent to Training Command at Home. As the Germans gained air superiority while conserving their pilots, the RFC's Western Front position deteriorated.

Meanwhile the extent of the RFC-RNAS problem was still misunderstood. It was not fully resolved when Lloyd George became prime minister on 7 December 1916. He established the four-member War Cabinet, made Churchill his successor as the munitions minister, and added a fifth sea lord for air to the Board of Admiralty. Churchill assumed control of the design and supply of air matériel while the new Air Board was empowered to coordinate RFC and RNAS policies. In 1916 the aircraft industry produced 5,716 aircraft and 5,363 engines of the 7,227 needed.

War-winning aircraft were on their way for 1917—the SE-5A fighter, the Sopwith Camel, and the two-seat Brisfit, not to mention the DH-9 light bomber and the Handley Page HP-100 heavy bomber.

In 1917 aggressive tactics on the Western Front protected the observation planes spotting for the artillery. However, the Germans were better and the RFC suffered disastrously in the spring. But reequipped with modern aircraft by September, the RFC was regaining the upper hand. Surprised by the German counteroffensive at Cambrai (November–December 1917), RFC officers began to criticize spreading their assets all along the front versus concentration, one of the elementary principles of war. By late November HQ understood, and training for the spring of 1918, together with conservation, became the mode. Well-trained crews, thanks to the Gosport method, were filling the squadrons. Still the High Command stayed with the peculiarly British notion that bombing would bring peace.[30]

By late 1917 Sir William Weir, a marine steam-engineering executive from early 1917 in the Ministry of Munitions, controlled aeronautical supplies. Under his stable administration these deliveries doubled. But the daylight German bombings of London in mid-1917 led to the Smuts Report, and that to the Act that created the British Air Ministry from 1 January 1918 followed by the amalgamated RAF on 1 April.

By the end of 1917 there were 771 firms in aviation employing 173,969 workers producing 14,382 airframes and 11,763 engines, though few engines of the higher horsepower needed. Munitions had placed its faith for 1918 in the new ABC Dragonfly, but it proved to be a disaster, and the alternative Hispano-Suiza was unreliable. Rolls-Royce made up some of the gap, as did the dependable American Liberties. And thus, by the end of 1917, Weir could plan a 240-squadron RAF. But early in 1918 he had to warn that 65 percent of the 20,000 new engines on order would suffer crankshaft failure due to a shortage of suitable forgings. Plans to expand the RAF in 1918 thus collapsed because of that shortage, as well as the lack of skilled tool-room labor, alloy steel, and ball bearings.

Anticipating the German March offensive, the new commander of the RAF in France, John Salmond (Trenchard had gone to be chief of the Air Staff [CAS] of the RAF) ordered airfields to be selected and trailers supplied to facilitate squadron moves overnight. Though Salmond lost 1,302 aircraft in a month, he had by low-flying attacks regained control over the front. By the Armistice on 11 November 1918, the RAF had consumed 2,692 machines but had absorbed 2,647 replacements. In other theaters, the RAF had air superiority. When in June 1918 Weir became secretary of state for air, he supported grand-strategic bombing and ordered the giant Handley Page V-1500 to be able to attack Berlin.

Meanwhile the German March offensive had taken 100,000 workers out of the industry and production in France dropped. Nevertheless, by October 1918 the workforce was 347,112, which delivered 32,565 aircraft and 22,088 plus 9,181 French engines through October 1918.

Production for the war totaled 67,987 French, 58,144 British, and 48,537 German aircraft. The World War I story should have informed the planners for World War II. The French story, especially, as John H. Morrow noted, seems to anticipate 1934–1940.[31] But France was so anxious for peace and security that it chose to ignore the lessons of 1914–1918.

Conclusions

World War I marked a watershed between the Napoleonic nineteenth-century colonial, limited conflicts, and modern industrial war. In its aftermath were lessons to be learned at all levels. Grand-strategically, it was becoming evident that even the great powers had to manage their wars and that these had to be in coalitions. National and international resources of all sorts—economic and financial, industrial, military, and the manpower pool—had to be integrated into an overall plan that took into account not only military necessities, but also aviation. With the whole nation at war, food and morale, as well as civilian psychology, had to be of concern.

The Franco-British legacies included the need for an overall cabinet management of the struggle and the necessity of having a means to integrate the national economies on both sides of the Channel into a seamless system, and a fear of casualties.

On the strategic level, manpower was as critical as armaments. The total of what was available, both male and female as well as the underaged, had to be rationed among agriculture, industry, shipping, and the armed services, which required both priorities and mathematical analyses of demands. It led to conservation on the battlefield and on the home front. At sea, it meant convoys, and on the land, trench warfare and a search for technologies to make the fighting more efficient, a theme also carried into the air. While the French produced and consumed the larger share of air matériel, the British wasted the great number of personnel by their offensive, hunting approach.

Though the French turned out more engines, a weakness was evident in the French failure to undertake thorough testing, analysis, and modification, due in part, of course, to demand. Moreover, aviation was in constant flux because of the stimulation of competition with the enemy and paradoxically the need to standardize for efficiency. The RAF understood this in 1917 when it began to specify common fittings and tools.

The strategy and tactics of production, whether of pilots or planes, were different on the two sides of the Channel. French production in *ateliers* around Paris plus French politics meant that neither the higher direction (overall planning and execution) of the Arme Aéronautique nor production advanced as far as it did in London. The German air raids inspired fear of an air menace in the French capital, while in London they brought on positive responses—an air ministry, a ministry of munitions' supervision of production, and the creation of the prototype Air Defence of Great Britain (ADGB). The index of French industrial production dropped from a basis in 1913 at 100 to 57 in 1919, rising to 140 in 1929, then dropping away, not reaching 140 again until the 1950s.

Overall, the larger lesson of World War I was that trench warfare, a very territorial state of siege, was too costly. There had to be a better way of war with far less consumption of manpower and money. This conclusion led thinkers in Britain and Germany to mobile armored warfare; the French response, though, was the Maginot Line and the deliberate-battle artillery approach, the legacy of Verdun. Postwar the French were concerned with their security and the gold standard. The British took a more insular and imperial view. The old entente was viewed differently across the Channel, as was the idea of appeasement. Both perspectives were legacies of the Peace of Versailles.

PART II
THE INTERWAR YEARS, 1918–1934

POSTWAR, 1918–1932

The Two Peoples

The Channel clearly has been a divider down through the centuries between a continental Gallic people and an insular Anglo-Saxon. Oxford don Salvador de Madariaga, a Spaniard who was a British delegate to the Geneva disarmament talks of 1928, described the then–cultural differences between the two nations.[1] Madariaga noted that the French stood for the *droit* (the right to do something) and intellect. They liked to think about prospective action, theorize and rationalize about tomorrow, and define and study schemes looking for ordered principles and preestablished laws—and that approach led to a "war" psychology. The average French person's foresight was self-defensive, and he expected to produce order. The French were irritable in action and lost their sangfroid, whereas the English were phlegmatic. The French favored the *attaque brusque* (sudden attack) and surprise. The French person's forte was knowledge, not action, and thus he judged activities by intellectual standards. The divisions of the Revolution of 1789 had healed somewhat in 1871 by shock when a beaten France came together as a nation, but a de Gaulle–like man on horseback was still lacking.[2]

French order was not spontaneous, but official and imposed from above, regulated, and accepted from below. This led to action being preceded by a complicated series of written laws or orders that aimed to foresee all possible cases, a network of principles to which all future action must conform under the *droit* and the *règlements* (rules) dictated by foresight and inspired by distance. The structure in France was political, whereas in Britain it was social. Social and political organization in France was thus externally imposed and tended to become rigid. The bureaucracy was centralized and, as the saying goes, as went Paris, so went France. The French colonial empire was much a governmental affair of map coloring—indicating territories of little economic value directed, if at all, from Paris.[3]

Parliament in Britain, with its opposing benches, was an exclusive club; its members, mostly gentlemen, also belonged to exclusively men's clubs when the members were in town. Parlement in France was a semicircular chamber with constantly shifting attitudes. These continuing mores were reflected in the air forces. In France, Ministre de l'Air Pierre Cot, a Radical Socialist, met with hostility when he attempted to train lower-class pilots at what they viewed as pretentious flying clubs. In Britain, the flying clubs were much more egalitarian, though the Royal Auxiliary Air Force's county squadrons carried on the élite club tradition on a territorial basis.[4]

As Fernand Braudel pointed out in the second volume of *The Identity of France*, there were few large merchant-traders in France, few large entrepreneurs, few risk takers.[5] Gaul up to 1939 was a nation in a rural setting with a large peasant economy as well as an economy of separate individual small traders, but no gamblers. In part this was because of a lack of primogeniture, each family member being assured of only a small part of the estate. Britain, however, in spite of the ingrained derisive Napoleonic French view that it was a nation of shopkeepers, was in contrast a country of primogeniture and risk-taking merchants and adventurers. It was maritime and not continental in outlook and—especially after the repeal of the Corn Laws in 1842—was willing to gamble on an overseas food supply to the benefit of industrialists at home.[6]

Alfred Thayer Mahan's 1893 determination of the factors that governed naval success—locations and resources, population and government—also indicated why France was a military rather than a naval power, focused on the army and the land frontier rather than on the navy and the sea. While Britain could enjoy splendid insular isolation coupled to imperial and commercial success, France from at least 1871 on feared the new German state. In the seventeenth century, Louis XIV had sought a frontier on the Rhine as a national barrier, and that was echoed again in the 1919 peace settlements and in the Allied occupation of the Rhineland. Versailles left the French feeling insecure, and rightly so, as Hitler showed from 1936 on.

As French military thought and plans developed, the Arme Aéronautique conceived the notion of a bombing force that would strike German industrial targets. The problem with this independent Douhetian approach of focusing on strategic enemy targets was that there were far too many of them, and the Armée de l'Air after 1933 never calculated the force and logistical support needed to do the job. For British planners, the objective already had been set in 1917 with the intention to use the giant Handley Page V-1500 to bomb Berlin, while at the same time developing the Home-based air defenses against German air raids—the air menace of the interwar years, seen first as emanating from Paris and after 1933 from Berlin.[7]

Geographic location as well as national outlook caused France to think in terms of army and linear defense, whereas Britain thought as a naval maritime power with a mercantile empire and a steady refusal to engage in a continental commitment in spite of the Duke of Marlborough, the War of Spanish Succession, and the Crimea. World War I was the exception. It was not until the spring of 1939, on the eve of World War II, that conscription was introduced and the army set to expand to fifty-five divisions.[8]

These realities affected the air arms. The French were shackled to the army and to the defense policy dominated by its Haut Commandement. In contrast, the RAF's independent role was approved in 1923 as Home Air Defence with, in theory, a strong offensive deterrent component, reinforced in 1935 as the handmaiden of appeasement.[9] The RAF saw Army Cooperation Command as a lip-service command.

In Britain all railways led to and from London so that the fastest route between two disparate points was through the capital. But the political system was quite different, in that provincialism was countered by members of Parliament not having to reside in their constituencies. Instead, the central party organization selected candidates to run, and the local constituents were free to choose whether to accept these nominations.

North of the Channel, then, there lived a body of people who saw themselves in sharp contrast to the French. They believed they were of the time, self-controlled, self-disciplined, easy-going persons who were not intellectuals but who worked with forces in a utilitarian way so that action would be fruitful as measured in a solid and weighty manner and in which ends could be achieved by compromise. They saw themselves as people wholly devoted to action, common practical sense, and the liberty of supreme disinterestedness.

The British believed that they had a genius for cooperation and spontaneous organization within well-defined groups, and that they were honest and had little patience with or concern for fraud. They believed that the parliamentary system of a loyal opposition led, on the whole, to constructive criticism rather than to challenges over principles.

In the British view, the laws sought and obeyed were not natural but practical—those of the sea, the road, and hunting. Restrictions were placed on the individual for the commonweal and that led to the concept of fair play. There was the idea, too, of the right man in the right place, and the acceptance of the disinterested leadership of the aristocracy, who recognized noblesse oblige. The class system generally was accepted. And, while the English might be shy at home, they were not self-conscious abroad.

To Victorian British minds and on into World War II, the Empire was something of which to be proud—even if occasional actions against its colonial natives were played down. Nevertheless, the British were concerned that this Empire might dissolve. However, at the coronation of King George VI in 1937, proud contingents from across the British realm would two years later join the country in another "Great War." Certainly in the past there had been incidents such as the 1857 Sepoy Mutiny in British-ruled India, but they had not yet been colored by post-1945 humanitarianism and anticolonialism.

It is easy today, far removed from the milieu of the interwar years and the knowledge and prejudices then present, to lay strictures on what had been done in years past. The morality or immorality of the grand-strategic bombing campaign can be seen quite differently in the twenty-first century than it was at the time. Coastal naval bombardments by Kaiserliche Marine (the imperial German navy), and its zeppelin attacks on London were much in the minds of planners in Britain in those interwar years. The intent was to destroy the will of the enemy people to make war economically, as opposed to once again racking up immense casualties in another land campaign.[10]

As British Bomber Command found out very quickly after 1939, its prewar technical assumptions were all wrong, and more than five years' time would be needed to put them right. The Command determined that bombers could not hit a target smaller than a city unless they adopted an entirely different approach, one using Mosquito light bombers instead of Halifax and Lancaster heavies. Similarly, incendiaries used by the Germans in 1915–1918 had been more effective against the cities than against the factories.[11]

The languages of the French and British even show interesting contrast. English is a monosyllabic language of action and community. Words are representative of acts. French, on the other hand, is multisyllabic, intellectual, and passive. English elides and eliminates unneeded syllables, whereas French emphasizes each one, producing a language that is accurate, precise, and unambiguous, though perhaps leading to a tendency toward abstraction as well as a desire for logic and clarity. But this character of the French language leads to a love of theoretical planning for many eventualities as opposed to what can be seen as a more typical British lethargy that prevails until necessity compels them to carry out a newly made plan tailored to a specific situation, a result reached, no doubt, by compromise.

In France patriotism was the drawing force of *patrie*—a glorious intellectual vision, the pageant of the military past, indicative that France was universally the homeland of all people. In contrast, patriotism in Britain was almost purely Anglo-Saxon and instinctive—and less emotional. Individuals were part of the country. Men went to war for "king and country" and not for "*la patrie*."

Politics in France were fluid due to the semicircular shape of the Sénat and the Chambre des Députés and the fact that members could easily shift their allegiance from Left to Right, or to parties in between. This was in contrast to the two sets of opposing benches in the House of Lords and Commons in the British Parliament, one set of which was occupied by His Majesty's Loyal Opposition. After World War I Parlement ruled through large permanent committees while a kaleidoscope of cabinets passed, averaging tenures of six months. Parlement was filled with members elected in their own constituencies and who sometimes still retained positions there. The president of France was elected and not impartial, in contrast to the sovereign in Britain.

One of the weaknesses of the French system was that the *patronats* and other leaders shunned politics; as a result, the senators and deputies never heard them speak but derived their knowledge of the industrial and business segment from the Parisian newspapers—a tainted and self-serving source. By contrast, persons such as the chair of Lloyd's of London, the large insurer, sat in the British Parliament and advised on proposed legislation.

Politics in Britain, though moving quite remarkably to democracy in the nineteenth century, was still a gentleman's game. There was a sense of fair play, there were few committees, and the generally long-lived (five years) governments enjoyed the confidence of the House of Commons. Private incomes helped avert corruption, lobbyists for special interests were known members of Parliament, and the armed forces were generally left to carry out policy laid down by the Cabinet. From the time of Edward VII (1901–1910), there always were some subcommittees of the Committee of Imperial Defence (CID), and occasionally, notably in the contentious 1920s, special advisory bodies to adjudicate interservice disputes. Even when the two-party system in the twentieth century was destabilized by the sudden election in 1924 of Labour, many of that party's leaders were scions of the upper class. The peaceful general strike of 1926 was as close as Britain came to class warfare in the interwar years. The British liked to think that their tradition was that of the Glorious Revolution of 1688, not that of the bloody French Revolution of 1789.

In the ten years preceding the British general strike of 1926, such protests had involved 1 million workers each year. In the ten years following 1926 they never involved more than 300,000. This reduction was due to a change of spirit rather than to discouragement and defeat. The showdown between the coal miners and the Welsh owners over lowering wages and adding hours was the ultimate workers' strike, but it failed during 1925–1926.[12] The 1926 action brought to the front labor leaders who put conciliation above strife. The events of 1926 also were a warning to the owners, themselves now more conciliatory. Outside the coal industry, wages remained stable until 1929, by which time, with the fall in the cost of living, the worker was better off, until the Great Depression.[13] And then when employers eschewed conflict, wage rates declined far less than in other countries because wages had become a fixed charge.[14]

Comparing and contrasting Britain and France in the interwar years, the nature of the people appears sharply different. One of the reasons for the delayed Rearmament and modernization of the Armée de l'Air and for the defeat in June 1940 was that France in the critical period of 1935–1938 was plagued with industrial conflict and politics. There were bitter strikes among the metalworkers, and in 1936 the newly victorious Socialist Front Populaire nationalized the arms industry. In Britain, the course in general was more one of compromise and progress.

Perhaps a factor here was the monarchy, which unlike the French presidency was not political in any but the very highest sense of guidance and stability. Within this framework it was possible to have the Royal Navy, the British Army, and the RAF go about their tasks—and to have the country warned from 1932 of world dangers, the need to rearm, and above all to have the funding supply, provided by Parliament, as the king's ministers urged. Not only were the armed forces apolitical in a party sense, but they also were apolitical in a partisan sense. Officers of the armed forces, like civil servants, loyally followed their political masters. Whereas in France policy was heavily determined by such as the Sénat and Comité Aéronautique de la Chambre des Députés (the aeronautical committee of the chamber of deputies), in Britain policy was a Cabinet matter based on the proposed annual estimates submitted by the responsible ministers and vetted by the CID. Yet, when Sir Thomas Inskip in 1936 became the nonexecutive minister for the Co-ordination of Defence and Admiral Lord Chatfield succeeded Sir Maurice Hankey as the secretary of the CID, they remained impartial in using their best judgments for the commonweal.

These differences in approach, constitutional structure, and service roles can be seen in the way the two air forces evolved during the interwar years. The very physical nature of the French legislative chambers affected the decision-making process, for the Chambre des Députés had derived from the Greek amphitheater and the warm Mediterranean climate. It also was acoustically practical. But it meant that there was no clear division of opinions and parties, and thus French governments were too often coalitions that lasted only as long as the compromises agreed to form them.

The British House of Commons' ancestry was the Viking longhouse with benches facing each other. The Government sat to the speaker's right, and the Loyal Opposition to the left. Minor parties sat below the gangway halfway down the chamber. Members were, therefore, either for or against the government, which generally made for decisions and not for waffling.

In the case of defense expenditures in the latter 1930s, the Government in London, holding a majority, could propose and have its policy accepted, because the Cabinet had already decided in 1934 that the RAF was crucial to the security of Great Britain. Part of this decision also was a British understanding of the lag in developing production and the placing, therefore, of large orders early on. The French were hampered by the inability to develop viable designs, notably due not only to the dominance of the army but also due to the narrow niggardliness of the Ministère des Finances and of the impact of inflation. Though the Socialists thought about national defense, the Banque de France and the Ministère des Finances were concerned about the gold standard, the value of the franc, and the flight of capital, all of which constricted the effective view of the dangers facing the *patrie*.[15] All in all, the two countries were not only physically and geographically different—they also saw the world and thought differently, and still do. This was reflected in the way they procured aircraft, as noted later.

Appendix I, Presidents, Ministers, Chiefs of Staff, France (1914–1940), and Appendix II, Prime Ministers, Foreign Secretaries, and Air Ministers of Great Britain (1914–1940) herein are illustrative of the ongoing changes in French politics as compared to what was seen and perceived in Britain to be a time of more basic continuity.

The Decision-Making Process

Among the comparisons and contrasts between the French and the British was the way in which each approached the making of policy, the definition of doctrine, and the ordering of technical procurement. Each had the same objectives: (1) protection against the air menace, (2) an independent counterstrike force, (3) army cooperation (*aviation d'assaut*) close support, and (4) colonial security.

Grand strategy is a continuous policy plan that guides the national destiny. It has to take into account not only possible enemies and their strengths and weaknesses, but also the need for alliances and the assets and debits of such. In addition, the makers of grand strategy have to consider, weigh, and plan to secure the nation's resources at home and overseas. Overall, grand strategy has to take account of the time and resources needed to implement any action. None of this can be done without intelligence (knowledge) and the means to bring it to the attention of decision-makers.

Part of the in-depth background delineated in Higham and Harris' *Why Air Forces Fail* points to the fact that the outcomes of the Battles of France and Britain in 1940 had their roots in events before and during World War I.[16] One of the major controversies of the disarmament era of 1922–1934 was over the international Armée de l'Air the French favored versus the independent Air Arm the British wanted. Part of that argument concerned the ability to convert airliners into bombers.[17]

This aspect of foreign policy was in theory the purview not merely of the cabinets on either side of the Channel, but also of the militaries. Yet advice came to the cabinets by different decision-making routes. The late nineteenth century saw the French, in the wake of the perceived success of the Prussian general staff in 1870–1871, develop their own such apparatus. North of the Channel, the long influence of Wellington and of the royal Duke of Cambridge as commanders in chief, plus lack of involvement in other than the Crimean War and colonial skirmishes, caused a wait until after the ignominy of the Boer War of 1899–1902. Then Lord Esher's 1904 report caused reform to be undertaken and the appointment of the chief of the Imperial General Staff (CIGS) in the War Office. Over and above those changes was the creation, in 1904, of the CID, a policy-making body chaired by the prime minister or his deputy.[18]

In London, where the civilians clearly ruled and a Wellington as prime minister was a rare exception, the CID became the funnel through which most defense matters reached the Cabinet and became policy. The CID soon had its own secretariat and so ordered business. Until David Lloyd George became prime minister, there had been no Cabinet agenda and no minutes. Lloyd George changed all that during his 1916–1922 term. A secretary of the Cabinet was appointed and an agenda was prepared beforehand; the secretary ensured that necessary papers were circulated to colleagues before the Cabinet met and that conclusions were accurately recorded in the minutes. The new system was essential; the old one hid secrets. British civil servants did not disclose government secrets, and this applied also to the official printers (His Majesty's Stationery Office). It was the ministers who sometimes were guilty of leaks, and parliamentary "lobby" correspondents who were, and still are, adept at drawing conclusions.

Importantly, in 1908 Maj. Maurice Hankey became the assistant secretary of the CID, in 1912 the secretary, and in 1916 the secretary of the Cabinet Office. This "man of secrets," as Roskill called him, gradually became immensely powerful behind the scenes.[19] Across the Channel in France, however, such a simple routine as keeping minutes of Cabinet meetings and following them up was not introduced until 1945. The nature of the bureaucracy and its processes and the structure of government were also quite different on either side of the Channel. The philosophies of ruling in a historical fashion affected the way business was conducted.

The French military system, though no longer dominated by aristocrats, was still run in a hierarchical manner. It was yet a preindustrial command arrangement, which was entirely unsuited to conditions of 1940, though it had just survived the war of 1914–1918. That war had removed HQ to châteaux well behind the lines, where the realities of the artillery were muted by distance. The German blitzkrieg of 1940 eviscerated national concepts, and on the ground and in the air by 14 May the French, and to a lesser extent the British, were defeated.

Organizational change combines continuity with new ideas, and that takes time. In the case of the French and British air establishments and the milieu in which they existed and grew, they had to fight battles against entrenched professionalism and prejudices with a shortage of experience and staff expertise in a climate of technological innovation and change and legacies of the Victorian century. In France by 1936 the national organization for war was the CSDN, chaired by the prime minister and attended by the Cabinet and the chiefs of staff. In 1936 a defense minister was appointed to coordinate the work of the Ministère de la Guerre, the Ministère de la Marine (ministry of the navy), the Ministère de l'Air (ministry of air), and the Ministère des Colonies (ministry of colonies). In January of that year Édouard Daladier, as both defense minister and war minister (and one of the founders of the Front Populaire in 1935), had taken powers to intervene by decree in Rearmament. That October, ten years after the founding of the two-year Imperial Defence College in London, the Institut des Hautes Études de Défense Nationale (college for the advanced study of national defense) came into being in Paris with a six-month civilianized course.

Defense in Paris was dominated until 1930 by the marshals of France, but after them by Marshal Pétain alone and his successors, Gen. Maxime Weygand and Gen. Maurice Gamelin. Because the Armée de l'Air was subject by precedent to the laws governing the army, airmen were frustrated in getting their views across. Anthony Adamthwaite's exposition of France and the French people in *Grandeur and Misery* provides a number of clues as to why the Armée de Terre and eventually the Armée de l'Air failed to develop policy and doctrine as well as the machinery for carrying them out.[20] To start, few of the military hierarchy were graduates of the École Libre des Sciences Politiques (free school of political science) and were thus excluded from the élite, who not only served in the cabinets, averaging two a year during 1919–1940, but also did not attend the salons and the literary clubs. One of the rare military members of the 1930s élite was Marshal Pétain. And though in theory France was a rational country, in fact it was run casually by persons who on the one hand passionately believed in spoken words solving problems, yet on the other were suspicious of the state and a strong executive. The result was casualness and a lack of preparation. In aviation terms this translated into the failure to realize the nature of the new warfare—in part because many French people were provincial and had little knowledge of or interest in international affairs.[21]

There had been no overall coordinating machinery, and key Cabinet decisions were made, in Adamthwaite's words, by gesticulating huddles of senior ministers. Moreover, those responsible tended to concentrate on details while the major important decisions were constantly put off to another day, and then rarely was there the necessary scrutiny of the proposals. A member of the Comité des Forges described one of his group's meetings: "We splutter and argue, conversations go on forever and everyone talks at the same time."[22]

In Paris, the making of policy was vastly more complicated and squalid than it was in London. Politicians and members of the other services could attend the deliberations of the GSAF, thus inhibiting discussion in such a way that the Armée de l'Air never clearly defined its purpose and the means to achieve it. Moreover the Armée de Terre, in the person in the latter 1930s of General Gamelin, who wore several hats, dominated these higher councils. But even worse, the Chambre des Députés and the Sénat of Parlement each had a services committee, which also exerted a great lethargic and baleful influence, such that few ministers lasted long enough to accomplish their programs. Small wonder then that there was confusion both as to activities and to structure. It is not, therefore, at all surprising that a later chief of the Service Historique de l'Armée de l'Air (historical service of the French air force) complained that he could not figure out the structure of the Haut Commandement of the French armed forces.[23]

Of forty-six French prime ministers from 1914 to 1940, only five did not also hold another portfolio while trying to keep a fragile Cabinet together (and still have time for their dalliances).[24] Daily survival took precedence over grand strategy and departmental coordination, and too much was ad hoc and dependent on personalities, preoccupations, and political clout. Moreover, for a long time voters had chosen the leaders for their lack of independent spirit, thus assuring the domination of mediocrities, including those in the chain of command of the armed services.

By the Constitution of 1875, the Cabinet made foreign policy without reference to Parlement. In wartime the military also acted on its own responsibility, though in peace Parlement's legislative, military, and economic committees had the same say. The road to the Munich Agreement in 1938 was paved by the almost complete independence of the foreign minister and his personal Cabinet, which enabled him to bypass his own senior bureaucrats. In addition, grand strategy and diplomacy were seldom coordinated, because the CSDN had been set up in 1906, but it rarely had met and did not have a planning section until 1921. The Ministère de la Guerre suffered from a rapid succession of ministers and chiefs of staff, and a sprawling, duplicated, and overlapping structure. Those officers who had served before 1914 had learned to spout only the official line so as not to be the victim of inquisitions as to their religious and political views. And the civil servants were lethargic and more concerned with defending their ministerial prerogatives than they were with acting, which when combined with sectionalism meant multiple solutions, if any, to a problem. Officials treated files as their personal property and locked them away. And while teatime is always thought of as an English foible, in the ministries of Paris it was the highlight of the day, with prestige gambled on the cake served. The overoptimism and structural deficiencies of 1914 surfaced again in 1939.

In the brief twenty years between World War I and World War II, very few years made a vast difference—though the Armée de l'Air came too late in the game and suffered from Parisian indecision. The RAF, however, enjoyed a very different national climate and was just the two essential years ahead. The French lost the Battle of France during May–June 1940, but the RAF avoided defeat in the Battle of Britain from the summer of 1940 on.

The differences can be epitomized in Gen. Joseph Vuillemin, chief of the GSAF in Paris, and Air Chief Marshal Sir Hugh Dowding, air officer commanding in chief (AOC-in-C) of RAF Fighter Command. Vuillemin, a colonial flying hero, was very pessimistic about the Armée de l'Air surviving more than two weeks of a new war, whereas Dowding had long studied the technical necessities, confidently planned to defend Great Britain against the air menace, and had grasped the old and new tools with which to do so. In addition, he stood firm against 1940 French importunities to come to France's aid in a battle already lost.[25] This is a classic story of command, control, and communications (C_3) at all political and military levels.

The French and British Air Arms, 1919–1934

Of the principal powers in the interwar years, Britain and Italy had air ministries and independent air forces.[26] In Japan and the United States, separate army and navy air arms existed, and in both countries the naval air arms developed aircraft carriers and philosophies on their use. In America, military airmen, influenced by Billy Mitchell, sought independence and fought the Army over support of the ground forces as opposed to strategic—or rather grand-strategic—bombing. The U.S. Army Air Corps came into being in 1926 under Gen. Mason Patrick.

Many of the arguments in these air forces were the same as the arguments in France, but with at least two advantages. The first was that the politicians had less power and drive to alter the roles the airmen were to play. For instance, in Britain the postwar debates allowed the creation of the Fleet Air Arm (FAA) in 1924 after Parliament approved a fifty-two-squadron Home Defence Air Force (HDAF), essentially a deterrent. Related to this was the apolitical nature of the RAF, which was never represented in Parliament by a senior officer until the newly retired Trenchard was ennobled in 1930. In contrast, France was going through the usual throes of multiparty ministries, which left the Ministère de l'Air, created in 1928, to be led by junior politicians such as Laurent-Eynac, Cot, La Chambre, or a senior general, Denain.

Second, the approach to technical development differed in the various countries. Russia and the United States were well ahead until the late 1930s when they went out of synchronization with powers closer to war. Thanks to the Treaty of Versailles, the Germans had time to go to the basics. Britain's RAF had a deterrent doctrine but was totally unprepared to apply it in 1934. What the British, Russians, Germans, and Americans had going for them after 1934 was expanding aircraft production and manpower.

Perhaps in France this disastrously unsettled state of affairs was in part due to the absolutes to which debates led. In that land of realists, politicians, the press, and the airmen themselves argued passionately, yet indecisively. The military needed to make calculations of power relations, military strengths, and logistical requirements, as did their masters, the politicians and the bureaucrats.

A constant theme of the interwar years was the attitude of the Armée de Terre, long claimed to be Europe's most powerful. The story is of especial importance here as the needs of the Armée de Terre dominated the Arme Aéronautique and the new Armée de l'Air when it was created in 1933. Across the Channel, however, such discussions were essentially academic because until the spring of 1939 there was no British field army for a "continental commitment." The basic question was only between the bomber deterrent and Home Air Defence fighters.[27] Because in 1919 the British Cabinet had laid down the Ten Years' Rule, specifying that for planning purposes no major war was to be expected for that period, and because in 1928, as chancellor of the exchequer, Churchill had extended that rule on a rolling basis, Britain would not need to be prepared for a major war until 1939 or 1942.

In the period from the Armistice of 1918 to the 1935 emergence of the Luftwaffe and the start of Anglo-French Rearmament, each of the Allied air forces retrenched and stabilized, but along very different lines. The independent RAF staved off the attempts to dismantle it and managed to consolidate its position as the air defender of Great Britain, while at the same time being an economical force in colonial rule. In contrast, the Arme Aéronautique (established by the law of 8 December 1922) enjoyed organizational stability, yet remained a part of the army and was plentifully supplied with 1918-type aircraft for army cooperation. Not until a decade after the Air Ministry in London came into being did a similar office appear in Paris. And whereas the RAF had been created by an Act of Parliament in 1917, the Armée de l'Air only came into being by decree of the president in 1933.

The related aircraft and ancillary industries shrank from their 1914–1918 expansion. The French industry was buoyed up for a while by sizeable orders for standardized machines, and then declined after 1924. On the other side of the Channel, the British industry enjoyed survival through the recognition by the Air Ministry of the Ring, a minimal number of contracts, but a steady experimental developmental program.[28] Basically the structures on either side of the Channel in the interwar years were steps along the road to managing modern war with its enormous industrial base and unwieldy mass armies, but both France and Britain saw the next war faultily, thinking they would have time to sit on the defensive and build up their forces. In the RAF case, at least, there was to be a grand-strategic air offensive against France as part of the plan for the ADGB from 1924 to 1936. The problem was that neither ally considered what the opponent would do, never putting themselves in the enemy's shoes.[29]

Arme Aéronautique, 1918–1922

As Robert J. Young has pointed out, the French from 1916 on developed an impressive tactical bombing doctrine aimed to support the forces on the ground, but made air power subordinate to those forces. And the army had no doubt that the next war would be decided on the ground, thus air power was inserted into that vision. But France had to have time to build up for the decisive strategic offensive later, not an initial *offensive à outrance* as in 1914, and so the Arme Aéronautique had to provide *couverture* (cover). Internecine fighting in the 1920s occurred because the army believed the Armée Aéronautique was an auxiliary, whereas the airmen thought it was a war-winning weapon.[30]

After the 1918 Armistice, the Aéronautique Militaire (to 1922 the Arme Aéronautique) had had as its first responsibility the protection of Armée de Terre mobilization and covering of the opening battles. It was to be able to respond to war without waiting for reserves to be mobilized. After the end of World War I and demobilization, the Armée de Terre engaged in endless internal discussion of the role of the Arme Aéronautique: Was it to be dispersed to units or Duvalized? Complicating the rational conclusions and the establishment of a system were the ideas espoused by airmen, influenced by the Italian general Guilio Douhet, that the next war would be of very short duration and that it would largely consist of devastating bombing campaigns waged by both sides against the infrastructure and the civilian morale of their opponent. Thus both offense and home defense had the potential to become roles for aviation, but at the same time the army, and to a much lesser degree the navy, insisted that it had to have, as 1914–1918 had shown, direct air support.

At the Armistice on 11 November 1918, the Aéronautique Militaire had 299 aircraft squadrons. Ground personnel quickly went off to the old prewar life, but many of the fliers (cadets, reservists, and active) wanted a career in aviation. The older men who had civilian positions departed and the service was worse off. In the 1920s the Aéronautique Militaire was top-heavy with officers at higher ranks, but few of the captains had graduated from the military schools and nearly all the lieutenants had risen from the ranks.

Very few officers had been trained in staff work. These factors placed the Aéronautique Militaire in an inferior position to *l'état majeur* (the general staff), which placed pedigree above competence. The command of squadrons went to nonfliers with the requisite rank. The lieutenants of 1918 had little hope of reaching captain or major, as to do so required they be in the upper half of the seniority list. The officer corps itself was divided between the fanatics of flight and those veterans disinclined to take risks. The latter were encouraged not to do so by superiors who had become administrators and would have preferred to run the Aéronautique Militaire sans aircraft. Yet these structural faults lay hidden until the 1930s.

In 1919 France enjoyed the prestige of being No. 1 and of having excellent war-tested matériel and doctrine, before Douhet's ideas were well known. But at the same time, the Armée de Terre resented the publicity given to aviators. By the end of 1920, the Aéronautique Militaire had shrunk to 119 squadrons and 39,055 personnel, its aircraft from 11,023 to 3,940, of which 3,050 were in storage; and the bureaucracy had shrunk to 40 percent of its strength in 1918. Surplus matériel was stockpiled and lived off for years to come. The government continued aircraft production into 1919 to avoid unemployment, and thus some 5,000 airframes and 15,000 engines were delivered. Still, in 1919, 8,000 airplanes and 11,000 engines became war surplus and had been disposed of by 1923. Ministre Pierre-Étienne Flandin supervised this, and ordered new designs and subsidized the new civilian airlines. Nevertheless, by 1921 the workforce was down to 3,700. The government's technical bureau had shrunk from four thousand to forty persons. Some 32 percent of the Aéronautique Militaire was stationed on the World War I airfields in eastern France and 41 percent outside France, with 17 percent in Germany and the remainder in the Middle East and Morocco.

After 1921 when traditional recruiting resumed, 69 percent of the new lieutenants came from the major schools (46 percent of the total from Saint-Cyr), 21 percent from the *sous-officier* (NCO) schools, and 13 percent from the ranks. Shortage of personnel led to dilution with draftees and reservists, but the low esteem of aviation in the public view still created recruiting problems. However, Bordeaux could not train the 350 new mechanics needed each year, and thus other schools at Courbevoie, Lyons, and Nîmes gave one year's training for a mechanic's license. The demand was still so great that two additional schools were opened in 1923 and one more in 1928. But the basic problem was pay. Civilians on base were better off than their service supervisors, yet it was hoped that service mechanics would reenlist after their first four- to five-year tour. They did not.

Unfortunately, moreover, the Duval Division, that 1917–1918 concentration of airpower, did not become the nucleus of an independent air service, but was disbanded. What air assets were left and not used in Syria, Algeria, and Indo-China once again were dispersed within the Armée de Terre. When their champion, Marshal Émile Fayolle, retired in the early 1920s, airmen were left as impotent juniors to argue their case over and over within the military hierarchy. Though Marshal Ferdinand Foch was converted to their view in 1921, he retired and his place was taken, in effect if not always in command, by the generals who were defrocked in 1940, Gamelin and Weygand.[31] Their legitimate concern was to obtain support for the Armée de Terre on the battlefield. They did not understand, however, that the airmen inevitably had to see their role as threefold: (1) the Douhetian bomber striking force with which to destroy the will of the enemy, shortly the German people; (2) the air defense of *la belle patrie*; and finally (3) support aviation, including reconnaissance. Underlying all the bitter rhetoric was the basic lack of funds until 1938, which left the new Air Arm without the means (the numbers) of men and machines to fulfill any of its roles, whether self-imposed or decreed by the Armée de Terre–dominated Conseil Supérieur de la Défense Nationale (CSDN; its name varied in the 1930s). The Armée de l'Air had not the *mentalité* to consider that a tactical air force should be its top priority, even though in the 1930s Italian colonel Amadeo Mecozzi countered Douhet by arguing exactly that.[32] By then it was too late.

As James Corum asked of the Luftwaffe, (1) What was the operational doctrine? (2) Who developed it? (3) What was the process of development? (4) What were the strengths and weaknesses of that doctrine? (5) When was it spelled out? (6) How did it relate to the technical means available? and (7) Were aircraft and equipment designed, built, tested, and evaluated in terms of approved doctrine?[33] These queries are equally applicable here.

The Aéronautique Militaire was revamped to provide air cover for the Armée de Terre's mobilization and early operations, and to be ready to do this at all times without calling up the reserves; it thus was organized as three brigades of thirty-nine squadrons, forty-nine brigades of observation machines, eleven brigades in the Levant and the colonies, and seven battalions of balloonists and five DCA regiments, all controlled by a *groupe*. The weakness was the leeway allowed in training and operational procedures. Each regiment had roughly one thousand personnel, with each squadron having ten to fifteen pilots, only one-third of whom were commissioned.

Colonial Operations

In Morocco the 1925–1926 uprising of the Berbers under Abd el-Krim was defeated by Marshal Pétain.[34] The Arme Aéronautique accompanied columns and did observation and photography, as well as liaison between isolated posts. But it lost aircraft to rebel rifle fire or when flying in the Atlas mountains where the guerrillas were above the machines. During the Rif War (1920–1926) after 1924, French aircraft dropped supplies to beleaguered garrisons, scouted, protected the flanks of marching columns, carried messages, and transported senior officers. The Rif rebels were efficient and well organized, had some artillery, and understood the value of entrenching. They quickly adopted countermeasures against aircraft and tanks. While lessons were learned about ground-air cooperation, these said little about a future European war.

French air involvement in colonial policing was both in active military operations and in long-distance exploratory flights. Significant of these latter were those "raids" carried out by Joseph Vuillemin, later to be chief of the GSAF. On the whole, French imperial air action was in many respects similar to that of the RAF in Iraq and in India, and yet in other ways different. Methods of army-air cooperation were not yet satisfactory. There was no arrangement to pick up messages from the ground and little use of wireless. Air liaison officers were not always available with columns—all of which was in sharp contrast to RAF practice. Air supply maintained by four Armée de l'Air airplanes kept seven hundred men alive in besieged Suwayda, and used French ambulance planes, as well as airfield preparation troops.[35]

Senior officers flew personally to reconnoiter areas and used airplanes to deliver secret orders to their troops, as Gamelin did for his concentric night march onto the gardens east of Damascus. On other occasions bombers were used to put down a rising in Hama in October 1925 and earlier joined with cavalry to break up a march on Damascus by the Druze, an Islamic reformed sect. A mass attack on Suwayda, however, involved only twenty machines armed with only ten 50-kilo bombs, which could not penetrate to the Druze cellars. Air attacks were generally not heavy enough to be effective, and Syrians learned how to deflate them.

The Druze brought down three French aircraft in 1926 and killed six pilots in one squadron, all of whose aircraft were badly in need of repair. Frustrated, the French went over to a deliberate terror policy. Local troops engaged in looting villages. Such acts backfired as the natives moved to rebellion rather than a more pacific stance. Destitute refugees from destroyed villages either drifted into Damascus as another volatile element, or became active rebels. (The British Army suppression of Iraq's rebellion of 1920 was temporarily harsh as well.)

On 6 May 1926 the French bombed and bombarded the Maydan quarter of Damascus without regard to civilian life and for three days fires raged. But some in the French Haut Commandement worried about the cost to French prestige. In the rural areas the French arbitrated to reduce tribal conflict, but in 1927–1929 further rebellions led to effective use of air power.

In Syria a series of outbreaks in 1925 saw General Gamelin leading a column against the rebel Druze capital, but it had to withdraw for want of supplies. Not until the spring of 1926 did the French begin to regain control of the mandate awarded them in 1920, but fighting lasted until June 1927. In the meantime the French had reinforced the army of the Levant to the extent that by mid-May 1926 thirty-two battalions were present, many of which were colonials, as well as local militia and *gendarmerie* (the police). French airmen worked closely with these ground forces to suppress the rebellion.

The Aéronautique Militaire, 1922–1928

By the end of 1920 there had been 119 flights, and the airmen were frustrated by the lack of an independent superstructure, but its doctrine and

fiscal allotments were up to the army general staff. In October, Marshal
Fayolle, inspector general of aviation, received from General Buat, the chief
of staff, authorization to redistribute the air squadrons in peacetime—the
divisions at Metz, Paris, and Pau, with brigades at Dijon, Tours, and Lyon. It
gave hope of centralization of the Arme Aéronautique. However, Buat died
in December 1923 and his Instruction was revoked by the new chief of staff,
General Debeney, and his friend on the CSG, Marshal Pétain, who brought
in 1923–1930 their World War I ideas and observations. Nevertheless,
Fayolle's plea that the Arme Aéronautique pursue battle planes became a
historic turning point, and the bomber force was quietly expanded. After
Douhet's *Il dominio dell'aria* (*The Command of the Air*) was translated into
French in 1932, the Italian's name was much heard. However, most Armée
de l'Air officers did not accept the idea that air power alone could win a war,
though they did recognize bombing as important and saw to it that much
of the Armée de l'Air's meager credits went to bombers. Yet not intending
themselves to launch preemptive air strikes, they suspected that less moral
enemies might do so—hence talk of the air menace.

General Debeney was the architect of the organization, recruitment,
and training systems that shaped the French ground forces to 1940. He was
a key figure in the development and siting of the Maginot Line. In the technical aspects of doctrine, his influence was at least as great as Pétain's, in
Col. Robert Doughty's view.[36] Yet the creation of doctrine was a large and
complex enterprise over which no one person held sway; it should have
combined the best available thought and as such influenced military education and training.

Meanwhile, as the occupation of the Rhineland phased down, the units
were reassigned in France. Bombers were taken out of their regiments and
reestablished into a general aviation reserve group at Paris in October 1930.
These same regiments in 1932 were transformed into squadrons bearing the
same numbers, and air bases were established. Pursuit squadrons were created, each of two groups of three flights. Because the air force did not have
territorial responsibility, air bases were established at Dijon, Le Bourget,
Lyons, Nancy, and Pau, each with a brigade HQ, training facilities, and so
on. This organization was quickly extended to all the air service and made

explicit in the decrees and orders of 1933 as technological progress required the application of new principles. On 22 November 1933 the Ministère de l'Air decreed that squadrons were to be purely tactical organizations, with the fundamental organization being the new group, the brigade, which took over training, supply, administration, mobilization, and protection. Meanwhile, the creation of an air ministry had been delayed until 1928. The Royale was given control of shipboard aviation, yet in 1939 the Aéronavale (naval air arm) was almost impotent.[37]

Up to 1928 the Aéronautique Militaire improved its performance only slightly. But the popular air salon at Paris and the air shows annually at Vincennes, Villacoublay, and Le Bourget, together with long-distance flights, left the public with the impression that France was still on top. One result of the long-distance flights was the introduction of navigators, as no one in the Armée de l'Air knew how to use a sextant. By 1929 the number of Aéronautique Militaire hours flown per year had risen from 1924's 163,000 to 234,000, and the hours flown annually per pilot from 1924's 100 to 1929's 130. Serious accidents occurred once for every 2,633 hours flown in 1929 versus every 2,000 hours in 1924. Not until 1928 was a Service de Société Aéronautique Centrale (central safety service) created and the real causes of accidents other than pilot error investigated and remedies applied. In the meantime, a special decree of 19 February 1925 defined the conditions to be met to be considered *personnel navigant* (aircrew) and the annual tests to be passed to retain that status. In 1938 an insurance fund for military and civilian aviators was established.

The Centre d'Aéronautique (center for aeronautics) became in 1925 the École Militaire et Application de l'Aéronautique (military school of air application) at Versailles, with the observer certificate issued at nearby Villacoublay and the pilot's at Avord. But slow development meant that by 1936 the officer corps was aged, with effects felt into World War II.

In 1926 the war minister was warned that the Arme Aéronautique would be ineffective in ten years, immobile even on the defensive, but still it lost DCA capability to the artillery. The latter failed to develop it, as became obvious in 1940.[38] Regulations and the development of matériel were worked out, and in 1923 the army chief of staff divided the force into general reserve and ground-support formations.

From 1925, in the wake of the Locarno peace treaties, the government of France cut the services, turned its back on the value of the military, and in 1933 stopped voluntary enlistments, cutting the regular officer corps 20 percent, reducing compulsory service to ten months, and stopping annual maneuvers of an army that during 1927–1928 had been converted solely to a training establishment. Doctrine reverted to the defensive of 1918, and the military bureaucracy became rigid and protective. The success of the Front Populaire protests in 1934 caused the isolated officer corps to see their future as doomed. As the French Arme de l'Air remained basically dominated by the army, how that service developed is of considerable relevance to the outcome of the Battle of France of 1940.

The 1921 Instructions for the use of large units remained the bible until 1936. As the weight of weapons increased, the chief of staff, General Gamelin, as an artillerist, saw more and more the burden of the commander as being to move these big guns, and thus the idea of mechanical battle developed. The new 1936 Instructions were firmly based on their predecessors, though they included sections on aerial forces and air defense.

Nevertheless, Colonel Doughty concluded that France went to war in 1939 with basically 1918 ideas and an inflexible use of doctrine. The Haut Commandement had become ossified and defensive, especially against Charles de Gaulle's radical armored concepts. By 1940 doctrine had become a substitute for thought. The French mismatched new technology to old doctrine, because—according to Eugenia C. Kiesling—they did not believe it needed to change, in spite of the reports of the Deuxeième Bureau on German developments.[39] The basic problem was the French institution of conscription. Worse, in Kiesling's view, was the shortage of trained *sous-officiers*, who are the heart of any military service.

On top of this, the methodical battle depended on communications, on telephones and wireless sets with which many units were unfamiliar. And the intent was to spare France itself the devastation by fighting forward along the line of the Dyle River in Belgium. But the problem, as the official British air historian Dennis Richard has noted, was that the Dyle was not a water barrier but a stream, across which he could jump.[40] Hoping to fight the next war in Belgium, the army adopted motorized divisions to rush to defensive positions on and beyond the northeast frontier.

Doctrinally there was a frustrating stalemate with the airmen arguing that their legacy of Verdun was the fight for air superiority over the battlefield. The Grand Haut Commandement, however, believed that the idea of gaining air superiority was a "battle" that would deprive them of air support. The airmen argued that their battle was exactly what the École de Guerre thought. But the army went the other way to argue à la Douhet that French cities would be devastated if the army did not win the first battle on the ground.[41] This led to talk among civilians of terror bombing and then to condemnation of all such action.

France sought only to defend itself. Fighters were even designated light defense aviation and bombers heavy! Stubbornly both sides chose to ignore the evidence of 1918, which contradicted the École de Guerre and the cooperation of aircraft and tanks. This doctrinal debate went on until 1939. The building of the Maginot Line from 1929 on, as a safe-haven replacement of the 1914–1918 trenches, strengthened the argument that the next war would be won in the air. But the Douhetian doctrines, including the idea of aerochemical war, were especially frightening in pacifist post-1918 France. Bombing was condemned as an offensive weapon, though viewed as protecting French mobilization.

While airmen argued for an independent air force, their army-bred Haut Commandement, which rarely flew, opposed the idea. Then, too, it seems strange that there were few air maneuvers, let alone joint ones, with the army or the navy.

Why did the French tend to glue themselves to rigid systems of war? True, Pétain and de Gaulle both proposed the mid-1930s mobile reserves and strategic air forces, but these were not yet in being in May 1940. General Gamelin's plan to fight in Belgium consumed all the forces available.

Perhaps the answer lies in the peasant-noble hierarchical society, the lack of a notably strong mercantile middle class—bourgeoisie—and the geographical position of France. The former placed the military strength in drilled regiments commanded by aristocrats and the latter required cumbrous armies. Stolidity ruled.

The Cavalry Exception

The 5 percent of the army's officers in the cavalry were not so alienated. They ignored the defensive of 1918 and sought instead new means of mobility and closer cooperation between ground and air forces. Within five years they had laid the foundations for armored warfare as it would be practiced in the 1939–1945 war, as exposed in Maj. René Prioux's series of articles, 1922–1924.[42]

Others talked of divisions of tanks, motorized forces, and self-propelled artillery that could smash through fortified zones and debouch into unprotected rear areas—ideas also being advocated across the Channel by J. F. C. Fuller and Basil Liddell Hart. Other officers spelled out the details, including the essential radios and organic aviation.

In the 1924 maneuvers a cavalry division was supported by an integrated modern regiment. But in the 1928 exercises the infantry arranged to kill the idea and there were no further experiments, as Faris Kirkland has noted, for another seven years. The cavalry persisted with its own mechanized forces, even using them in Morocco coordinated with horsed cavalry by radio. Maneuvers in 1927, 1928, and 1929 proved the usefulness of motorized forces and the need to refine radios and obtain better air support. Senior cavalry officers advocated the revolutionary step of allowing younger officers free rein to respond to unforeseen events. Yet May 1940 would prove fatal to the rigid Armée de Terre rule of no action without orders from above.

From 1929 the cavalry began to realize its ideas, with junior officers commanding and maneuvering motorized forces. In the critical fiscal year of 1933, cavalry officers began to work out the details of what Kirkland asserts was the first armored division in the world, writing at the time that cavalry officers predicted what the Germans would do in 1940, in fact, including overrunning airfields before bombers could take off. One of the new cavalry-armored divisions, a Division *légère mécanisée*, took part in the revised maneuvers in 1935. It used pressed officers to rethink time and space in a new intellectual and organizational setting. Moreover, always accustomed to improvising, cavalry officers, in contrast to the stick-in-the-mud infantry and artillery, went ahead with experiments before their new equipment was delivered in 1936. And though by 1940 there were four armored divisions, the Haut Commandement, not knowing how to use them, broke up three into penny-packet support of the infantry. As Kirkland points out, the aristocratic cavalry officers could only have survived by adapting mechanization, by being progressive, and by having an image of themselves as the dashing shock leaders.[43]

It seems strange that there was no bonding between the cavalrymen and the airmen because the horsemen recognized the role aviation had to play in breakthrough armored warfare in the future. But without communications they could not fit into mechanical battle—they created chaos. French commanders doubted the efficacy of tanks because they saw them as unlikely to survive long during methodical battle, and therefore as being too costly. The rise of antitank weapons and training was also discouraging. French studies concluded that the infantry had nothing to fear from tanks. But after the establishment of the first three German panzer (tank) divisions in October 1935, these ideas began to change. It was soon seen that the only antidote to the panzer was a French tank of similar characteristics, which were developers' improved models. It was armor-advocated organization and integration that gave problems.

The Armée de Terre and the Arme Aéronautique

The creation of the Ministère de l'Air in 1928 and the ratification of the status of an independent air force in 1934 affected the army. Armée de Terre historian Marcel Spivak noted (in 1984) that this occurred at a time of international dangers, of *la malaise politique française*, and at a time when aviation was fast advancing. At a moment of great uncertainty, the human element could not be overlooked. It was, said Spivak, a very complex problem that needed a multidimensional analysis.[44]

In June 1922 the then–army inspector general, Pétain, had seen the necessity of hiving off aviation. But upon the creation of the Ministère de l'Air in 1928, Pétain insisted that where cooperation was involved, it be sub-ordinate to the decrees of the Ministère de l'Armée de Terre (ministry of the army), the Ministère de la Marine, and the Ministère des Colonies. While the new ministry would decide on its equipment, eight regiments and five groups of fighters and reconnaissance machines as well as two aerostation (lighter-than-air) regiments would be involved.[45]

In 1929 the CSDN refined the terms so that the new order was "*réserve générale aéronautique*," though the concepts were the same as the discarded "mass of maneuver" and "*armée de cooperation*." Pétain resolutely opposed the new Ministre de l'Air André Laurent-Eynac on freedom of action for the airmen, believing that the generalissimo should control all means for waging war. He recalled what he had had to do at Verdun, and the status of French finances, and that foreigners regarded France as militaristic. He argued that preparation of the air force for war should be the responsibility of the war minister. The result was that the new "adjoint" inspector general of the army for aviation was created, which after a tortuous course ended up as the delegate of the chief of the GSAF to the CSG, where he argued with the new vice president of the council, Gen. Maxime Weygand. The same occurred with the post of CAS, which came into being on 27 August 1931.

The army chief of staff, General Debeney, had in the meantime in November 1928 established a liaison between the Ministère de la Guerre and the Ministère de l'Air, and established that the Ministère de l'Air should attend the CSDN on the same basis as the Royale. Debeney wished, however, that both Pétain as inspector general and himself as chief of staff should attend. Weygand agreed, with suspicion that in time of war there would be disputes as to who controlled air assets, and thus he wanted clarification of the general organization of aviation in peace and war; the cooperation of the air force in army, navy, and air defense; the question of the recruiting and training of air force personnel; air force combat tactics; the establishment of procurement programs; the putting into service of new weapons, and their impact on their conditions of employment; and industrial mobilization. Weygand believed the CSG needed to complete organic action regarding consultation, to fin-ish studies for the war minister and the army Haut Commandement. At the same time, he believed that the chief of staff did not have enough voice on the CSG. Weygand seemed more flexible than the aging Marshal Pétain, but he still saw the state of the army's air support as grave, for what existed was a façade. Weygand wanted a national policy related to industrial mobilization, especially with regard to prototypes. Particularly he wanted long-range, high-speed, well-armed reconnaissance machines and fighters equal to any of those of the neighbors. He also was concerned that on the outbreak of war personnel would be available to man these aircraft.

When in November 1931 Gamelin became chief of staff of the army, he raised the issue, unclear in the law of 28 November 1928, as to cadres and effectives—the precise problem with which the army was faced by the advent of the Armée de l'Air. The army saw any gains by the Armée de l'Air in credits, officers, and so on, as losses to itself; but it did admit the need for the Défense Aérienne du Territoire (DAT; air defense of the territory), the DCA arm, and the creation of a fighter arm. Gamelin wanted an equilibrium of personnel and equipment.

In 1932 Weygand refused to accept the Air Staff's proposed reorganization and any shift that would reduce the fighters under his command; he was doubtful of stripping the regiments of their fighter and observation assets because that was prejudicial to their common role and would only delay satisfying the army's needs. Further proposals ran afoul of the idea of a ministry of national defense, which Gamelin wanted. He was concerned about the execution of the Plan de Défense Nationale (national defense plan) on the outbreak of war, and thus he wanted a meeting at which the defense minister and the three chiefs of staff would make the allocations. It was this task that went to the new military Haut Commandement in March 1932. It would be succeeded in wartime by the Comité de la Guerre (war committee). The idea was to set this higher organization in stone in peacetime, both to handle military affairs and to establish close contact between the three chiefs of staff, as Britain had done in 1923.

In June 1932 the military Haut Commandement was chaired by the civilian president of France to whom Weygand submitted the grave differences as between the army and the air force staffs.

Pétain had been the inspector general of the DAT and had raised the question of the constitution, employment, and command of the air reserve, the day and night fighters, and the bombers. Weygand saw this as taking time due to emerging aviation technologies and capabilities. Pétain was skeptical of the effectiveness of the air force attacking enemy vital points without ground action. He envisaged that in war the armed forces would be controlled by the chief of staff of the armed forces, who would direct the bombers to make independent sorties at the start. Pétain reckoned that the general reserve would need FF900 million (French francs) the first year, and FF200–300 million more annually thereafter, FF250 million of which would easily be obtained for the defense of the northeast. Gamelin wanted a large long-range bomber force, but not at the expense of cooperation aviation. He noted it was contradictory to argue at Geneva against such a force while creating one in France.

These debates of 1932 were not resolved, and thus the president of the CSG ordered Pétain to develop a triservice solution. The military Haut Commandement remained concerned. It wished to put off a resolution until the government decided by law on the nature of the general reserve and its wartime command. Personal influences also came into play as elder states-man Poincaré wanted the new Ministère de l'Air to control in peacetime, but the Ministère de la Guerre to control on the outbreak of hostilities. Article 24 laid down how the Ministère de l'Armée de Terre, the Ministère de la Marine, and the Ministère des Colonies would exercise their powers. On mobilization, the general reserve would be divided by the government as a function of operations. However, Spivak notes, the principal contentions remained unsolved until 1938. The discussions of doctrine in the global atmosphere of the 1930s were related to concern for the conduct of the war itself. The creation of the Armée de l'Air required these discussions; that this happened in France in the 1930s was due to its international position, the fatigue from World War I, France's democratic nature, and its wariness of another war. And we must remember, Spivak cautioned, France was not the only country to have made errors of judgment.

Creating the Armée de l'Air, 1928–1934

A coalition was already working against the French commerce minister when he died in a 1928 plane accident; Poincaré then appointed Laurent-

Eynac as air minister. The new minister had to undertake the Herculean work of dealing with the moribund aircraft industry and commercial aviation, and obtain legislation to authorize an independent air force. In 1928 and 1933 the Armée de Terre and the Royale both opposed the hiving off of the Arme Aéronautique as an independent service. However, in 1932 the navy kept its own air arm because of the necessities of shipboard naval aviation, having commissioned the carrier *Béarn* in 1927. The biggest howl went up from the army, though in the end the largest part of the Armée de l'Air was placed under its command in wartime. The army persisted in creating a manual reflecting its views. Others opposed a new service as lacking the esprit and traditions of the older organizations, while the fear also was bruited about that the airmen might pull off a coup d'état. The French had a long tradition of coups, and times were very tense after 1930.

Laurent-Eynac wanted a single air service—army, navy, and colonial— that could attack enemy nerve centers and affect the morale of enemy urban dwellers. In 1928 he noted that France lacked technical research, doctrine, instruction, and standardization; had too many prototypes of poor quality; and had an overabundance of obsolete military stocks and decrepit airliners. He at once called for four times as much of the budget to go to research and development (R&D) as before, and for concentration and consolidation of the industry. He brought in Albert Caquot, a skilled World War I aeronautically experienced engineer, who took charge of the Ministère de l'Air's technical programs of 1928–1933, reestablishing policies that advanced French aeronautical technology to the fore. But he had no production orders to give out; with only prototypes he was unable to prepare the *atelier* industry to be capable of moving these prototypes into wartime mass production.[46]

In 1928 too many firms were concentrating on production with too little R&D, having lived for a decade off war-surplus stocks. The manufacturers resented young engineers brought in to try new ideas, an excellent policy that did produce advances but that was abandoned in 1932–1933 in favor of large numbers of "transition" aircraft, which led to the new Armée de l'Air being saddled with outmoded planes and no new models from 1936 on. The result was that private enterprise was not challenged by new specifications—as in Britain—and showed little interest in corporate consolidation or in dispersion from the Paris environs. Nationalization thus was thrust on the manufacturers by the Front Populaire after their 1936 victory.

The policy of prototypes included some large aircraft that could be used by both the airlines and the air force. This was a good example of that concern of the 1933 disarmament conferees. As director of the Ministère de l'Air, Caquot had changed the prototype policy to provide for large payments in advance in order to enable brilliant but impecunious engineers to compete. However, the government owned the designs and had the right to have other firms build them, while paying a royalty. Nevertheless, this resulted in nearly 180 different types and 40 different engines being ordered in 1928–1933; fewer than 50 were kept for tests, fewer than half of those were military, and more than half of these were of metal construction in 1929. The new policy concentrated on long production runs so that no new tested designs were ready for production in 1936. But the government's approach still left design in private hands, and that survived the nationalization of 1936. The result overall was that the aircraft industry was neither consolidated enough to enjoy economies of scale nor dispersed enough for safety. The solution had to await Caquot's return in 1938, for he was forced to resign in 1933 to return to his engineering career. And prices remained a mystery. The arsenal at Villacoublay was proposed in 1930 as a yardstick "dockyard," but this was not established until 1936, and may not have been the sought-for solution as the products of His Majesty's Dockyards in Britain were about twice as expensive as private companies even in World War II.[47]

The problem with sharp changes in emphasis, such as the abandonment of the prototype policy of 1928–1933, is that it takes a while for people to learn to think differently, especially if they are asked to be innovative when they have been conditioned to produce what is acceptable to the bureaucracy. Emmanuel Chadeau has provided an excellent history of the French aircraft industry up to 1950.[48] It does as much as Claude Carlier's *Marcel Dassault* to explain the mess that the aircraft business found itself in the years from 1934 onward.[49]

The great problem for designers and manufacturers was to harmonize military requirements with industrial design. In France the process after 1918 had been hampered by relatively few orders from an army living off war surplus that was unsure how the air arm fitted into its doctrine, and by the lack of interest in export sales. French air doctrine was very unsettled and thus the aircraft requested tended to be compromises influenced by Douhetian concerns to smash enemy factories and morale, or to defend French population centers from the "air menace," or to support the army. The industry was more successful with commercial designs because the airlines had plainer requirements governed by economics.

The arguments over an independent air force were settled finally during 1933–1934 by establishment of the Armée de l'Air. These arrangements were complicated by theories about the control of the aircraft industry and by the continuation theoretically of the debate over the allocation of support aircraft to the army and navy, as well as by the formation of a bomber force and an equally independent fighter corps. These discussions were far from easy to resolve for a number of reasons. One reason was changes that around 1934 forced costs up, due to the Technological Revolution and other causes. A second reason was the awful political decision because of costs, among other things, to build the BCR—the bomber-combat-reconnaissance multipurpose aircraft, a compromise, obsolescent, general-purpose machine— not for a colonial war, but for a European one. Third was the stinginess of the Parlement, which gave the bulk of the funds to the army. And fourth was the fact that the aircraft industry was still in its artisanal, handcrafts state and could not turn out large orders.

Most critical of all, perhaps, was the fact that theory was unrelated to the physical distribution of the Armée de l'Air in regions different from its war stations and that plans that would have needed at least three thousand to four thousand modern aircraft were standing on feet of clay of obsolete and obsolescent types—and very few of these. As a result, few maneuvers or air exercises were held to test for flaws. The dilemma was accentuated by the arrival of Italian colonel Amadeo Mecozzi's ideas of support aviation including level, dive, and low-level bombing, which began to eat away the Douhetian certainty of annihilation of the cities by air battleships in a sudden surprise attack.[50] The latter was a very real danger especially since Intelligence knew it was to be the favored German tactic on the outbreak of war. In fact, in September 1939, since the Armée de l'Air had only roughly four hundred fighters and thirty-eight heavy bombers, the Haut Commandement was cloaked with fatalism.

As Julian Jackson has revealed, the study of the reports of the Deuxième Bureau (intelligence) in Paris shows that from 1933 its analyses of German strength were accurate. They provided timely warnings, but the politicians, who distrusted the military, bore the burden of trying to act within major political, economic, and strategic bounds, and within shortages of matériel that allowed them only to make limited responses.[51]

Winston Churchill stated elsewhere that the French had allowed the lotus years of 1928–1935 to be wasted in endless debate while the aeronautical world leaped from post–World War I to pre–World War II following the collapse of the disarmament talks at Geneva. Here, too, rationalism defeated pragmatism on the needs for parity in classes of machines. Thus at a time when the Duval concept had been destroyed in France and the Arme Aéronautique parceled out to army units in a force whose chief of staff had little understanding of the triple threats the airmen had to meet, French airmen were reduced to grumbling auxiliaries.

But before relating how the Aéronautique Militaire became the Armée de l'Air under the new independent Ministère de l'Air, it is necessary to step across the Channel to see how differently the events unfolded to the north for the RAF during 1918–1930.

The Royal Air Force, 1918–1930

In contrast to the story of the Armée de l'Air between 1918 and the Battle of France in 1940, the story of the RAF was quite different.[52] Its structure dated from 1915 and its enabling act from 1917. The Air Ministry came into being on 1 January 1918 and the RAF on 1 April. Almost from the start, the Air Ministry was headed by a veteran secretary of state for air, Winston Churchill, recently munitions minister. After briefly being the first CAS in 1918, Sir Hugh Trenchard returned in early 1919 and remained in that post until 1930. It was he, with Churchill's approval, who in December 1919 laid down the blueprint for the new air service before Parliament in what was called "Trenchard's White Paper," *Command (Cmd.) 467*.[53] Given the limited funds available, most of the active squadrons were based in the Empire while the emphasis at Home was on the building up of a cadre of well-trained professional airmen and ground crew with the necessary support apparatus. Maj. Gen. Sir Frederick Sykes, the second CAS, was appointed controller general of Civil Aviation, but when Trenchard returned as CAS, the two old enemies clashed—one at home in Whitehall and the other in the field—and Sykes resigned.

In August 1919 the ranks and titles, the new blue uniform, and the light blue ensign with the red, white, and blue roundel came into being officially. While the Air Arm's operations could be independent, it was firmly established before the end of World War I that it had to be subservient to and an instrument of national policy. For these ends it required a staff to plan and to ensure that the machines would suit strategic purposes.

Trenchard, as the former general officer commanding in chief of the RFC, had opposed the formation of the RAF independent of Field Marshal Haig on the Western Front. When the Armistice terminated his command of the Independent Bombing Force, he regarded that group as a colossal waste of effort. But then, once again CAS, he extended his view that the best defense was a solid offense and deemed the Air Arm an attacking force. This coalesced with the necessity to defend Britain against air attack, and the best way in which to do this, in Trenchard's view, was to strike enemy cities where he believed the moral effect of bombing to the matériel would be on the order of twenty to one. By the time Trenchard had become CAS in 1919, the 188 combat squadrons, 22,647 aircraft, and 291,270 officers and men had been reduced to 33 squadrons, of which 8 were still forming.

Circumstances had dictated in late 1918 that Churchill be both secretary of state for war and for air. This encouraged the First Lord of the Admiralty to try to get the RNAS back. Indeed, many had assumed that the 1917 RAF Constitution Act was a temporary wartime measure. However, Trenchard was determined to protect his new fief, and therefore he proposed an RAF half the size that Sykes as CAS had advocated—and a cadre one at that, but with a Cabinet-approved civil aviation department. The 1919 Cabinet dictum that there would be no major war for ten years, and thus no BEF, helped Trenchard's scheme.[54] As CAS he protected the essentials, but gave way on everything that could save money, says Montgomery

Hyde.[55] Trenchard made an immense impression and became known as the "Father of the RAF," an accolade he deserved, even though his battles with the War Office and especially with Admiral of the Fleet Earl Beatty, the first sea lord, were disturbing and caused a neglect of the necessities of the RAF as an instrument of policy.

Yet the Ten Year Rule gave the Treasury the upper hand at least for 1924. The silver lining to this cloud was the Air Staff decision to cut the operational RAF to the bone and concentrate on preparing a professional cadre for war. Officers, who were all to be pilots, were to be trained at the new RAF College at Cranwell, and fitters and riggers (mechanics) were to be trained in an apprentice scheme at No. 1 Technical Training School at Halton.[56] Both of these programs provided current personnel and a trained reserve, each essential to the Expansion from 1934 onward.[57]

Vital to the Trenchard approach was laying the foundations of an air force spirit, providing increasingly reliable engines, eliminating flying accidents, erasing the idea that pilots were chauffeurs, and viewing airmen as technical experts in the science of aeronautics, navigation, meteorology, photography, and wireless. Of these experts only 50 percent obtained permanent commissions; 40 percent had short-service commissions, and 10 percent were seconded from the navy and army. Cranwell graduates were trained in the imperial tradition. They did gunnery at the RAF Staff College at Andover (established in April 1922) and then were posted to a squadron for what would later be called service flying training. After five years they were expected to choose a technical specialty in which to become proficient and then rise to higher command. Flying instructors were trained at Gosport, where Maj. Robert Smith-Barry had initiated the dual teaching approach of academic classroom work and verbal flight training; staff courses were taught at Andover. Given limited funds, the RAF College at Cranwell was built first, as the war-legacy RAF technical training school at Halton already had excellent shops and useable huts; the latter were only slowly replaced by barracks. Supply and research was moved from the extinct Ministry of Munitions, but the facilities at Farnborough (now the Royal Aircraft Establishment; RAE), Biggin Hill, and Matlesham Heath for testing aircraft were retained, as were the two airship establishments, Cardington and Howden.[58]

Politics played a part in the appointment of Churchill's relative, Lord Londonderry, as secretary of state for air on 3 April 1920 since the 1917 Act required the Air Council be chaired by the secretary of state, and Churchill was too busy at the War Office. Londonderry soon successfully carried through Parliament the Air Navigation Act of 1920, the basis of international civil aviation rules.[59] Only in the summer of 1921 were the first three Home squadrons formed. But the demands of the Middle East soon sent these three there, leaving behind in late 1922 four Navy Cooperation squadrons, two fighter flights, one Army Cooperation squadron, and one Communications squadron.

The French menace of its large air force scared the politicians, thanks to the writing of P. R. C. Groves and others, and thus several Cabinet committees and subcommittees were appointed, with the result that in 1923 the Cabinet decided to create an HDAF of fifty-two squadrons, of which two-thirds were to be bombers capable of striking Paris at this time of tension over the Ruhr and reparations.[60] In the meantime, British airlines had been forced off the airwaves by subsidized French rivals, leading to the appointment of the irrepressible Sir Sefton Brancker as director of Civil Aviation. There followed the Hambling Committee, and in 1924 Imperial Airways came into being as "the chosen instrument," with a ten-year, £1 million subsidy and the long-term goal of linking the Empire to London.[61]

In the meantime, a significant part of its route to India had come into Air Ministry hands through the March 1921 Cairo Conference in which Churchill, now colonial secretary, arranged for the RAF to take over control of Mesopotamia (modern-day Iraq) and other mandated territories at a saving of fifty-five battalions of infantry and six of cavalry, and sixteen artillery batteries. They were replaced by eight squadrons of aircraft and four of armored cars, and it was decreed that the air officer commanding, Sir John Salmond, was not to be subordinate to any army commander. At the same time, Frederick Guest, another Churchill relative and a pilot, became secretary of state of the independent Air Ministry.

Trenchard's struggles against the Admiralty and the War Office stemmed in part from Admiral of the Fleet Beatty's fear that in the next war the commander in chief would be an airman.[62] An Air Staff paper on the role of air power in imperial defense led to the former Prime Minister Arthur Balfour's CID committee, which noted that the air force had to be autonomous in administration and education and have the primary role in air defense. In surface campaigns, however, it would be subordinate to the navy and army commands, but in other cases there had to be cooperation so that the RAF was not treated as an auxiliary.

In the meantime, the Cabinet-appointed "Geddes Axe" committee on government expenditure had noted that to redivide the RAF would be wasteful and would not allow that service to develop properly. Nevertheless, Geddes cut the RAF budget from £18.5 million to £10.75 million. Trenchard postponed rehousing and reintroduced noncommissioned officer (NCO) pilots. Churchill headed the Cabinet committee that approved these measures, while noting that further cuts would be damaging to the RAF's future. Churchill then headed a committee on navy–air force relations, which gave the Admiralty control of aviation at sea but required it also to pay for airmen and aircraft on ships. Then in April 1922 a CID subcommittee reported on the dangers that Britain actually faced, especially from France, a threat that did not concern the three chiefs of staff, but did alarm the politicians.

In October 1922 Prime Minister Lloyd George fell and his successor, Bonar Law, consulted his new son-in-law, Sykes, who recommended that to save money the Air Ministry and the RAF be abolished. Sir Samuel Hoare was named secretary of state for air and told he would not hold the position long and that Iraq would be abandoned. But Trenchard rapidly converted Hoare, who soon had the Air Ministry moved to Whitehall alongside the Admiralty and the War Office, with Christopher Bullock, who was formerly Churchill's private secretary, as secretary of the Air Ministry.

As the Admiralty was obdurate, Hoare asked Bonar Law for an impartial CID inquiry. The lord president of the council, Lord Salisbury, presided and appointed the Balfour subcommittee to look into the proper strength required by the RAF. In the meantime, tension with Turkey and the inducements of the Mosul oil fields led to Air Vice Marshal Salmond's victory in northern Iraq. When Bonar Law subsequently resigned, Stanley Baldwin became prime minister. He had been financial secretary to the Treasury from 1917 to 1921, president of the Board of Trade from 1921 to 1922, chancellor of the exchequer from 1922 to 1923, and would be prime minister during 1923–1924, 1924–1929, and 1933–1937. He admired Hoare and gave him a seat in the Cabinet.

The main Salisbury Committee recommended that the RAF meet the essential requirements of the navy and army and of Home defense; the RAF was to guard against the strongest air force within striking distance, the Air Staff was to draft proposals, and a first-line force of six hundred machines was to be created to equal the opponent's independent striking force and to be capable of expansion. In addition, £500,000 was to be allocated for land for additional aerodromes, research, recruiting, and increases in personnel and Air Ministry staff. And for public consumption a statement was also to be made in Parliament as to the desire for disarmament.

Prime Minister Baldwin announced the fifty-two-squadron HDAF to the House of Commons on 26 June 1923. The approach was Trenchard's— only an offensive could win a war; therefore the force would be two-thirds bombers without escort fighters so as to be able to deliver the maximum bomb load. By the end of five years there would be 394 bombers in 35 squadrons and 204 defensive fighters in 17 squadrons. At the time, however, there were only 2,500 men and women left in the aircraft industry, and aerodromes recently sold as surplus had to be bought back at higher prices. Secretary of State for Air Hoare had to constantly battle the Treasury for funds. The senior services did not give up, however, even though the British Cabinet in mid-1923 had decided on the RAF's role. Yet by 1924, the RAF had a grand-strategic assignment different from the two older services and was to have parity with France's estimated threat to Britain. Economy and efficiency in the RAF helped, plus the fact that the parliamentary Air Committee was chaired by Rear Admiral Sir Murray Sueter, founder of the RNAS and a supporter of Trenchard.

In Montgomery Hyde's view, by 1924 Trenchard was indisputably the winner, and he did not lose when Baldwin was defeated in the election and Labour came to power, for the latter confirmed on 18 February 1924 the new defense policy and agreed to the Air Ministry's request for an additional £2.84 million for eight new squadrons. As a result, the air estimates rose to £19.742 million, including money for medical and educational services. Trenchard also received approval for his inexpensive Auxiliary Air Force.

In 1924 the ADGB Command came into existence as essentially a bomber command, but with the detection, reporting, and defense against raids still led until 1929 by Maj. Gen. E. B. Ashmore, who had worked out the basics in 1918. The dispute over the defense of Singapore and the Far East was postponed until the Japanese invasion of Manchuria in 1931, which triggered the end of the Ten Year Rule. In addition, the Admiralty and the Air Ministry clashed over the 1923 Balfour Report on the naval Air Arm. The Admiralty tried to claim for the FAA coastal area shore stations and schools. But the chancellor of the exchequer (Haldane) told Vice Admiral Sir Roger Keyes and Trenchard to settle the argument—they were married to sisters! A sensible solution was agreed to, so that by 1937 when the RAF was large enough and busy with Expansion, the FAA was officially transferred to the Royal Navy.

When Baldwin returned as prime minister in late 1924, Winston Churchill was the surprise choice as chancellor of the exchequer and Hoare returned as secretary of state for air. The 1925–1926 air estimates contained money for seven new squadrons, including four planned for the HDAF. Being regional, the HDAF enjoyed the bonds of stability of personnel. The Cambridge University Air Squadron came into being in 1925 to link RAF officers studying engineering and the aircraft industry, and squadrons also were added at Oxford and London. In addition, in 1924 the short-service commission scheme started with 5,400 volunteers on five-year contracts. These new expansions were the best way to enlarge the RAF inexpensively and to provide a body of officer pilots for war, and the program was encouraged by qualified membership in the Institution of Mechanical Engineers at the end of five years of service.

International events such as Locarno peace treaties of 1925 lessened the dangers of conflict, and thus the 1923 plan for RAF Expansion was slowed so that its completion would be in 1935–1936 rather than in 1928. At the same time, the Colwyn Committee examined the armed forces' expenditures and concluded that the Admiralty needed to learn modern management practices, and recommended its budget be cut by £7.5 million. The British Army and the RAF cuts were £2 million each. The Colwyn Committee also criticized the Air Ministry, but this was tempered by recognition of its inexperience and constant government changes of policy. While Trenchard tried to oblige the Cabinet to say that Colwyn would be the last attack on the independent RAF, Baldwin only went so far in Parliament as to commit that the government had no intention of reopening the question of a separate Air Arm; the RAF was the coequal of the older services and attacks on it should cease. Baldwin went further, and in letters to the first lord and the secretary of state for air urged the two services to "grow up" and to stop questioning government policy. The two ministers then agreed to joint staff meetings, and the CAS wrote to each air vice marshal to explain the prime minister's rulings, expressing a belief that as of August 1926 the controversy was at an end. Yet in early 1928 Lord Salisbery had again to adjudicate the FAA problem with Baldwin's approval.

In 1928 Churchill at the Treasury placed the Ten Year Rule on a rolling annual basis. At the same time, the RAF development policy on engines enabled Britain to win the Schneider Trophy in 1927 and 1929 and, with Lady Houston's £100,000 to supplement RAF funds in 1931, also to set a world's air speed record of more than four hundred miles per hour. The French had dropped out of the competition in 1923 and their engine development suffered in consequence and left them in 1940 with inadequate power.[63] Also of significance was that the Air Council had won Treasury approval in 1924 for a Scientific Research Department, and in 1925 the experienced H. E. Wimperis was appointed to keep tabs on foreign developments. At the same time, Trenchard obtained an American Curtiss D-12 in-line engine and had it designed into the Fairey Fox light bomber and fighter biplane.

In 1928, the last Indian battalion left Iraq, one of Trenchard's great achievements, noted Montgomery Hyde, as the RAF was left in sole control. In 1929, the CAS' last year, the RAF was active in Iraq, the Sudan, Aden, and the Northwest Frontier, but there was only one death. Elsewhere Trenchard argued for further substitution of RAF for surface forces and for a thorough overhaul of imperial defense.

As all this was proceeding, however, a series of fatal accidents caused official examinations and the publication of reports by the civil aviation inspector of accidents. This led to work on the reliability of engines and later to looking at accident causes other than engine failure. In addition, public pressure led to the 1929 adoption of parachutes for aircrew, though due to the failure of the British design the American Irvine chute was adopted. Hoare directed that the human factor in accidents be studied and then focused attention on retention of flying skills and factors affecting the human body. Along with these developments, the Canadian professor of psychology at Cambridge and the director of RAF Medical Services worked together to study nervous and physical stress on pilots in Iraq.

Tied to all of this, earlier in 1923, the Chiefs of Staff Committee had been established to provide service advice to the Cabinet, and in 1926 the Imperial Defence College had come into being to deal with matters concerning the nation's defense, including that the principles of war were stated the same way in each of the three services' war manuals. The result was that in 1928 the Air Staff produced a paper titled "The War Object of an Air Force," which stated that the RAF would use a new method of defeating the enemy by attacking his means of waging war without first defeating his surface forces.[64] Attacks on such facilities would inevitably produce civilian casualties, as did long-range naval bombardments, but terror bombing would be illegitimate. Trenchard was convinced that in the next war no area would be free of air operations and therefore officers and men had to be prepared to meet and counter such attacks. But because the other two chiefs of staff disagreed with the Air Staff's assessment, no common imperial defense manual was ever issued.

The search for strategy for a doctrine for the RAF, according to A. D. English, took place earlier at the new RAF Staff College at Andover during 1922–1923. It was the work of officers on the first two courses (classes), who Trenchard had selected for their experience and brightness. The result was a combination of working syndicate discussions and interaction with the directing staff and outside speakers, with the CAS frequently in the chair; the economy was an ever-present theme.[65] By 1928 there had come to be an RAF Staff College view on strategic bombing: to attack the enemy's vital centers in order to weaken or break its will to war, to destroy its morale and not its air force—and the essays of the first five courses had been promulgated annually as air publications and circulated within the RAF.

Candidates for the RAF Staff College were recommended to have read seven books, among them Sir Charles Callwell's *Small Wars*, Sir Julian Corbett's *Maritime Strategy*, and *AP1300 RAF War Manual*, the latter having been a revision of the confidential document *CD22 RAF Operations Manual*, based on war experience from 1914 to 1922.[66] The RAF Staff College view was that the British population could withstand bombing better than the more imaginative French and that close formations of day bombers could defend themselves successfully against enemy fighters. The first part was clearly Trenchard's belief in his 1928 testimony, while the second was quickly destroyed in the fall of 1939 over what was the first World War II aerial battle between the British and the Germans, over Heligoland Bight, when Wellingtons in tight formations with powered turrets were shot down by cannon-armed Messerschmitts.[67]

In 1927 the *Basic Principles of Air Warfare*, authored pseudonymously by "Squadron Leader," was published as Air Marshal Sir Hugh M. Trenchard's *Clausewitz*.[68] The work probably was authored by S/Ldr. C. G. Burge, who had been personal assistant to Trenchard from 1926 to 1927. The book was seen as a semiofficial work that relied heavily on the CAS and RAF publications. It did not achieve a viable reputation.

A. D. English notes that the RAF Staff College was influential in feeding CAS-selected graduates into the Air Ministry, especially into its Directorate of Plans. By 1938 all eight officers in Plans were "p.s.a."—graduates of the RAF Staff College—and had all the strengths and weaknesses of such a trained and select group. Nevertheless, by 1931 the RAF had an officially accepted body of doctrine as contrasted to the Armée de l'Air's lack of such. As Scot Robertson pointed out, a real weakness in the Air Staff in London was that they tested their ideas of the offensive against their own concept of the defenses.[69] Tactics were limited to formation flying and methods of bombing; there was no bomber development unit. Only in January 1938 did Air Marshal Edgar Ludlow-Hewitt, the AOC-in-C of Bomber Command, ask for investigation of topics for which he needed answers, such as the best formation in which to fly and what to do if new long-range fighter guns could fire from beyond the range of his bombers' own guns. By early 1938 Bomber Command had yet to convert theory into useable strategic and tactical doctrine.

The problem of how to bomb accurately was not yet solved by September 1939. The high-level error was 150 yards in daylight and 1,890 yards at night. Therefore, the RAF had to choose clustered targets, such as the Ruhr. At low level the error was only 50 yards without a bombsight, but balloons were a hazard. For the Advanced Air Striking Force (AASF)—Bomber Command's force sent to France in 1939—the Air Staff recommended low-level attacks or dive-bombing. As early as 1937, Ludlow-Hewitt reported that, owing to Expansion and lack of operational training, his Bomber Command was inefficient and incapable of offensive operations. A Bombing Development Unit was at last set up in June 1938, but the bomb tests at Gretna Green did not take place until the spring of 1939.

Scot Robertson viewed RAF planning in 1939 as "mythological," and botched by a pious hope that there would be time to fix it: it was based "upon suppositional wishful thinking." Moreover, the Air Ministry was not motivated to avoid a continental commitment as its budget depended on the "air menace" belief, even though the CIGS pointed out that the RAF view of the purpose of the Luftwaffe was incorrect. Nor was the attack on enemy morale quantifiable, though from 1934 the Air Staff had to develop specific plans; yet these were flawed by the mirror effect, assuming the Germans thought like the English. Politicians on both sides of the Channel indeed were in a funk due to the air power forecasts of the devastation that raids would create.

Marshal of the RAF Sir Hugh Trenchard retired on 1 January 1930 and was made a peer of the realm in the New Year's Honours. He left active duty at about the same time as the marshals of France, except Pétain. One of Trenchard's failures was in not establishing schools for observers and gunners and in not making these crew members full time in bomber squadrons who would be facing the enemy in the air.[70] Was this an Air Staff failure? The basic approach, as Colin Sinnott would note, was the approach governed by the supposition that the bomber would always get through and that it would have to protect itself. Nevertheless, that being so, to ignore the training of professional gunners was, if not criminal, at least stupid.[71]

In reviewing the Trenchard years, Scot Robertson, in his 1995 study of the development of RAF doctrine, noted that the history of the RAF was a classic case of the failure to relate theory to technology and vice versa. The Air Staff never thought through what war would require, never related the parts of air power to each other. Equipment policy was not seen, as it should have been, as all-encompassing. Fed with war surplus, the RAF failed to read the lessons of World War I and to keep abreast of aeronautical developments. Thus, by 1934 the HDAF lacked the necessary grand-strategic bomber and could not play the deterrent role. The Air Staff used "received doctrine" and exercises that proved preconceptions about the offensive, with no intellectually honest counterpoint. And, as Sinnott has made plain, the bomber side of the Air Staff and fliers did not know what the fighter side was accomplishing—nor was the defense credited sufficiently for its successes on exercises.[72]

Airmen have not been great readers, and thus they did not carefully scan Salmond's 1932 report, as AOC-in-C of ADGB, and missed some points. In addition, in 1935 the annual report was still subjective. On the other hand, the Air Staff was developing *Memorandum No. 50* (in its 1936 version as secret document *SD98*) on wastage and consumption, which would prove prophetically accurate. Yet how to reach targets and how to deliver attacks were not studied, and navigation was such a special field that there were only fourteen professionals in the RAF in 1935.[73]

But by the time the French Ministère de l'Air was formed in Paris in late 1928, as yet without an independent air force, after eleven years working with a small coterie of powerful politicians—notably Churchill and Hoare—Trenchard had placed the RAF on a firm independent professional footing.

FRENCH AND BRITISH AIRCRAFT INDUSTRIES, 1918–1934

Introduction

In the period roughly from 1918 to 1930, the strength of the French and British air arms was not measured solely by the number of first-line machines they possessed nor by their personnel and bases, but in terms of air power of the whole structure, which included both the political economy of the day and the aircraft industry.

The watershed in aviation development was during 1929–1935. The Technological Revolution started at the front of an aircraft, so to speak.[1] That radical development enabled more efficient machines to be built by a consolidated and heavily capitalized industry very much in need of modern equipment. The aircraft industry suffered from a severe shortage of machine tools, vital for the employment of women, as well as for series production. Émile Dewoitine bought tools in Switzerland and Italy, as well as in France, but at the time of the 1940 Armistice had only 373 such pieces of equipment of the 575 needed; the bulk of what was required did not reach Toulouse until later. Yet, at the same time, British designers and the Air Staff were looking ahead. In Britain the designs of 1932–1934 evolved into a few types that served in modified form throughout the 1939–1945 war, but in France the designs of 1934 were obsolete by 1939, and the follow-ons were dead in June 1940.

By the 1920s the sheer size of French food processing, textiles, retailing, banking, railways, and shipbuilding faced administrative challenges of coordination and control, in part—and if nothing else—because they were doing more than ever before in geographic scale. Because of this and more workers, the old central office was now in need of departments manned by white-collar workers who would have to deal with Taylorism and Fordism to achieve greater efficiency. With diversity came subsidiaries, leading to firms that were both centralized and decentralized. By 1919 most of the new managers came from the *écoles polytechniques* (engineering schools). But not until the 1950s did the French begin to see management as a real profession. Sales took a back seat to production, even in the aircraft industry where the impact of mass production was dominant during 1914–1918 and again from 1936.

Meanwhile, in the wake of World War I, France had made a searching evaluation of the country's economic performance and therefore was in comparatively better shape during the 1930s than most realized.[2]

The French Aircraft Industry, 1918–1928

After World War I the French aircraft industry remained on a higher production plane longer than did the British.[3] The 1918 French aircraft industry had 180,000 employees in 115 establishments owned by 62 companies, of which 29 were research firms. The Breguet firm was pioneering metal tubular construction and Hispano-Suiza had developed the cast-block aluminum engine.[4] Shortly after the war, high altitudes were achieved with unparalleled instruments and *télégraphie sans fil* (radio, or wireless). But by 1921 employment in the industry had dropped to 3,700.

Of all the firms operating in 1918, only ten remained in 1920. Many of the ancillary machine shops had converted to other work. Manufacturers hoped to sell newer models to both foreign and domestic buyers, and the Office Général de l'Air (general air office) was created to help. At the same time, though, the four thousand employed in the technical bureaus in 1918, which had controlled aircraft production, dropped to forty, leading to a quick decline in research activity and the consequences. In 1919 the whole of the Département Aéronautique (aeronautical department) was reorganized and enlarged to include air navigation (essentially civil aviation).

French aluminum production had begun in the nineteenth century, but expansion was delayed until 1914 when new electrochemical processes, which used Alpine and Pyrennean hydropower, were developed. In World War I aluminum enabled the aircraft industry to become major fabricators, especially in the last months, both in engines and in airframes.[5] The use of the lightest metal in aeroengines was promoted by Hispano-Suiza with its in-line cast blocks. France was fortunate to have large bauxite deposits, and thus in 1920 its domestic production of 13,000 tons of light metals was 10 percent of the global, and it had tripled by 1939.

In June 1919 the Organisme de Coordination Générale pour l'Aéronautique (office of general coordination of aeronautics) was created to put all technical agencies under General Duval of 1918 Division Aérienne (air division) fame. But on 20 January 1920 Under-Secretary Flandin was reinstalled to handle all civil aviation. Pierre-Etienne Flandin, pilot, lawyer, and wartime director of the Inter-Allied Air Services, at once moved the Organisme de Coordination Générale Pour l'Aéronautique from the Ministère de la Guerre to the Ministère des Transports to handle technical, manufacturing, air navigation, and later meteorology. These areas were to be managed by an inspector general, and were to be the purveyor of all matériel to both military and civilian users. One poor result, however, was that the general staff lost its authority over the industry.

The Arme Militaire was served by the Service Technique d'Inspection Aéronautique (aeronautical technical inspection service) with a director-general of Matériel Aéronautique (aviation matériel and supply). Four specialized storage units accumulated matériel for mobilization, general aviation storehouses issued matériel to units in their areas, and two units crated and shipped stores to overseas establishments. By 1920 there was a central matériel establishment at Chalais-Meudon.

The French aircraft industry was managed to meet the same necessities of colonial operations and army cooperation in the 1920s because the Arme Militaire was part of the military. In the meantime, the airframe firms worked on the need to reduce the operating costs of airliners. To do so they used better aerodynamic ideas and both French and British engines. The

French aircraft industry was little interested in overseas orders in the 1920s and basically left the government salesmen in Latin America out to dry.[6]

From 1918 to 1922 the French aircraft industry produced 150 to 200 aircraft per month, after which the rate dropped to about 30. Yet postwar sales eventually went to twenty-eight countries. The most-produced aircraft were: more than 8,000 of the 1917 three-place Breguet XIV bomber; 1,187 of the 1921 Nieuport-Delage 29; more than 1,500 of the 1922 Breguet XIX; and some 4,000 of the 1925 Potez 25. These figures were far above RAF procurement and British aircraft produced until the Rearmament orders from 1936 on. Jean-Louis Crémieux-Brilhac published in 1990 a scholarly analysis of France and its aircraft industry in Rearmament.[7] It clearly shows, as have the economic and labor historians, that France was behind in preparing for war. Moreover, when the veteran engineer Albert Caquot was recalled to the Ministère de l'Air at the time of the Munich Agreement in 1938, which had allowed the German annexation of the Czech Sudetenland, he tried prodigiously to push aerial rearmament. For his efforts and pains, however, he was fired in February 1940. The story is reminiscent of World War I, when politics determined production and the fate of entrepreneurs. Caquot was born in 1881 and was the founder of the antecedent of the Musée de l'Air et de l'Espace (air and space museum) at the Aéroport de Paris–Le Bourget (Le Bourget airport) near Paris. He had served in World War I, and from 1928 to 1933 and 1939 to 1940 was the director of air prototypes and then president of the nationalized aircraft industry.

Caquot had wanted 1,600 aircraft to be produced per month, but Crémieux-Brilhac noted that there was not sufficient manpower to do that. In early January 1940 Caquot approved recruiting three to four women to every man, who would be their leader. But still there was a severe shortage of men with professional skills, and the small to medium-sized factories suffered from the calling-up of their engineers. These shortages, along with that of the machine tools, even affected the 247 Curtiss Hawks landed at Casablanca in December 1939. Only six had been completely assembled by 4 April 1940. In addition there was an acute shortage of raw materials, especially of the metals that composed 80 percent of an aircraft and its engine. In February 1940 the armaments minister told the aircraft firm

Caudron-Renault that it would receive only 40 percent of its needs. And because of the lack of sufficient suitable oils, engines overheated and endangered aircrews. Because the specialists were overemployed, weeks were lost creating substitutes.[8]

All of this meant that Caquot's demands for vastly expanded production were not possible. In April and May 1940, 10 percent of the aircraft ordered were not *bon de guerre* (operationally war ready) because of the lack of equipment. The minister was to blame here for the failure to place orders for propellers and ancillaries until late 1939. In part, too little forethought, said Crémieux-Brilhac, had been devoted to war because of pacificism in France. Even when delivered to units, many aircraft languished because of various breakdowns and the shortage of mechanics. Essentially, both the general staff of the Armée de l'Air and the constructors were overwhelmed by Expansion and could not focus on the future because of current problems—difficulties aggravated by the bureaucracy, which caused Caquot in January 1940 to cry that it was not possible to save France.[9]

Of the three leading French aircraft designers and managers, Marcel Bloch and Paul-Louis Weiller were attacked as Jewish. Bloch was fired because he was not a manager but a prototype expert. Weiller, of the firm Gnome et Rhône, was blamed for the shortage of high-powered engines. Émile Dewoitine survived, but was unable to realize his expansion plans because of time, financiers, and the German victory.

In 1924 the French aircraft industry had appeared to be doing well, with numerous records held by French aviators, but that soon soured due to the administrative complexity that separated users from suppliers, causing unacceptable delays in deliveries. As a result, for instance, aircraft of a 1924 program did not go into service until 1930, although only one of those six years was needed for manufacture. New planes were therefore out of date when they arrived at their assigned units. La Service Technique Aéronautique (technical service) became the center of all this. It issued orders and paid the bills, but it criticized the industry, which took refuge behind it, and all innovation ceased. So the industry remained artisanal—handcrafted in ateliers—and needed government help to survive. Prototypes were ordered, but, as in the United States, production was spread around to others, and set prices were high and automatically had a 10 percent profit added. Along with a slow and experimental process, there were too many types. In February 1926 there were 1,858 machines on charge (on the government's books) of sixteen different types.[10] In 1928 there were twenty-two types on order. All of this led to maintenance headaches, especially for mechanics who were not fully trained. In addition there was a lack of spare parts, resulting in many unserviceable aircraft.

From 1925, the French began to fall behind German, British, and American manufacturers, who were by 1935 using all-metal monocoque structures. Both in America and in Britain reliable air-cooled radial engines and in-lines came on the market together with new cowlings and variable-pitch propellers, as well as sophisticated test facilities, including wind tunnels. After 1927 the world passed by the French, and they were stunned by Lindbergh's flight that year; it took their crews until July 1930 to take off to fly east from France.

French military aviation had rested on its 1918 laurels, with new types being but modifications of the wartime designs. In 1930 the latest Farman airplanes were still open-cockpit wooden monoplanes. These were no French all-metal machines, and the first large air-cooled engines were just beginning to be available from Gnome et Rhône.[11] But the lack of capacity and capability in the aircraft industry in the interwar years was not unique. The French defense industry as a whole had shrunk as manufacturers chose to concentrate on the civil market rather than take the risks involved in accepting defense contracts for which payments were likely to be delayed; by 1936 contracts for vehicles alone were technically too demanding for factories with obsolete machine tools and assembly lines that were too small.

In this period of pacifism, belief in disarmament, financial stringency, and reduced orthodox budgets, subsidies for modernization and expansion were nonexistent. Unavailability of suitable tank prototypes, for instance, for testing and extremely small orders meant that the best tanks in the world actually were handcrafted and deliveries very slow, as Jeffrey Clarke noted in his study of Renault.[12] And of great import were the developments in the air services and their supporting industries, as well as emergent personalities.

In the 1920s unit prices remained high because the government divided orders for aircraft among various constructors. For example, orders for two hundred aircraft were split among four manufacturers who set their own prices and added 10 percent profit. The troubles of the French aircraft industry, said Emmanuel Chadeau, were not solved until the nationalization of 1936.[13] The years 1919 to 1937 were characterized by uncertainty. The pioneers survived until 1933 when a number fell in a financial miscalculation, as noted below. Another of their problems, of course, was ministerial instability, which was one of the reasons for the failure to develop an air policy. Yet aeronautical affairs to 1931 were handled by men with both experience and an interest in them.

While most firms liquidated at the end of the war, Hispano-Suiza disposed of FF11.5 million worth of war surplus for FF40 million, thus being able to retire its FF37.5 million debt. Salmson, another engine-maker, who also built aircraft, paid off its debts as well. Hispano-Suiza went into luxury cars, Salmson went into motorcycles, and Lorraine-Dietrich returned to automobiles. Renault put its aviation research on hold until 1927, Gnome et Rhône barely avoided liquidation in 1921, and the owner of Clerget committed suicide. Other firms, however, diversified. The survivors threw themselves into commercial aviation, usually in combination.

Significantly, Pierre-Étienne Flandin entered the French Cabinet in January 1920 and lasted eighteen months with a legacy that shadowed air affairs until 1928. He was an expert financier who controlled the matériel for civil, military, and colonial aviation. He started to rebuild by liquidating war-surplus stocks so as to restore markets for the firms. The Sociéte pour la Liquidation des Stocks de l'Aviation (air liquidation company) was chartered for six years, with the state holding a 50 percent interest. By 1922 it had sold FF45 million worth of surplus. By the end of 1923 it had cleared the market, in spite of the shoddy condition of much of the matériel. Flandin ordered limited quantities of new machines, spreading the building of two types among twenty-one firms. The Armée de Terre added orders for 1,023 other aircraft to the 93 Flandin had requested. Flandin's actions affected the industry until 1928, especially in trying to match demand and supply, while his policy of support allowed the firms to opt in or out. The whole was run by the Aéro-Club de France.

Hanriot and Dewoitine entered the market directly with trainers and fighters. All together, five constructors during 1920–1925 offered an average of fifteen prototypes per year, and all combined the state bought 215 during 1920–1928, which benefited twelve airframe and fifteen engine firms. At the same time, the credits for aviation rose from FF160 million in 1921 to FF400 million in 1927 and 1928. The state was paying for at least 1,000 airframes (*cellules*) and 1,300 to 1,600 engines per year. Overall production ran at 3,500 to 3,600 per year until 1928, when it dropped to 10 percent of those numbers and went even lower as series of any type ceased to be ordered during 1929–1930.

Flandin argued—as Trenchard did in a different way in Britain—that France needed to retain the necessities for industrial mobilization, and that required a sufficient number of factories for series production. All of that needed design bureaus, research facilities, and skilled workers. Flandin, moreover, argued that France had to take advantage of peace to rectify the mistakes of 1914. It had taken three years of improvisation, 1914–1917, to be able to produce what was needed for 1917–1918. However, Flandin's policy was not understood even by 1928, when it was abandoned with brutal consequences, according to Chadeau.[14] People wanted the best airframes and engines at the least cost—an old problem. Already in December of 1922 the general staff had abandoned the triple tactics of 1918's bombers, fighters, and observation craft, and procurement policy had reverted to the dilemma of 1912—quantity versus quality. Prototypes were presented but not adopted until six years later with the result that by 1928 there was not a single bomber of quality in service. The solution was seen to be the use of one principal supplier, yet that would have destabilized the system.

It was at this time that Charles Lindbergh's arrival at the Aéroport de Paris–Le Bourget in late May 1927 shocked France—he had flown more than three thousand miles in a diminutive, single-engined aircraft! The idea of an air ministry was then ongoing, and the fortuitous death of Ministre de Commerce Bokanowski allowed André Laurent-Eynac to be appointed air minister. Laurent-Eynac, born in 1886, was a barrister and had served with the Arme Aéronautique during 1914–1918. He then was under-secretary for aviation during 1921–1926 and air minister during 1928–1930 and 1940. In addition, Albert Caquot was brought back as technical czar during 1928–1933. Caquot was passionate about infrastructure and tooling with standardized techniques in the building of airframes and engines. He obtained funding and nationalized the École Nationale Supérieure d'Aéronautique (superior school of aeronautics) to produce civil and aeronautical engineers to run the state bureaus and industrial and civil aviation offices. Caquot also was able to have the budget raised from FF400 million to FF950 million in 1929 and FF988 million in 1930. He managed the system that was supervised by a commission of young engineers who had not experienced war at all. The costly new prototypes were seen as part of a whole set to be modified to produce new families. Caquot believed that fewer new types would continue to appear, but with adequate credits they would be better and come from fewer consolidated factories. Interchangeable parts, which were logistically essential, would also lower costs.[15]

A bank was established to help decentralize the aircraft industry, which was then becoming too vulnerable to the manipulative banking of Paris. Funds were also made available for sport aviation and for commercial research and purchases. The impact of this was fifty-four new transport and touring aircraft, all monoplanes and most multiengined. The policy of prototypes also stimulated engine development by Hispano-Suiza (300–650 horsepower, then to 780 horsepower) and Gnome et Rhône (200–250 horsepower). From 1931 all-metal airframes began to appear, such as the Farman 200 open-cockpit monoplane, and fighter speeds consequently rose from 156 miles per hour in 1928 to 218 miles per hour in 1933.

Remarkable in the period 1920–1932 was the Breguet firm, which at times received 100 percent of the government's available monies, reaching its peak with orders for sixty-eight machines in 1925–1926.[16] But in 1927 the Breguet firm had to downsize, and in 1932 the firm was merged into a Caquot naval enterprise. It had meanwhile shifted its exports to the commercial, as no one predicted another "Great War." Some six thousand of the eight thousand Breguet XIV biplane bomber and reconnaissance aircraft had been manufactured by subcontractors. After having decided not to liquidate in late 1920, the Breguet firm raised its capital from FF2.4 million to FF3.6 million and proceeded with the new type XIX, many of which were sold abroad. Both the XIV and the XIX appeared in many versions. The XIX had a Duralumin frame and wing longerons as braces. With its ovoid fuselage, cowled engine, and better aerodynamics, it had a useful load of 1,320 pounds. Its 400-horsepower engine gave it a speed of 113 miles per hour and a ceiling of 23,100 feet.

The Breguet XIX was produced under license in Spain, Japan, and Belgium. When in 1926 sales to France began to decline, Louis-Charles Breguet moved production to Yugoslavia, and by 1928 the Poles, Czechs, Greeks, Turks, Spaniards, Belgians, Romanians, and Yugslavs all were flying the XIX. In France by 1926 the factory at Vélizy was on a Taylorism system with a conveyer belt for wings and fuselages moving through the assembly line. The whole operation was gigantic and costly, needing years to amortize. Tooling had been installed for the manufacture of 3 aircraft per day, but orders received averaged only 1.9 aircraft per day due to the spreading of contracts. The Breguet firm went into financial decline and could raise just 25 percent of the capital needed for operations in 1928. During the next six years the firm did research and went into the manufacture of flying-boats, taking a license for the English Bristol-powered Short Brothers machine in 1930. The firm was caught by the Great Depression and the pervasive and unintended consequence of the policy of prototypes.[17]

Manufacturer Henri Potez had managed by 1926 to have sufficient orders to carry him to 1930, after being in the motorcycle and bicycle business and subcontracting to Breguet and Nieuport. Orders for his own all-wood Potez 15, which outclassed the Breguet XIX, sustained him. With family connections, Potez built a factory at Méaulte in the Somme region, where he also produced tractors for farmers from 1927. With Reconstruction money he built a second factory at nearby Albert; both were in lower-wage areas. By 1928 Potez was getting 35 percent of the French military orders, which with foreign orders totaled 1,500, to be delivered by the summer of 1929. The Potez 15 cost only FF58,000, as compared to FF130,000 for the Breguet XIX.[18] In 1930 Potez rolled out the all-metal braced wing observation monoplane P-39. All together, including the Caquot prototypes, Potez sales totaled FF60 million during 1929–1932.

Aviation also was only one of the activities for the firm Frères Farman and its Billancourt works. The firm built Breguet XIVs and Lioré et Olivier aircraft as well as a limited number of its own F-50 twin-engined night bombers and F-60 Goliath biplane heavy bombers in 1918, in addition to a few airliners and, during 1923–1926, a large three-engined aircraft that did not sell until 1932. The Farman works was not an organization of innovators; their machines flew low and slow, including a four-engined bomber of 1930 with a variant that was still sent on operations in 1940. But Frères Farman earned FF90 million building Caquot prototypes, and like others, they subcontracted out at a 10 percent lower price than the design company charged.

At the time, there was a certain amount of replacement work in the industry. Lioré et Olivier built fifty bombers during 1920–1921, but did not sell them until 1926. Amiot, Lioré et Olivier, and Hanriot, however, did little for Caquot and were absorbed in the 1930s into other firms. In 1929 Nieuport was reestablished as the Société Générale d'Aéronautique (SGA; general aeronautic society); in 1932 Morane-Saulnier failed, and in 1933 Aéroplanes Caudron was absorbed by Renault aviation engines. Engine-makers like Gnome et Rhône went into aircraft engines as well as automobiles and railway materials. The most famous aviation pioneer of these interwar years, Louis Blériot, merged his company with SPAD (Société pour l'Aviation et ses Dérivés; society for aviation and its derivatives) in 1920. His designs were not very successful, and he drifted into being a salesman for prototypes, rapidly on the way to becoming a "has-been."

For Emannuel Chadeau, the lessons of the years 1920–1933 had become clear: the young designers had not the sagacity of Marcel Bloch to leave the business in 1919 nor the ability and wealth of Potez.[19] This new generation had small *ateliers* with only a dozen or more employees. They searched for a sponsor to help their precarious existence, ruled as they were largely by the state. These entrepreneurs had been born between 1886 and 1894, were contemporaries of Bloch and Potez, and came into the business via the "back door" of a wartime education in construction and, in the interwar years, followed a variety of careers.

Trained as a mechanic, Émile Dewoitine had the only bureau in 1928 that had become industrialized. He had returned to France from Russia after the Revolution and in 1920 founded his own company in Toulouse, Constructions Aéronautiques Émile Dewoitine; the next year he introduced a 300-horsepower monoplane *chasseur* (fighter). He received prototype contracts from the state, and from one of those contracts he received orders in 1925. His 1923 all-metal D-9 attracted Swiss orders and was built at the Eidgenössische Konstruktions Werkstätte (EKW; Swiss federal construction works) at Thun; it was followed by the Swiss-financed D-26 trainer of 1928 and the D-27 fighter. The D-5 fighter was built in France by Amiot and licensed to Yugoslavia. Later designs were built in France by Hanriot, and licensed abroad. Of the some six hundred built, Dewoitine's Toulouse works fabricated only thirty-three. But Dewoitine's revenues were sufficient to launch a factory with nine hundred workers employed up to 1933, and to have built eight hundred aircraft, of which the Royale took seven hundred. Still, Dewoitine hesitated to become "industrial"—to convert into a production industry. He founded a new company in 1924 in which Hispano-Suiza held the majority of stock, along with Mitsubishi of Japan. Dewoitine was the designated administrator and the technical director and consultant to foreigners. When his base at Châtillon closed, he moved to become the technical director for the Swiss factory at Thun.

In 1928 Dewoitine founded a Paris-based company that enabled him to obtain enough capital for the Toulouse factory. Again, Hispano-Suiza had shares, with 81 percent held by Edgar Brandt's munitions enterprise, which also held Lioré et Olivier stock. And thus Lioré et Olivier became the constructor of Dewoitine aircraft. Émile Dewoitine eventually counted on the French government to build his designs. He got through the early 1930s with two hundred to three hundred employees, and had completed three prototypes by the end of 1932 when the D-500 *chasseur* appeared. Lioré et Olivier built two hundred, paying license fees. The arrangement with Brandt and Lioré et Olivier was effective.[20]

Perhaps the most significant yet disappointing development of these interwar years was the founding of the Société Générale d'Aéronautique (SGA) in November 1929 by Lorraine-Dietrich, the automobile and aircraft-engine manufacturer. The intent of the prototype policy was to increase machine-tool hours and the organization of skilled work on the eve of the Technological Revolution, but it was misunderstood. Instead of consolidation, the policy of prototypes actually spread orders to thirty-six establishments for fifty-four different types. So rather than the anticipated large orders, the funds dried up and the manufacturers of the SGA faced a loss in 1932. Innovative research clashed with the original desires of the clients.

Belgian financier Charles Nicaisse of Lorraine-Dietrich had been the initiator of the SGA. By February 1930 the organization was based in Paris, and Nicaisse also was the administrator of the Banque Nationale de Crédit. The SGA had been established to compete with Britain's Vickers company, and with Ford and General Motors of the United States. The SGA consortium was rapidly put together and included Hanriot, Nieuport, and Caudron, as well as smaller players.[21] The capital was an impressive FF325 million, backed by several banks and Lorraine-Dietrich's stockbroker, Paul Robert. The SGA had hoped to obtain FF222 million in sales during 1928–1929, which would allow the amortization of 10 percent of the cost of installations and a 10 percent return to the subscribers. By February 1930 the capital had risen to FF400 million in hopes of selling Lorraine-Dietrich engines and profiting from the policy of prototypes with stable sales.

Unfortunately, during the four-year period of 1930–1933 the SGA group lost money, which in 1933 alone amounted to some FF46.5 million. Nicaisse's fulsome predictions never bore fruit, and thus even starting in 1931 the parts of the SGA consortium were being sold off. By the end of 1933, SGA existed only on paper. The group faced imminent deflation and then the Great Depression. The competition Lorraine had faced since 1926 had seen a decline in its sales versus Hispano-Suiza and Gnome et Rhône, and so it was not as viable as claimed. The problem also, in Emmanuel Chadeau's view, was that SGA had concealed its debts, which had grown to FF149.6 million by the end of 1932.[22] The organization had not tried to be a monopoly, yet its values were inflated to the stock market. The scheme actually had been launched only thirteen hours after the Wall Street collapse. Eventually the whole enterprise was refinanced and Lorraine devoted its time to research for the Ministère de l'Air. A resolution of the problems finally came in May 1934.

Chadeau concluded that for several years the senior firms had been semiparalyzed.[23] Nicaisse returned to the seclusion of his Belgian estate and remained elusive and evasive. However, the dissolution of SGA did not solve the problems of "groups," or how to transfer the active firms to those who were able to run them. The whole was complicated by the collapse of the pioneering aviation company Aéropostale in 1932, which also had lowered the prestige of aviation. All of this led to the need in 1933 for a renewal that brought Pierre Cot to be air minister to put aviation on a new course, which would include the formation of Air France as a national airline and the creation of the Armée de l'Air. This led to the need to enthrone the military and eliminate the engineer-constructors. One outcome of this change would be the nationalization of the aircraft and armament industries. Cot, born in 1895, held doctorates of law and economics and politics. He had been elected a deputy in 1928 and became under-secretary of foreign affairs in 1932, then air minister in January 1933.

Specifications and the British Aircraft Industry, 1918–1934

The importance of the following exposition of the Air Staff's development of various types of aircraft is that it shows both what was possible and what was necessary in order to create a first-class air force; it also shows that there were differences of professional opinion and of success.

As the political and diplomatic processes lessened tensions and made France only a theoretical enemy, so the demands of the 1920s faded, only to be replaced by a far more complex situation in the 1930s because there was no recent European theater combat experience and, until 1931 in the Far East and 1934 in Europe, no visible enemy. The future state of technology on the eve of an actual war was something that had to be guessed. Twice in 1931 the Japanese had disrupted the Far East, but their abilities were severely discounted or distorted by xenophobic lenses worn by "superior" Europeans. The first close testing ground was the Spanish Civil War from 1936 to 1939.

As Colin Sinnott in *The Royal Air Force and Aircraft Design* has noted, a primary Air Ministry concern was the defense of London and the need to develop an interceptor that could climb to height in time to get above an incoming bomber force and with sufficient speed to overtake it rapidly from astern, the best attack position. But inability to do this in the early 1920s led to the deterrent-strike idea and to the necessity for precision daylight bombing; but that would require high-speed penetration of enemy air space by aircraft that could defend themselves.[24]

Sinnott notes that his work restores the balance, because Postan, Hay, and Scott in the official *Design and Development of Weapons* had to talk to industry because they could not access the Air Ministry files.[25] We now know that thoughtful men on the Air Staff defined requirements for an unknown future and that the Air Ministry funded firms to meet these operational requirements. France was for long the enemy because there had to be some basis for planning. Specifications were directly related to the aircraft industry in terms of visions of the future, design acuity, management talents, and manufacturing techniques. Sebastian Ritchie has explored that side of the subject, and it is on his work and Sinnott's that the following is based, as well as on my own writings.[26]

The RAF failed for some time to develop a clear management regimen for formulating operational needs, the follow-on specification and tender requirements. Moreover, in the interwar years new specifications were drafted to replace older types and as innovations to meet freshly perceived demands and to take advantage of new technology. Before a specification could be written, the Air Staff had to decide on the RAF's intended role and the desirable aircraft characteristics. Once the operational requirement was agreed upon, it was incorporated into a specification, which included what the Air Ministry Department of Technical Development deemed feasible.

The next step was to ask firms to tender and to test their designs and any private ventures also submitted. Eventually one or more production contracts were allotted, but after 1934 the system changed. The initial need was to speed up the process, and so in the 1930s the one-year squadron test was omitted. In October 1933 the Air Council agreed to announce the date when "specs" would be issued and a limited number of firms would be invited to tender. A significant cause of delay had been overloading the Air Ministry with testing of new designs.

A 1923 study of the German Gotha attacks on London and the failure of the defensive fighters led to the evaluation that bombers could defend themselves, but others came to a different conclusion, pointing to the German air force's attacks on the bombers of the independent air force in France in 1918. On the one hand the RAF pursued the idea of fighters mounting heavy guns (one was a Coventry Ordnance Works piece called "the COW"), and on the other the RAF believed that no one would use escort fighters. In 1926 the ADGB became conscious that all fighters needed to be able to counter a knockout blow against London. As for bombers, the Air Staff vacillated between day and night types, finally in the late 1930s settling for short-range day and long-range night bombers.

To get the required interceptors to be able to climb so as to be above and ahead of the incoming bombers, the 1927 specification, tested during 1931–1932, called for high performance, heavy armament, limited endurance, and no radio (those at the time being 20 percent of a fighter's weight). Also specified was a clear view forward, but only two rather than six guns. However, in 1934 this evolved into the eight-gun Spitfire and Hurricane specifications.

In the meantime, the antidote to the two-seat fighter was thought to be the two-seat bomber, using the same airframe so as to make interception difficult due to little airspeed advantage. At the same time it was found that the tactics of fighters being ahead of and below the bombers did not work. The Air Staff bomber development plans, as Sinnottt noted, seemed to have no awareness of new fighter thinking.

Biplane bombers were only slight improvements over those of 1918. In 1936 the twin-engine bomber still could not maintain height on one engine. This type also was confused with a transport (one of the stumbling blocks at Geneva on air disarmament). By 1930 standard hangar-door widths made the Air Ministry decree that a one hundred–foot span for aircraft was the maximum. Designs also were limited by a requirement for a bomber landing speed of less than sixty-five miles per hour. In the early 1930s, Vickers took a great loss on a private venture "battle plane," à la Lanchester and Douhet.[27]

It had first flown in 1931 at a time when the Technological Revolution was becoming visible in the Boeing B-9 in the United States, followed shortly by the Martin B-10, both twin-engined monoplanes. Thus in 1932 Vickers began work on what would emerge in 1936 as the Wellington, which would remain in service throughout World War II because it was a quantum leap forward in concept and design.

In 1927, 1928, 1931, and 1932, the Air Ministry exercises used 1920s aircraft to attack London, except in 1932, which was a paper practice. Only in 1931 did the French hold an exercise that was similar to these of the RAF, which were designed to test the operational efficiency of units and the detection, tracking, and interception of raids—and as such were quite artificial due to the rules. This led to a reconsideration of the interceptor type and to the return of radio. The Air Staff, believing in the knockout blow, was disturbed by ADGB's amalgamation of day and night fighter designs in the Hawker Nimrod, arguing that this would see half the defending fighter force unavailable.

At the same time, there was some concern over the ability of bombers to find and hit their targets, but not enough to break up confidence in the deterrent strategy. On the fighter side, worry over the effectiveness of fighter armament led to the maximum-speed eight-gun fighter, but to no consideration of what would be the consequences for the RAF's own bombers if that concept were successful. And while the RAF had the world's best fighters in the 1920s, the Air Staff failed to see that the strategy of the continuous night and day bombing of the enemy was not matched by the machines it sought—a major omission in the analysis of operational requirements. The Air Staff was fascinated by the performance of the high-speed day bomber. The RAF relied too much on its own concept of a self-defending bomber force and so undervalued its own progress in fighter defense—a case of myopic staffs in different rooms and of a service pecking order.

And in spite of the Supermarine S-6's demonstrated superiority in the Schneider Trophy by 1931, the RAF still eschewed monoplanes in favor of biplanes as compared to American advances in monoplane structures and aerodynamics. In part this was due to Air Ministry specifications wanting too many things indifferently stated, as Sinnottt noted; there were too many experimental contracts at one time for the design staffs available. Ritchie noted that Blackburn, the most successful firm in the early 1930s, tendered for everything. This was a legacy of 1914–1918 when a new design needed only six months from drawing board to operational service.

In the first seventeen years that followed 1918, Paris at 240 miles was the objective; but after 1934, it became Berlin at 600 miles. The attack on London in the later period was seen as coming by unescorted bombers from German airfields. The view was that to stop these raids the fighters had to attack in formation to bring sufficient firepower to bear. This led to a twisted search for how to aim close formations to concentrate firepower with the constant of maximum speed. Encouragement of the aeroengine builders saw speeds rise from 180 miles per hour in 1930 to 330 miles per hour in 1936. The Air Ministry's high-speed research program led to the Spitfire and Hurricane. Spec. F7/30, started in October 1929, was sent in draft to the Deputy Chief of the Air Staff (DCAS) in April 1930, when arguments arose over a monoplane design including flaps and slats to keep the fighter landing speed to fifty-five miles per hour (brakes were then only under development). Delay also came because of money and the installation of Air Marshal Dowding as the new air member for supply and research (AMSR). In October 1930 pictures arrived of the new U.S. B-9 and B-10 bombers with retractable undercarriages, the U.S. National Advisory Committee for Aeronautics cowlings, and metal propellers. The CAS subsequently ordered a six-month delay while thorough investigations were made. In June 1931, after the Department of Technical Development assured the CAS that 190 miles per hour maximum with a landing speed of 60 miles per hour was the best the RAF could achieve, the Air Staff sent a fresh draft specification to the new DCAS. Additional discussion led to the CAS plumping for mono-planes and the view that the Air Ministry would only receive innovations if it insisted on them.

Engine development then led to reconsideration of air-cooled or liquid-cooled, a battle that Rolls-Royce won thanks to the cost-plus-10-percent development contracts it held. But the AMSR then pointed out that Britain could not afford to lose the air-cooled potential in war, and a typical

British compromise ensued. The CAS, however, again decided that best performance was the sole criterion, and thus finally on 31 September 1931 the Air Ministry issued the amended Spec. F7/30. Because all tendering firms chose the in-line liquid-cooled engines, the Air Ministry requested private venture designs with air-cooled engines. The Air Ministry was encouraged by the responses. The initial Supermarine design proposed a speed of 244 miles per hour. This eventually rose in the Spitfire to 365 miles per hour, due to the accelerating design progress, better fuels, engines, and aerodynamics, which enabled the long-held Air Staff dream of heavier armaments to become possible. And, thus, at a time when the Armée de l'Air was issuing specifications for the BCR, the RAF was well on the road to excellent fighters suitable for a modern war.

In the bomber field, the specifications that led to the Hampden and Wellington were issued in 1932, but those for the Stirling and Halifax four-engine heavy bombers not until 1935. By 1933 Edgar Ludlow-Hewitt was DCAS and he argued for a number of squadrons to test new designs to get the best fighter possible. This was a sound approach at a time of technological flux, but CAS Ellington put a damper on it by instructing the Air Staff to put its priorities on fighters under development. The CAS was skeptical of the single-seaters because they could not fight in formation, and one of the CAS' pet projects was a "formation fighter" called the "novel." At the same time, the basis for calculating endurance was changed in 1932 to "maximum continuous running" at maximum normal revolutions per minute as opposed to full power. The criterion then became time-to-climb to 20,000 feet. At this point the Air Staff's new Flying Operations I ruled that speed was more important than climb, overturning a long-standing RAF demand. The Air Staff also accepted loss of maneuverability, as it appeared that all attacks would be made from astern.

Then came the information that foreign fighters would soon be faster than RAF fighters. Thus in 1934 the specifications were changed to 1.25 hours at maximum continuous revolutions per minute, which would give 277 miles per hour top speed and 3.5 hours on patrol at 150 miles per hour. In November 1934 this was formalized as Spec. F5/34 for an eight-gun monoplane; F10/35 circulated in April 1935. Then came cannon and new larger aerodromes, which would allow a higher wing loading, flaps, and a speed of 330 miles per hour.

In September 1934 Hawker submitted a new high-speed design four-gun fighter that was accepted by the Air Ministry in ten days, with no specifications issued for this item F36/34; the price was to be £8,000 each. Supermarine's experience was similar with the Rolls-Royce PV (private venture)-12 (later the Merlin), instead of the unreliable Goshawk as Spec. F35/35. The AMSR ordered these two new prototypes without the Air Staff being involved. But the project to try to get tenders for a fighter of more than four hundred miles per hour showed so little promise over the Spitfire that it was abandoned.

In August 1935 the difference between day and night fighters, still sought in the then–Fury replacement, was eliminated. This "*critical* change," as Ritchie calls it, came before RDF was known. In addition to speed, the Air Staff also studied firepower. But new tactics came in from 1936 to take advantage of the new high-speed single-seaters such as the Spitfire and the Hurricane. Both CAS Ellington and DCAS Ludlow-Hewitt saw the turret fighter as a viable solution, though Ludlow-Hewitt also sought a heavily armored single-seater to lie astern of the enemy bomber, and gave priority to the high-performance single-seater. He also advocated boosting the rates of fire.

AMSR Dowding accepted this, but believed in aimed fire. At the time of this discussion, the RAF envisaged that in a war against France it would pit fighters with speeds of 165 miles per hour (1928 Bulldogs) to 205 miles per hour (1930 Furies) versus French bombers with one fixed and two moveable guns with speeds of 122 miles per hour. The RAF had problems visualizing enemy bombers as fast as their fighters (in spite of the De Havilland DH-4 two-seat biplane day bomber and its revision, the DH-9 of 1918) and enemy bombers with multigun positions. When very shortly in 1935 the Luftwaffe appeared, with its fast bombers, as indeed the RAF would have the Blenheim, the game accelerated.

The analysis of the evidence of firing trials confirmed that eight guns with 1,000 rounds per gun were needed. Though the AOC-in-C of the ADGB was opposed to the weight, he realized that eight guns had to be wing-mounted, and as a result of the 1934 Air Exercises he urged that speeds be raised by 100 miles per hour to 280 miles per hour (the U.S. Army Air Corps was then talking of 300 to 350 miles per hour). The arrival of new reliable American Browning guns meant they could be wing-mounted for a drag penalty of only 1 percent. And all presighted eight guns could be aimed at once by the pilot, using his aircraft, to get a concentrated cone of fire at a set distance. By 1935 the Air Ministry also was aware of the new Swiss and French cannon with explosive shells; the new larger British airfields then being built as part of Rearmament, even without runways, would be large enough to take the extra weight of the new fighters. These fields had been increased to 1,100 yards diameter versus the standard peacetime 500 yards.

One result of the cannon approach was the Spec. F37/35 for a twin-engine four-cannon fighter that was to become the Westland Whirlwind. When this aircraft was delayed, cannon were installed in the wings of Spitfires and Hurricanes. In Sinnott's opinion, the RAF with its eight–machine gun or four-cannon fighters was way ahead of any other contemporary air force.

Air Ministry procurement policies affected both design and production in the interwar years as, except for De Havilland, the companies were influenced by the work being done at the National Physical Laboratory and the RAE, and generally adhered to the specifications issued. Nevertheless, aeronautical research received £15 million between 1925 and 1934. Fairey was prosperous in the 1920s.[28]

In 1917 the British Air Staff had adopted standard tool kits and required that nuts, bolts, and other common items be of standard design so as to have the fewest different parts in RAF aircraft and for ground crew a limited number of mechanics' tools. The Air Ministry also adopted in 1935 the blind-flying panel of six essential instruments always placed in the same relationship to each other to make cloud- and night-flying safer.[29] However, metal construction was not standardized. There was the Junker-style pure aluminum stressed-skin, the Boulton Paul high-grade steel strips, and the Blackburn's and Hawker's mild-steel tubing. From 1926 to 1930 these were the norm, but in the latter year Vickers began to look at geodetic structures. Metal construction led to savings in cost, increased strength, less maintenance, and less storage space, and thus was desirable for wartime production.

In 1926 the new Principal Supply Officers Committee (PSOC) concluded that in the first year of a war the engine industry would fall 80 percent short and the airframe industry 60 percent short. In 1927 the AMSR was forced to conclude that the aircraft industry was in a perilous state regarding a new war, and he therefore supported the PSOC's proposed five-year procurement of ten types as a means to stabilize the firms, to reduce in-service modifications and costs, and to trim the number of types in service. However, CAS Trenchard disagreed, as like most air marshals he saw production as a wartime problem only, proposing instead to reduce the number of types flown by the RAF and to give new types a one-year squadron trial before placing large orders, and then to keep these models operational for seven years. The difficulty was that so many World War I types were still in storage that in the interwar years production was not seen as serious (and this would also be CAS Newall's belief in 1937).

The PSOC's warning, however, did spur the Air Ministry to devise a plan to transition from peace to war on the principles of conversion, concentration, and organization. As this in its turn involved the motorcar industry accustomed to metal and not wood, the Air Ministry ordered all future aircraft were to be of metal construction. At the same time, the number of types was to be limited to those proven, and efficiency was to be gained with economies of scale. This would mean that a number of firms would produce one operational design. A war-production organization was to be established in the Air Ministry to plan and coordinate the supply of materials and equipment, especially those the Air Ministry normally purchased or supplied free to the airframe firms. The first were to form committees to allocate resources to their own groups. In practice, for instance, the Armstrong-Whitworth Siskin fighter was ordered from four firms in 1923 in order to keep them in business and to provide them with experience in metal construction. By 1931, in spite of the Great Depression then descending, the aircraft industry was thought to be in fair shape. The Air Staff noted, however, that Air Ministry procurement still impeded the development of improved production methods, the problem lying in the way that aircraft orders were placed. This was related to cost controls and to ideas of quantity versus quality.

By 1928 the PSOC had taken over the problem of peacetime capacity in contrast to wartime demand. By 1931 PSOC decided that Daimler, the luxury car-maker, had been educated for aeroengine production, and the next year it established that in wartime, Standard, Daimler, Humber, and Singer would be allocated airframe production, and Daimler would be contracted to machine 5,800 engines for Bristol. But these plans were based on the RAF's forecast of its needs only for overseas in the 1930s, with 7,444 airframes needed in the first year, which indicated a surplus the following year. However, if Home needs were added, the total was 15,000 the first year and then 20,000 annually thereafter. After 1934 the deficiencies grew even more acute.

In 1933 Lord Weir criticized the selection process, which took ninety-six months for a bomber, including forty-three devoted to official procedures, so that aircraft were obsolete when finally ordered. In 1934 the Air Council had at last recognized that the AMSR was overburdened at a time of rapid technological change, and thus it created a separate Department of Research and Development and the supply directorate was transferred to the air member for supply and organization (AMSO).

Until 1934 the Air Ministry had seen a sudden war, with a shortage of aircraft during the first year; the ministry's role therefore had been to organize coordinated output of the various sectors of the industry. The planners did not envisage an interim period between peace and war, what I labeled in 1963 as "rearmamental instability."[30] Nevertheless, the Air Ministry was concerned over mobilization and the ability of the aircraft industry to supply the RAF's needs in a new war. For example, the estimated need of engines was 15 million horsepower, but Rolls-Royce was seen as only able to produce 1 million. The industry was thought capable of only 55 aircraft per month as compared to the 2,500 of 1918. The weak procurement cycle was unsteady, and aircraft were neither fully tested nor modified.

The fall of 1938 to the end of 1939 was the critical time when the RAF was almost powerless as squadrons reequipped and trained, and took in new air and ground crews and reserve aircraft and spares. The British airframe industry was no better prepared perhaps in 1934 than the French industry was for large orders. The Ring had been kept in being as a cadre production organization in case of war. Imperial Airways had only been able to provide very small orders, until in 1934 the Air Ministry and the General Post Office were persuaded to inaugurate the Empire Air Mail Scheme and to use flying boats for it. Mail, not passengers, was the key, and since the Air Ministry had to provide the necessary facilities, alighting areas, as less expensive than air-fields, were chosen. The new C-Class Empire flying boats were a technical leap forward based on Imperial Airways rather than Air Ministry concepts. These 40,000- to 50,000-pound machines were in sharp contrast to the offi-cial 1932 specifications for the Wellington—not to exceed a Disarmament 8,000 pounds; in 1934 the constructors forced the Air Ministry to scrap that limit in favor of a 32,000-pound aircraft that might actually carry 4,500 pounds of bombs 1,200 miles.

It is important to recall that not until the Technological Revolution—which in 1929 produced transports such as the German Junkers Ju-52, the Dutch Fokker, and the American Ford Trimotor, as well as the Douglas DC-3 in 1936—were airliners cost-effective. The airlines were enabled to make money and attract investors because a host of technical improvements became available, from high-octane fuels and constant-speed propellers to brakes and flaps, as well as such labor-saving devices as automatic pilots.[31] That these were of influence to the aeronautical powers almost at the same time was due to the international nature of the field, with free exchange of information via periodicals and technical publications and the worldwide nature of oil companies, such as Royal Dutch Shell, which promoted flying with a long-term self-interest in mind. However, it was crucial by 1935 that the ministries and companies, knit together as they were by close personal contacts, keep up with and anticipate the use of new developments.

What had held back Air Ministry specifications besides the lack of money and no official enemy was paucity of the operational experience necessary to develop doctrine. The Air Staff had not planned out realistic activities and had not done the sums to see what was feasible and what was needed. In this sense Peter Fearon is correct that from 1927 to 1934 techni-cal progress in RAF equipment lagged—but not so on the civil side.[32]

Airframe manufacturers were generally design offices with workshops attached. Of necessity, Air Ministry orders meant that designers were tied mentally to what would bring a contract. A few firms, notably De Havilland after 1930, were able to do serial production of light aircraft, and Hawker specialized in a line of fighter–light bomber aircraft, producing about three and a half aircraft per month. But the system did not encourage innovation. Its greatest weakness was that the firms did not need production engineers. This was a serious handicap when mass-production began and the foreman no longer had time to hand file parts to fit. Another problem was that, while new machines came with a small set of spares and flying hours were limited to about 250 per annum with professional maintenance, the number of spares for the life of the aircraft was not settled until about eighteen months after the machine's introduction to squadron use. By that time production was on the decline and the factory was happier to get a contract to produce the necessary parts.[33]

Engines, however, were a different matter. In the early 1920s quite a lot of engines were needed due to frequent breakdowns. Then starting in 1927 a secret program was initiated that saw reliability increased from just a few hours between breakdowns to more than 1,700 hours after an engine type had been in service for four years.[34] Moreover, it was only in the early 1930s that accident investigations stopped blaming pilots for mishandling engines and crashing in forced landings, and began to realize that airframe faults and poor maintenance were also likely causes of accidents.[35]

Yet another reason for the stultification of design was not only the consumption of war surplus up to 1924, but also that those aircraft and engines served on into the 1930s. The Westland Wapiti, a radial-engine version of the DH-9 light single-engine bomber, and the Vickers Valentia (1934), a heavy twin-engine bomber, were simply further extensions of the same old designs, the DH-9 in use until 1939 and the Valentia until 1944. Fortunately, by 1939 there was a close unity of RAF, Air Ministry, and the aircraft industry thanks to the feeding of ex-RAF tradesmen to the industry and to development funding. The RAF's generous support of industry and research gave it the tools for victory.

In Eric Lund's industrial history of strategy as opposed to production, design effort was much more important than historians have realized. For example, aircraft tire pressure was related to airfield real estate and to the costs of runway maintenance.[36] Blame has been placed on Imperial Airways for not being more innovative, but it suffered both from long leisurely routes without much competition and from the need to make a profit.[37] The aircraft industry was hampered by the belief that 130 miles per hour was the greatest speed needed. However, behind the scenes by the 1930s the Air Staff was beginning to move ahead of Imperial Airways' thinking, and private ventures were also picking up the Technological Revolution. That involved, when emergency Expansion began in 1934, a highly technological industry in managerial, scientific, and engineering problems of grave magnitude, according to Sebastian Ritchie, as well as financial strains. And the Air Ministry use of the Admiralty Technical Costs Branch further reduced profits to such an extent that even a fully occupied production line in 1935 was not profitable. Yet Ritchie concluded that the so-called lean years were in fact lucrative, as the industry gained some experience of quantity production.[38]

Another issue that arose in early 1931 was the question of competitive bids for aircraft designs. The Society of British Aircraft Constructors opposed the idea; but subcontracting was tried with the Hawker Hart, because the Air Ministry refused not to be competitive. As a result, the cost of the first batch of Harts in 1931 was £3,140 each, whereas that of the second lot in 1933 was £1,475 each. But the Hawker-Siddeley merger this spurred was anticompetitive. The leaders saw the Society as ineffective because there were too many firms, and Vickers rejected a proposed merger with Hawker-Siddeley, believing the Air Ministry would let the conglomerates sink or swim on their own. In 1934 Vickers, Hawker-Siddeley, Rolls-Royce, Bristol, and De Havilland together had 22,000 employees, or 66 percent of the aircraft industry's personnel, so these key companies had a head start when Rearmament began.

Mergers

In the dry years to 1935 a number of mergers took place. When Supermarine was absorbed into Vickers in 1928, the larger company found the flying-boat facility behind the times and poorly organized. Vickers cut labor by dilution, simplified design, and made a profit, just as the larger union with Armstrong-Whitworth took place. The Armstrong-Siddeley Development Company was the joining of Armstrong-Whitworth with Siddeley Motors, to which was added A. V. Roe and High Duty Alloys in 1928. And in 1935 Amstrong-Siddeley was taken into Hawker-Siddeley, which included Hawker Aircraft and Gloster. Outside these groupings were De Havilland and, in engines, Rolls-Royce and Bristol Aero Engines.

In aeroengines, Armstrong-Siddeley was satisfied with its trainer-engine market and neglected to do R&D; it thus failed to get its engines into first-line machines. Napier sold the World War I Lion engine until 1930, but had no successor, having turned down an Air Ministry request to develop the American Curtiss D-12 until it was forced to the edge of bankruptcy.[39] The company in 1928 brought in F. B. Halford, the engine genius, to develop the Dagger, though it was not a great success, being of too low horsepower. Napier hung on until it had a winner at the end of the piston-engine era with Halford's 2,000-horsepower Sabre (and Halford went on to design in seventy-seven days De Havilland's first jet engine).[40] Bristol Aero Engines had a major export business, and both its Roy Fedden and Rolls-Royce pursued R&D on cost-plus-10-percent contracts with the Air Ministry, which led to successful lines of radial and in-line engines.[41]

In contrast to the weak engine situation in France, in Britain the Air Ministry used the cost-plus-10-percent incentive contracts to keep the engine-makers doing R&D. The outstanding example was Rolls-Royce, which developed the 2,350-horsepower "R" for the Schneider Trophy races and applied the knowledge gained to design the 1,000-horsepower Merlin in-line, which was developed to 1,650-horsepower and used in a variety of successful World War II designs, and the Bristol family of highly successful and licensable radials.[42]

Procurement Practices

A most important fact of decision-making was the creation of procurement policy. Here the French system was more convoluted, involving as it did

Parlement at the technical level, perhaps because not infrequently the war ministers were generals. In contrast, the British system was almost silent, much of it done by minutes and in committees in private, with the benefit of technical advisers.

Patrick Facon described well the 1938 Armée de l'Air approach to specifications.[43] The start of the process should have been to determine what France required in the way of an air arm as part of the national grand strategy and then to harmonize air doctrine to that need. The trouble started at once because the GSAF was filled with 1914–1918 wood-and-canvas experienced fliers who had no training as aeronautical engineers, so that they were learning on the job at the same time that the Technological Revolution and Rearmament were taking place. But on 5 March 1938 Ministre de l'Air Guy La Chambre laid down the general framework. La Chambre, a barrister, was born in 1898 and entered the Judicaire (judicial chamber) in 1928. He was under-secretary of state for war during 1932–1933, then served in the Ministère de la Marine, 1934, and subsequently was president of the Commission Militaire (chamber army commission) during 1936–1938, until he became the new air minister.

The GSAF then worked out the requirements and submitted them to the Conseil Supérieur de l'Air (CSA; supreme air council), which had been created in 1931 as an advisory body to examine organizational questions, recruitment, and the provision of aircraft. It also had to consider the effects that the introduction of new types of aircraft would have on operational doctrine. (Given rapidly changing technology, this was gazing into a murky crystal ball.) And finally it had to mull over the problems related to Armée de l'Air preparation for war. After the CSA reported back, the minister, in consultation with the GSAF, had to decree the solution. However, it has to be borne in mind that the minister already had sat in the chair at the CSA and the chief of the GSAF was his vice president. The CSA also consisted of the five major generals who had held the post of inspector general for at least a year, an air region commander, an air corps commander, and a section head from the GSAF.

However, the defense minister and members of the government could attend any session if it was appropriate. These additional visitors were ex officio—they could speak but not vote. So, too, the chiefs of staff of the Armée de Terre and the Royale could participate. In practice this meant that General Gamelin could be there—a determining influence.

In the Ministère de l'Air, matériel questions were dealt with by such a committee—the Comité du Matériel (matériel committee)—that handled those relating to armaments, programs, and technical problems. The air minister chaired the Comité du Matériel, members of the minister's military and civil cabinets, the chief of the GSAF, the CAS, the head of the Comité de Technique et Industriel (technical and industrial department), and the head of the Comité Aviation Militaire (military air matériel department). Sometimes representatives of the Armée de Terre and the Royale were also in attendance.

Overall decisions in the last stage were taken by the CSDN as part of the nation's general military policy. The CSDN was presided over by the prime minister, with a host of senior officials, including the chiefs of staff of the three services, the secretary general of the Ministère de la Défense Nationale, the comptroller general of the army, and the secretary of the CSDN.

In 1942 the Riom *procès* offered the observation that the conception and birth of a new type of aircraft were the sole responsibilities of the GSAF. The GSAF started by proposing a paper in which were stated the required characteristics and performance of a new aircraft. This paper was then forwarded to the Comité de Technique et Industriel of the Ministère de l'Air, which distributed it to the designers, who subsequently created prototypes to meet the specifications. The command of the Armée de l'Air then examined these submissions and asked for modifications or improvements. Once a prototype had been approved, the GSAF on its own responsibility drafted contractual requirements. The conclusion at the Riom *procès*, however, on the basis of La Chambre's testimony, was that the Ministère de l'Air had no responsibility for the 1940 disparity between the Armée de l'Air and the Luftwaffe.

Gen. Joseph Vuillemin, when he appeared in 1942, agreed that the process had been correctly described. However, he pointed out that the GSAF program was prepared, taking into account only the technical possibilities and the progress that could reasonably be expected in the near future, information provided by the Ministère de l'Air's Comité de Technique et

Industriel. The GSAF drew up the requirements, based on feasible or possibly feasible designs, but these were then presented for discussion to the CSA, over which the minister presided. Vuillemin strongly objected to the man who had presided over the CSA trying to blame all failures on the GSAF, which was subordinate to the minister.

Official Historian Patrick Facon believed that there "was a lack of clarity in the delicate matter of the requirements for the FAF [Armée de l'Air], especially as it related to Plan V, the relations between the Minister, the Plan, and the aircraft industry."[44] The whole story of 1931–1940, in Facon's view, would fill a shelf of volumes. The period 1938–1939 was well documented in the minutes of the CSDN, in the reports of the CSA, and in those of the Comité d'Équipement et Matériel (equipment and matériel committee), as well as in the papers of La Chambre and Vuillemin. Facon concluded that up to 1931 the engineers had worked on multiple distinct types, but that the GSAF officers lacked expertise. In 1931 the idea of a Douhetian BCR aircraft emerged, but soon, because of the Technological Revolution, it became obsolete. In 1934 there was a return to diversity of types, but by then the BCR had set France back. In 1936 there was another revision as to the number of types, each designed to allow the Armée de l'Air to meet the German challenge. These rapid changes disrupted the design teams. These offices, in fact, forgot that a prototype was a design to be refined before production of an aircraft whose requirements had been determined, without any thoughts as to, as Chadeau noted, "industrial construction."[45]

At the Riom *procés*, said Facon, the blame was spread around, as all shared the responsibility for technical and industrial policies, especially the failure to provide the infrastructure to support the projects. Everyone made some mistakes and many had not done their best to rearm the Armée de l'Air successfully: "As for those responsible in the Air Force, caught up in doctrinal contradictions of a service suffering from mental sclerosis, they were able neither to recognize the realities of modern warfare nor adapt to them when they should have done so."[46]

In contrast, the RAF in the 1930s worked out secret tables for the guidance of Air Officers Commanding in planning the size of their forces. Air

Staff Memorandum No. 50 (*SD98*) of 1936 gave calculations as to wastage and consumption of men and equipment.[47] The AOC-in-C of Fighter Command used it for what became the Battle of Britain, and it proved to be quite accurate in its estimates of wastage and consumption in intensive-, moderate-, and low-activity periods. Secret document *SD98* was also a basic logistics document.[48]

In the meantime, RAF procurement practices had been established by the RNAS and the RFC to 1918, and by the RAF thereafter. Specifications were drawn up by the Admiralty or the War Office and issued to the companies, who then designed a machine and submitted those drawings for approval; if they were deemed satisfactory, the Air Ministry issued a contract for a prototype and hopefully then for production. In peacetime the system was much slowed down and limited both by war surplus and by money. Orders were carefully spread around to keep the sixteen airframe and four engine firms of the Ring as a nucleus for future war production. In addition, the writing of specifications became much more serious, as Colin Sinnott has explained.[49]

The Delivery Process in France

The procedure in France by which aircraft moved from factories to operational units was the subject of much postwar criticism by the Service Historique de l'Armée de l'Air (SHAA; French air force historical service).[50] The interface management of supply and completion in the French aircraft industry in 1939–1940 reflects a major weakness in the supposedly rational French system. When the constructor presented an aircraft to the inspector and he accepted it, it was considered delivered and was classified as having left the factory. The constructor, however, kept it for testing and it was then classified as in the course of being *mise au point* (readied). When the constructor delivered the aircraft to the Centre de Réception d'Avions de Série (center of reception of airplanes of a series), the aircraft was said to be *présenté en recette* (checked in as property of Armée de l'Air) though it lacked such essentials as propellers and engines. And when this *recette* was done, the aircraft was classed as accepted. It was then taken on charge by the Armée de l'Air and the Direction du Matériel Aérien Militaire (DMAM, office of air matériel) discharged the constructor, who was then paid.

This procedure was full of delays between when the aircraft was delivered and accepted, and thus three statistics appeared: (1) machines leaving the works, (2) Centre de Réception d'Avions de Série aircraft accepted, and (3) taken on charge by the DMAM. Data are still needed on those aircraft serviceable and ready (*bon de guerre*). Winter affected these statistics because of shorter daylight and bad weather, so that fewer aircraft were completed, but there were too few aircrews to man the machines available, serviceable in depots and in schools. In addition, there were other aircraft that were unserviceable for lack of parts.

In France an aircraft was held at the receiving unit until all the missing pieces had been supplied and fitted, and then air tested. However, although ready to be issued, it was still unlikely to be *bon de guerre*. One of the major complaints in 1940 was that of every thirty-two aircraft "accepted" by the Armée de l'Air, only twenty-two could go to squadrons and that many of those delivered were "unserviceable"—unfit still for war, as the system was not vigorous but rather was haphazard. The first aircraft of each new series was sent to the Centre d'Essais en Vol (experimental test center) at Reims where it was assigned to an experimental squadron manned by air and ground crew from the squadron that would first receive it. The squadron at Reims carried out tests and then drafted pilot and ground crew notes. In addition, an officer from the Centre d'Essais en Vol was attached for one month to the first unit to be issued the new type.[51]

In Britain, in contrast, after experiencing the financial difficulties of manufacturers in World War I—since the same experienced men such as the former Director-General Lord Weir were still around in 1935—deliveries and acceptance were handled somewhat differently, not only with capital loans and shadow factories, but also with equipment that was supplied to the factories so that in mid-war up to 40 percent of an aircraft was government issued.[52] In the British system, aircraft were completed at the factory, where they were approved by an Aeronautical Inspection Department man who signed off on them. The machine was then flown by a company test pilot and handed over for delivery to either an aircraft storage unit or to a repair and salvage unit for installation of final service items and readied in four to five days for delivery.

Aircraft were delivered from the factories after air testing, almost—if not completely—equipped, and went to a storage unit, from which they were issued on demand. Usually in peacetime the receiving squadron would send pilots to pick up the aircraft after a brief air test.

Squadrons would work up new types and recommend modifications, if needed. When taken on charge against the initial establishment, the machines were expected to be ready for action. It was at the other end of their operational career that if the squadron personnel could not fix battle damage within three days, they were taken off charge and pushed into a neighboring field to await collection by a repair and salvage unit, which would rebuild them or return them to the factory. Category 6 machines were complete write-offs, to be picked over for spares and then collected for scrap. After the Battle of Britain, rebuilds became a significant number of the aircraft issued to units, as they had been in World War I.

PART III

THE ROAD TO WAR, 1932–1940

FROM THE ADVENT OF HITLER TO WAR, 1933–1940

Introduction

The French political scene in the 1930s was a spectrum of fancies and fears, a milieu that prevented politicians from doing what needed to be done, a world in which on the Left were those who wanted a Marxist proletarian utopia, and on the Right, neo-Fascist authoritarianism. Economically it was a France stuck with dull nineteenth-century ideas glued to the gold standard. If it was a land of petite bourgeoisie, it was also one of peasants, and it was a land of militant workers and of women employees.

In the 1930s all the peoples of France became more economically insecure and internationally afraid. In a way, what bound them together was hatred of politicians and conscription. In the depressed 1930s the autoworkers fought discipline because employers imposed it as they ceased to tolerate slack attitudes in the workplace; the owners vigorously modified working conditions. Workers became more adept at saving time by skipping stages in a process and by restricting output when time-checkers were present.

French Fordism was only partial, and the workers received paid holidays and the forty-hour week with weekends free. But from 1933 on there was a growing shortage of skilled labor, a talent critical to production strategies.

Although Renault was a modernizing factory by the late 1930s, the owner had decided it would benefit to really make it modern. At the same time, in the November 1938 strikes, the government sent in the *gendarmes*, lockouts occurred, and firms dismissed workers. Renault installed turnstiles at the entrances, and productivity soared. The influence of the unions was reduced, and the breaches in Fordism closed, though they reopened under the Vichy government during 1940–1944.[1]

Eugen Weber's *The Hollow Years* depicts in great detail France in the 1930s when the combination of war casualties and the low wartime birth rate meant that conscription had to be extended from one to two years.[2] The result was that the grace period of the Phoney War was wasted by inaction. The thought was that France would parry a German offensive and then rest on the defensive for several years.

As Weber noted, French thinking had become defensive. Moreover, there was a subtle undercurrent of pacifism and fatalism in the population. In part because of rotation-in-office of civilians, military planning and budgetary proposals were increasingly left to the military professionals, dominated by General Weygand and General Gamelin, the former chiefs of staff to the leading World War I generals.

At the time, the Royale was impotent and the Armée de l'Air neglected. Rearmament was both helped and hindered by politics and ideology on the part of management and labor, while production accounting made the Armée de l'Air appear much larger than it was in reality.

The fear and insecurity regarding Germany during the interwar years had been seen as early as the 1920s, and it accelerated during the 1930s from the publication in 1932 of the French translation of Douhet's *Command of the Air*, the penultimate discussion of the "air menace." Civil defense in France was only begun in 1936. Moreover, it was disconcerting to the French people, after Hitler had annexed Czechoslovakia in 1938, to subsequently discover in 1939 that a large percentage of civilian gas masks had been ordered from the Czechs, and now there was no immediately available supply.[3]

During the 1930s, with Hitler's victory at the polls in 1933 and guns-not-butter economic plans, Germany, already with a larger population than France's, surged ahead on a wave of nationalist enthusiasm. At the same time, in Italy Mussolini turned from a sometime friend of France to an ally of Hitler and a threat to North Africa. Ethiopia fell to his forces in 1936, and the League of Nations was proved ineffective in the wake of the 1934 failure of the World Disarmament Conference at Geneva. Shortly thereafter Hitler began dismantling France's Eastern Bloc alliance. Then came the Spanish Civil War of 1936–1939, with Soviet and then German and Italian participation. France and Britain stayed neutral, which shocked Paris and the Front Populaire as the Spanish people's choice went down to defeat in the face of the Fascist powers.

Looking back to 1934, however, it is evident that the pace of events overall had quickened and everything had become more complex. The state of the Armée de Terre before 1940 not only fooled foreign observers, but also the French themselves. The weaknesses of General Gamelin's forces has been well covered by the writings of Robert Doughty and Eugenia Kiesling, among others.[4]

The story of French military aviation is depressingly complex. It reveals that the blame for the French defeat of 1940 must be spread so wide as to cover the whole of French society, not just the leadership of the political parties, of the unions, of the Armée de Terre and the Armée de l'Air, nor even of the manufacturers alone.[5] Striking at the opponent's mobilization was in French doctrine a strategic, not a grand-strategic, action. In spite of its birth by decree in 1933, the Armée de l'Air was blighted by its past. The new chief of the GSAF, Gen. Victor Denain, could not stand up to the Armée de Terre's General Weygand and the Royale's Admiral Darlan because the wording of the law was, according to Young, "vacuous."[6]

Denain was born in 1880, graduated as a cavalry officer from Saint-Cyr, and received his pilot's brevet in 1915. He then was chief of the Service Aéronautique de l' Orient (aeronautic service of the East) at Salonika until 1919, after which he went to the Levant until 1923. In 1928 he became chief of the French military mission in Poland, then from 1931 was commandant at Tours. As of April 1933 he was commanding general of the GSAF.

The Armée de l'Air soon found 86 percent of its strength handed over to the surface commanders and dispersed to surface units, which simply aggravated the older airmen's resentments. Airmen fought for a week's unfettered action on the outbreak of war as a strategic strike force against the enemy's principal communications and transportation centers, munitions depots, military and naval bases, and production establishments (which World War II would prove was far beyond the capabilities available at that time). The aim was not Douhet's knockout blow, but merely slowing the enemy's mobilization.

Calculations of the likely effectiveness of bombing needed to be made. If we accept Holley's statement that only 27 percent of the aircraft produced in the United States during World War II ever reached a target, and combine that with the fact that 50 percent of the bombs the Germans dropped on London during the 1940–1941 blitz fell on open spaces, then the possible bomb damage was only 13.5 percent of the number of aircraft dispatched.[7]

From a planning point of view, if a bomber could carry four thousand pounds of bombs (eight 500-pound bombs) to a target, the force needed in early World War II was thirty aircraft for every one ton of bombs dropped on the target.

Further regarding the Armée de l'Air, from 1929 to 1931 both the air minister and the war minister appointed chiefs of the Air Staff until the air minister gave in and accepted them. To regain their power, the aviators moved (as in Britain) to get the role of grand-strategic bombing of the enemy's heartland. They ordered heavy bombers, but only broke free of Armée de Terre and Royale resistance in 1934 when the army still kept the Armée de l'Air "children" under control in 118 of the 134 squadrons. In that year Marshal Pétain, the new war minister, transferred Armée de l'Air credits (funds) to the Armée de Terre; at the same time the umpires of that year's maneuvers urged the abolition of the Armée de l'Air Haut Commandement because it was an obstruction. The 1935 maneuvers report rejected the Armée de l'Air's claim that strategic bombing could be decisive and demanded that air assets be distributed to the surface services. But the Armée de l'Air was backed in grand-strategic bombing by the Left, which had supported Disarmament and collective security to protect the *patrie*. Their real target, however, was not an external but rather an internal enemy—the Right and the Armée de Terre.

Quite suddenly in the early 1930s the centrist coalitions, which had kept France steady, came unglued and political power coalesced on the Left. The Right, fearing the consequences, marched on 6 February 1934 on Parlement. The Left also appeared on the streets, while a thin line of *gen-*

darmes tried to maintain order. The situation played into French fears of another 1789. The only military force available in Paris was the new Armée de l'Air, which General Denain sent to defend the senators and deputies. In the calm that followed the dispersal of all the antagonists, the Left coalition, the Front Populaire, won the first round of scheduled elections.

In the interval, before the second round, the *gendarmerie* arrested Alexandre Stavisky, a Jewish peddler of a fraudulent municipal bond scheme who died in custody. A new Leftist government under the Socialist Léon Blum then took power.[8]

From the economic and political history of the 1930s in France it is clear that orthodox finance, the task of a strong leader able to stay in power, and the lingering Depression were part of the reasons why the Armée de l'Air was behind the air forces of other countries; other reasons were the mistaken air force policies and the artisanal small-firm nature of the aircraft industry and its ancillaries in the midst of the Technological Revolution. Although aircraft production finally caught up in terms of numbers in late 1939, the types produced were still two years behind, technically and in performance. In 1937 the RAF had begun to take delivery of Bristol Blenheim and Vickers Wellington bombers; the French equivalent types did not appear until 1939. The late Rearmament meant that the debacle of 1940 was not just a military matter. France, the French people, and the system of government they condoned were at fault.

Britain, a smaller country with a larger population, did not hold its politicians in such low esteem as France did. Parliament was regarded as the stamp of approval on the Cabinet's actions. That small, élite body aimed to lead, even if it did not always well understand the needed solutions. Moreover, strongly in mind on the subject of colonies was the Empire—the red coloring on the global map—in contrast to the vacuum in Paris.

Britain had participated in League of Nations debates and treaties during the 1920s but pursued the policies of traditional settlements of dangerous situations by appeasement and splendid commercial isolation. From 1932 on Cabinet committees had called for the abolition of the Ten Year Rule and Rearmament, as disarmament by example had placed the country in a dangerously weak condition. From the only global power in the

1920s (the United States was isolationist), the Commonwealth in 1926 (and so declared as of 1931) was rapidly slipping into a diplomatic, military, and economic position of equality. Rearmament helped reduce unemployment and coincided with modernization, especially that of the RAF HDAF, which Neville Chamberlain deemed the least expensive and most evident solution to the need to rearm. Chamberlain had been a member of Parliament from 1918 to 1940, a manufacturer, and chancellor of the exchequer from 1923 to 1924 and from 1931 to 1937.

Fortunately for the country, the aircraft industry and its allied engine firms were prepared to design and build the new all-metal types needed, and the Air Ministry foresaw the requirement for aircrew and ground crew, as well as airfields. And while the British Army began to prepare for war, it was only allowed to develop a limited mechanized force—at least as a mobile armored one—until the spring of 1939 when the government decreed conscription and the goal of a fifty-five-division military. Still, while staff talks had started in 1936, it was not until after the Munich Agreement in September 1938 by Britain, France, Germany, and Italy, allowing the German annexation of the Czech Sudetenland, that the potential allies began to realize they had to coordinate their plans against an increasingly hostile world. Worthless guarantees were given to Poland and Greece, and a pact with the Soviet Union was sought, but too slowly. And so it was that with the ultimatum to Hitler regarding Poland being ignored, Britain and France declared war on Germany on 3 September 1939.

As Talbot Imlay has pointed out in *The Fog of Peace and War Planning,* 1932 to 1939 were years of great uncertainty. War planning had to be done in a vacuum until 1935, and over that planning lay the pox of the fear of another "Great War" and the Bolshevik threat with the mainstay Russian, Austria-Hungarian, and German Empires no longer on the playing field. And the economic crisis impelled by orthodoxy was compounded by the uncertainties created by the tank and the airplane. The fog was not penetrated by too-small intelligence agencies, except in Britain in a limited way. But to 1935 this perpetuated the myth that Germany was weak and France strong. All of these inducements increased the risk factor and, after 1934, government intervention in the German, Italian, French, and British economies.

Planners were themselves forced to try to assess economies as well as military strengths. In France, the Troisième République never succeeded in passing legislation to prepare for a new war—there were too many complications—and Paris, like London, in 1935 envisioned a new war as still distant. Moreover, the staffs of the military and foreign offices were too small to deal with the incessant crises, as well as the increasing lead times of the new technology, and at the summit of these woes was the youth of the French and British air staffs.

The Armée de l'Air, 1933–1939

In 1936 the Armée de l'Air was organized as decreed in the Law of 1934, which was basically a copy of that of 1927 governing the Armée de Terre, using regional commands. Under these measures the essential task was to condition the forces and prepare them for mobilization, the coverage of which was to be the prime Armée de l'Air action in wartime. The Law of 1927 gave the army the power to create large units in peace that could go into battle immediately without mobilization. But no one thought to use these forces in March 1936.[9]

The Armée de l'Air enjoyed comparative stability at the top. In 1933 Pierre Cot, a Radical Socialist, became the air minister and shortly made General Denain chief of the GSAF.[10] Denain succeeded Cot as air minister from 1934 to 1936, followed by Marcel Déat who was air minister for six months, then by Cot again until January 1938. Cot realistically sought a policy of returning to an 1890s-style alliance with the Soviet Union to squeeze Germany, but this was denied. Guy La Chambre followed Cot as air minister until March 1940 and appointed Gen. Joseph Vuillemin as chief of the GSAF, who led the Armée de l'Air through defeat into the Vichy regime.[11]

Earlier in the winter of 1932 Premier André Tardieu had tried to create a single defense ministry, but he left office before it could be established; in 1933 the Ministère de l'Air was still a skeletal organization where habits were still in opposition, not fused into a whole. It was complex and uneconomical with Directorates de l'Arme Aéronautique de la Terre et de la Mer (land and sea air arms) not under a general staff. The Direction Technique (technical directorate) was a state within a state. The rift between airmen and soldiers remained over the matter of close support, which no more met the desires of the army chief of staff than of the Armée de l'Air.

Made aware of the coming crises by, among others, the Deuxième Bureau de l'Air (French intelligence agency), the French Haut Commandement needed to act rapidly to ensure France's safety.[12] But haste was not possible owing not only to political instability, which led to the Front Populaire government, but also to the unsettled quarrels between the Armée de Terre and the Armée de l'Air as to their roles.

It was Cot's Decree of 1 April 1933 that had laid down the principles of the use of the new Armée de l'Air.[13] This was based on the 1914–1918 war, but edited with reference to a hypothetical conflict. After discussions, the Armée de l'Air was expected to cooperate with the Armée de Terre and La Royale. Then there was the Commandement de Région Aéronautique (regional air command), but its command was highly debated. However, the inspector general of the service that would use it in wartime had the right to inspect it during combined exercises or maneuvers. Chief of the GSAF Denain wagered that the text of the October 1928 decree gave the Armée de Terre certain units and rights, their location, and choice of matériel, numbers of aircraft, and their use in liaison with other arms. Like Daladier, Gamelin and Weygand held to the October 1928 terms, insisting especially that the Armée de Terre should choose the aircraft. But just at this critical moment, the question of new aircraft types arose, as did a five-year plan that had shortly to be decided, along with the organization of the Armée de l'Air and allocations to the Armée de Terre. These were the background to the law of 2 July 1934.

The Commission Aéronautique de la Chambre (chamber air commission) was impressed by Cot and Denain and the compromise victory defended against Pétain in the Sénat. The Royale fought bitterly against a separate Armée de l'Air during the 1933–1936 period and used its journals to campaign especially against Douhetism, as noted by Thierry Vivier.[14] Under the Law of 1934 the country was divided into air regions whose commanding generals were directly responsible to the air minister and who were to command the troops there. In time of war the government would decide on the allocation of air units to operations with the reserve Armée de l'Air units under the chief of the GSAF, who had the right of inspection of all air units and would direct any air operations the government entrusted to him. The air assets allocated to the Armée de Terre were to be commanded by an Armée de l'Air general under the authority of the army theater commander. The same applied to the Royale.

Unfortunately, this organization had two major defects. It went against the principle of unity of command and action, largely because the Armée de l'Air was so small that the chief of the GSAF could not conduct general maneuvers. In addition, it violated the principle of permanence as laid down in the Law of 1882. Thus on the outbreak of war the Armée de l'Air would have to be totally reorganized from a territorial to a functional basis that did not exist in peacetime. In spite of precautionary measures, the Armée de l'Air therefore was entirely unsuited to action when war broke out. That this disparity was allowed to occur flew in the face of concepts of a short modern war, but is explained by the fact that the French Haut Commandement was determined to begin a new war from where World War I had ended in 1918.

In 1933 the Directorates de l'Arme Aéronautique de la Terre et de la Mer had been abolished and the Conseil d'Administration (directorate of military aerial matériel) under the general staff created in their place, together with the directorate of personnel, and a central work-installations service. The idea was to solicit greater staff input, but this was denied to the director general for engineering. When in 1934 General Denain became the air minister, he carried out a new reform based on making the technicians subordinate to the users.[15] The new Directoire de l'Ingénieur (directorate of engineering) was abolished and replaced with a Directoire de Fabrication Avions (directorate of air manufacturing) with control of everything dealing with civil and military matériel, from prototypes through production, with a central works and installations so as to concentrate everything concerned with the air infrastructure. From then on the Air Staff as users would control both civil and military aviation, and all of this was embodied in the Decree of 5 March 1934 followed shortly by the setting up of the Comité du Matériel (aviation matériel and supply) and the Comité d'Essais en Vol (flight test commission). While Denain had now placed the Air Staff over the technicians, this did not in itself guarantee results. Denain also set up regional air circles synonymous with the military districts to allow reserves to be trained and mobilized with ground units. Denain did not understand the need for prototypes, and his actions here help explain 1940.

At the same time he needed to instill in personnel a love of flying and a bad-weather capability. In 1935 the École de l'Air (air school) was established to handle the direct recruitment of fliers, advanced air training was revised, and a new Centre d'Études Tactiques (center for tactical studies) was planned together with an École Supérieure de Guerre Aérienne (advanced military aviation school), all intended to train the top leadership of the Armée de l'Air of the future.[16]

A principal organizational problem under the 1934 Law was that while the Armée de l'Air was divided into regional commands, these did not correspond to Armée de l'Air wartime needs, which were not by any means only to support the Armée de Terre. The latter were only concerned with the opening battle on the ground, yet there was no organization to re-create the idea of the Duval Division of 1917–1918. Thus in October 1936 the Air Staff argued that a new air organization was needed in peacetime to meet the needs of the opening battle. This meant creating a new structure separating the territorial and operational commands with the air units involved reporting directly to the air minister. Each new heavy air corps consisted of three divisions divided into eight air brigades themselves, divided into *escadres* (wings). In addition, there was to be a light air corps of three divisions of balloons, also divided into *escadres*. Regional air commanders were to be the technical advisers of the surface (Armée de Terre or Royale) regional commanders.

While criticized, this nevertheless was a step along the way to a functional organization. At last the Armée de l'Air was released from the type of structure decreed after the Franco-Prussian War of 1870–1871. Yet this was inept, as there remained a large gap between fliers and base operators. It was not economical—the expanded staffs had too many captains. The Decree of 15 August 1937 only marginally affected the Armée de l'Air by separating operations and administration, making, for example, air bases central.

In one way the Armée de l'Air was five years ahead of the RAF in that the Centre d'Aéronautique Militaire Expérimental (military air experimental centre) established at Rheims pioneered new techniques including pathfinding and bombing tables. Also set up were inspectorates of air reconnaissance and of defense aviation.

One of the most arguable decisions of the Denain tenure was the ordering of the BCR, the long-range heavy battle plane with all-around defense à la Douhet, who had however also espoused a very fast escort fighter. In contrast, the RAF did not take much note of Douhet, though the then–U.S. Army Air Corps did.

The BCR went back to 1918's multiseat Caudron R-X1 used to escort bombers and its descendant, the Blériot 127 of 1933. But the true reason for the BCR, according to historians Christienne and Lissarrague, was the inability to put all the limited Armée de l'Air resources into bombers while also needing to support the Armée de Terre and escort heavy bombers. Under the proposed Rearmament Plan I, this led to the Bloch 200 and 210 and to the Amiot 143, which were bombers, but not really support aircraft. The ideal BCR was the Potez 540, which began to reach units in mid-1935 and equipped most of the Armée de l'Air reconnaissance units from 1936 to early 1939 and then soldiered on and suffered heavy daylight losses in May 1940.[17]

Plan I had been approved by the CSA in June 1933 and by Parlement in July 1934. It called for 1,010 aircraft—350 fighters, 350 bombers, and 310 reconnaissance bombers. The use of old designs would not have mattered so much if there had been a follow-up plan, but there was not. Some considered the BCR an ideal civil aircraft. It was a compromise between the Douhetian bomber extremists and the Armée de Terre's desire for total collaboration with the ground forces.[18] According to Thierry Vivier's work, *La Politique Aéronautique*, General Gérardot in 1951 said it was "everything and nothing," an excellent civil machine.[19] But the BCR was soon outclassed by the 20-mm cannon-armed fighter. As a result, only the Potez 540 was retained in Plan I, but the civil war in Spain showed it to be totally unsuitable for daytime combat.[20]

One wonders, then, if Pierre Cot's 1,010-plane order of 1934 was a deliberate break from the Armée de Terre purchasing system of driblets, and if it also was designed to prepare the industry for a massive Rearmament in the face of the German menace.

This situation with the new Armée de l'Air was exacerbated by the sudden emergence of the Luftwaffe in early 1935 with its fresh designs. Parlement refused to accelerate Plan I, so the government used its special powers to add another segment, to be completed by late 1935. This was disastrous because it simply added to the disorder in the aircraft industry, which was not only incapable of turning out aircraft on time, but also was still caught in the atelier stage because of lack of large orders for so long. Plan I's completion thus was extended to the end of 1937, and that interfered with newer plans.

Meanwhile, the Deuxième Bureau had at first overrated the new Luftwaffe, then failed to see that German production was four times the French and their population twice as large—and that the Luftwaffe received the monies it needed. The new German aircraft types vastly outclassed the 1934 Plan I prototypes. The Deuxième Bureau kept the Air Staff well informed, so that the Me-109E of 1939 was no surprise to the Armée de l'Air. Already at the Zurich Air Meet in July 1937 French officers had seen the Me-109 versus the Dewoitine 510 and had gone home depressed. The fighters reaching squadrons in late 1938 were useful for training, but the Dewoitines were notoriously inadequate in performance, as again was the BCR.

On top of these problems, the Armée de l'Air was short of manpower and had a weak officer corps. This had not been a problem when there was relatively little flying, and that in good weather. But the new types coming into service demanded much more vigorous maintenance on the ground and precise handling in the air, by specialized personnel, and much more training. These needs were not always synchronized with manufacturers' delivery schedules. Insufficiency and inferiority of material was covered up with flying displays. Part of the problem also was, as the RAF realized, that the training of personnel took far longer than the building of an aircraft. In 1936 the Armée de l'Air had 30,000 personnel who were becoming super-annuated, while the bulge in officer ranks meant that the flying personnel especially were in their forties, which was acceptable in peacetime but not in war. In July 1936 the youngest major general was fifty-three, the young-est brigadier general fifty-one. Half of the colonels were over fifty; of all the lieutenant colonels, 16 percent were over fifty, 58 percent between forty-five and fifty, and only 26 percent below forty-five years of age. The youngest was forty-one. Half the majors were in the forty to forty-five bracket; the youngest was thirty-eight, and 7 percent were over fifty. Of the 672 captains in 1936, 313 had entered the service in the 1914 war, and unless they were in the top half of the seniority list, they were not eligible to be promoted to major. Of those 336 on the July 1936 promotion list, only 29 were younger than thirty-six years old. Unfortunately, there was no purge of superannuated officers in France as there was in the United States and Britain, or more brutally in the Soviet Union. All of this helps explain why many aircrews had difficulties converting to the modern aircraft beginning to enter service and why they also were not very able instrument fliers.

Cot also had wanted to change the sociopolitical complex of the Armée de l'Air officer caste by purges, by ceilings on age for rank, and by commissioning senior NCOs. These measures cost eight hundred (40 percent) of the officer corps and all eight top generals of the CSA. The air minister brought in 392 NCOs and some reserve officers to fill the void, having also set out earlier in the Law of 1935 to make a drastic reform in the officer corps, starting with reducing the previous age limits by five years, achieved only for brigadier generals, and two years younger for others. By 1938 the number of captains aged over thirty-six had dropped from 60 to 48 percent, while the number of lieutenants over thirty-five had risen from 17 to 27 percent. No more could be done because of lack of time and money.

Intelligence from Berlin indicated the Luftwaffe would have rearmed by 1938–1939 and that the French would by that date have to have an experienced and well-informed Air Staff. But to obtain them meant that such had to be set up in 1936. Cot told the Comité Aéronautique of Parlement that he would keep General Fèquant as chief of the GSAF, he would promote five brigadiers to major general (including Vuillemin), and add four new brigadier generals. At the lower end, he proposed to promote more senior NCOs to lieutenants. This led to charges of politicizing the air force, which was partly true. By the twenty-first century, his approaches were considered standard management practice, to encourage NCOs and the graduates of the large military schools by freeing room and creating the possibility of promotion.

Cot set out in his second term in 1936 to reorganize the Armée de l'Air with command structures for operational units, logistics, and mobilizing Reserves. He created two cadre corps HQ to command one hundred *escadres*, each staffed with politically suitable officers. Yet, when war came, nine out of ten Armée de l'Air HQ had no function and so squandered manpower. However, apparently doctrinally coherent and politically plausible, which would both take the war to the enemy and support the Eastern Bloc allies, Cot's reforms were not implemented because the Front Populaire government was not in tune with the times, technology, and strategic realities. Moreover, Cot's measures aroused fear, mistrust, and uncertainty in Armée de l'Air officers, including those just recently advanced. The firing of the experienced Gen. Paul Armengaud of Moroccan fame left the Armée de l'Air with no one to lead army cooperation. Thus in 1938 Guy La Chambre, the new air minister, abolished grand-strategic bombing and ordered a return to close support.

Another important aspect of Armée de l'Air preparation was personnel. This was far more important than production and would prove to be a real air force Achilles heel in 1940. Though the Air Staff recognized the needs, the Ministère des Finances opposed any greater load on the budget and the politicians did not press the issue. Staffing was detailed in organizational manuals based on theoretical needs. These were treated with respect but never honored.

The basic problem was that while material needs were understood, personnel requirements were not. Thus the manpower for the new matériel on order was not synchronized to its delivery. Nothing was done in the budgets of 1936 and 1937; only in the latter year was the Centre d'Instruction Avancé (advanced training center) opened for its first class from the École Supérieure de Guerre Aérienne and from the third class at the École de l'Air at Salon. As a whole, the Armée de l'Air lacked the necessary schools and had to use civilian ones.

Since few if any French pilots had had general staff experience before 1914, they lacked an understanding of the organization and administration as well as the industrial-economic base needed by their highly technical new service. The Germans, in contrast to the French and British, did evolve the Luftwaffe out of the old Great German general staff. And they understood the limits not only of the bombers, but also of the countervailing effect of attacking the will or morale of an enemy population insulated by buildings and hard to cripple because of the multichannel nature of a modern industrial society. Both the Armée de l'Air under Cot and the RAF under Trenchard and his successors convinced themselves of a mythological power that was a war-loser.

The immediate need in 1936 was for pilots because those in the reserve would not be available until mobilization. As the years from 1934 passed rapidly, as the lead time for new aircraft lengthened, and as France faced the series of crises from internal revolutions to the remilitarization of the Rhineland (1936) through the Munich Agreement (1938) to war and defeat (1939–1940), France fell further and further behind Germany, even as Britain in 1939 became an ally. The harsh reality of France's situation was absolutely clear in the summer of 1938 when chief of the GSAF, Vuillemin, visited the Third Reich where he was psychologically overpowered by displayed personnel and new machines.[21]

Plan V of 1938 should have played a vital role in the regeneration of the Armée de l'Air, but it was delayed both by the industry and by lack of vision; to catch up to the Germans, France needed much more than reaching pure numerical parity with them in 1937, even without spares and wastage taken into account. In addition, Gamelin faced increasingly complex managerial problems. The Front Populaire's forty-hour law hampered the defense industry, and resulted until 1938 in owners' determination to break the unions. But arms production was also hampered by a shortage of skilled labor in spite of unemployment, in part due to the failure of the state to add to the few technical schools. Modern war demanded modern arms, which needed machine tools and operators. France was deficient in these. Pierre Cot's attempted dispersal of the aircraft industry as a protection against bombing set back production because of the scarcity of useable labor in the provinces.[22]

Unfortunately, just as France began to rearm, the political Left and Right reached into the armed forces and in 1936 severely affected morale in the services, whose reaction was "a plague on both your houses."[23] By 1938 the Armée de l'Air was also split between the Douhetian school of bomber offensive defense and the Mecozzian philosophy of attack aviation in support of the Armée de Terre on the ground.[24] While this real quarrel over roles was largely theoretical, it failed to consider the number and types of aircraft needed to be effective and it ignored the serious question of wastage of aircraft and crews, let alone the size of the ground structure and reserves needed to support active operations. In other words, as this history explains, the disastrous defeat of 1940 was already on the books before the Munich Agreement and its origins can be traced back to 1918. The victors talked and paid some of their debts while the vanquished planned to reclaim their great-power status. Organizationally only the changes of 1937 finally produced the definitive structure of the Armée de l'Air, and this was symbolized by the new dark blue uniform and soft cap, instead of a kepi.

Pierre Cot as air minister attempted to widen the base of aviation by the *aviation populaire* (popular aviation) movement (which was the equivalent of the Royal Auxiliary Air Force across the Channel), but it ran afoul of the social élite in the flying clubs, there being no assurance that they were either sympathetic to or understood the Armée de l'Air's needs.[25] Scholarships were provided for the costly flying time, but the results were mediocre, primarily because sport aviation was a luxury practiced at expensive, "highbrow" clubs that resented lower-class students. Pilots were recruited from only 2 to 3 percent of the French population. The Armée de l'Air moreover desperately needed younger men. Cot's additional proposals along this line also met with resistance.

Unfortunately, the Germans were on a different timetable and had conceived a way to upset the French schedule. The acquisition of new weapons has to be paralleled to the training of personnel to use and maintain them; otherwise, they simply languish in warehouses and depots. A modern air force in the late 1930s needed manpower, both aircrew and ground staff. Moreover, war operations were at least eight times as intensive as operations in peacetime. The RAF looked at manpower in 1934 and decided that pilots could be trained in eighteen months, though fitters and riggers needed seven years, as in medieval crafts. The RAF took action; the Armée de l'Air did not.[26]

This foresight led to various training schemes and to the introduction of the RAF Volunteer Reserve (RAFVR) in 1936. Thus by the Battle of Britain the RAF contained already more than 300,000 personnel. In contrast, the Armée de l'Air, in part because of lack of assets, had barely one-third that number, with many aged pilots. In addition, the Armée de l'Air was so short of mechanics that its serviceability rates dropped rapidly after 10 May. More than that, new machines were stored at bases in the rear as they could be neither manned nor serviced. Even so, the flow of new aircraft was smaller than it might have been due to the clumsiness of the newly nationalized factories having to go through the tedious competitive bid process, complicated by the increasing complexity of the new aircraft and misleading accounting.[27]

For the Armée de l'Air and the RAF it was not only important that the state of their prototypes, production orders, and arrival on operational squadrons be adequate, but also that they understood wastage and consumption, as well as the necessity of commanding numbers. Neither the French nor the British had much concept of how many of everything, including aircraft, they would need. The British did not realize it would take five wartime years to create an effective Bomber Command, and the French weakness was to talk of reaching par with the German forces of 1939 by 1940–1941. There was generally a lack of vision, as in the case of RAF chief of Air Staff Sir Cyril Newall (1937–1940), who when asked about reserves, replied that 225 percent should do as factories would be up to full war production ninety days after hostilities began.[28]

Air Commodore Peter Dye, RAF, has recently argued that the effectiveness of air power is entirely dependent on the delivery by the national technological industrial base of adequate logistics and a solid infrastructure. Not only aircraft and their cost, but also the availability of suitable bases are part of the equation. Although he was writing in 1999 about the newly issued RAF doctrinal document *AF 3000*, his remarks are equally applicable to the 1930s.[29]

The Armée de l'Air also suffered from organizational and doctrinal defects. There were insufficient fighters to protect bomber and reconnaissance units, and the BCR concept made no sense, though at least it satisfied the Armée de Terre. The Armée de Terre's 1936 Instruction noted that the progress made in DCA methods almost negated the technical progress made in aircraft. The tactical role of aviation was reaffirmed, but this contradicted the 1935 Armée de l'Air vision of the use of the air force in that role. The Armée de l'Air indeed resisted developing either dive or fast tactical bombers. The difference in conception was not, as Young notes, even seen to exist, and this was evident in the ill-conceived BCR, which could only really be a lightweight strategic bomber. In qualitative terms, the Armée de l'Air by 1936 already was outclassed by the nascent Luftwaffe.[30]

When Cot returned to the Ministère de l'Air, he, in part to blame, tried to overhaul the Armée de l'Air to give it some teeth. Cot, chief of the GSAF General Féquant, and General Jauneaud, Féquant's private Cabinet chief, abolished the general-purpose BCR and proposed a new perspective. But it was still theoretical, there being no force behind it, in this attempt to make the strategic role more relevant to national security. To achieve this new demand, France had long needed a centralized and coordinated bomber force. Thus on 31 March 1937 Cot issued a new Instruction, which clearly defined the Armée de l'Air's role as offensive-defensive against the enemy's rear and hinterland.

As Wesley Wark has noted, Cot declared that the Armée de l'Air had reached its majority, obviously a healthy development.[31] But the new challenge was the need for fighters to defend metropolitan France, especially Paris, from the obviously superior Luftwaffe, whose new mass-produced bombers cruised at speeds equal to those of the top French fighters. Cot sought to develop the grand-strategic bomber force as a counter to raids on French cities. He raised the bomber force from twenty-seven to eighty-six escadres, while at the same time doing away with thirty-five Armée de Terre observation escadres. This caused the Armée de Terre to withdraw its contacts with the Armée de l'Air.

The essence of Cot's work was to revive the Armée de l'Air. It needed a clear definition of doctrine and employment of airpower, on which plans could be issued, designs drafted of new aircraft to meet those needs and those of Allies, and recruitment and training of the necessary personnel to fulfill the anticipated roles. What was needed were plans based on reality and not dogmatic solutions. Cot broke new ground when he sought to over-

come the weaknesses of the organization of the Armée de l'Air by breaking it into territorial and operational commands (similar to the RAF's 1936
functional reorganization), with in war the chief of the GSAF as AOC-in-C,
which put him on a par with the leaders of the other two services. But in
1938 Guy La Chambre, Cot's successor, did not like all this and reverted to
the 1934 plan, at a time when the public was getting increasingly concerned
about the German air menace. By then, the deterrent value of the Armée de
l'Air had evaporated, while the Armée de Terre and Armée de l'Air staffs still
refused to acknowledge their different perceptions.

To remedy this standoff, La Chambre had to try as rapidly as possible to
modernize the Armée de l'Air. To compete with the Luftwaffe it needed super-
charged engines, cannon, radios, and the developments of the Technological
Revolution. Top priority had to go to the fighter force in the new Plan V, as
those planes were faster and less expensive to build. Moreover, as the demand
emanated from the Air Staff, it was the staff leaders' tacit admission by ordering 1,081 fighters as compared to 876 bombers that France's air defenses were
very thin. And as the Arme Aéronautique was part of the Armée de Terre
until 1928 and its personnel well steeped in the military service mentality,
what applied to vehicle ordering also applied to aviation.

The 1936 election of the Front Populaire, opposed to European
Fascism, opened the coffers for a comprehensive Rearmament program
announced in September 1936. But the Front Populaire also ordered the
forty-hour workweek, higher wages, and paid vacations to reduce unemployment and stimulate the economy. At the same time, the Socialist prime
minister, Blum, was pledged to greater regulation of arms producers at a
time of the Nye Committee in the United States and the Royal Commission
in Britain investigating arms profiteering, with Blum aiming again at international disarmament.[32] One of Blum's first proposals was to nationalize
parts of the French arms industry.

The Royal Air Force, 1934–1939

As Malcolm Smith concluded in 1984, there was a fundamental shift in the
assessment of the 1930s after 1940. The view of air power is central to this

shift from economic recovery as the focus to confronting Hitler and Stalin, Fascism and Communism, as well as Hirohito from 1931 and Mussolini from 1935. The appearance of the Luftwaffe focused British attention on Germany and questioned how the RAF response should fit into imperial defense. All of this created the vexing problems of how to balance fiscal and imperial security. The RAF seemed the ideal counter: it was thought the bomber would always get through as there was no defense against it. Moreover, the greatest part of the air menace was a surprise blow.[33] Thus the RAF had to be instantly ready to deter such an attack and to launch a counterstrike.

The Air Staff favored first a massive bomber strike force, then an international agreement to ban the bomber. The Cabinet favored the latter until 1937–1938 when it realized that air defense was possible. Moreover, Britain did not have the commercial infrastructure that had enabled the Royal Navy to dominate the seas, and that service relatively had weakened as other nations emerged as naval powers. The Rhineland in 1936 upset the strategic applecart. Hitler's raising of Germany once again to be a great power was too swift for Britain to be able to mobilize its moral and military strength to resist it. Air Rearmament was therefore designed to keep the Germans at the table.

By late 1934 Air Ministry operational requirements clearly stated the proposed role of aircraft and their required performance. After a delay due to Lord Weir's fresh production scheme in an urgent situation, it was agreed new aircraft could be ordered "off the drawing board." To counter the new Luftwaffe, the Air Ministry put forth Expansion Scheme A (see Table 2), for a total of 1,252 aircraft in 111 squadrons by March 1939. This plan was soon out of date because the Germans had cleverly hidden the boom in their production by benefiting from the pre-Hitlerian work, so that the Luftwaffe received modern aircraft from the start. In June 1934 the CAS had written a warning memo which, however, Hankey did not forward to the CID because he considered it to be too alarmist. The new secretary of state for air, Sir Philip Cunliffe-Lister, set a precedent when he called the Air Staff together in an auditorium and told them exactly what they had to do.

Events then moved rapidly. Scheme F was promulgated in November 1935 for a total of 2,704 new aircraft and there was a move to modernize

TABLE 2. Summary of Prewar RAF Expansion Schemes, 1934 to 1939

SCHEME	DATE SUBMITTED	ROYAL AIR FORCE				GERMAN AIR FORCE (estimated)			REMARKS
		TOTAL STRIKING FORCE	TOTAL FIGHTER COMMAND	TOTAL INCL. OVERSEAS	DUE FOR COMPLETION	STRIKING FORCE	TOTAL GERMAN AIR FORCE	DUE FOR COMPLETION	
A	July 1934	500	336	1,252	March 1939	—	—	—	The first prewar expansion
B				1,500	April 1940				
C	March 1935	840	420	1,804	March 1937	800/950	1,512	March 1937	The result of Sir John Simon's and Mr. Eden's visit to Hitler in Berlin
F	Nov. 1935	1,022	420	2,704	March 1939	840/972	1,572	March 1937	Further German expansion and the Abyssinian war
H	Jan. 1937	1,631	476	2,770	March 1939	1,700	500	March 1939	Withdrawn after consideration by Cabinet
J	Oct. 1937	1,442	532	3,031	June 1941	1,458	3,240	Dec. 1939	The first scheme based on estimates of minimum overall strategic requirements
K	Jan. 1938	1,360	532	2,795	March 1941	1,350	2,700	Summer 1938	The "emasculated J"
L	April 1938	1,352	608	2,863	March 1940	1950	4,400	April 1940	After Austria
M	Oct. 1938	1,360	800	3,185	March 1942	—	—	—	After Munich. The first "all-heavy" program.

by introducing the Bristol Blenheim high-speed medium bomber into production versus older types and at the same time providing for adequate reserves, a move to create war production capacity at once, the starting of the RAFVR, and the establishment of the balloon barrage. AA guns were an army responsibility, but were inadequate, as noted later, against a knockout blow (the air menace) until 1941.

Scheme H of 1937 was withdrawn and replaced by Scheme J to take into account an operational Luftwaffe of 1,458 out of a total of 3,240. At the same time the emphasis was placed on fighters.

Scheme J was further amended and approved as K in early 1938, but with less than the 2,251 reserves considered adequate. The government did not yet realize what was necessary for the defense of Great Britain. However, these schemes did move British aircraft production forward so that by September 1939, when war came, British production was equal to German.

In the meantime, when Austria fell in March 1938, the Cabinet approved Scheme L for 2,863 first-line aircraft with full reserves by March 1940, which meant that the 1936 rate of 1,000 per annum had to be increased to 12,000 in 1940. As this was beyond the capacity of the aircraft industry and the 1936 shadow factories (where aircraft were produced by the motor industry), purchases were made in the United States. Readiness was not great in the fall of 1938; less than 50 percent of the striking force was prepared for war, and reserves were only 10 percent, not 225 percent. Of 666 fighters available, only 93 were modern, and of the 29 Fighter Command squadrons, none could engage in combat above 15,000 feet due to unheated guns; there were no reserve aircraft in storage and only a 40 percent reserve on squadrons. Only 30 percent of the needed AA guns and balloons were available.

Scheme M thus aimed to provide an effective fighter defense in 1939. The Air Staff postponed the offensive, but nevertheless the RAF was held back by problems in training, in part because the Central Flying School was by 1937 having trouble converting open-cockpit biplane instructor pilots to fly the new monoplanes of the Technological Revolution.[34] Because sending an officer pilot to each manufacturer was too slow to provide pilots' notes, new types were delivered to the Central Flying School and then teams dispatched to orient each squadron about to receive them.

Nevertheless, in October 1938 the new secretary of state for air, Sir Kingsley Wood, said training would limit the RAF to an output of 1,600 pilots (more than five times the 1935 intake of 300) annually as compared with the Luftwaffe's 4,000, due to limited facilities and a shortage of instructors. On 3 September 1939 the actual strength of the RAF was 536 bombers, 608 first-line fighters, 96 Army Cooperation, and 206 Coastal Command aircraft for a total of 1,456, with only 2,000 (137 percent) in reserve. At that time the Luftwaffe had 1,738 first-line aircraft, with 1,600 reserves (92 percent). Fighter Command by September 1939 had fifty-five of fifty-seven planned squadrons, of which twenty-six had Supermarine Spitfires or Hawker Hurricanes, as compared to none at the time of the Munich Agreement (1938). Nevertheless, there had been a failure of the Air Staff, in historian Colin Sinnott's judgment, to investigate scenarios and contingencies.[35]

Both the Spitfire and the Hurricane were eight-gun monoplane fighters powered with a Rolls-Royce Merlin engine of 1,030-horsepower. The Hurricane was first conceived in 1933 as a private venture; the Spitfire design emerged from earlier work to meet Air Ministry specification F5/34. The Hurricane flew first on 6 November 1935 and the Spitfire on 5 March 1936. Three months later, the Air Ministry ordered 600 Hurricanes and 310 Spitfires. By 3 September 1939, 2,309 Hurricanes had been assigned to eighteen squadrons and 1,400 Spitfires to nine.

By January 1935, when Air Chief Marshal Sir Christopher Courtney replaced Air Chief Marshal Sir Edgar Ludlow-Hewitt as DCAS, it was agreed in the Air Staff that the RAF needed an overall assessment of its requirements. In May 1935 this indicated the classes of aircraft acceptable, but showed that there was a shortage of bombers and fighters and that what would have been the zone and interceptor types should be merged into one higher requirement. Industry, according to Sinnott, did little to initiate designs because the Air Staff regarded fighting qualities as its bailiwick. The industry thus worked in the familiarity of Air Ministry proposals; by the late 1930s this had become almost a partnership. At the same time, specialists were emerging in aerodynamics, structures, and engines. In 1928 the RAF went to the all-metal, stressed-skin aircraft of superior performance using higher horsepower, better cooling, and lower drag. The beneficiaries of these developments were at first the ADGB fighters of the later 1920s, which led to great advances in the 1930s in speed, armament, and ceiling, but the emphasis was on defensive fighters rather than on offensive bombers, due to the Ten Year Rule and the Geneva disarmament limitations. Trenchard favored the general-purpose aircraft used in Iraq to be used also for raids on Paris. Actually the pattern was the reverse, in that the older aircraft at Home went to imperial duties and so the latter had little design influence.

By 1938 the shift had been to husband resources for a long war while showing Hitler that because of Fighter Command he could not win a quick short war. Looking back, the Air Staff, according to Malcolm Smith, have to be blamed for taking the view that Rearmament had only one choice—between the air and the surface forces. Chancellor of the Exchequer Neville Chamberlain, that thoroughly decent and opinionated Englishman, saw the RAF as a less expensive alternative to another infantry war on the Continent. He saw the RAF's deterrent as an instrument of the pacifist policy of appeasement. But he realized neither how much it would cost nor how many years it would take to make it believable, nor how impotent the then-deterrent bomber force was. Britain, of course, in the end was saved by its defense, which was quietly built into an effective fighter and RDF force under the right commander, Air Chief Marshal Sir Hugh Dowding.[36] Chamberlain wanted to cut the £76 million recommended by the Defence Requirements Committee to £50 million, but to add thirty-eight squadrons to the RAF, close to Scheme A of July 1934. The CAS used the new money to take in short-service officers, Reserves, apprentices, and semiskilled workers, as well as to buy new aircraft and another aerodrome on Malta.

On 19 July 1934 Baldwin announced Scheme A of £20 million to be completed in five to eight years. On 10 November Air Raid Precautions was announced. It had been under consideration as part of Home Defence by the CID for ten years and, as a military matter, was placed under Maj. Gen. M. L. Pritchard, Commandant of the Royal Engineers.[37] The CID report of October 1925 had led to continuing Air Staff guesses as to casualties likely from French bombing raids in spite of War Office counters that only 50 percent of the German bombers had reached London during 1917–1918 and that 22 percent of these were destroyed. Nevertheless, air raid precautions measures proceeded, which proved of great value according to Montgomery Hyde, but AA was neglected.[38]

By 1930 there was concern that the public could not be relied on to clear roads and decontaminate after a gas attack. Ministers feared civilian morale would collapse. In 1935 when Major General Pritchard retired, a wing commander was appointed to succeed him; this officer was made assistant secretary of the new air raid precautions department in the Home Office. Local authorities were contacted to discuss how to cooperate with each other, and to encourage them to build their own shelters.[39] CAS Ellington was at first opposed to the changes made under Scheme A, but had to realize 1934 was not 1923 and that a German bomber range of 375 miles put at risk the country east of the line from Portsmouth to Middleborough. Thus there was a need for a minimum of twenty-five fighter squadrons. The Air Ministry was not happy as the prospects for successful fighter defense seemed to be lessening—but ironically Robert Watson-Watt, a Scottish physicist, was just discovering RDF, which shifted the advantage to the defense. On 17 October 1934 a new CID subcommittee chaired by the AOC-in-C, ADGB, Sir Robert Brooke-Popham, started work on air defense plans. It was at once found that foreigners were ahead of the RAF in navigation and that the majority of raids would be at night or in poor visibility, making interception chancy. With speeds approaching two hundred miles per hour, the searchlighted zone needed to be not fifteen, but twenty-five miles deep. The new bomber speeds put a critical pressure on time-to-climb of the defending fighters. These would not be able to catch incoming bombers, if they were only spotted over the coast, before they reached London or the Midlands, so standing patrols (costly in hours flown) would be needed.[40]

As to bombers, the less expensive light ones ordered could not attack Germany. The deterrent thus did not exist, as there were no satisfactory medium or heavy bombers in production—nor were there adequate reserves. The silver lining was that the light bombers could be used for pilot training while the small reserves meant fewer obsolete aircraft on charge. It was expected that the new heavies would be based on the Continent. In the meantime these new heavies just being delivered—the Heyfords and Hendons—were 1928 designs. Newer bombers had been delayed by the wrangles at Geneva over banning bombing.[41] Sadly, in 1934 the only RAF aircraft that was ahead of the world was the Gloster Gauntlet biplane fighter—still basically a World War I type.[42] While there was a radical change in aircraft development due to the Technological Revolution, the new all-metal designs took time for the constructors to master. In the end quality prevailed over quantity.

The 1931 Air Exercises showed that the bomber would always get through, though when the scientist Dr. A. P. Rowe examined fifty-three Air Staff files on air defense he found that everything except the use of science had been considered. This was called to the air minister's attention and very soon scientific advice was being taken. Professor Henry Tizard, a World War I Farnborough expert and by 1934 chair of the Aeronautical Research Committee, pointed out in October that the solution to air defense early warning had to be electrical. This led shortly to the Air Ministry Committee for the Scientific Survey of Air Defence (CSSAD), chaired by Tizard, unpaid and advisory only.[43]

In the meantime, CAS Ellington had not been able to persuade the Chiefs of Staff Committee to circulate to ministers the Air Staff estimates of the growing strength of the new Luftwaffe, which included the German production potential. The Air Staff estimated the Luftwaffe would have 1,300 first-line machines in 1936 with a production rate of 60 to 140 monthly. Scheme A would give the RAF only 884 first-line aircraft by April 1939.[44]

Concurrently a thorn in the side of the secret Tizard committee was the appointment to it of Churchill's *éminence barbé* Professor F. A. Lindemann, in spite of Air Ministry opposition.[45] Then in February 1935 the Daventry test, run by Watson-Watt, showed that an aircraft could be detected by radio reflections on a cathode-ray tube. As AMSR, Air Marshal Hugh Dowding was enthusiastic and the next month RDF was born.[46] Churchill, Lindemann, and Austen Chamberlain had attacked the Tizard committee before Prime Minister MacDonald, but Secretary of State for Air Lord Londonderry saved it. However, the CID then set up a subcommittee advocated by the ubiquitous, if not omnipotent, Hankey, that included Tizard and with Sir Philip Cunliffe-Lister as chair. Soon after Baldwin became prime minister, Cunliffe-Lister, as Viscount Swinton, succeeded Londonderry.

Just a month prior to the first meeting of the Swinton committee, Gen. Herman Goering announced the Luftwaffe and Hitler told the British Foreign Secretary Sir John Simon and Anthony Eden on their visit to Berlin that the new air force already equaled the RAF and would soon enjoy parity with the French metropolitan and North African air forces. Hitler claimed the Luftwaffe had 11,000 aircraft, but the British air attaché in Berlin reported that of these only 910 were first line.[47]

Critical for grand-strategic decision-making was intelligence from the embassies. This was of limited use, or rather biased, due to the fact that those in the British diplomatic service came from a largely Etonian and other public schools' background and had entered the service by oral interview and written examinations, which by the interwar years had begun to assume that the candidates were graduates of Oxford or Cambridge. The emphasis was on the ability to draft communications, knowledge of two foreign languages, and inbred social sensibilities. The selection, accreditation, and circulation of service attachés remains for the period something of a mystery. We do know that the RAF's F. W. Winterbotham, later the man who oversaw the Ultra Secret decipherment, who had been shot down in World War I and who as a POW had spent eighteen months learning German, was reporting on Germany. His reports were not believed until May 1935 when he appeared before the Air Parity Subcommittee of the Cabinet and substantiated his words. He went independently to Germany from 1930 on, visited the Luftwaffe, and had by 1939 drawn up a highly accurate assessment of the Luftwaffe. The trouble was that this excellent "gen" did not always percolate to the top where it was needed in the making of policy and doctrine.[48]

After the Germans in 1938 found that Winterbotham was in the Secret Intelligence Service, he stayed away and teamed up instead with the Australian Sidney Cotton to develop high-altitude (30,000 feet) photography, the origins of photoreconnaissance units. In 1939 he set up the secret scientific intelligence section of MI-6 with Tizard, Watson-Watt, and R. V. Jones. In August he was involved in setting up the Government Code and Cypher School, which acquired an enemy Enigma machine and soon had moved to Bletchley Park, which became the site of the United Kingdom's main decryption establishment.[49]

The Air Ministry reaction to this new intelligence was one of grave anxiety, especially as the RAF was short of Reserves. But neither the secretary of state for air nor the CAS wanted a large immediate Expansion, preferring to wait for the new modern designs either on the drawing board or in the prototype stage. This led them to Scheme B, to have 123 squadrons and 1,500 aircraft by April 1940, assuming Germany would not go to war before 1942. Delay also occurred because of a shortage of design staffs, time needed to develop and manufacture new types, time needed to train personnel, and so on. Expansion would temporarily lower standards, but the end result would be quality.

Sir Robert Vansittart, permanent under-secretary at the Foreign Office, had argued strongly that the Germans were likely to go to war in 1938, not 1942, and that airpower had to mesh with foreign policy. CAS Ellington responded that lack of resources and unclear government policies had caused delays, which only time could now overcome. Concurrently, Baldwin appointed the Cabinet Air Parity Subcommittee, which, after interviewing the service officers, concluded on 8 May 1935 that Britain had to match Germany by April 1937. Two days later Cunliffe-Lister (shortly Viscount Swinton) told the Cabinet Disarmament Committee that by Secret Intelligence Service estimates the Germans had eight thousand pilots rather than the four thousand the Air Ministry had reckoned.

On 17 May 1935 the Cabinet accepted that absolute necessity required the ordering in bulk off the drawing boards of the needed medium and heavy bombers as well as two new fighters, in spite of Air Ministry concerns that the latter were monoplanes, a type banned from the RFC and RAF since before 1914. But Dowding, now air member for research and development, strongly backed the new fighters. Lord Weir, the production czar of 1918, was called in for industrial advice.[50] The problem was how to manufacture 3,800 new machines by April 1937; Weir noted that the technical structure was too weak to carry such a load, especially in the new all-metal airframes industry—a parallel to the dilemma in Paris with Cot's 1,010-plane order.

On 23 May 1935 the Cabinet approved Scheme C, which had no reserves, but did provide for personnel expansion. The gadfly Churchill noted, however, that by the time it would be completed the Luftwaffe would be three to four times more powerful. Baldwin accepted this criticism because the government had underestimated German aircraft production and thus was to blame. In November 1935, after the election, Baldwin gave Swinton support for the radical transformation of the RAF, including linking fighters to RDF, ordering multitudes of new aircraft off the drawing boards, and integrating scientists into the Air Staff.[51]

Under Scheme C there would be seventy-one squadrons by April 1939 with 2,500 new pilots and 20,000 other personnel, as well as fifty new air stations on top of the existing fifty-two of 1934. The estimates for 1935–1936 were £31 million. New specialist schools—navigation, gunnery, and so on—were established. Initial flying training went to the old Civil Training Schools, and advanced training was shifted from the squadrons to new RAF schools. In 1934 the RAF had 31,000 officers and other ranks; by 1 September 1939 it would have 118,000 with 45,000 in reserve. Before 1935 the average annual intake was 300 pilots and 1,600 other ranks; between 1935 and 1938 the aggregate intake was 4,500 pilots and 40,000 other ranks and fourteen- to eighteen-year-old boys. The Royal Auxiliary Air Force rose from eight to twenty squadrons, with 4,600 flying personnel and 18,400 in balloon squadrons. To balance the drain on the Reserves caused by calling up these trained men, the Air Ministry founded the RAFVR as a citizen air force, adding eight hundred aircrew per year without social distinction, trained at thirty-five aerodromes.[52]

The RAFVR was soon expanded to include air gunners, observers, and wireless operators. The secretary of state for air, the Air Council, and the king approved new, more comfortable RAF uniforms, which was good for morale, recruiting, and efficiency. (All of this was in sharp contrast to French inactivity during the same period.) The Expansion push resulted in Spitfires and Hurricanes reaching squadrons in two years after prototypes were tested, rather than the usual five.[53] In parallel, the power gun turret was developed and constructors were forced to incorporate it in the bomber designs.[54] But on the other hand, one thousand Hawker Harts and Hinds, though basically colonial aircraft, were ordered for day bombing and dive-bombing of enemy airfields.

The Defence Requirements Committee was ordered to do another review and concluded that a reasonable state of preparedness was needed by 1 January 1939. For this, 150 percent reserves of aircraft were required by 1 April 1939, together with 75 percent initial and maintenance reserves, to cost £78 million. This was the basis of Scheme F, approved by the Cabinet in early 1936 when the Ministerial Defence Committee became the Defence Policy and Requirements Committee.

While critics called yet again for a Ministry of Defence, the German occupation of the Rhineland led to the appointment of the attorney general, Sir Thomas Inskip, as minister for the coordination of defense (instead of, for political reasons, Churchill, as in the past).[55] Inskip challenged the Air Ministry thinking and reversed the ratio of fighters to bombers so as to protect the island arsenal.

The Defence Policy and Requirements Committee was convinced that Hitler would use a highly mobile strategy to strike through the Netherlands and around the French and Belgium flanks in order to establish air bases in the Low Countries long before a BEF could reach the Continent. Thus the Defence Policy and Requirements Committee wanted the most terrifying deterrent—not in theory but in reality—to the German plan. Squadron initial establishments were to be increased from twelve to eighteen aircraft.

Scheme F was designed to have 1,736 aircraft in 124 squadrons by 31 March 1939, with a total of 187 squadrons of 2,516 machines at Home and abroad. With the consolidated reserves, this would amount to 225 percent expected to cover losses in the first few months of a German war, by which time industry would be able to keep up with war wastage. There were also to be eight hundred pilots in reserve, more than the Armée de l'Air had in the *chasse* total in May 1940.

By March 1936 the Air Ministry had created the Directorate of Aeronautical Production to deal with airframe, engine, and equipment contractors. Lt. Col. H. A. P. Disney had to cope with archaic management suffering from years of few orders, and then with the impact of requirements for five hundred rather than five machines. One outcome of Scheme F was the creation of the "shadow" factories run by the motor and shipbuilding industries as an immediate boost to production. Due to the previous paucity of orders, the British aircraft industry was just able to cope with those of 1934 and 1935, but those for 1936 called for far larger numbers than they were accustomed to producing—all at the same time as they had a shift to all-metal construction, which needed new tools. It took awhile for "the learning curve" to reach efficient production. What Scheme F did, then, was to create the war potential talked about since 1924. But a balance had to be struck between overexpansion during 1937–1938 and overcapacity in 1939, as well as capitalization.[56]

To get enough of the four thousand Bristol engines needed, the air minister helped create a consortium so that Bristol could limit the dilution of its talent in teaching and assembly. On the whole, shadows were sited near the parent company because decentralization against bombing was not at first thought vital. The new shadows were producing engines successfully within twelve months. Lord Nuffield of the Morris Motor Company, however, opposed the Bristol scheme in 1936, but in 1938 opened a Spitfire factory producing complete machines, and the Air Ministry built a factory for Merlin engines in Scotland, which Rolls-Royce managed from 1939.[57]

In September 1935 the experimental RDF establishment was moved to Bawdsey on the Norfolk coast and the Treasury authorized the first five Chain Home (CH) RDF stations. By March 1936 Robert Watson-Watt and his team of scientists could locate an aircraft by height, distance, and direction. In the fall of 1936, Biggin Hill had abandoned mathematics for simple direction by vectors of fighters to intercept incoming bombers, using the "Tizzy Angle."[58] CAS Ellington opposed, but the AOC-in-C of the new RAF Fighter Command, Dowding, approved and had all fighter stations practice the method.[59]

By the fall of 1936 the Chiefs of Staff Committee was persuaded by the Joint Planning Committee that war with Germany was both possible and probable, and that it would start with a knock-out blow, which would last at least fourteen days and would have to be countered by the new Bomber Command attacking Luftwaffe airfields and maintenance depots. If, however, the Germans opted for a land attack and the BEF was sent to France, then the RAF would have to bomb the German lines of communications. The Joint Planning Committee was surprisingly accurate in its forecast, except for the estimated 150,000 British casualties in the first week of the war. The Allies would have to parry a rapid attack and then hang on for a long war. However, as the Air Staff began to realize that Bomber Command could not blunt a German offensive, it swung more in favor of fighters.[60] When in 1936 the Air Staff realized that the Germans would in April 1939 have a strength of 1,700 bombers and 800 fighters, the Air Ministry hastily produced Scheme H.

An exchange of visits with Gen. Erhard Milch, the head of the Reichsluftministerium (German air ministry), gave both sides considerable knowledge of the other's status.[61] But the Germans had moved faster than they had admitted, the spring 1938 program being completed in the fall of 1937. Milch knew the RAF in 1937, and, he said, the Luftwaffe had a better system.[62]

On 1 September 1937 Sir Cyril Newall succeeded Ellington as CAS to the disappointment of Dowding, who objected to a civilian (Lord Swinton) making a service appointment without consulting the CAS or the Air Council. Newall's director of plans was Group Capt. J. C. Slessor, who at once raised the question of the real strength of the RAF versus the Luftwaffe.[63] This led in fourteen days to Scheme J, so that the Defence Plans (Policy) Committee could review that scheme along with the proposals of the other two services. It was the best of the schemes submitted, as Montgomery Hyde pointed out, because it was based on a full appreciation of German air strength and intentions and also on the RAF's overseas needs.[64] It could not be completed in mid-1940 because the Cabinet was not yet willing to put the country on a war footing. The Air Staff insisted on the increase of Bomber Command to ninety squadrons, as it was the heart of air policy and had at all times to be ready to strike on the outbreak of war, which Inskip noted in December 1937 would be short, using a knockout blow. The RAF therefore had to have a fighter force to destroy the Luftwaffe over Britain. After a stiff Cabinet debate, Inskip's view prevailed, policy was sharply reversed, and personnel were to be recruited up to war strength, not for reserves. Because Prime Minister Chamberlain was concerned about financial stability, Scheme J was limited to £100 million and referred back to the Air Staff.

On 21 January 1938 the Air Staff produced Scheme K, which put the emphasis on the less expensive fighters and reduced the bomber squadrons to seventy-seven, with only nine weeks of reserves, in part because reserves would involve greater wastage if there was no war. War industrial potential was an asset.[65] Scheme K marked the end of the race to parity; it was based on political and financial needs, and upset the Air Staff. It saw the radical shift from an offensive to a defensive air policy. But by the time the Cabinet agreed to the scheme, Hitler had taken Austria and thus K was referred back and emerged as Scheme L. Director of Plans Slessor argued that the RAF needed a year of consolidation so personnel could be trained and thus allow the RAF to go to war in March 1939. Slessor's views were not accepted. CAS Newall resisted cutting the defense estimates below £157 million because, in his words, "The issue was the survival of British civilization."[66] He won, and at last aircraft production was not financially limited, and a mission was sent to the United States to purchase aircraft.[67]

Another seven hundred pilots were needed, but could not be ready until September 1940 unless squadrons were denuded of instructors. At the same time, the industry needed the 347,000 used in 1918, but had only 90,000 in the spring of 1938, up from 30,000 in 1935.[68] In 1938 the aircraft industry in Britain was still using only 25 percent of its 1918 workforce, when, as Collier noted, aircraft needed only 10 percent of the man-hours required in 1938.[69]

By the time of the Munich Agreement in September 1938 Fighter Command was being equipped with RDF as well as Observer Corps intelligence, with fighters directed by R/T (radio telephone) from sector control aided by AA searchlights and balloon barrages. Hurricanes and Spitfires were just beginning to reach squadrons. The public did not know what had been going on behind the scenes, and so criticized Lords Swinton and Weir, though they opposed rationalization because they believed scientific progress depended on the imagination and enterprise of individuals, as it certainly did in engine and RDF development.[70]

The Society of British Aircraft Constructors was asked to obtain a full-time chairperson to liaise with the Air Ministry and to attend meetings of the RAF Expansion Progress Committee (until 1936 the Air Council). Thus

Sir Charles Bruce-Gardner attended and proposed changes that stream-lined relationships, with the CAS having executive power regarding service requirements and the AMSO approving all modifications made by the technical departments.[71] Churchill, aware of RAF needs, criticized the Bruce-Gardner proposals. As a parliamentary opponent, Weir called for the Air Ministry to be organized on a war footing with Air Marshal Sir Wilfred Freeman appointed as air member for research and development responsible for supply and equipment. In May 1940 Freeman was transferred to the new Ministry of Aircraft Production.[72] Air Vice Marshal Arthur Tedder was brought in as director general of R&D.[73]

Reserves for fighters were on a scale to cover sixteen weeks' wastage in time of war. Fighter squadrons were enlarged, though they would only go into action with twelve machines and 75 percent of the Ideal Programme's thirty-four fighter squadrons.[74]

Owing to the perceived political need to have the secretary of state for air in the House of Commons, Swinton was summarily dismissed on 13 May 1938. Weir resigned and received a viscountcy from the king. In Montgomery Hyde's view, Swinton was the most outstanding interwar air minister in spite of fiscal and other restraints imposed by the Appeasement-minded Prime Minister Neville Chamberlain. His accomplishments could not be told at the time.[75] He was succeeded by Chamberlain's friend, Postmaster General Sir Kingsley Wood, who quickly understood his task and at once began to disperse the aircraft industry as protection against air attack and to reduce the number of designs so as to get rapid and economical production. He supported subcontracting and taking work to laboring men, and he encouraged the shipbuilders and also the Vickers takeover of Supermarine with its Spitfires. He pushed firms into production groups, and he brought in the World War I fighter pilot, member of Parliament, and businessman Harold Balfour as vice president of the Air Council and chair of the Air Council Committee on Supply, which met thrice weekly with its Treasury representative having spending authority.[76] Balfour was the only active pilot on the Air Council; in September 1938 he flew one of two Spitfires available. He attempted the reform of the ill-functioning Air Ministry bureaucracy, but he was unable to persuade senior officers of the value of concrete runways until June 1940.[77] The senior officers also opposed the use of American aircraft and the limitation of modifications.

During the Munich crisis, the RAF was impotent. Bomber Command could not afford to attack Germany; of its squadrons, some were either reequipping or flying obsolete aircraft, or were short of aircrew, and even more were short of spares.[78] Those with new aircraft were either not up to establishment or were still unfamiliar with their equipment. Of the 29 squadrons able to be mobilized in Fighter Command with 406 aircraft, only 7 had modern Hurricanes and 14 had Spitfires. Dowding needed 688 modern fighters, but had only 84; and of the 2,500 reserve fighter pilots, only 200 were fit to go into the line at once, so there was no reserve of such personnel.

If war had come at the time of the Munich crisis, the RAF could have lasted perhaps three suicidal weeks, said the Mobilization Committee Report. Thus the days gained were critical where the impact of Expansion on a small professional force and an unprepared economy had inevitably caused delays. There were not yet enough personnel to man the system, and war would have simply collapsed it. Changes were made, but recruiting and training of staff officers took time.

Post-Munich Scheme M aimed to increase fighter strength to roughly 30 percent above Scheme L, raising the thirty-eight Home squadrons to fifty and the twenty medium and forty-seven heavy bomber squadrons to eighty-five heavies, who would have parity in bombs dropped with the Luftwaffe. The Cabinet agreed to Scheme M on 2 November 1938. Yet once again, in late 1938, Churchill and Lindemann gave the secretary of state for air a hard time on the Tizard Committee. It was decided then that Churchill would go off the committee and "the Prof" was allowed on, to promote yet again his 1933 idea of aerial mines.[79] On 20 June 1939 Tizard opened Churchill's eyes with a tour of Bawdsey and Martlesham Heath test center and enlightened him on the role and effectiveness of the Observer Corps.[80]

Air Staff plans were based on air intelligence reports of the Secret Intelligence Service, and on German industry gathered by the Industrial Intelligence Centre, which, however, did not glean enough target information for planning. The Foreign Intelligence Center had been set up in June

1936, but died in 1939 because of Air Ministry opposition, which believed that its own Intelligence Directorate was capable in itself.

In the meantime, a small group of intelligence committees had been gathering data.[81] Before Slessor was made director of Plans in 1939, in October 1937 thirteen Western Air (WA) plans had been developed and sent to Bomber Command HQ with instructions to concentrate on three of them. After March 1938 the limitations of Bomber Command became depressingly obvious. Detailed studies under Group Captain Don, the former air attaché in Berlin, revealed that Plan WA-1 was unworkable because the Germans had many unknown airfields that Bomber Command could not locate. The Joint Planning Committee pointed out that even a highly successful attack on the aircraft industry would have too slow an effect to stop an attack on London, and Bomber Command's losses would be prohibitive. By the Munich Agreement, WA-1 had been abandoned as it was concluded that even if the RAF were based in France, it could not effectively execute any of the thirteen WA plans, nor was its effectiveness helped by Chamberlain's announcements in June 1938 and September 1939 that it would attack only military targets to avoid civilian casualties.

WA-4, designed to thwart a German attack through the Low Countries, was subject to War Office versus Air Ministry views of the best rail targets. The problem in the Low Countries was the density of railways and differences in the possible routings. Slessor's 1936 book of his lectures at the British Army Staff College, *Air Power and Armies*, drew lessons from 1914 to 1918, showing the best places to disrupt the networks.[82] So Bomber Command settled on WA-5 against the Ruhr, but the Air Staff disputed the former's estimates.

After the Munich Agreement the planners had problems defining military objectives, as retaliation was a factor, and some attacks might open up London, supply systems, and seaborne trade. Given his organizational strengths and weaknesses, including navigation, Ludlow-Hewitt, AOC-in-C of Bomber Command, wanted WA-14 leaflet raids to train crews in night operations.[83] Slessor then pointed out that bombing civilians could increase patriotism rather than destroy morale. Little help could be obtained to break morale in the German regions. The Air Staff believed that Germany had no specific problem, so therefore the whole country was fair game.

By the end of the first year of the new war, the Air Staff came to realize that the four previous years of air strategy had to be junked, as Bomber Command did not have the tools to do the job. By March 1939 the net air estimates had reached £66.5 million while the real expenditure authorized was £220,626,300 versus the real French equivalent of £87.98 million.[84]

In 1938 the Civil Air Guard had been created to train the RAFVR, guided by a board headed by Lord Londonderry. It was wound up when war began and the personnel transferred to the RAFVR or to the new Air Transport Auxiliary. Concurrently the Women's RAF of 1918 was revived as the Women's Auxiliary Air Force. On 9 March 1939 it had 230 officers and 7,460 airwomen.[85]

By April 1939 Fighter Command had 270 Hurricanes, 130 Spitfires, and 170 biplane Gladiators, with a 50 percent reserve. It needed seven hundred first-line aircraft in squadrons. There was still a shortage of pilots and so group pools were formed to replenish both Fighter Command and Bomber Command squadrons. Serious deficiencies remained, but April–May fighter production was 25 percent above predictions. By June seven hundred modern aircraft were available, and two hundred new RAFVR pilots were in group pools for operational training.

Meanwhile in addition to the British Purchasing Commission sent to the United States, another mission in mid-1938 persuaded the Canadian prime minister, Mackenzie King, to switch from anti-British isolationism to accepting the British Commonwealth Air Training Plan, which was only agreed to in April 1939. By the time it started, Canada was also at war and Canadians were volunteering.[86]

By the outbreak of war, Fighter Command had thirty-nine squadrons and also the wider duties to protect the fleet and coastal shipping. But the most onerous new commitment was for squadrons for the Field Force (soon BEF). When Anglo-French staff talks opened in London, the French pressed strongly, as they had earlier, for more fighters to be sent to France. The British refused, as it was vital in the long-term grand strategy to thwart a "knock-out" blow. It was at this time that Slessor, representing the RAF, noted that the French were afraid of an armored 1914-style thrust through the Low Countries supported by the Luftwaffe. And a knockout blow against Paris could only be halted by five hundred to six hundred aircraft based in France. At this point Slessor saw the need for a common air-defense system from Scapa Flow to the Med with a backup of twenty mobile fighter squadrons. The CAS then authorized six squadrons to be mobile and to go to France as needed. Dowding protested: he believed Fighter Command needed a minimum of fifty squadrons.

In August 1938 the War Office and Air Ministry agreed to four squadrons and others as needed. But when the Cabinet decided in the spring of 1939 to double the size of the Territorial Army, the information was not communicated to the Air Ministry, because neither the secretary of state for war, Leslie Hore-Belisha, nor the CIGS, Sir Edmund Ironside, understood the air consequences.[87]

Increasingly, the British believed that Hitler would strike east and not send a knockout blow against the west. The Anglo-French forces were nonaggressive, which left an undecided bomber policy that put the burden on Fighter Command. Even with more than five hundred modern fighters, Fighter Command was still inferior to the Luftwaffe, though it was in a position to fight.

Ludlow-Hewitt of Bomber Command, in Montgomery Hyde's view the most brilliant RAF air marshal of the day, was ignored by the Air Staff as to the need for escort fighters and for armored aircraft. Whitehall believed that armor would reduce bomb load. Due to a lack of gunnery training and of regular air gunners as opposed to the casual use of fitters and riggers, aircrew had little faith in their ability to defend themselves; thus they would not, said Ludlow-Hewitt, press on to their objectives.[88] Bomber Command also lacked a development unit, such as Tizard supported. In September 1939 Bomber Command would have been incapable of undertaking a grand-strategic air offensive against Germany. CAS Newall saw the August Nazi-Soviet Pact as granting the West time, so it would be unwise to expend the RAF in the early days when it was still ignorant of many of the factors of air war.

War came to Poland on 1 September 1939 and the French and British declared on 3 September.

Comment

While on the surface it appears that French technical aviation development was comparable to that across the Channel, in reality this was not so. Within the Air Staff in London there was a continual process of creating both the specifications and the practical applications needed to keep the RAF on the cutting-edge.[89] Due to the lag between specifications and operational aircraft, the impact of the Technological Revolution on airframes was disguised. Prototypes began to change quite radically in the period 1934–1937, with the fully fledged new models beginning to reach squadrons in 1937, but with the effective upsurge not coming until late 1938 to 1942.

Whereas the French and British wasted the time the Phoney War gave them, the Wehrmacht and the Luftwaffe started early in October to dissect the campaign in Poland and to distribute staff papers on the lessons learned. They also refined what had been learned in Spain. The most important conclusions related to the needs for decisive commanders, a superior communications net linking all involved, and a mobile logistics system reinforced by air transport. In contrast, the French concluded that there was nothing to be gathered from the Polish experience, not even that the Germans concentrated on the *schwerpunkt*, the focal point of both panzers and the Luftwaffe to achieve a breakthrough. And as a corollary to this, air superiority had to be obtained as quickly as possible by destroying the enemy air forces on their airfields, and then disrupting their lines of communications. What the story shows is that the RAF was evolving presciently and at the same time was paradoxically blind to certain operational realities. More than seven years of peacetime and turnover of personnel had led to lack of institutional memory. The Armée de l'Air was four years behind.

5

TECHNICAL INFRASTRUCTURE, 1928–1940

The French Aircraft Industry, 1928–1938

In order to help understand what happened to the Armée de l'Air on the road to 1940, it is necessary to delve deeper into the background of the state, the workers, and primarily the employers—the *patronats*—from 1933 to 1940.[1] The French aircraft industry labored under a number of difficulties, including the problem of owners who were remote and aloof and did not know how to talk to the workers. The latter had developed grievances since World War I, but as the owners refused to consider effective bargaining, the workers had no outlet. The Communist Party played on this head of steam and brought professional, practiced organizing skills to the workers' aid. Thus on 9–10 June 1936 the *patronat* delegation at the Matignon talks was badly defeated by a knowledgeable workers' delegation. Although labor gained the forty-hour workweek, weekends, and holidays, employers determined to regain control of their premises and to rid themselves of collective representation and compulsory arbitration.

Michael Torigian has explained the factory occupations of early 1936; Edward Shorter and Charles Tilley have set the strikes into the context of industrial action; and Herrick Chapman has covered the story on the capital–labor strife angle to May 1940. Chapman's work is wider, looking as it does to technical sectors as well.[2] According to Shorter and Tilley, the 1936 social explosion was one of the most compelling of historical problems for French scholars, and the popular unrest was equaled only by the Great Fear of 1789. What is puzzling is the brief duration and the impermanence of labor's achievements. Patrick Fridenson notes that the auto industry in France had considerable success in the introduction of Fordism to the factories, but never gave up paying on a piecework basis rather than with hourly wages.[3]

In 1934 the air forces were boldly experimenting with new models based on the Technological Revolution then occurring. The Germans, Russians, British, and Americans, as well as the Japanese, understood that industrial progress needed money, loans, or credits. Some in Paris did grasp this, but the Armée de Terre and Ministère des Finances blocked the idea until 1938. By then Paris was four years behind London, and then, too, cross-fertilization was taking place. Premier Daladier was persuaded to order one thousand American Curtiss Hawks (the exportable P-36 Model 75) and the British were seeking American designs. However, the United States had a strong isolationist sentiment and had in 1935, 1936, 1937, and 1939 passed the Neutrality Acts. Among other restrictions these laws required buyers to pay cash and to carry the arms purchased in their own ships or in neutral bottoms.[4]

In the meantime, London had evolved from World War I the shadow factory scheme, which in 1936 the French examined and considered adopting. Industrialization involved calculating numerical, capacity, and fiscal sums. Those costs had to include the recruiting and training of workers, mechanics, industrialists, bureaucrats, and aircrew. And while in a few cases the sums were done, progress could not be made without time and money. The artisanal approach had to be replaced by mass production methods, management, and money. The vital four lost years, 1934–1938, could not be made up even if by 1940 French aircraft production exceeded that of both Germany and England (Table 3). It was useless to build and store aircraft when neither mechanics nor aircrews nor the logistical facilities were available to make them viable and efficient, as the Battle of France clearly would demonstrate.

This deficit reflected a variety of French theories alluded to earlier. In part, at the heart of the matter was the workers' familiarity with the process of both industrialization and of modern war—Verdun 1916 coming to

TABLE 3. Production and Distribution of Armée de l'Air Aircraft

DATE	AIRCRAFT PRODUCED[a]	TO METROPOLITAN AIR FORCE: AIRCRAFT ACCEPTED	TO METROPOLITAN AIR FORCE: PERCENT OF AIRCRAFT PRODUCED
Jan. 11, 1939	1,580	586	37.09
Dec. 1939	1,739	654	37.61
Jan. 1940	1,855	686	36.98
Feb. 1940	1,927	735	38.14
Mar. 1940	1,991	765	38.42
Apr. 1940	2,111	799	37.85
May 1940	2,166	865	39.94

[a]Total aircraft to the French Air Force at home and overseas was generally less than 45 percent of the aircraft produced.

mind—which made the French worker and family demand liberty, equality, and fraternity once again, vis-à-vis the capitalists. Hence the demand for ownership of the means of production, for the Maginot Line, and for policies and strategies that would defend France without senseless costs.

For some five years there had been talk of reorganizing the production side of a distracted French aircraft industry. Denain had tried to concentrate enterprises, to tool-up the industry for mobilization, and at the same time to disperse it geographically to make it less vulnerable to bombing. He had been partially successful regarding airframes, but not at all with the engine-makers. The problem was tooling for mass production, as across the Channel the proprietors were afraid that if programs were cancelled, they would stand to lose substantial investments.[5] With the state buying 98 percent of its products, the industry was accustomed to state aid.

In the design and development of aircraft and engines, the French did not have the advantage of the stimulus of successful Schneider Trophy racers of the later 1920s, nor the benefits of advanced engines or concepts. In part this was because Paris did not have an air staff to draft specifications. In Whitehall, however, specifications and doctrine interacted to produce a few squadrons of each design to prove the type and provide information on the consumption and wastage of spares. The critical years were 1927–1934, during the Technological Revolution. Even before it was acknowledged, F. R. Banks had been mixing aromatic fuels and doping racing engines; one result of this work was new fuels that enabled the Rolls-Royce Merlin engine of 1936 to produce twice the horsepower of the American Liberty of 1918 on the same 1,650-cubic-inch displacement.[6]

In post–World War I France, only the Hispano-Suiza company pushed ahead with cast-block engine development, concentrating on in-lines and producing motors of 700 and 1,000 horsepower by 1934. These engines were widely licensed in Britain, Spain, Japan, Switzerland, Czechoslovakia, and the Soviet Union, but in 1939 French industry could not produce them as fast as the Morane-Saulnier MS 406 and Dewoitine D-520 fighters needed them, so some twenty-five engines per month were imported from Skoda in the Sudetenland and a few from Switzerland. In 1938 Hispano-Suiza had a 1,350-horsepower engine evolved from its earlier 1,000-horsepower engine, but it did not go into production until after 1945.[7]

In the meantime, the speed of French fighters was limited by the largest production engine they had, the 950-horsepower Hispano-Suiza. To get adequate speed, the designers reduced armament to four 7.5-mm machine-guns of less lethality compared to the Spitfire's and Hurricane's eight. It was this lack of horsepower that made the American Curtiss Hawk H-75 seem such a good buy. The Hawk (the RAF Mohawk) had lost the fighter competition in 1935 to a rival, but nevertheless the U.S. Army Air Corps had placed a substantial order for them. The Hawk went into service in April 1938 with the U.S. Army Air Corps, at the same time that the Armée de l'Air ordered one hundred of them, with a 1,200-horsepower radial engine that gave 302 miles per hour at a loaded weight of 6,600 pounds.

Hispano-Suiza took a license for the American Wright R-1510 radial engine, but these were unreliable, losing their propeller shafts; in the Potez 630 the cylinder heads lasted about ten hours, and in the Lioré et Olivier 451 even less.[8] The well-known airframe manufacturer Farman also produced engines, but their few designs were of too little horsepower too late, or had no commercial value. Groupe Latécoère was in the engine business as well, but left it during the Great Depression; neither of the automakers Bugati or Delage ever put their aeroengines into volume production.

Gnome et Rhône had reached a peak in 1917 when it limited itself to 160-horsepower engines. After almost collapsing, the firm in 1922 obtained licenses to produce the English Bristol Jupiter 280- to 420-horsepower engines until after 1929, when its first new engine appeared. By 1938, following American ideas, the company was marketing a 1,080-horsepower air-cooled radial engine. Meanwhile, the organization had combined an aggressive sales force with bringing in house formerly subcontracted items as well as increased financial support. It also created a market not dependent on French military orders, and devoted roughly 5 percent of its annual revenues to R&D. Its laboratories studied and enhanced performance and production, and it excelled in follow-up service. By the end of 1936, Gnome et Rhône was able to assemble complete engines and variable-pitch propellers.[9]

However, even the Gnome et Rhône–licensed Bristol engines were only of marginal use in 1939, though the 710-horsepower could have been developed for a twin-engine single-seat fighter. According to Herschel Smith, they were mounted instead on a three-place aircraft of only vaguely defined mission. In the meantime, the Gnome et Rhône eighteen-cylinder 1,400-horsepower engine was abandoned as too heavy and bulky. Later, after France had fallen to Germany, Smith notes, Free French pilots continuing the fight against the Axis forces flew British aircraft and rejoiced in the reliability of their engines.[10]

The second generation of aviation entrepreneurs arrived in the 1920s. They had modeled themselves on the "pioneers," but also made changes. However, they managed small firms and so had to find market niches. Often their innovative designs were—as in the case of Marcel Bloch—completed by a rival and friend, in Bloch's case Henri Potez. Ironically, he suffered the failure of success in that his 1924 Potez 25 was easily modified for all sorts of roles and stayed in production until 1934—a fine design, it could be produced by poorly educated labor.

By 1935 the Potez firm's traditional approach was severely challenged by unfamiliar elements and could not meet the demand; it was nationalized in 1936. It had great difficulties in making the leap to the Potez 63, which could beat the twin-engine German fighter, the Messerschmitt Me-110. The fault lay in Henri Potez's refusal to see the problem as technological rather than managerial.

The process of innovation in France was also hindered by the rigidity of the training system, even though in 1909 the École Supérieure de l'Aeronautique (high aeronautics school) had been founded. This course was divided between classroom and *atelier*, and by 1923 had graduated more than 460 engineers. Yet the government did not reopen other engineering schools until 1917 because of the wastage of engineers during the war, but after the Armistice the Écoles de Mineurs et Génies (schools of miners and engineers) gave government engineers increased prestige. A 1924 law created a Corps de Génie Aéronautique (corps of aeronautical engineers), which turned the older schools into the *écoles polytechniques* whose students could obtain practical experience in aviation, though only for a year. Then in 1928 the creation of the Ministère de l'Air led to the nationalization of the École Supérieure de l'Aeronautique. This, however, did not advance the cause of modernization so desired by the very first air minister, André Laurent-Eynac, as the instructors were government engineers trained before 1914 or during the war when the army engineers dominated the "golden-era age" of aviation. In addition, the best students were sent into state service and became embroiled in paperwork beneath their talents, far removed from the technical problems on the shop floors.

In 1937, of the 218 state aeronautical engineers, only 12 were actually organizing and conducting research and 13 headed ministry directorates or advised the minister. It is clear that the government neglected training the middle-level personnel essential to aviation production. Foremen and supervisors came either from the trade apprentice schools or from the post-1916 military schools set up to train NCOs. Otherwise aviation was left to the practitioners without incentives for future vision.[11] During the war the Armée de Terre had created a special technical section at Chalais-Meudon but its main duty was either to adapt new designs to standard usage or to reject them. From 1915 through 1918 it had passed on 125 different types of aircraft and engines. Converted to the technical service, in the interwar years it was a filter between manufacturers and users, producing program specifications and translating general staff requirements into drawings and standards for contractors.

In the interwar period a further problem was the very small sum allocated for military aeroresearch as compared to monies to private manufacturers for production. In 1938 FF9.7 million (in 1914 economic terms) were spent on aeronautics, of which only 0.9 percent went to research. With most of its equipment not far from 1919 ideas, Chalais-Meudon was seen by practicing aviation leaders as a hypercritical authority unequal to the task rather than as an ally. In 1928 Ministre de l'Air Laurent-Eynac wished to set up a research establishment on a par with the German and American organizations, but it was 1935 before this was realized at Villacoublay's nearby Arsenal de l'Aéronautique (aviation arsenal). By 1938 the leaders there had perfected the VG-33 fighter design, authorized for production in the national factories in 1939; few were ever built.

At the same time, a technical experimental establishment was created nearby at Issy-les-Moulineaux, whose engineers averaged thirty-three years of age as compared to forty-four years in the technical and production sections. Half of the new group was chemists, physicists, and scientists. Their hiring was symbolic of the modernization that in 1938 included a large new wind tunnel, the first exclusively for aviation in France. Nevertheless, all of this was, unfortunately, too little too late. Official proposals failed to ask basic questions of people in the know. And that was what was wrong with French aircraft design and production up to 1934–1938.

As historian Emmanuel Chadeau concluded after carrying the story to 1950, the aircraft industry in France continued with the nineteenth-century habits and traditions of small firms and artisans, isolating innovators and research teams from each other. There was no effective communication system for sharing and evaluating specialist knowledge and new products. Small innovators were soon absorbed into commercial organizations, and visionary long-term projects were stillborn because public direction demanded solutions for short-term goals.[12] At the same time, the Armée de Terre general staff attempted to persuade manufacturers to disperse their factories because it was feared that in a new Franco-German war they would be easy bombing targets, clustered as they were close about Paris (see

Appendix VI). But dispersal was unappealing on commercial and financial grounds, given the uncertainties of future orders. Moreover, with limited management resources and shortages of skilled labor, firms were reluctant to make such moves. Small orders begat high unit prices and were inefficient as well as not encouraging expansion and modernization of factories and their dispersal.

The Discussion Expands

Not until Germany in March 1936 remilitarized the Rhineland did the Chambre des Députés and the presidency become concerned about the relationship between Rearmament and the industrial base. The links between planning, contracts, funding, and increased manufacturing facilities were then seen only as the cause for the armed forces' chronic shortages of modern equipment. Thus in August 1936 this led to the nationalization of select defense industries in a move, at last, to create a war economy.[13]

In September 1936 massive expansion for Rearmament was at last decided on with a consequent spreading of orders and subsequent higher maintenance costs due to lack of standardization of parts. The French government's Plan I of 1934 to rearm the Armée de l'Air was delayed, as were Plans II, III, and IV before Plan V started in 1938. It was revised upward a number of times, but the retardations proved fatal. On 3 September 1939, of the roughly 1,400 modern machines, only five hundred were really such. Injecting new orders into the industry with modifications did not simplify things, either. The 1936 Five-Year Plan assured the industry of long-term work, but coming after nationalization it had reduced impact. Plan II aimed at parity with the Germans in heavy bombers, with as many reconnaissance flights as needed, and also fighters to defend France (at that time so short of the number of fighters that Paris had asked London for the RAF to defend Paris). Thus Plan II was to provide 2,795 aircraft (1,277—45.6 percent in reserve). As in Britain, the emphasis was shifted to the defensive with thirteen new "light aircraft" groups (fighters). But the omnipresent Conseil Permanente de Defense Nationale (permanent council on national defense) scratched Plan IV in favor of staying with Plan II (Tables 4, 5, and 6).

TABLE 4. Armée de l'Air's Credits on 20 June and 20 July 1938 (in 1935 pounds sterling) vs. RAF's

YEAR	1935 ARMÉE DE L'AIR INDEX 100 (IN FRANCS)	1938 ARMÉE DE L'AIR INDEX 154 (IN MILLIONS OF POUNDS STERLING)	TOTAL RAF BUDGET (IN MILLIONS OF POUNDS STERLING)
1933	1,665	9.35	16.78
1934	1,899	10.62	17.63
1935	1,451	8.15	27.50
1936	2,912	16.35	50.13
1937	3,355	18.84	82.29
1938	4,793	26.93	133.8
1939	24,120	135.50	220.63

French Price Index (with 1935 as the 100 base):

1933 = 114	1935 = 100	1937 = 135	1939 = 165
1934 = 109	1936 = 108	1938 = 154	

Source: The Times (London), "Financial and Commercial," 20 June 1938, 22; 20 July 1938, 22; Higham, *Armed Forces in Peacetime*, 326–327; Christienne and Lissarrague, *A History of French Military Aviation*, 276–278, 304.

Note: On 20 June 1938, 1 franc would equal $0.28; 1 pound would equal $4.97.

TABLE 5. British Defense Estimates (in millions pounds sterling)

DATE	TOTAL DEFENSE (£)	AIR
1921–1922	189.4	13.5
1925	129.4	15.4
1931–1932	110.5	17.8
1934	113.9	17.6
1935	139.9	27.4
1936	185.0	50.1
1937	193.3	82.3
1938	254.4	216.1
1939	3,840.4	133.8
1940	4,840.0	269.5

Source: Christienne and Lissarrague, *A History of French Military Aviation*, 276–278, 304.

Note: By reducing the French credits and British appropriations to the common base as in Table 4, it becomes quite obvious why the Armée de l'Air was well behind the RAF by 1939. The disparity was £26.93:£133.8 millions.

TABLE 6. The French Air Programs, 1938–1940

PROGRAM (AIRCRAFT TYPE)	ORDERS DATE	ORDERS QUANTITY	SCHEDULED START	SCHEDULED FINISH	IN PRODUCTION START	IN PRODUCTION FINISH	AIRCRAFT PRODUCED QUANTITY	AIRCRAFT PRODUCED % OF TOTAL	BALANCE NOT PRODUCED QUANTITY PLANNED	BALANCE NOT PRODUCED % OF TOTAL
Morane-Saulnier MS 406	Mar. 1938	1,082	Apr. 1938	Mar. 1939	Mar. 1938	May 1940	1,080	99.8	2	0.2
Potez 63	June 1937	170	Nov. 1938	June 1939	Nov. 1937	June 1939	170	100	0	0
Potez 63	Aug. 1938–July 1939	1,123	Apr. 1938	May 1940	Apr. 1938	May 1940	880	78.4	243	21.6
Potez 63	Sept. 1939–Jan. 1940	662	Jan. 1940	Apr. 1940	–	–	0	0	662	100
Bloch 151/152	Apr. 1938–June 1939	532	June 1938	Mar. 1939	Mar. 1939	Apr. 1940	532	100	0	0
Bloch 151/152	Sept. 1939–Dec. 1939	1,090	Dec. 1939	Apr. 1940	Apr. 1940	May 1940	65	6.0	1,025	94.0
Bloch 174/175	Feb.–July 1939	250	June 1939	Mar. 1940	Dec. 1939	May 1940	57	22.8	193	77.2
Bloch 174/175	Mar.–May 1940	484	Nov. 1939	Sept. 1940	–	–	0	0	484	100
Dewoitine 520	Apr.–July 1939	710	June 1939	Mar. 1940	Jan. 1940	May 1940	137	19.3	573	80.7
Dewoitine 520	Sept. 1939	1,163	Jan. 1940	June 1940	–	–	0	0	1,163	100
Lioré et Olivier 45/45.1	Sept. 1937–May 1938	242	Feb. 1938	Mar. 1939	July 1939	May 1940	242	100	0	0
Lioré et Olivier 45/45.1	May–July 1939	627	Apr. 1939	Mar. 1940	Apr. 1940	May 1940	96	15.3	531	84.7
Lioré et Olivier 45/45.1	Sept.–Dec. 1939	301	Feb. 1939	July 1940	–	–	0	0	301	100
Amiot 351	1938	285	May–Sept. 1939	Mar. 1940	Oct. 1939	May 1940	46	16.1	239	83.9
Amiot 351	July–Dec. 1939	595	Sept. 1939–Jan. 1940	Sept. 1940	–	–	0	0	595	100
Breguet 690/691	Nov. 1938–Jan. 1939	224	Apr. 1939	Mar. 1940	July 1939	May 1940	147	65.6	77	34.4
Breguet 690/691	July 1939	237	Dec. 1939	June 1940	–	–	0	0	237	100
Breguet 690/691	Sept. 1939	245	Feb. 1940	Aug. 1940	–	–	0	0	245	100
Arsenal VG33	Sept.–Dec. 1939	820	Feb. 1940	Sept. 1940	Mar. 1940	May 1940	3	0.4	817	99.6
Total		10,842					3,455	31.9	7,387	68.1

Source: Adapted from Emmanuel Chadeau, "Réalisation des programmes aéronautiques français (1938–1940)," in L'industrie aéronautique en France, 1900–1950. De Blériot à Dassault (Paris: Fayard, 1987), 488; and based on sources in SHAA, 3 B 7-14, 3 D 493; LE, 1/6.

At the end of 1937 the industry was still struggling with small quantities of poor matériel. Deliveries under Plan I were about completed, but those of Plan II were only just starting. Of the 771 aircraft ordered under the five-year plan and under Plan II, only 83 had been delivered, and these were all prototypes. France still had 382 planes on order, which would be outdated when delivered. Modernization of the Armée de l'Air, in fact, say Christienne and Lissarrague, could not have been completed until 1941–1942 at the earliest.[14] But if the shortfall could have been obtained abroad, an idea heavily opposed in protectionist France of the day, the difference, Cot argued, could have been made up by U.S. industry. Unfortunately, the latter had not yet shifted to Rearmament. It would be some time before U.S. Ambassador Bullitt in Paris, President Franklin Roosevelt, and others in Washington could accelerate American production so that eventually the U.S. industry in 1940 would be able to meet Roosevelt's demand for machines, thanks to Franco-British cash orders of 1938–1940.

After 1937, perhaps in part because the factories and not the design offices were nationalized, the French industry began to make up lost ground with the new Luftwaffe designs constantly challenging them. But another reason for the slow French aircraft productions was the rapid growth of labor in an industry that was itself in the learning curve. The industry employed 21,500 in 1934, mostly artisans, 48,000 on 1 May 1938, 88,000 on 1 June 1939, and then a rocketing expansion to 177,000 on 1 January 1940 and 250,000 six months later.[15]

The new Dewoitine D-520 only began to leave the manufacturer with 9 in December 1939, rising to a maximum 136 in May 1940. Of the *chasse* aircraft taken on charge—*prix en fin en compte*, and the manufacturer paid—only 37 percent were issued to Armée de l'Air units in France during November 1939–May 1940. Only in mid-1938 did the Armée de l'Air have more monoplane all-metal single-seaters in service than metal-framed and fabric-covered biplanes, and, though a real step forward, the French could not catch up (Table 7).

TABLE 7. French Aircraft Production, 1939–1940

DATE	AIRCRAFT PRODUCED	AIRCRAFT ACCEPTED
Sept. 1939	284	267
Oct. 1939	254	283
Nov. 1939	296	267
Dec. 1939	314	233
Jan. 1940	358	178
Feb. 1940	279	192
Mar. 1940	364	346
Apr. 1940	335	335
May 1940	330	303
June 1940	434	

Note: Acceptances were well below production, except in April 1940.

The Problems Magnify

Amid all of this, the German planning process for aircraft production, according to R. J. Overy, was at first, up to 1936, quite simple. The German air-staff planners determined the requirement, passed that to the Reichsluftministerium, which studied the industrial capacity needed; the two then were melded into a plan by the Hoch Kommando.[16]

At the start of the war, the French aircraft industry suffered from problems other than dispersion. Engines, in which the French had been a leader in World War I, came to be that country's Achilles heel in the interwar years. Thus it was that by the time of the later Schneider Trophy races, engine failures helped force the French out of the contest, though their development of the three-bladed metal propeller might have given them an edge. Yet because in the 1930s there had been no dedicated French engine-development program, the Armée de l'Air had entered World War II with inferior engines and thus inferior fighters regardless of airframe.[17] So on 25 July 1939 during their talks in London, Kingsley Wood offered La Chambre 403 propellers and 291 Rolls-Royce Merlins to be delivered by June 1940.[18]

The malaise that affected the French aircraft industry is further illustrated by what happened next. The Rolls-Royce side of Sir Kingsley Wood's allocation of Merlins to France in July 1939 is told by Ian Lloyd, and is revealing.[19] Lloyd concluded that the evidence made plain that the "French government and its representatives in 1939 were quite incapable of formulating and executing a precise, definite, and realistic policy."

Added to the above, Fordair, the American Ford auto subsidiary in France, could not obtain the machine tools there, but had to order them from Detroit. In France tools and draftsmen were lacking, as indeed was much ability to manufacture parts. As a result Rolls-Royce agreed to ship enough parts for 225 almost-complete engines by August 1940 when French production was expected to mesh. Then on 21 August 1939 Henry Ford decided to stay neutral and all work was suspended in Detroit and at Bordeaux. Moreover, most of the staff at Bordeaux were called up on the outbreak of war. Thus on 12 September the Ford subsidiary in Bordeaux proposed they become subcontractors to Derby. However, Rolls-Royce could not supply the expertise needed.

Mixed in with all of these negative elements, the Ministère de l'Air did not seem to be much behind the Merlin project, and always wanted something for nothing, or so it seemed to Derby; Paris became indignant when Derby pointed that out. The cancellation of the project on 18 December 1939 was, Ian Lloyd averred, "the result of high-level intrigue in French military, political, and commercial circles. The French in 1940 clearly preferred politics to production."[20] The French, in fact, had decided to produce the Hispano-Suiza at Bordeaux since the Merlin was beyond their capabilities. But as the Armée de l'Air still needed Merlins for the Amiot bomber and the Dewoitine fighter, 143 were delivered by the fall of France.

Yet, the number and quality of all engines supplied were inadequate, which delayed the production of aircraft, and thus 5,229 U.S. engines had to be ordered from Pratt & Whitney, Wright, and Allison. The same was true for accessories, particularly propellers. The solution here also was orders from the United States. Aircraft armament were provided by the Ministère de la Guerre, but were fitted at the Châteaudun Arsenal; they were the cause of numerous delays due to tardy suppliers who also were rapidly expanding, and not due to delays within the aircraft industry.

Another perspective on the French aircraft industry is to be found in the Tsarist émigré pilot and designer Alexandre P. de Seversky's *Victory Through Air Power*. In it he describes the seven months he spent in Europe in 1939 trying to sell his P-35, which had won the 1935 U.S. Army Air Corps contest versus the P-36. He was not, in his own words, impressed, and came away empty-handed.[21]

The French aircraft industry had systemic problems that went far deeper than the noted troubles; its owner-labor relations were, to say the least, antagonistic. Owing to the provincial nature of France, at least to 1939, business lacked a stable market, but at the same time that was seen as stagnation. Many companies had their main offices—*sièges*—in Paris, away from the factory. Small companies had fewer than fifty employees, and in 1936 only twenty-five companies had five thousand or more; these twenty-five dealt largely with each other and the state, and thus were further isolated and under suspicion. Most important was the fact that the bulk of French industrial leadership was in family firms and heavily influenced by business politics, and the leaders ensured that the legacies went to the heirs and not to charities. The *patronats* never thought of divorcing business and family; they were assisted by a large class of professional managers, graduates in law or engineering, especially of the *écoles polytechniques*. And Taylorism, that system of intense task management, was enthusiastically supported by the *patronats*, though not by their managers. As a result, notes Richard Vinen, industrialists and politicians seemed to live in different worlds: "The Chamber was dominated by the chattering professions."[22]

In contrast to Parliament in London, the legislature in Paris contained almost no businesspeople. Economic discussions in Paris focused on small business and agriculture. The supposed two hundred families who controlled the Banque de France were normally targets, especially of conspiracy theories. Charges against the *patronats* were easy to bring, since they had no public defenders, while sheer ignorance of industry encouraged suspicion. Politicians, moreover, received most of their information from the lurid tabloids.

The *patronat* was an aloof, élite group. It reigned, according to Torigian, and did not negotiate, and lacked a way to communicate with the shop floor.[23] Their actions were distant, unilateral, and offensive to the democratic sensibilities of the workers. As the paternalistic patrons, the *patronats* believed that any troubles were caused by agitators.

Labor Changes Its Approach

As the Front Populaire grew with its Communist ideas, so did attacks on big business, which was viewed as Fascist. However, the social conservatism of the system and the bourgeoisie attachment to property acted as a shield. It was this isolated safety of big business that was shaken by the election of the Front Populaire in 1936. The *patronat* response was in the short term the Matignon Accords, and in the long term their efforts to restore their power by defeating the unions, with state help.

However, the metalworkers, commonly called the *métallos*, which included the automobile and aircraft industries, took matters into their own hands. Before 1936 strikes had rarely been very large, often not involving more than a few *ateliers*; because employers could rarely afford a work stoppage, the strikes were settled rather quickly. But shortages of labor resulted in high rates of turnover, as Renault had learned in World War I. The CGT Unitaire organizing efforts in 1935 won victories at Bloch, Gnome et Rhône, Farman, Lioré et Olivier, Caudron, Hispano-Suiza, Salmson, Lorraine-Dietrich, and Amiot in the aeronautical industry. All had been enjoying rapid growth, increased employment, and union activities, especially among the *métallos*. At Bloch, they won an "English week" and a guaranteed hourly wage, as well as an improvement in piece rates.

The *métallos'* offensive began on 26 May 1936; they occupied the Nieuport factory for five days; then the management, which had refused help from the *gendarmes*, capitulated. At this time the Communists did not see the mass movements their actions would provoke. The strikes then hit Farman, the primary aircraft manufacturer in the Paris area, and then others. The grievances were local after five years of depression. The workers insisted this was not about revolution, but purely about economic matters and caused by the *patronats'* intransigence. The Communist Party sought control with social clout, and the government damped down class hatred by negotiations.

Blum then asked for calm and broadcast a promise of a forty-hour week, an annual paid vacation, a pay raise, and a system of collective bargaining. On 6 June the Chambre des Députés gave him a vote of confidence. Over the next few days, in the Salon de Matignon (Matignon room) of the Palais de l'Élysée (presidential palace), accords were reached. But by then there were 2 million others on strike who refused to go back to work. The issue was a guaranteed wage and nationalization of the arms industry.

These strikes put fear into all those who wanted to maintain the existing order, including the French Communist Party. On 10–12 June the Chambre des Députés passed new laws. Daladier, as the bourgeois defense minister, urged Blum to prepare to use force, and thus the French Communist Party leadership succeeded in getting the strikers to support the Matignon Accords and to go back to work peacefully.

By late 1936 the membership of the CGT had swelled to more than 5 million, and it was the authentic representative of the working classes— even more so when in late June 1936 it merged with the CGT Unitaire. From almost nothing, the *métallos* now controlled almost 90 percent of the industry's workforce, but it was still volatile and undisciplined.

In addition, the Matignon Accords created problems. The petite bourgeoisie and small owners now had too much paperwork to be able to support outside activities. The *patronats* had been humiliated and determined to get revenge, refusing to accept an adversarial relationship. To counterattack, they needed to turn their loosely structured Confédération Générale de Patronat Employeuses (general confederation of *patronat* employers) into the more organized Confédération Générale du Patronat Français (CGPF—general confederation of French *patronats*), which was not only for economic, but also political and social reasons, and its president received a reforming mandate. Now the group challenged the unions and the state and their solidarity held the key to social problems.

Complicating all this was the inability of the *métallos* to control their swollen ranks because the new union representatives were young and inexperienced, and their ideas invoked conflict. Aviation workers resisted management attempts to reclassify jobs, and workers at Nieuport struck until the stopwatch engineers were removed and management promised not to alter piece rates. By early 1937, the Front Populaire was falling apart, as strikes caused the state and the *patronats* to coalesce, and a helpless Blum was forced to resign. Layoffs and firings mounted, and by fall the CGT was losing members who did not trust the leadership.

By early 1938 labor relations in Paris were in turmoil. Conscious of the union predicament, management held fast, and Blum resigned when the *patronats* refused to budge. By 11 April 1938, fifty-four factories with 130,000 *métallos* were out on strike. The Front Populaire was gone. Daladier was in power, and the "Jacomet sentence" gave the aircraft workers a 7 percent increase in pay if they would accept the forty-five-hour week. The Jacomet sentence was finally ratified on 14 April, as the workers had lost faith in their leaders. On 19 April they got the forty-five-hour week and the extra pay. Employers applauded the dismantling of much of the Matignon Accords. Union membership dropped dramatically, and apathy again prevailed. A new national contract was in place by 30 April. Then in August the Ministère du Travail extended the earlier Ramadier Decree, making the aircraft workers the best paid in the nation with the 7 percent increase and forty-five-hour week.

Prime Minister Daladier shortly declared the longer week as standard in the defense industries. When Albert Caquot of the nationalized aircraft companies tried to abolish the weekend, workers voted with their feet. By 12 November, after the September Munich Agreement had been signed, the CGT was on the defensive. The aircraft industry saw the index of production, which had been one hundred in 1928, drop to sixty-six by August 1938; not until March 1939 did it top its 1925 level. With fifteen French Cabinets between 1932 and 1938, the system of Parlement had already failed.

When Ministre des Finances Reynaud launched an attack on the forty-hour week, returning to the principles of competition to restore a free market in labor, a wave of strikes and lockouts occurred, the latter being a fourteen-day government order. The 30 November symbolic general strike was quickly put down; the government kept transport running, the *gendarmerie* controlled the streets, and radio discouraged the affair. The *patronats*, with Daladier's victory, had a free hand for revenge. After that, workers had to reapply for their former jobs, which in Herrick Chapman's view was a disaster.[24] Though the unions lost ground, production was expanded and rationalized with La Chambre, Caquot, and other officials pressing Expansion at the end of 1938, including the use of automaker firms as subcontractors, and uniform contracts and wages.

By April 1939 all aircraft workers were under the standard 1938 *métallos'* contract, and work rose to sixty hours weekly, partly due to the shortage of labor. But the employers agreed to grant holidays due. By summer, militant workers were out, and there was an internal management–older workers consultative process. The industry was safer for the capitalists, but the militants believed Daladier had destroyed the old relationship of the ministries, labor, and employers. The militants later were shocked by the August 1939 Soviet-German Non-Aggression Pact.

Robert Frankenstein, a French economist, looking back from 1982 saw the problems as deep-seated; industry, finance, and personnel, among others, needed to make choices with expediency and confidence. The public was afraid of another 1917 and the Front Populaire. France was divided between the liberal Atlanticists who favored an Anglo-American alliance and the Europeanists who were for authoritarianism. Whether or not to fight Hitler was seen as a capital versus labor issue. Global devaluation, in Frankenstein's view, coupled with the massive fiscal inputs of Rearmament, saved capitalism in France.[25]

War Preparation and Industrial Change

The approaching, unavoidable war posed two particular problems—among many others—for French society. The first was solved by outlawing the Communist Party, and the second by agreeing to raise production from 750 to 1,500 airframes per month by June 1940 despite the shortage of machine tools, aluminum, and labor, as well as the very essential engines, without perhaps perceiving the difficulties: management stress, labor recruitment, location of land, and purchase and building of new works. When Raoul Dautry was made armaments czar, Daladier told him that La Chambre ran the top priority task—aviation. In spite of the best-laid plans, the war mobilization absorbed 20,000 skilled workers; it was not until nearly 1940 before they all returned. In the meantime, the semiskilled workers, women, and immigrants filled in. By June 1940 the industry employed some 250,000, of whom 20 percent were women that were cared for by the specially trained *surintendants* (superintendents) who also helped make production more efficient. As Vicki Caron has noted, France had an immigration policy regarding refugees in the 1930s that alternately sought to get rid of them and to allow some to stay to strengthen France economically and militarily.[26]

Laura Lee Downs aptly describes the gradually reshaped factory culture in interwar France in *Manufacturing Inequality*.[27] The *surintendants* were given a two-year course that trained them to evaluate health conditions within the factory as well as the potential for improving industrial efficiency. The now 218 *surintendants* were considered collaborators as the protective economy came to fruition in the struggle to modernize an industry still using piece rates. The *surintendants* began to use stopwatches to measure work, and appeared to be gratified by a well-ordered factory floor that matched individuals to tasks. But the new women also extended their interest, as the employers had done in the past, to the worker at home.

June 1930 was the peak of French industrial supremacy, and the country started downhill from there. By 1932 overall industrial production was only 23 percent of 1913. Relevant to an understanding of French business is Charles P. Kindleberger's 1976 analysis, "Technical Education and the French Entrepreneur," which reveals some of the same descriptive evaluation of French character and systems as are found elsewhere.[28] In 1913 France lagged behind Europe in the preparation of its students in technical education. Kindleberger notes that among the criticism of the French system were admissions to technical education that were limited to those who could afford it; instruction was too theoretical, mathematical, and rigid; and schools were élitist and cliquish. In essence, the weakness of the French system lay in the arrogance of its élites and the French incapacity for personal relationships. Kindleberger concluded that the French person needed exposure to other cultures to help in resolving his weakness in handling personal relations.

Other War Influences

All of this evaluation is informative in the effort to determine the underlying causes of the failure of the French system in those interwar years. It is evident that the late war both helped the expansion of French industry and created new problems. This was particularly so in the case of financial and administrative precedents. Little by little these were changed so as to have the state guarantee needs. At the Armistice in 1940 there were some seven thousand French industrial enterprises that had been involved in the war effort.

Mobilization for the war also greatly affected industry. But the first major difficulty was *main-d'oeuvre*—manpower. Regulations regarding workers, promulgated just before the onset of war, reached the aircraft industry only on 1 September, and affected it more than other munitions work because of the large number of manufacturers added during 1938–1939 who were not allowed to foresee a need for special skills. Moreover, the call-up to war service of skilled artisans created difficulties, as they were hard to replace; nevertheless, they were rapidly demobilized from the services. This affected the Armée de l'Air as it lost its mechanics and lowered air force morale, for these people had been destined to show newcomers the way.

The second problem immediately pre–World War II was the regrouping of the munitions industries under a new Ministère de l'Armement (ministry of armament). The air minister did not accept this, as the aircraft industry had been recently reorganized. The dispute, however, was resolved by the president of the council, Daladier, who gave absolute priority to the delivery of aircraft.

And, once again, the Armée de l'Air was not able to put up a maximum effort in May–June 1940 because 55 percent of the machines accepted by the Armée de l'Air were not serviceable. Charles Christienne, chief of the SHAA, provides figures that are damning. In July 1940 Vuillemin claimed that the Armée de l'Air had throughout the battle only 30 percent serviceability.[29] The Armée de l'Air's ready reserves thus were only about 40 percent, and even these could not be delivered to units that could not spare, or did not have, the pilots to collect from the depots the machines that were in fact ready for war service. This would have been drastic in a 1918-style fixed

"Great War." It was disastrous in a mobile battle. How many replacements were lost on a former airfield because the *chasse* had moved, again it can only be guessed, as well as how many were made unusable because inexperienced pilots were involved in accidents during delivery.[30]

French fighters were inferior compared to those of other nations. The MS 406 and Bloch 152 were ancient (1934) in conception. The MS 406, the first of the modern *chasseurs* to be put into production, was prime when it appeared but outclassed by 1940. By that spring it was being phased out. Like other French fighters, it had been designed to the same GSAF request C-1 of 1934, as refined in 1935. Originally appearing as the MS 405, this single-engine monoplane first flew in 1935 and passed its trials. Orders for this 405 version were placed, and in 1937 further orders were placed for the MS 406. Both entered service in early 1938, but the MS 406 needed 16,000 hours to assemble—double that of the Me-109, yet more than 1,000 MS 406s were delivered to the Centre de Réception d'Avions de Série.

The Bloch MB 151/152 was an unsuccessful *chasseur* single-engine monoplane, the number reflecting the engine fitted. Submitted in response to the GSAF request of 1934, the first prototype could not even get off the ground in 1936. A revised design flew in September 1937, but was unstable and underpowered. It was further redesigned, and orders began to trickle in during the spring of 1938. However, the aircraft was not suited to mass production and the design still needed to be reworked. When modified, it finally flew on 18 August 1938, but it was no match for the Me-109.

In contrast, the D-520 in 1940 equaled the British Hurricane, though it was still inferior to the Spitfire and the Me-109. The Arsenal VG-33 would have been equal, if not superior, to its opposite numbers but was not produced, and the D-550 when it appeared was also at least the equal of its contemporaries, but both were too late.

At the time of Munich in September 1938 the Armée de l'Air had not a single modern airplane in service and was then powerless against the Luftwaffe, as Vuillemin cautioned. Yet it was not the weakness of the Armée de l'Air but the unwillingness of the government to go to war that resulted in the debacle at Munich. A year later the situation of the Armée de l'Air had changed for the better when it had seventeen of the twenty fighter groups in

France equipped with Morane, Curtiss, or Potez fighters, though all twenty-one bomber groups had obsolete machines and could not carry out offensive operations in daylight. And of twelve reconnaissance groups, only four had the Potez 637, which could fly above the Luftwaffe. Thirty-five groups of reconnaissance aircraft had to be withdrawn as their equipment was useless in a modern war.[31] In the fall of 1939, then, all the French needed was time, money, and management. But the Germans would not wait. All that the Armée de l'Air could do in 1940—as Christienne, Facon, Buffotot, and Kennett have noted—was to fight not for victory, but for honor.[32]

In contrast to the muddled state of French air rearmament due to the almost revolutionary split in France between the Right and the Left, the story was, as will be shown, quite different in Britain.

Nationalization

In July and August 1936 Ministre de la Guerre Édouard Daladier had introduced a bill that gave the state wide powers over arms industries and including rules to reduce war profiteering. It was also aimed to help the services in peace and enable the state to mobilize the economy in war. Which factories would be nationalized would be decided by industrial priorities in due course.

The air minister engaged in "cartelization" of a number of small airframe manufacturers to centralize the fragmented aircraft industry under state control. It was the learning curve and the lack of credits that then hampered progress in air rearmament until late 1938. By January 1937 the factories were 80 percent nationalized; the owners had been indemnified for two-thirds of their stock. As Christienne and Lissarrague comment, "Nationalization, far from robbing the manufacturers, was an exceptional financial bargain for most of them." Six regional national manufacturing companies had been created, though a few companies were not taken over due to their lack of funds. The industry as a whole had only FF60 million in tooling as compared to an annual turnover of FF1,200 million.[33] The long failure to devalue the franc and go off the gold standard hurt French finances.

What was important was whether or not the Front Populaire's action slowed rearmaments, as the Right claimed. There were, in fact, other causes of delay.[34] The Law of 11 August 1936 created a limited nationalization essentially for mass-producible weapons, and thus it had aided the French military but upset business. There were political and physical constraints that did not allow Daladier to clarify his intentions, but the great increase in French military budgets from 1936 made nationalization less necessary. German threats and France's traditional arms procurement melded to restore the state to a dominant position in arms procurement.

Nationalization did not go smoothly, though, and aircraft production dropped from a monthly forty-five in 1935 to only twenty-five in 1937 due to labor unrest—as well as to the introduction of more complex metal airframes. But compared to the RAF, which was getting one-third of the British defense budget, the Armée de l'Air was receiving only one-sixth of the French defense spending due to inflation, making it worth only 50 percent of the 1935 franc. Moreover, France had started three years behind Germany and had a hypothesis of parity with the RAF against the Luftwaffe, which, however, had never been agreed to by the British.

Rearmament

In November 1937 following Premier Chautemps' visit to London, Chief of the GSAF Féquant began an urgent study of Armée de l'Air needs. Yet still in early 1938 the new chief of the GSAF, Vuillemin, and his staff also successfully argued the case apparently for a substantial bomber force. But Plan V of 15 March did not reconcile the doctrines of the Armée de Terre and the Armée de l'Air, though it also provided aircraft for reconnaissance and tactical support.

Plan V was really a renovation of the Armée de l'Air. The approval of the new scheme was complicated by the fact that Chautemps had dissolved his alliance with the Front Populaire, which meant that there were acute social and economic problems during 1938–1940. Efforts were focused on combating the worldwide Great Depression—restoring the government's finances and putting people back to work. Once these goals had been attained, the foreign policy debate was whether or not to intervene in Spain and whether or not, or how, to appease Germany.

The organization of the French higher direction of defense was as convoluted and as disarrayed as French Cabinet meetings, with no clear channel of command down from the top, nor a clear line of communication from the bottom up. There were critical—even crucial—players, especially in the latter 1930s: Daladier and Reynaud, Gamelin, Cot, Denain, La Chambre, and Vuillemin. However, it is hard to construct a national organizational chart because Daladier wore at least two hats and Gamelin, the manager, had fingers in many pots, as well as the weight of military prestige and budgets behind him. There was no one in Paris equivalent to Secretary to the Cabinet Sir Maurice Hankey (1916 to 1938), with long experience and organizational skills to facilitate policies and progress. Contrary to tradition, Paris muddled through, whereas London remained structured.

It was thus that by 1938 French Rearmament had developed against a constant international backdrop. At the Ministère de l'Air on the Boulevard Victor the Minister, La Chambre, had the advantage that the reorganization of the French aircraft industry was beginning to pay dividends and the ministry was finally getting much larger credits (at least on paper). Plan V gave absolute priority to fighters, in spite of the official view that all should be put into the bomber offensive.[35] By the outbreak of war, the emphasis was on warding off the German air menace. At that time the Armée de l'Air was still weak, but had the twenty fighter groups in France, of whom seventeen were equipped with modern aircraft. For the first time a coherent set of actions was defined that would make possible an air force capable of using the matériel provided. La Chambre demanded an immediate increase in personnel, but trained recruits would not be available until March 1941. When the Franco-German Armistice was signed 24 June 1940, the Armée de l'Air was still at least six to nine months from being ready for war.

On the other hand, General Gamelin and Daladier, deputy prime minister and also defense minister and war minister, had been allies since 1933.[36] The latter was a veteran of the 1914 war, a petit bourgeois commissioned on the battlefield, a deputy since 1919, and an academically trained historian. He and Gamelin enjoyed a close relationship from June 1936 to 18 May 1940 through five governments. Daladier was a bulwark between the services, the antimilitarist Left, and the conspiratorial Right.

The Decree of 16 February 1936 had created the Ministère de la Défense with Daladier as minister and Gamelin the chief of the Armée de Terre general staff and head of the Ministère de la Défense general staff. But while this fulfilled a long-felt need, airmen anxiously distrusted the new defense minister, and the Comité Aéronautique of the Chambre des Députés objected to the prime minister also holding that position, believing that the chief of staff of the Ministère de la Défense should also be the chief of staff of one of the services and that land-bound thinking would impinge on a rapidly changing air force.[37] The Comité also urged study of the immediate enlargement of the Armée de l'Air and charged that the new decree ran counter to both the decisions of the Comité and of the Chambre des Députés. La Chambre, formerly of the Ministère de la Guerre, tried to defend the decree as hypothetical and pointed out that the 6 June 1936 Decree had made the war minister also the defense minister with a common secretariat, so that rather than coordinating, the war minister gave final approval, which the air minister insisted was a guarantee of fairness as opposed to a separate defense minister with a whole new hierarchy.

Adding to the stress was the fact that neither Daladier nor Gamelin had sufficient experience to direct the Ministère de la Défense. La Chambre insisted that air force decisions needed to be made by the CSA without outsiders present. To improve morale, La Chambre appointed the noted long-range pilot Gen. Joseph Vuillemin chief of the GSAF, but the minister's motives in this were questionable. Vuillemin's predecessor, General Jauneaud, was controversial.[38] General Bouscat seemed the logical choice to succeed Jauneaud as head of the minister's military cabinet, but adding to the confusion was the fact that General Féquant, who knew a great deal about the Armée de l'Air and had a remarkable team, died suddenly on 24 December 1938. Six possible major generals were in the running to succeed Jauneaud, all with wide experience. Nevertheless the choice of Vuillemin, who had no staff background, was accepted enthusiastically for he was a flier with more than five thousand hours, and was a World War I ace with ten victories. His assistants were General Mendigal, a graduate of École Spéciale Militaire de Saint-Cyr, and Colonel Bergeret, both of whom had long served at the army École de Guerre and had a breadth of view.

La Chambre then at once tackled the problem of matériel, with the industry about ready to absorb the new appropriations, while at the same time realizing the need for a new plan in two and a half years. But only three designs were ready to be mass-produced: the Morane-Saulnier MS 406, the Potez 63, and the hard-to-erect Lioré et Olivier 45. La Chambre needed more designs while large-scale tooling took place.

Of the 4,739 Plan V planes to defend against a German attack in mid-1939, 2,122 were for the reserve, and 41 percent were fighters, 34 percent were bombers, and 24 percent were reconnaissance. But better matériel was essential, as that of the Armée de l'Air was thought inferior to both German and Italian. Plan V thus was compressed for completion from three to two years, 31 March 1940 to 31 March 1939. However, the start was far too late to realize the planned objectives.

In June 1939 the CSA approved bombers for *outre mer* (overseas), multiseat, bomber-escort fighters—and an increase in reserves to 120 percent for fighters and 200 percent for bombers, the latter to let industry keep up its production rates to produce a total of 8,094 aircraft. But the modern planes France so badly needed had yet to be designed. The air staff had been so slow that 1934 planes had to be ordered in 1936, and those needed in 1939 had still been under study from 1936 through 1938. Not until 1939 did the air staff hope to be able to order the 1936 designs, which had been under test for two years at least. By 1 September 1939 only 6,858 of the 8,894 ordered had been produced, and of these only 1,410 had yet left the factories. And in spite of all the personnel activities, in September 1939 the Armée de l'Air was short 9 percent of aircrew, 31 percent of nonflying NCOs, and the same percentage of specialist NCOs, notably mechanics, electricians, radio operators, maintenance airmen, and photographers. Again, everything had been begun too late and would not be rectified until 1941.

One of the reorganizations combined the offices of the chief of the GSAF and inspector general in a functional office with five subordinate inspector generals. La Chambre had recognized that one of the chief advantages of the 1936 and 1937 changes had been that the Armée de l'Air could switch from peace to war without having to change its structure. But the lack of imagination and personnel problems stemming from the Armée de

Terre led to the rejection of all the innovations of 1936–1937 and going back en bloc to 1934. The Decree of 2 September 1938, on the eve of the Munich Agreement, made it impossible for the Armée de l'Air to launch any large-scale attacks on the outbreak of war. Luckily, the Phoney War nullified this edict by allowing time to form an air command. The May 1940 German attack emphasized the main defect of the Armée de Terre strategy—fighters were allocated to army units in such insufficient numbers that the air force was kept on alert on the ground, much to the great benefit of the Luftwaffe. The extreme common sense and clear-sightedness of General Vuillemin regarding the urgency of training was not felt until under the Vichy regime in early 1941. At the end, France showed what would have been done if only it had been started four years earlier in 1935 and not in 1939, when it at last got going faster than any other European country.

Even after the Munich Agreement, when the need for a deterrent force was more intense, the Luftwaffe had a much greater retaliatory potential. Thus in the fall of 1938 Cot's strategic force was dismantled and parceled out once again to the infantry divisions. But the squadrons were even less prepared for the tactical role than they were for the strategic. What happened in France was that after 1918 there developed two mutually incompatible doctrines—that of the Armée de Terre and that of the Armée de l'Air. And what was more surprising, wrote Robert Young in his 1972 and 1974 articles on French air war doctrine, was that there was no resolution until May–June 1940.[39] Both services declared they were doing the opposite of their actions. The result was a total inability to defend France.

The Royale, the French Navy, appears virtually as a bystander in this story of defense in France.[40] The blame for this circumstance is to be found in part in the defense decision-making process, which has been heretofore described.

Indicative of the French difficulties was the complexity of the MS 406 design. The *chasseur* was erected out of two sets of seven thousand different parts; it needed six thousand special tools, for which there was a delay in procurement. Completion of this first-generation modern fighter took twenty-three weeks. When one of the factories lost the tooling for the wings and fuselage, all work stopped. Added to this, the new forty-hour week of

1936 increased the days required to complete a single aircraft.[41] At the same time, Bloch asserted he could produce three hundred of the MB-151/152, while Morane-Salnier turned out only sixty-five of the MS 406.[42] But Bloch badly underestimated the delays his firm would encounter. Unfortunately, when in May 1938 these became evident, it was too late to accelerate MS 406 production. Still, the MB-152, with its cooling problems at last solved, only began to enter squadron service in October 1939.

By the end of 1939 it was clear to La Chambre that engines for the MS 406 that were more powerful would not be available until the latter part of 1940, and not for the MBs until almost 1941. As for the shortage of propellers, Bloch proposed to make his own, starting in 1940. When in January 1939 La Chambre had asked his staff about 1940 production numbers, Caquot said they would need to expand manufacture from 370 machines per month to 600–700. However, Vuillemin was opposed to this, as he would not have the aircrew to man the planes, and thus, in March 1940 the minister, La Chambre, settled for 330 per month for the year.[43]

Across the Channel the British were again in splendid isolation. By the 1930s much had faded, including memories of World War I, but France still remained a threat as a continental commitment. The literary disenchantment with the 1914–1918 war also paralleled a coolness to France, historian John C. Cairns has noted.[44] Chancellor of the Exchequer Neville Chamberlain believed France made the most of its misery, and the Cabinet in London remained skeptical of Paris. The 1934 proposal of staff talks foundered on Gamelin's sympathy for Rome and Laval's concern to befriend Mussolini.[45] By the time of the Rhineland crisis in 1936, the British thought the French a liability regarding settling German affairs without destroying Versailles, and thus French inquiries of London received only bleak replies. In addition, the Baldwin government showed no urgency for staff conversations. No alliance was desired in 1936 with the French and the Belgians, and thus the latter declared neutrality.

British Technical Aircraft Development

The British Air Ministry and the RAF developed operational requirements against a political, fiscal, strategic, and technological background. The

Air Staff's visions must be judged against the times, as Sebastian Ritchie and Colin Sinnott note.[46] The story of these deliberations and subsequent specifications also has to include, as in most armed services, a mental gap between branches—the offensive-minded "bomber barons" and the defensive "fighter boys." The result was an interesting dysfunction between the bomber concepts of effective defense against enemy fighters and the RAF's own development of that weapon. Thus the deterrent force kept blissfully on with the idea that the bomber would always get through and could penetrate to German targets in daylight.

The time from specification to squadron of the new modern types was twenty-four and a half months for fighters, eleven and a half months for light bombers, and twenty-six months for medium bombers. The heavies were not available until months after the fall of France. What is important to note is that during 1932–1936 the RAF was ordering advanced prototypes that far exceeded the specifications for the then-standard aircraft in squadron service. If the Fury I was the first machine to exceed two hundred miles per hour in RAF service in 1931, the Hurricane passed three hundred miles per hour only seven years later. The Blenheim IV of 1938 was the fastest World War II bomber until the De Havilland Mosquito became operational in September 1941.

The importance of Colin Sinnott's work is that it provides a detailed overview of the process by which the Air Staff worked out operational requirements and transmitted them to industry, which then responded with designs. The process was divided into desirable types, which were related to strategic and tactical needs as limited by technology, and the Air Staff's and the manufacturing designers' vision. Space does not permit much discussion or exposition of the Air Ministry's development of bombers and fighters. Colin Sinnott in *The Royal Air Force and Aircraft Design: The Expansion of British Aircraft Production, 1935–1941* has laid that out very well in parallel with Sebastian Ritchie's *Industry and Air Power: The Expansion of British Aircraft Production, 1935–1941*.[47]

The appearance of the cannon-armed Me-109 of 1935 did not enter into the bomber staff's calculations. They had little World War I experience to analyze. Nevertheless, heavy bomber specifications did evolve, but the 1927 proposals, which only entered service in 1936, were totally obsolete; they were replaced by the new heavies—the Whitley and the Wellington. The Armstrong-Whitworth Whitley was a twin-engine night bomber of 21,680 pounds, designed in 1934 and first flown in 1936. The Air Ministry had ordered 80 of them in August of 1935 as heavy bombers, and by June 1943, 1,466 had been delivered. The Whitley was notable during the Phoney War for its leaflet raids.

The twin-engine Vickers Wellington became the backbone of RAF Bomber Command during World War II. The design started in 1932 at 6,500 pounds and was radically revised in 1934 when the World Disarmament Conference at Geneva failed, thus emerging as a 28,500-pound heavy bomber. The Wellington first flew in 1936 and the Air Ministry ordered 180 of them. By 3 September 1939 it began to enter service in six squadrons.[48]

The Whitley and the Wellington were followed by the 1936 heavies, ordered off the drawing board, but not operational until 1941. Though fitted with the newly developed four .303 gun turrets, they were never provided with the 20-mm guns needed to meet the Luftwaffe fighters and thus suffered losses throughout the war to VE-Day 1945. Nor did the designers calculate the required ammunition supply for extensive penetration of enemy territory.

Fighter development was slow in the 1920s, yet the need for Home defense existed from World War I. Though the German Gothas of 1918 appeared to always get through unescorted, they provided a challenge, and the fighter side of the Air Staff worked on how to stop them. The assumption was that whether the enemy was French, as in the 1920s, or German from 1935 on, the air-menace bombers would be unescorted. Due to the changed circumstances of the German access to Norway and France, the Battle of Britain in late summer 1940 forced RAF Fighter Command finally to come to grips with escorted bombers.

In the meantime, the Air Staff had concentrated on maximum speed and the heaviest armaments possible. Coupled to the Air Ministry's twin pushes for higher horsepower engines, the Technological Revolution, and the springboard of the Schneider Trophy races, fighter specifications moved rapidly from the 200-miles-per-hour four-gun Fury to the eight-gun 330-miles-per-hour Spitfire and Hurricane, equal to the Me-109.

In these developments the RAF was fortunate that many of the same personalities were in key positions, that a methodology was in place, and that there was vision in both the Air Staff and in the private design offices. Moreover, politics played little role below Cabinet level, in contrast to the situation south of the Channel. Though an Air Staff operational requirements office had been proposed in 1924, it was not established until 1934. In the meantime, all new aircraft were labeled "experimental" and appeared each year at the Hendon Air Show.

On the other hand, there were not always clear lines of authority and thus the AMSR ordered aircraft without Air Staff approval, a case in point being the high-speed research machines that became the Hurricane and the Spitfire. At about the same time, in 1935, the operational research section was moved into the Directorate of Operations and Intelligence, and designers were given early copies of operational requirements. And a further change was that the DCAS suggested that the CAS get advice not only from Flying Operations (1), but also from the commands as the new 1935 Operational Requirements Committee (ORC) was set up. From then on the committee recommended to the CAS, and if he approved, the AMSR would draft specifications; if the DCAS then approved, these then would go to industry. The Air Staff also saw the need to have an overall review of RAF requirements in order to have a stable and orderly procurement policy. This was accomplished in early 1935.

As in other ways, Rearmament pushed the RAF along new paths. According to Colin Sinnott, the Air Staff worked with industry and, contrary to the published historical works, often led with demanding specifications. The process linked the operational requirements to the aircraft industry's design offices, as seen in both specifications and requests to tender.

The specifications themselves were influenced by both grand strategy and by the Air Staff's interpretation of whether it was technically possible to carry them out. Bomber design was much affected in the 1920s by the fact that the enemy capital was Paris, whereas in the 1930s it was Berlin. Range, speed, bomb load, and defensive armament all had to be harmonized in a complete equation, to which late in the 1930s altitude had also to be fitted.

As Peter Fearon has pointed out, on the eve of Rearmament the RAF was equipped with biplanes whose top speeds scarcely exceeded those of the new monoplane airliners coming into service in the mid-1930s. Thus the RAF had to be reequipped with brand-new monoplane fighters and bombers, designed in 1934–1936 in the case of fighters and in 1934–1940 in the case of bombers. The production people had to learn to build all-metal stressed-skin aircraft, and the RAF had to learn how to maintain as well as fly them. This also called for imagination and a willingness to shift from wood to metal, and to hydraulic and electrical systems.[49] But it all took time and it posed problems—physical, labor, and capital dependent on continuity of orders. After 1936, as demand escalated, the costs of metal airframes dropped below those of wood, but in spite of mass production the cost of new aircraft rose with the attendant weights and complexity. In all of this, in Britain the Air Ministry played a dominant role. Until 1933 "no major war for ten years" was the rolling premise.[50]

The British Aircraft Industry, 1933–1940

The British aircraft industry had been kept in being through the Ring. Once the Ten Year Rule was rescinded in 1932, only the Geneva World Disarmament Conference failure in 1934 and lack of money prevented the RAF from moving ahead. New aircraft designs were in the wings, but they were to be drastically affected by the switch of political targets from Paris to Berlin, as well as by the rise of Hitler in 1933.

In the interwar years Britain had seen depression—especially in its basic industries such as shipbuilding and mining—as well as the rise in the standard of living in the boom of 1925–1929. Moreover, British manufacturing had made a radical change in a short period to new industries requiring new skills and new materials, different locations, and salesmanship to the Home market. Some of the difficulties came from the normal British lack of planning, just as across the Channel the *planistes* (advocates of planning) had experienced little success, caused in part by rapid technological change with new machines, new consumer products, and advertising as never before. All of this demanded training, research, and development. From the Department of Scientific and Industrial Research and its followers came the scientific layout of factories, especially in the aircraft industry, as well as the study of fatigue in the workplace. The level of production taken as 100 in 1924 had risen to 150 by 1937, and the growth rate went from 1.7 percent per annum in the 1920s to 2.7 in the 1930s.

The leaders in growth were the electrical sector and electrical engineering. The motor industry moved forward as it pioneered Fordism with the first mass-produced Austin in 1921 and the Morris production line in 1925. In addition, the industry consolidated from ninety-six companies in 1922 to twenty in 1939. Closely related to the motor industry was the development of aircraft engines. At the same time, the population shifted south to the new industries from the dying export-staples towns in the north. The shift came because of the completion in 1919 of the national electrical grid, and because of the availability of capital; that countered unemployment, which in some districts topped 80 percent. By June 1938, 54 percent of the population was in the south of England.

Other changes had occurred as well. Under the 1921 Railway Grouping Act, a permanent system of negotiation and conciliation of labor disputes for all levels of staff was made compulsory to counter the prewar refusal of the companies to even recognize unions. The Act also authorized the transport minister to require the companies to standardize equipment and rolling stock, and to establish common working procedures and other economizing means. The state granted the companies monopolies for efficient working. Indicative of the progress, as well, was the fact that by 1939 the General Post Office had 3.25 million telephone subscribers—far more than in France. And by 1939, 9 million wireless licenses were in force, enabling citizens to listen to the BBC (British Broadcasting Corporation).

The joint-stock company expanded in the interwar years, but increasingly the self-perpetuating boards of directors and management controlled with little input from stockholders. And as firms grew, they employed more women, some 21 percent of the workforce, for instance, in firms of more than one thousand employees.

In 1938, 95 percent of the large employers were in the aircraft industry due to economies of scale. There was a rationalization of business with
either cooperative agreements or mergers. Overcapacity was by these means
reduced, old factories razed or sold, and work consolidated in new factories. By 1931 industries had been streamlined and whole industry organizations could operate so that regulations, control, and planning could
create efficiency. The state played a mature role, with public corporations
becoming more popular; even the General Post Office was exhumed from
the Treasury and made one. However, the whole British economy, with its
worldwide investments, in 1929 four times that of the French, was much
affected by the Great Depression. But tariff protection was delayed until
1931's imperial preferences, a mercantilist theory, a "grossly anachronistic
idea," in the words of Sidney Pollard.[51] Balancing the budget was a peren-
nial problem and was to be influenced by John Maynard Keynes' 1936 work
General Theory of Employment, Interest and Money, which argued that in a
depression it was the duty of the government to spend and to create incomes
by public works, and to encourage investment by low interest rates.[52] Keynes
was not a recognized guru until the 1940s.

Nevertheless, the chancellor of the exchequer faced declining revenues
and increased expenditures for social services. Britain had gone onto the
gold standard in 1925, but dropped off again in 1932, and deflation followed. That eased exports, as the pound sterling had been overvalued by 10
percent. Yet the British problem was not that the Banque de France hoarded
gold, of which it had a surfeit in 1931 but a deficit in 1933 and 1936. The
basic problem in Britain was the orthodox financial mentality, which did
not end until 1939 when the chancellor of the exchequer asked the banks
to end speculation. And meanwhile, in 1931 the Macmillan Committee had
told the banks to invest in industry, which had been self-capitalized to 1914,
but which by the 1930s was undercapitalized.

Unemployment between the wars was largely localized and declined
rapidly in the 1930s with the new industries. In those interwar years there
had been mergers in the armament industries.[53] In 1928 Vickers and
Armstrong-Whitworth joined together, extending their organization with
small aircraft divisions. These aviation consolidations were expanded

in 1935 by pressure from the secretary of state for air when the Hawker-Siddeley Aircraft Company was formed under one financial control, though the companies kept their design offices in competition, with a modicum of production. The potential capacity of the firms was much greater than that in use.

On 1 March 1933 Prime Minister Baldwin called for a report on the private armament industry. The result pointed to the terrible deterioration that had taken place, but also indicated a tendency to underestimate the potential capacity of the inactive facilities. The Supply Board of the CID then convened a committee of three experienced industrialists, including Lord Weir, who reported in February 1934. That subcommittee based its conclusions on improving resources within the existing industrial structure. Thus, apart from firms like Vickers and Armstrong, the committee suggested engineering firms be brought in to create in 1936 a "shadow industry" attached to the main organization to help increase production. In May 1934 the Supply Board was given the go-ahead for the armament industry in general, and in February 1936 the Cabinet decided that the shadow scheme should be adopted at once; similar action was taken to expand aircraft production.

Now aircraft quality production was essential, but up to 1934–1935 there were scarcely the orders to keep the industry alive. There seemed to be supply capacity, but the impact of the Technological Revolution with the resultant increase in complexity, number of parts, and especially weight and size soon made Expansion desirable. In 1935, the aircraft industry, like shipbuilding, was professional yet, still, in Hornby's words, "an industrial embryo."[54]

Between 1925 and 1935 the Air Ministry concluded that the aviation industry was not large enough for war and would need considerable help from the outside—a shadow industry, which would come into being in 1936. This became the predominant factor in Air Ministry Expansion policy. Still, the government left it up to the industry to develop that shadow industry, though after 1938 the government underwrote its financial needs, which created a hybrid—part private, part public—for war production. Under the Capital Clause, the Air Ministry started with a guarantee of £6.5 million in 1938, rising to £110 million by August 1940. At the same time, the Air Ministry pushed all firms to subcontract, eventually to 50 percent of capacity. Added to this was the program by which several firms, often from the motorcar industry, contracted to produce multiples of the same aircraft type. The Air Ministry pushed these firms to establish some form of group organization, with sometimes more than one professional aircraft firm in the group. These new factories were then dispersed around the country for security.

As designs became more complex, more specialty ancillary companies came into being to meet the demand. By 3 September 1939 most of the factories that would determine wartime production were in place. A second shift had still to be imposed because the Expansion schemes kept demanding greater increases, from zero in 1937 to 7,000 aircraft in 1939, and to 24,000 in the twelve months from March 1940. The new challenge then was to match engines, propellers, carburetors, magnetos, and armaments as well as instruments and raw materials to the flow from the factory.

In Britain, labor supply in the munitions industries went through somewhat similar phases to that in France, with a shortage of skilled engineers in the Rearmament period, to which employers, the government, and labor adjusted, learning to hire within a chronic shortage, by training semiskilled to become skilled, and by upgrading the unskilled.[55] The government helped, and the unions accepted the need for dilution. The supply of unskilled workers in the war years was sufficient until 1943 when manpower shortages became of general concern, together with a scarcity of "green" (newly employable) labor. In October 1940 there still were 800,000 unemployed. Prior to the Holidays with Pay Act of 1938, working-class Britons could not afford to take unpaid leisure time.[56]

The demand for workers in the aircraft industry was limited until 1938 when "business as usual" was abandoned and money flowed more freely. This was at the same time when the new aircraft types, apart from the Blenheim and the Wellington, Hampden, and Whitley, were finally ready for mass production. From then on the limitations were thought to be what the firms believed they could produce, and the supply of labor. Production rose from an average 700 per annum during 1928–1933 to 1,800 in 1936, 2,800 in 1938, and almost 8,000 in 1939 when the estimates called for 2,300 aircraft per month (27,600 per annum). The lag in production that year was also due to the shortage of skilled engineers.

The British government forwarded its needs to both employers and labor in advance, so that they could be met by the mutual agreement of the parties involved. But there was as yet no administrative machinery by which workers could be distributed or directed to the firms that needed them. However, from 1940 new War Office and Ministry of Supply factories were established in areas in which there was no shortage of labor. Estimates of labor surpluses for planning purposes first arose in the aircraft industry, though difficulties were encountered due to the lack of statistics, especially on the hours needed to produce the new, much larger, all-metal aircraft; difficulties were encountered as well with the guesses as to the impact of dilution and with the lack of government control over the movement of labor to the higher-paying aircraft industry. The first attempt by the Ministry of Labour to estimate was made in 1936. The CID Defence Requirements Committee objected to estimates because it needed counts of actual workers. On the other hand, the Air Ministry found the estimates to be a great help in formulating schemes insofar as these numbers showed the principal firms the need to subcontract. Employment in the industry went from 79,000 in December 1938 to 790,000 in August 1940.

The problem of shop stewards was solved by excluding them from the new factories, and that of military call-ups was met in January 1939 by issuing a schedule of reserved occupations (badging), which did not, however, prevent individuals from volunteering. On the declaration of war, some 15,000 skilled aircraft workers left, but most were recovered by 9 September. According to Miriam Glucksmann, women were needed in the new industries "because of their nimble fingers." By 1935 about 35 percent of all engineering operations were run largely with women in semiskilled or unskilled labor; a few were electrical engineers or fitters.[57]

The government had long supported R&D. Since before World War I the National Physical Laboratory at Teddington, and the Royal Aircraft Factory/RAE, were geared to the aircraft industry. Practically, the airframe industry suffered from the fact that both the RAE and the National Physical Laboratory were more interested in the theoretical than in the practical. The verso was that these establishments had to advise industry on problems with which they were not so familiar due to the fact that they could not build airplanes themselves—a ban engineered by the industry itself.

In the 1930s faith in planning was seen as the road to success, with the journal *Planning* founded in 1931. Science, technology, and modern administrative methods were also seen as the road to success. Agreements not to compete replaced competition, with the Imperial Chemical Industries in 1936 one of the last of the government-pressed mergers, with 42,500 employees. This persistent government intervention, as Glucksmann suggested, effectively created the industrial infrastructure necessary for wealth accumulation.[58]

Neither management nor labor challenged the new working conditions, nor did they challenge the new structure of production itself. Part of why conflict was averted was the development of fresh job descriptions, which placed new types outside the union contract, segregating those who understood and worked with machines from those who serviced them. This had the utmost significance on wages, the whole relying on educated production engineers and professional qualified technicians and related work activities.[59]

The first firms were helped by the system developed in World War I that after each stage of airframe production passed government inspection, 80 percent of the cost was paid. Firms were also helped by amalgamations in the industry and by the pooling of patents as well as by specialization by aircraft types. Erik Lund has argued that of the American, British, and German industrial strategies, as essential as much as an economic plan for victory, the British was the most design-intensive industrial.[60] That has to be related to the roles of the geographic and social substructures of the industry.

By 1939 the British national industry was the most experienced, had the largest order book, and the strongest R&D side. The RAF had preserved a legacy of operational strategy from the 1914–1918 experience of a great power. Moreover, from 1919 to 1934 aviation spending in Britain greatly exceeded that in Germany (not allowed an air arm by Versailles) and in the United States. Even by 1939 the Luftwaffe did not lead in arms, flexibility, and material equality. In scientific achievements the Germans were slightly ahead in 1939. The British aircraft industry was well capitalized, competitive, and research-intensive, yet the RAF was small because the Air Staff policy was based soundly on organization and personnel infrastructure and training of a cadre for a future expansion. As an example, the respected RAF aeronautical training school at Halton admitted one thousand boys annually for a three-year mechanic's course, from which almost all graduated to go on to serve in the RAF for twelve years in the ranks or as NCOs. The Trades Union Council agreed that Halton set the national standard for aviation engineering technicians and successfully appealed to the lower middle class. From 1920 to 1938 it is estimated that Halton trained 12,000 men for service in the RAF, more than in all the German aviation establishments and well beyond those of the French. In Britain, as interwar "Halton brats" left the service, they provided a skilled cadre for the expansion of the aircraft industry, which the first graduates were just entering in 1935 when the Air Ministry began pouring money into orders for the Ring.

As for production itself, batch (limited numbers) rather than American-style mass production was better suited to smaller orders at a time of rapid technological change, thus giving the firms expertise in new techniques. About 20 percent of the air estimates in the mid- to late 1930s went on prototypes. That the British did not outproduce the Americans was because they had too many types in production, manpower limits, and restricted imports of raw materials. The major British failure had perhaps started in 1935 with the policy of "quality over quantity" and the excessive number of types, but this was a result of the rapidly changing technology during 1932–1940 and of the "insurance policy" philosophy—a legacy of 1918—of developing two different designs for each specification of both aircraft and engines in case one failed. Most of the middle and upper managers recalled the events of 1918, whereas by 1937 RAF officers, due to the youth of the service and its narrow training, were unaware.

Although there were delays in Rearmament while Cabinet sanction was obtained for monies, on the whole Expansion moved steadily ahead once such a policy was decided upon. What no one realized were the complexities of instituting almost at once all-metal construction with the attendant ancillaries of the Technological Revolution. For both the manufacturers and the Air Ministry, machinery had to be developed to track progress. Thus into 1938 the manufacturers labored under many management burdens, from shortage of labor to that of machine tools. Everything took much more time, especially when the numbers increased dramatically.[61] Then, too, the creation of shadow factories, sometimes at great distances from the central factories or managed and staffed by persons unfamiliar with aircraft construction, wore down management. But gradually these problems were sorted out, with shadow-factory staff brought into classes, hands-on instruction at the parent factory, and liaison maintained through a special office.

The process was not, as in France, highly politicized, but rather businesslike. Orders for obsolescent types were continued to provide for the learning curve, with the end products useable in Training Command. As in France, 1938 was a watershed year. In July 1938 the shadow factories turned out only 72 engines, while two years later output had risen to 8,317. The decision to use machines paired with unskilled labor both expanded production and bypassed the unions with new job descriptions based on a noncontract vocabulary.

Of course there were failures, such as the Rolls-Royce Vulture engine, a pairing of two V-block twelve-cylinder engines sharing a crankshaft. Faced with the competition of the Napier Sabre, another twenty-four-cylinder engine, and the eighteen-cylinder Bristol Centaurus, Rolls-Royce revised the proposed 1932 twelve-cylinder, super-charged, liquid-cooled Griffon engine and redesigned it to fit into the Spitfire in place of the Merlin. Meanwhile the Merlin had been undergoing constant development so that the Air Ministry had to revise its engine needs.

It was the chronic shortage of spares that caused the new prime minister, Churchill, in May 1940 to create the Ministry of Aircraft Production under his 1917 wartime friend, Lord Beaverbrook. This relieved the Air Ministry of charges of incompetence deriving from its being forced to try to manage production as well as the RAF.

In the 1930s management techniques were limited; many of the leaders had come up from the shop floor or from wood-and-canvas days. There was a lack of clear doctrine and a systems approach. In the rush to get aircraft, there was an unnecessary overabundance of types and overwhelmed design staffs as they tried both to meet Air Ministry requests and to see that the shops had the necessary production drawings. Airfields could still be laid out almost by eye, but rule of thumb was no longer good enough for aircraft weighing up to 68,000 pounds, and flying at speeds and altitudes unheard of in 1932.[62] At the end of 1937 the Air Ministry calculated that the seven thousand aircraft to be produced in the first year of war production would be only half the RAF's requirements and that factory floor space would need to be doubled to 10 million square feet. It was questionable whether or not the industry could support such an enlargement.

After the Munich Agreement in September 1938, the planners envisaged the need for 17,000 aircraft in the first twelve months of a war beginning in October 1939 and a need for a wartime capacity of more than 2,000 aircraft per month by the end of 1941. By 1939 the development of wartime potential production capacity became an end in itself. In October 1935 a special production office had been set up in the Air Ministry with a staff of four, while the Air Staff formulated production policy. Meanwhile Lord Weir was especially influential with his friend, Secretary of State for Air Sir Philip Cunliffe-Lister (soon Lord Swinton), who sought to move the aircraft industry to a war footing without dictatorship. It started with incentives to industry to expand its facilities. The subcommittee on air parity of the Defence Requirements Committee urged the Treasury to save time and money by relaxing its rules to create greater efficiency. This was accepted, as Air Staff studies showed there were important industrial implications, and the industry went ahead on jigging and tooling in anticipation of large orders. Scheme F of 1936 put this on a three-year basis, which allowed large-scale tooling that paid dividends in a rapid increase in production in 1938 and 1939.

To meet all of those demands the Air Ministry had to provide increased working capital for Expansion, and a remaining problem was how to capitalize this and yet ensure fair prices for aircraft. The Air Ministry side of this was that it had neither the advanced data nor the staff to do costing. To assure the firms that they would not be penalized for overcapitalization and unusable factories, the Air Ministry assured the Society of British Aircraft Constructors (SBAC) in October 1935 that compensation would be paid when the Expansion program came to an end. In addition, the Air Ministry agreed to pay 80 percent of the costs of Expansion materials monthly and

90 percent of the firms' estimated total costs. Remembering the expensive settlement with Claude Grahame-White after the 1914–1918 war—the RAF's eventual 1925 purchase of his former Hendon aviation school that it had taken over during the war—this was an eminently sensible approach.[63] The Capital Clause and the Progress-Payment Schemes were later extended to cover the Rearmament programs where firms had limited capital and credit resources.

The major problem of the late 1930s, though, was the failure to standardize designs—as Sebastian Ritchie notes, a lengthy process when time was of the essence.[64] But at a time of radical changes, a modification process was inevitable. Because of the 1939 deadline, the Air Ministry had to order competing designs. The Hurricane first flew in 1935, but production did not begin until 1937, and thus Hawker could deliver only six hundred of the Air Staff's needs by 1939. As a result, Spitfires were ordered, although the type had not yet flown in early 1936. But, as Ritchie points out, to have ordered only one fighter type would have eliminated the superior Supermarine aircraft. Moreover, construction methods were not standardized, so that the Wellington could not be produced by one of the production groups because only Vickers had the necessary rolling and milling machines. But Vickers also had the Wellesley contract and thus could only produce half of the 360 Wellingtons needed. The Air Ministry thus ordered the Handley Page Hampden, while Vickers had to "prove" Wellington production.

The twin-engine Handley Page of 18,750 pounds was almost as fast as the Blenheim at 254 miles per hour, but could carry twice the weight of bombs twice as far. Designed in 1932 it first flew on 21 June 1936, had an initial production order of 180, and first entered squadron service in August 1938. The Handley Page was regarded as the worst of the early heavy bombers. The Bristol Blenheim was a fast 12,000-pound twin-engine medium/light bomber designed as a result of the private-venture challenge initiated by Lord Rothermere, the press baron. The first RAF version flew on 25 June 1936, though orders already had been placed for 150 in August 1935. The first delivery to the RAF started in November 1936 and by early 1939, 1,134 had been received, when production then advanced from the Mark I to the 260-miles-per-hour "long-nosed" Mark IV.

By 1937 the older firms without new types on order were building obsolete Hawker Hart derivatives under contract. On the other hand, Bristol Blenheims were being built by Rootes, Bristol, and A. V. Roe, with wing sets by Dobson & Barlow of Bolton for all three until July 1938, by which time the state was gaining more control through financing and the firms were gaining greater experience under their new managements. Because the next Expansion plans called for 90 percent more fighters than Scheme F, the Air Ministry had no choice but to commit to Hurricane, Spitfire, and Boulton Paul Defiant production, and so by 1939 had three different fighters on the way while still hoping to end up with Hawker's Vulture Tornado and Sabre Typhoon.

The dangers of standardized production were adequately demonstrated by failure of designs for the FAA and Coastal Command, leaving them both short of modern aircraft. The total failures of their own left Blackburn, Westland, Saunders Roe, and Boulton Paul producing other firms' designs. As progress was made, the groups changed, and by the end of 1941 the Wellington, Halifax, and Manchester airframe and Hercules and Merlin engine groups absorbed more than half the resources of the wartime aircraft industry.

The demands of 1936's Scheme F were such that the Air Ministry abandoned working only with the Ring and promoted the new shadow factories as a useful war potential; by September 1939 the motorcar industry was well into aircraft production as well. In contrast, in airframes Rootes produced Blenheims, but Austin was stuck with high tooling costs for one thousand obsolete Fairey Battles. Designed in 1933 and first flown on 10 March 1936, it went into production shortly after, and 2,200 were delivered between April 1937 and December 1940, starting in squadron service in May 1937. Although the Battle was a great advance on the biplane light bombers, with a 1,030-horsepower Merlin engine (and twice the weight of a Hurricane), it was a design that did not compare to the German Stuka as a ground-attack machine. Underpowered and poorly armed, it was obsolete by 1939.

The motor magnate Lord Nutfield took over Spitfires at Castle Bromwich and brought out 240 monthly. Others followed suit, and by the end of 1939 further airframe and engine groups were in existence, including a Merlin shadow factory at Manchester under Ford. By then the Air Ministry had enough experience to farm out new designs early to avoid obsolescence. The close linkage of design and production assured quality and quantity assisted by a very large number of subcontractors outside the Ring. The new schemes were much more successful than those of 1935–1936 in part because the Air Ministry was now willing to gamble on new designs and to the newly redundant managerial capacity of the professional aircraft industry. The principal cause for the success, however, says Sebastian Ritchie, was the slowed rate of change, which allowed 1935–1936 designs to still be operational in 1945.[65]

Early studies by the Air Ministry in 1938 were not reliable in measuring labor productivity, as a number of factories were not yet in full production. In 1939 the industry proved capable of much higher output, with by July more than 1,200 firms under subcontracts encompassing 15 percent of airframe labor. During the period 1935–1938, the ministry also had to come to grips with the increasing complex ancillary industry and the advent of variable-speed propellers, powered gun turrets, retractable undercarriages, and complex radios and electrical equipment. Thus schedules and shadow factories appeared for these as well. De Havilland eventually produced more than half the United Kingdom's propellers, and the Air Ministry persuaded Rolls-Royce and Bristol, the engine-makers, to found a rival in Rotol.

The basic problem of late deliveries at this stage was that the Air Ministry's own programming was, as Ritchie avers, pure guesswork. Yet as these schedules had been prepared with the firms, neither party thought they were optimistic. The quantum jump from Scheme C to Scheme F had far-reaching implications for both the aircraft and the engineering industries as time-consuming reorganization of production had to take place. Plans had to be redone, as well as jigs, and Grade A tools could not be justified until a production run of 400 aircraft were to be produced, whereas C-Scheme orders were only for 150. Once the 400 threshold was passed, however, costs began to drop, and the additional jigging and tooling allowed the use of less-skilled labor. But the Grade A tools were more complex and toolmakers were in short supply; new tools were backlogged as much as twelve months. Here again, the strains between standardization and competing aircraft types were a factor, as were the higher wing loadings of the new monoplanes.

Although most aircraft were nine months late starting in production, higher rates had erased the deficit by August 1939. Still the Air Ministry blamed the industry, and this caused ill feelings and the demand for changes in management at Fairey, Blackburn, Boulton Paul, Westland, Vickers, Bristol, and Airspeed. The industry was angry and feared shadow factories were a step along the way to nationalization, as in Italy and France in 1937 and in Germany where the state owned parts of the industry. Suspicions arose again during the war when the government demanded access to the firms' accounts. In the aftermath of the 1938 SBAC memo blaming the Air Ministry for delays, Weir and Swinton left and Downing Street told the industry to accept Sir Charles Bruce-Gardner as the independent chair of the SBAC or be nationalized. Relations remained tense until at last production accelerated, and only then did the Air Ministry begin to record the weight of aircraft produced, not just the numbers.

Having solved the standardization problems by 1938, production could be increased simply by adding more floor space and by duplicating drawings, tools, jigs, and machinery, and by training workers at the old factories to go back to the new and teach others. Aircraft were finally assembled from subassemblies in which it was also easier to install equipment. Moreover, aircraft such as the Manchester were designed with ease of production in mind versus the traditional view of the industry as a design office with a workshop attached. Yet not until August 1938 was the Air Ministry convinced of the value in speed and lowered costs of high-pressure presses, and thus sanctioned their purchase under the Capital Clause, which provided for government-guaranteed investments in factories.

The shadow factories had the advantages of being able from the beginning to use modern techniques and being managed by motor-industry executives who understood mass-production straight-line flow. After the outbreak of war, motor and electrical industry personnel were vigorously recruited to speed output. Production was also increased by a strong Air Ministry program of subcontracting starting with the Spitfire, which went to ten firms, but subcontracting also stressed staff and allowed errors to creep in, and thus further delays ensued. Nevertheless, by May 1938 the firms themselves realized that only by subcontracting could they meet their deadlines. By 1940 Hawker was outsourcing 50 percent of Hurricane production, and by then 50,500 workers, or 27 percent of total airframe employment, was at subcontractor establishments. Moreover they were now getting credits, unlike in World War I.

By September 1939 employment in the industry was double that in 1938, and production was up 200 percent. Manufacturers had delivered 633 aircraft more than the target set and had 8 million square feet of floor space, planned to be 19 million by 1941. But production still needed much to make it efficient, because labor, machine tools, and floor space became harder to obtain in wartime.

Though the Rolls-Royce share of engine manufacturing had declined from 1925 to 1929, it had an aggressive R&D supported by an Air Ministry cost-plus-10-percent policy. The result was that in 1932 Rolls-Royce began to develop the PV-12, the Merlin. Meanwhile, Napiers failed to keep up, only later developing the Sabre, and the Air Ministry increasingly bought the Rolls-Royce Kestrel for Hawker biplanes. Production of these rose from 123 in 1930 to 1,282 in 1935, and by 1938 had reached a total of 4,778 of twenty-seven different marks (variants) as development proceeded logically. Faced with the Air Ministry conclusion in 1934 that Kestrel production would be inadequate in wartime, Rolls-Royce refused to share its secrets with a potential rival and instead undertook an expansion of its Derby works and more subcontracting. The company recruited 1,300 new workers during 1934–1936, and its subcontract hours rose from 70,000 in 1934 to 670,000 in 1935. The general works manager had visited U.S. automakers in 1930 and been impressed with their methods and emphasis on cost reduction. He demanded in 1937 that aeroengines and autos be separated and that staff and machines be modernized. Rolls-Royce adopted cost accounting, and introduced mechanical calculators. Under Scheme C, Rolls-Royce easily met the demand for 33 Merlins a week. In August 1936, under Scheme F, the Air Ministry ordered 2,854, but Merlin production in 1936 was still delayed by lack of standardization.

Due to design, experimental, and development stages, Merlin II draw-ings were delayed from September 1936 to March 1937, which snowballed due to the much larger orders of Scheme F. Subcontracting, started in 1934, needed constant supervision, with failures meaning searches for other sources or making up the difference at the factory. Firms in depressed areas proved to have lost the art of rapid production. At the same time the Rolls-Royce foundry had to be radically reorganized to cure the rejection rate for light-alloy crankshafts and cylinder-head castings. To catch up on the drop of 50 percent in production, Rolls-Royce went to night shifts and overtime in order to be back on target by the end of 1937. By May 1938 the company had delivered 1,000 Merlins, but only 160 of those had been flown. By 1939, after these reforms, initiated by Ernest Hives, Rolls-Royce was ahead on deliveries and confident it could face further expansion.[66]

The detailed Rolls-Royce story is similar to Bristol's but with a differ-ent management approach to shadow factories due to the Rolls proprietary mind-set. The company also faced the dilemma of the demand for high pro-duction rates under Scheme L, the creation of wartime production capac-ity without follow-on orders. Rolls-Royce needed orders for at least four thousand engines at any one time, and this anxiety was not relieved until February 1939 when the Air Ministry could at last place new contracts. But the ministry changed the Rolls-Royce programs at least six times in 1939 as demand for Merlins rose and the uncertainties of the Vulture and the Peregrine made planning difficult. Liaison with the airframe manufacturers helped keep Rolls-Royce in the picture.

After Munich, the Air Ministry carried out a complete review of aero-engine supply and concluded it would be deficient. In Rolls-Royce's case this would be 2,100 engines a month, and thus a new factory was sanctioned and Merlin production shifted to Glasgow, Scotland, where manpower was available. Bristol went the shadow-factory route, which was hard on their technical personnel, while at the same time they resisted letting the motor industry into aeroengines and they opposed the ministry's desire to have each firm make only certain parts. Yet, on the whole, Bristol cooperated with the Air Ministry and took a complete team to meetings in London, a very practical and constructive approach starting in 1936 when the biggest shadow scheme was set up. Bristol had to train five motor companies to far more exacting engineering techniques. Its factories were simple in layout and easily controlled. Not until orders exceeded 1,500 engines would Bristol order better tools to cut costs, while demanding complete interchangeability of Bristol's own and shadow parts. Bristol only introduced modifications if they were justified by experience. Shadow factories, run by the Austin Motor group, were judged on Bristol working times. As work expanded, management introduced line production. Shadow personnel frequently visited Bristol and returned home with detailed drawings, manuals, and hands-on experience. The parent firms' shadow-industry office was central to success, a lesson learned from the export business, as Bill Gunston explained.[67]

The initial shadow order was for 2,000 Mercury VIII's, 1,500 complete and 500 in parts. Because further orders had to await Cabinet sanctions, the Air Ministry's Directorate of Aeronautical Production created a showdown in 1937 regarding interruptions of orders to ensure there was no shortage of work. But then came the Anschluss (political union of Austria with Germany), and by May 1938 all the aircraft industry was on night shifts. When in October 1938 the Air Ministry refused to expand the Humber factory, William Rootes went ahead anyway and billed the ministry retrospectively for £83,100.

Sebastian Ritchie praises the way in which the motor firms grasped the shadow factory scheme, how well they managed it, and how easy it was in 1939 to introduce a second set, while the sharp increase in output during 1938–1940 reduced costs, despite higher wages in the industrial Midlands.[68] A pairing of Bristol engine production allowed each couple of shadows to produce complete engines. These were mass-production facilities that planned to use unskilled labor, flow-production methods, and single-purpose machinery. Bristol and the shadow factories planned to turn out 510 Hercules engines monthly. Rolls-Royce did much the same and the ministry approved six works, which became mass-production factories.

By the war, the aeroengine industry had improved from 14,291 workers turning out 2,248 engines in 1936 to 30,983 workers providing 12,499—or from 6.36 workers per engine to 2.47 workers per engine. Correlli Barnett in his critical *Audit of War* argues correctly that, faced with the German air threat, the Cabinet opted to make airpower the centerpiece of defense.[69] And so it created a state aircraft industry, if not in name, at least in fact. What was a further difficulty, as Barnett notes, was that the Expansion schemes meant essentially creating a whole new industry with far higher requirements for accuracy than the general engineering talent practiced. And the unions were strongly opposed to dilution, though there was more than enough work to go round. What exploded the myth of Great Britain as a world power, according to Barnett, was that much of the armament, instrumentation, and even the manufacturing tooling, as well as ideas for the aircraft industry, had come from abroad. Britain lacked the imagination and drive to be a world leader after 1918, and success came because of foreigners' contributions, which Barnett carefully catalogs. John Ferris, in addition, has recently argued that the RAF's difficulties and disasters in the peripheral theaters went back to the failure of the Air Ministry and the aircraft industry to deliver modern aircraft in 1936 rather than in 1938 and 1939.[70]

ON THE ROAD TO WAR, 1933–1940

Introduction

As Robert Allan Doughty has noted in *The Seeds of Disaster*, civilian control of French defense failed because the committees met infrequently and because of Cabinet turnover. By 1939, 85 percent of the mobilizable French Army were reservists. Doubts about their readiness made for a cautious opening strategy. In production, the emphasis was on mass and not on quality new weapons. General Gamelin became ever more timid, with no real plan to aid the Little Entente (an alliance formed in 1920 and 1921 by Czechoslovakia, Romania, and Yugoslavia) in the east. And in 1936 Belgium sought refuge in neutrality, which left a northern gap between the Maginot Line and the sea.[1]

The short three years from the German seizure of the Rhineland in March 1936 to the outbreak of war on 3 September 1939 were filled with charged international events and domestic difficulties. Hitler was a gambler who was very perceptive with regard to his opponents, and who at the same time had a sense of grand strategy.

Hitler seemed to play the Ides of March game—declaring the formation of the Third Reich on 15 March 1933, invading the Rhineland on 7 March 1936, invading Czechoslovakia on 15 March 1939—though he did nothing rash in 1937. On 12 March 1938, however, he took over Austria, thus encircling Czechoslovakia and seriously weakening the Little Entente. At the same time, he and Mussolini supported General Franco in Spain. In 1935 Mussolini had avenged the Italian loss to Ethiopia at Adowa (Adua) in 1896 by invading the northern African nation and thus posing a threat to the Suez Canal on the British lifeline to India. More importantly, Mussolini threatened French North Africa. Hitler soon afterward issued the Sudeten ultimatum to Czechoslovakia and brought Daladier and Chamberlain by air to Munich in September 1938. As with their response on the Rhineland, Paris and London were not prepared or in a position to act. France and Britain bought time, and did begin really to rearm. But in March 1939 Hitler dismantled the rump of the Czech state and obliterated those divisions and aircraft that might have joined France and Britain to stop the Fascist dictators.

In August 1939, while the newly allied French and British debated the value of the Soviets and the desirability of reviving the 1894 Franco-Russian alliance, a Soviet-German nonaggression treaty was signed—the Molotov-Ribbentrop Pact—and the fate of Poland, the last strong Eastern bloc ally of France, was sealed. And so it was that the disarrayed French and the unified British declared war on Germany.

Back in 1918 the Armée de Terre had received 95.5 percent of the defense budget while the Royale received 4 percent. In 1938 the Armée de Terre received 52 percent and the Royale 21 percent. The French air service's share was 1 percent in 1918 and 23 percent in 1938, as compared to the RAF's 54 percent. By 1940, unfortunately, the Armée de l'Air was the least offensive-capable of France's armed services.[2]

Martin Thomas' careful study of French imperial planning in the interwar years shows that France disdained its Empire. Defense of the colonies was only handled by a junior ministry whose representatives had little say in Gamelin's councils. As a result, French imperial planning was never realistic, nor did it have resources. It was talked about, but never implemented.[3] The French deluded themselves after Munich that their Empire was solidly behind their policies in Europe and that there was unity all around. But the French imperial system, long a backwater, fell apart under multiple pressures, as Martin Thomas pointed out.[4]

The most serious and prolific of General Gamelin's defenders, Martin S. Alexander, has shown that in 1934 Gamelin wanted to discover what

Armée de l'Air thought and doctrine were on war so that he would know the handicaps his generals would be working under with this vital new dimension of warfare.[5] The French Haut Commandement did not treat the new weapon as the British had the rigid airship—get one and find out its capabilities and vulnerabilities.[6]

After 1933 the Armée de Terre had to negotiate, or argue, with an equal installed on the Boulevard Victor. The Armée de l'Air's search for independence then followed the incomplete British line—to be assigned the DCA—as well as the strategic-bombing role. CAS Féquant and Chef du Cabinet Jauneaud became strategic enthusiasts and published the *Instruction pour l'Emploi des Grandes Unités Aériennes* of 31 March 1937—touting mass in aerial battle. Thus they opposed any dilution to the Royale or to the Armée de Terre for cooperation. The army had by its intransigence created its own nemesis, and only General Weygand opposed the new independent Armée de l'Air. Otherwise everywhere orthodox soldiers had difficulty accepting military aviation. In 1936 the war minister, General Maurin, forecast a German blitzkrieg, but from the air, not on the ground. Maj. Gen. Alphonse Georges agreed. Ministre de l'Air Pierre Cot, a Socialist, resisted a proposal for air support of the Armée de Terre because he saw it weakening the Armée de l'Air by diluting its strength for strategic bombing.[7] At the same time, in 1936 the nationalized aircraft industry was disrupted by the move of twenty-eight engine and airframe factories from the environs of Paris to Bordeaux and Toulouse.[8] The industry could not possibly produce the 2,400 new aircraft called for in the then-current plan. Cot's ideological enthusiasm and stubbornness alienated the cautious Gamelin—the more so, as Martin Alexander has said, because Cot lacked the disposition for doctrinal change.[9] And as this was occurring, the Deuxième Bureau reported that the Wehrmacht had evolved from 1918 to a breakthrough force under air superiority with ideas also tried in Spain.[10] Gamelin believed this assessment—air power haunted him, but he refused to do anything about it.

The 1936 Rhineland crisis led to a call for a Ministère de la Défense and a *generalissimo* à la Foch of 1918. It did lead to the creation of the College des Hautes Études de la Défense Nationale (college of high studies of national defense), but still lacked a common purpose. Cot was for the idea and Daladier felt it was ambiguous and ill defined, so Gamelin by default became in January 1938 the supreme *generalissimo* and general in chief designate of all the armies—not an impartial leader. But he also lacked the executive authority to straighten out matters with the Armée de l'Air.

What was helpful was that at last the Chambre des Députés saw the fiscal weakness of the Armée de l'Air and gave it the needed credits, four years after the RAF. Gamelin now saw that there would be air-defense fighters, as with Inskip's decision in Britain, and a small offensive bombing capability. All through the summer of 1938 Gamelin and Vuillemin fought the classic battle of tactical versus strategic airpower. Gamelin could not force Daladier to make him supreme *generalissimo*, so he could only obtain air assets if he gave up his command of the northeast. These quarrels were disruptive to the aircraft industry as types to order could not be agreed. Thus one of the roots of the disaster of 1940 lay in the ideological side of Cot's nature, according to Martin Alexander, and not solely in Gamelin's management and Daladier's ambivalence.[11]

At the end of 1938, Gamelin was still trying to achieve a proper balance for the coming battle in terms of air intervention, and thus he concentrated on fighters and hoped bombers could be acquired from Great Britain. But the British were cautious and insular—they had to protect the island kingdom. At least by this point, in Alexander's view, French policy was clearly formulated and coherent.[12] Gamelin was not complacent, but until the attack on Poland sharpened the thinking of senior French officers, he fought an uphill battle, even on the theoretical cover.

In June 1937 people had been puzzled as to why the Sénat brought down the Blum government. According to Julian Jackson, it was not because Blum had asked for financial power by decree, but because he did not go far enough. Yet he was exhausted, depressed, and in June close to despair. He did not appear in public, for he always feared street riots, as the French system lacked adequate avenues of redress. Thus it was that the aviation industry owners won in 1938. The Left lost the forty-hour week and control of the factories, supposedly in the interest of national defense.[13]

When Guy La Chambre succeeded Cot in early 1938 the Armée de l'Air was realigned to meet the rising Luftwaffe, after the occupation of the

Rhineland now only one hour's flying time from Paris. Yet this new disposition of forces was complicated by the change in Italy's attitude after the
Ethiopian War, requiring both the allocation of forces to the southeast frontier and the retention of those in North Africa to face the Italians in Libya.
However, inflation of 154 percent reduced the purchasing power of the budget to FF3.112 million in 1935 francs. La Chambre had the great advantage
that credits for the Armée de l'Air were finally flowing in 1938, up from
1933's FF1.665 million to 1938's FF4.793 million. At last the Five Year Plan
of 25 August 1936 was fully funded.

Albert Caquot, back in Paris as head of all the national corporations,
from September 1938 took all orders and divided them among the factories by allocating a certain item to a particular factory. But in that month
the industry produced only forty planes, all of older designs; in August
1939 about three hundred modern aircraft came off the lines.[14] It was at
this point that La Chambre pushed the aircraft industry to mass production, and ordered machine tools and aircraft from the United States, the
Netherlands, Belgium, Switzerland, and Czechoslovakia. From the spring
of 1938 to the spring of 1940 production rose from 40 per month to 640,
totaling 4,000 new aircraft by the spring of 1940. However, Cot and La
Chambre had alienated the Armée de l'Air officer corps, which they saw as
the antithesis of the "Marianne" French image. Cot had put Jauneaud in as
CAS, but La Chambre sent him into exile. Under the La Chambre plan to
dismember strategic bombing, the air staff sat on its hands and developed
no subsequent support doctrine. During May–June 1940 the Armée de l'Air
was still bent on its own survival, as can be seen in personnel policies and
training, combat doctrine, organization of the ground environment, and the
June 1940 evacuations to North Africa.[15]

In the spring of 1938 the Armée de l'Air was so alienated that it did
not believe in Plan V and thus did not acquire the personnel to man 4,739
new machines. It reinforced this by refusing to accept new planes, and on 10
May 1940 was incapable of ground support. More than 1,300 Armée de l'Air
fighters equipped with 20-mm cannon had no armor-piercing ammunition.
The Armée de l'Air air staff had failed to prepare for a defensive battle over
France. The scarce RDF and ground observers were hardly organized and

lacked effective communications. The combined effect was low operational readiness, average pilots (thirty-eight- to forty-five-year-old reservists), and a sortie rate of fewer than one each day per aircraft, as compared to the German four per aircraft per diem. The Armée de l'Air bomber rate was one sortie every four days.[16]

Doctrinal debates on air superiority over the opening battles emphasized the need for a large concentrated air force; those who took this view supported Plan II. The opponents saw the Armée de l'Air merely as the handmaiden of the ground forces, needing only reconnaissance aircraft protected by fighters as in 1917. The latter group came to prevail, as the air force was too young, its appropriations could be cut, and its units needed to be concentrated to protect the army from the Luftwaffe. The argument was that in a general air campaign the Armée de l'Air would be forced to dissipate its resources against uncertain objectives. The air minister tried to work out a compromise to support the army in the opening battles, but thereafter to allow the whole air force to be brought to bear in the general struggle. La Chambre tried to do this under Plan V, but it was political and industrial situations more than doctrine that dominated. The Armée de l'Air was not against dive-bombing once air superiority had been achieved, but the Armée de Terre having no DCA was wide open to attack by the Luftwaffe Stukas. And, finally, mobilization was not regarded as peace, but it was not exactly war either. Unlike in 1914 the forces did not have time in Poland in 1939 and in Belgium and the Netherlands in 1940 to mobilize.

To remedy the lack of modern types, La Chambre followed Cot's initiative and sought U.S. fighters over the opposition of the French aircraft industry. U.S. export regulations would not allow military aircraft to be sold abroad until two years after they had entered American service. But in 1938 France received the first one hundred Curtiss P-36 Hawk fighters and then Martin 167 and Douglas DB-7 light bombers, as well as Vultee BT-9 trainers and Chance-Vought dive-bombers. The first P-36s arrived in September 1938; by the Armistice in June 1940, 489 out of the order for 980 had been delivered. Thanks to the work of the fighter schools, Armée de l'Air pilots thought they were equal to the Luftwaffe. Although by May 1940 the Armée de l'Air had in theory as many aircraft as the Luftwaffe, it had trained personnel for only one-fourth of them. In fact, many expedients had been developed by the Haut Commandement to refuse to accept new machines. And yet the Armée de l'Air perhaps could have beaten the Luftwaffe, if actions had been taken earlier.

Col. Faris R. Kirkland, a U.S. artillerist with psychological training, blames this remarkable state of affairs on psychological conflicts and fantasies that infected the republicans, the Socialists, the army, and the air force, saying that these fantasies affected the way in which they viewed others.[17]

Until the late 1920s (as in the U.S. Navy), French fliers were content to stay in junior ranks. As they aged, Armée de l'Air independence was driven by the desire to hold higher ranks. At the same time, from 1924 the Left gained control of the Chambre des Députés and proceeded to cut down the army. In contrast, an independent air force could be justified to keep up with the British and the Italians, as well as a more economical and centralized supervision of aviation as a whole. Public revulsion against the army and fear of the "aerial menace" allowed the new Marianne to arise. Armée de l'Air promotions were managed by the Ministère de l'Air, but the units remained under Armée de Terre control. Fliers lacked doctrine and the right to create specifications for the aircraft they needed. The 1935 Plan I included the Dewoitine 500 and 501, the Amiot 140, the Bloch 200, and the ANF-Les Mureaux 117. This order was followed in October 1933 by the BCR concept, which resulted in the Potez 540 and the Bloch 131.[18]

Equally fundamental was the absence of a training establishment capable both of expanding the air force as modern aircraft tardily became available, and of providing mechanics to maintain them, as well as the ability to meet wastage and consumption—sustainability. One root cause of this disarray was the lack of vision of an air staff hampered by all the points made above and its failure to see that from an inferior position, as was plain to Vuillemin in August 1938, it would take the French double the German production to achieve parity. And how long that would take was anyone's guess.[19]

In September 1938 Daladier persuaded the chiefs of staff that France was ready, but Vuillemin, just back from Germany, believed that the Armée de l'Air was not. He had been carefully briefed by the Deuxième Bureau's Captain Paul Stehlen in Berlin, whose dispatches were notably accurate.

Vuillemin believed that the Armée de l'Air would not last two weeks against the Luftwaffe, yet he sat silent on 23 August when La Chambre said the Armée de l'Air was better than in 1938. On 26 August he wrote the minister and they compromised, though in fact only the day and night fighter force was nearly operational and the reconnaissance forces were just about so. There were no heavy bombers, and there were major deficiencies in the DCA.[20]

Guy La Chambre was considered the best air minister of the interwar years. In the spring of 1938 he reorganized the ministry to comport with its responsibilities and needed resources. He remade the GSAF, removing the "clinkers," and he reconstructed the CSA. La Chambre appointed Vuillemin chief of the GSAF because of his competence and organizing ability. He had seen the appalling state of the aircraft industry in early 1938. On 1 January 1938 the Armée de l'Air had 1,350 aircraft, of which 80 percent were from Denain's 1935 program and obsolete. Of *chasse*, capable of 250 miles per hour, the French had 55, the British 90, the Germans 400, and the Italians 590. In November 1937 Neville Chamberlain had told the French foreign minister that France did not have and could not produce any modern aircraft.[21]

Due to the backward nature of the industry, a large gap existed between technical programs and the delivery of matériel. In 1936 Parlement had adopted a plan to renovate the air force fully by 1941, but there was a lack of prototypes on which production orders could be placed. Plans I and II had included this 1936 five-year initiative. Plan II never reached Parlement. And meanwhile the industry suffered from a lack of investment and national industrial policy.

The CSA in 1938 was charged to examine organizational questions, recruitment, and the procurement of aircraft, and to determine the impact of new equipment on Armée de l'Air operational doctrine. The CSA was only consultative, however: the final decisions were made by the minister in consultation with the GSAF, and in the end by the Comité Permanente de la Défense Nationale (standing committee on national defense) under the prime minister. Thus general air force rearmament under La Chambre was governed by Plan V. Armée de l'Air requirements had to be totally revised because of intelligence on the Luftwaffe and air force staff talks. Pierre Cot originated Plan V and La Chambre had it approved after the GSAF drew up the requirements: By March 1940 there were to be 2,617 first-line aircraft and 2,122 in reserve (81 percent reserves). There was to be an extensive training program to produce 600 officer pilots and observers, 100 engineer officers, 1,500 to 2,000 NCO pilots, 1,200 air gunners, 10,000 aircraft mechanics, 800 equipment technicians, 100 photographers, 600 balloon mechanics, 1,000 radio operators, and 1,000 electricians.[22]

But by the end of 1938 very few aircraft had been delivered. On 29 March 1939 the CSDN asked for 5,133 aircraft, and on 13 June La Chambre accelerated Plan V to be completed in the fall of 1940, and asked for 8,094 aircraft with 330 airframes monthly. By 1 April 1939 there were only 500 aircraft, with untrained crews. "Nor was it possible," Patrick Facon notes, "to understand how the Air Force General Staff determined the aircraft-requirement policy without considering staff training, which was essential."[23]

In January 1939 Vuillemin determined that 40 to 60 aircraft per month was adequate; the number later was fixed at 330. As a result, industrial investment was restricted, as were orders for raw materials. Vuillemin and Bergeret at the Riom *procès* in 1942 laid the blame on the aircraft industry. On 1 January 1938 the total that actually was considered possible to achieve by 31 March 1940 was 4,739. Facon notes that delays in production of the 1935 and 1937 designs, however, like the MS 406 and Bloch 151, were such that "there was no chance of having new aircraft for 1940."[24]

Priority was given to fighter production because the bomber prototype situation was deficient—they were not yet in the developed prototype stage due to the fact that Armée de l'Air engineers were military officers untrained in aeronautics. In addition, manufacturing was disrupted by attempts to modify aircraft to match German and Italian progress, and it was hindered by the BCR image.

What is today a very apparent gap between the aviation of the 1930s and that of the 1940s was not so evident then. France unfortunately lagged behind in research and the other aspects of the Technological Revolution. Older pilots had trouble adapting to the new aircraft and to all-weather flying. Though blind-flying (*pilotage sans visibilité*) had been introduced at Avord in 1936, few felt confident enough in 1939 to land under blind-flying conditions in bad weather. The Lorenz blind-landing system had been available in Germany since 1934, but did not reach France until 1940. Some improvement came with the introduction of primitive simulators in 1937 and a Link trainer in 1939 at Avord for 450 students, but new gunnery and bombing techniques, including a gyro-bombsight, were too late for the war. The new planes were ahead of the mechanics' knowledge and skill level, which meant low serviceability rates. And while oxygen masks allowed flight at higher altitudes, nothing had been done to heat cabins, camera lenses, and guns. Much new in wireless transmission, R/T, direction finding, and radio compasses had to be tested and absorbed, and operational practices developed.

By 1938, John Cairns noted, the problem became how to have close and practical cross-Channel relations without an alliance.[25] By then Chamberlain was trying to run the foreign policies on both sides of the Channel. All of this only confirmed and strengthened London's prejudices and stereotypes. The dilemma for Britain was to try to persuade the French to cooperate over Czechoslovakia without revealing that there would be no British troops available. For their part, the British suspected that the French wanted to involve them in Eastern Europe. Chamberlain wanted to know French strength while being sure Britain was not embroiled to the detriment of Appeasement.

By the spring of 1939 the British had come to realize they had to make a continental commitment with conscription. France was humiliated. The British had seized the initiative and carried the moral burden.

Appeasement

The idea of appeasing the Germans after the Treaty of Versailles of 1919 was a salient feature of both French and British foreign policy, especially in the later 1930s.[26] But Appeasement did not mean the same in Paris as it did in London and was not handled the same. Moreover, this policy of mollifying the Germans impacted the grand strategies of France and Britain in different ways, although both countries were fearful of the air menace.

Britain was fortunate that Chamberlain's traditional policy of appeasement, while regrettably naïve in the face of Hitlerian reality, nevertheless gave the island kingdom the arms vital to its survival in 1940. Chamberlain's decision to take the less expensive way in defense meant that money was bet on the RAF deterrent. While that bet was lost for technical reasons, Inskip shifted the emphasis in late 1937 from the impotent bomber offensive to fighter defense of the United Kingdom. Thus, while France and its policy was dominated by the army because of the weakness of the political system, Britain enjoyed consistency of policy with the fiscal emphasis on the RAF.

Martin Alexander's edited work *Knowing Your Friends* is a valuable resource for these interwar years.[27] In the 1920s the British imperial defense took precedence over European security. The British could afford to be nonchalant about the Continent, but the French could not. In London, France had once been viewed as the greatest military power in the world, but now was seen as a potential enemy, though never to the point of thorough investigation. British defense planning in the 1920s was haphazard, but with diplomatic cooperation in Europe while facing imperial defense problems. The British were antipathetic to the French who they regarded as cads—the French did not "play cricket." The British carried out liaison with an obstructive and superior manner. The question of "mobile" or defensive doctrine had still not been solved in 1940. The British judged the Armée de Terre by class standards, and the majority of French officers, in British eyes, were bourgeois.

In the 1930s the French appointed senior military attachés whose reports went directly to the Deuxième Bureau and were full of gen. Not so the British. The 1936 talks were more political than practical. Military liaison in the late 1930s was filled in London with mistrust of Paris and resentment at being placed in a subordinate role. The chiefs of staff were Francophobes. During Munich the CIGS did not believe that discussing military matters with the French would be opportune. Not until March 1939 did London consider having frank conversations with Paris that involved delegates of both general staffs.

During 1937–1939 French intelligence was concerned with the poor status of the British Army's manpower, especially in the Territorial Army. After 1935 Britain's main concern was the strength, modernization, and speed of transfer of the Field Force to the Continent. Not until the 1939 staff

conversations did the War Office in London begin to receive direct information on the size of the Armée de Terre, first in relation to disarmament and
then against Germany, in terms of divisions and limited manpower. There
was also concern as to the Armée de Terre's strategy in a future war, and
especially the morale and efficiency of the *poilus* and their leaders.

When Weygand was commander in chief he ordered a review of deficiencies, which led the British to conclude that the French army had become
a smaller, better-trained professional force with an interest in mechanization. The British complacency regarding the Armée de Terre changed after
Hitler's rise to power in 1933. By 1938 the British were concerned by French
dissimulation as to the impact of the Maginot Line, the new manpower
laws to counter the low World War I birthrate, and the lack of knowledge of
Gamelin's plans for war—until 1939. And the morale of the Armée de Terre
was suspect in British eyes.

In 1935 Colonel T. G. G. Hayward, the British military attaché in Paris
with a French wife, reported that the average Frenchman regarded military
duty as an irksome necessity, and never with enthusiasm. Concern increased
when the Front Populaire came to power. The Abyssinian crisis between
Italy and Ethiopia forced British leaders out of their complacency—the
French would not alienate Italy because of the Armée de Terre and Armée
de l'Air May–June agreements with Italy to oppose Hitler.

In March 1939 the confidential British War Office handbook on the
Armée de Terre was updated. In January 1936 the staff talks did not entangle
Britain, which was assured that France could defend its frontiers alone and
that the French should go to aid the Belgians. The French were naïve again,
but perhaps because they were at a low ebb and wanted to frighten London
into an alliance. Churchill was invited to the Maginot Line and Hayward
was replaced. Colonel F. G. Beaumont-Nesbit's reports were revisionist and
may have backfired for the French in that he was never positive. But the
RAF deterrent bomber school in London still held sway; there was no sense
of urgency among British planners because war was not expected until
perhaps 1942.

During 1937–1938 there was improved communication across the
Channel, but no joint strategy. The 1936 talks were not followed up. The

British had to size up the European situation using mostly basic statistics. And so the tendency was to judge the French in terms of the size of the army and the strategy of fortifications. But by 1940 military strength would go against France, especially as in 1938 the Germans dismantled the Eastern bloc. Secretary of State for War Hore-Belisha was dazzled on a visit to France by supposed French strength, but the CIGS was not.

In March 1938 the new military attaché in Paris, Colonel William Fraser, delineated a much-changed Armée de Terre in 1937 due to the shift in strategic geography. France would now go on the defensive on the Franco-German border and on the offensive against the Italians in North Africa. In London the CIGS guessed that France would not go to the aid of the Czechs; France would put fifty-three divisions into the field but could only sustain forty, as compared to the German one hundred.

In the last months of 1938 Gamelin visited London to meet Inskip and others. He painted a new picture: one hundred days in the field and assume the offensive at once to aid Czechoslovakia, then withdraw behind the Maginot Line for the winter and attack Italy with British help in the spring of 1939. However, the War Office believed it was mere bluster to bring in Britain. In October Fraser saw a new special light mechanized division, which he suspected, moreover, was deployed for his benefit.

From early 1937 the French were alarmed at the pace of British mechanization and failure to respond to appeals for a small but strong BEF. After the Munich Agreement, it was clear that the French would lead in a new war. CAS Cyril Newall wanted talks. The French plan revived memories of the Flanders mud of 1914–1918. Late in 1938 the British did assess the consequences for France's security of the loss of Czechoslovakia. The new CIGS report was pessimistic regarding France's chances without substantial assistance, but it was vague. If the Germans went through Belgium and Italy joined in, French survival until the BEF could arrive was not thought possible.

The foreign office and the chiefs of staff were fearful that French politicians would leak secret information, and there was concern that a BEF, as in 1914, would be irrevocably committed to a French battle line. Whitehall was too trusting of Gamelin's public statements as to the state of the Armée de Terre. Still, both reluctance and mistrust remained. Because the British, in the Phoney War, had believed the Armée de Terre's fighting capacity, the Haut Commandement, the fortifications, and the soundness of the strategic plan, they were surprised in May 1940. Yet CIGS Sir Edmund Ironside had believed he had to trust the Armée de Terre.

In the interwar years in the 1920s the French government had strong leaders who were able to focus on pacific policies, which both defended France and appeased Germany. But in the 1930s when a focused dictatorship came to power in Germany, French leaders lost their cohesiveness and appeasement changed from an honorable to a defeatist course. This coincided with the upheaval caused by the creation of the Ministère de l'Air and then of the Armée de l'Air, together with the revolution in aircraft and their production. French defense policy lacked cohesion and numerical realism. Internal politics and fear of another war created a ripple of uncertainty that dismantled the old Eastern alliances. Priorities were not sorted out in time for fiscal and physical action to place France on a sound military basis before the May 1940 Battle of France began.

Britain, in contrast, as apparently the one superpower of the interwar years, had a coherent foreign and defense policy, though it changed from one decade to the next. The important legacies from 1914 to 1918 were the fear of another "Great War," the need to modify Versailles, and the vulnerability of Britain to air attack. But self-confidence led to mirror image misinterpretation of Japan and Germany and delusions about the air menace. Yet the Defence Requirements Committee anticipated the failure of German rearmament and so the Cabinet took steps in 1934 to bolster imperial and Home defenses, and these coincided with new technologies.

While south of the Channel coalition governments came and went with a kaleidoscope of clusters of known persons, the turnover in the 1920s in Britain, when the Labour Party came briefly to power in 1924 and again during 1929–1931, still saw consistency of policies—all despite the Great Depression and its unemployment, and an appeasing foreign policy that did not, however, cripple defense spending. From 1931 to 1940 Britain had only three prime ministers—MacDonald, Baldwin, and Chamberlain, in succession.

Air Marshal Arthur
Barratt of the British
Air Forces France and
Gen. Joseph Vuillemin
enjoy an after-dinner
cigar—perhaps winter
1940.

SHAA Collection.

M. Laurent-Eynac and
René Fonck on a
1923 visit to a French
aircraft factory.

SHAA Collection.

At the christening of the airliner *Ville de Tananarive*, from left to right, Ministre des Colonies M. Rollin; Madame Denain; pilot Réne Lefèvre; sometime Ministre de l'Air Pierre Cot; and Ministre de l'Air General Denain, 1934.

SHAA Collection.

At the start of World War II, General Vuillemin, Admiral Darlan of the Royale (French navy), and General Gamelin of the Armée de Terre (French army).

SHAA Collection.

Early Supermarine Spitfires in prewar markings, but fitted with the new all-steel three-bladed propellers.

RAF Museum.

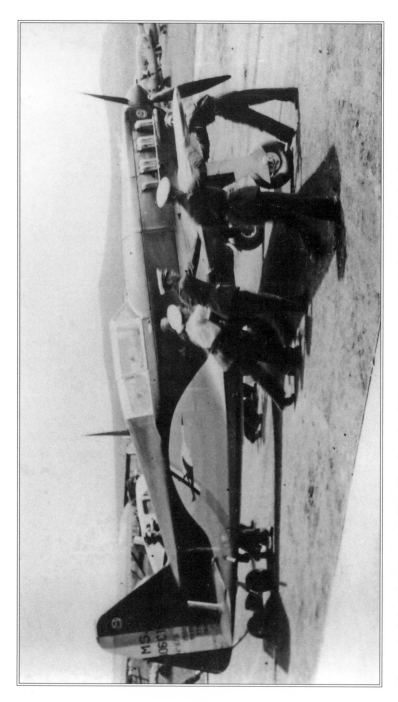

Morane-Saulnier MS 406 Armée de l'Air (French air force) fighter, contemporary but inferior to the Luftwaffe Me-109E.

SHAA Collection.

Bloch 200 heavy bombers with crews at Toulouse in 1935.

SHAA Collection.

RAF Fairey Battle light bomber. Such ungainly aircraft, with a crew of three, were slaughtered in the Battle of France.

RAF Museum.

Front Populaire workers during the occupation of a factory, ca. 1936–1938.

SHAA Collection.

Sir Philip Cunliffe Lister (later Lord Swinton), newly appointed secretary of state for air, seated at his desk at the Air Ministry, 1935.

Charles Brown Collection, RAF Museum.

Aerial view of Handley Page Heyfords of 7 Squadron on the ground at RAF Finningley, 1936, while this permanent station was under construction.

Charles Brown Collection, RAF Museum.

Hawker Fury I aircraft of 1 Squadron in flight, RAF Tangmere, 1937—the best of the biplane fighters.

Charles Brown Collection, RAF Museum.

Pilots of 601 [County of London (F)] Squadron Auxiliary Air Force standing in front of Hawker Demons, Hendon, 1938.

Charles Brown Collection, RAF Museum.

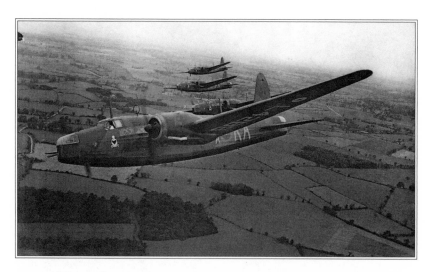

Vickers Wellington I aircraft of 9 Squadron in flight, RAF Stradishall, 1939.

Charles Brown Collection, RAF Museum.

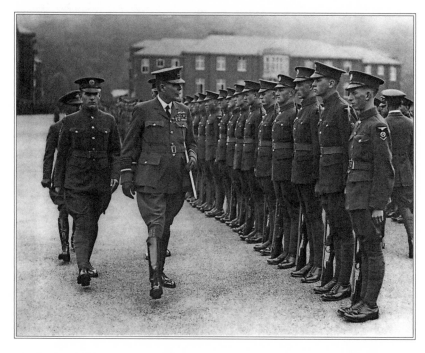

Air Chief Marshal Sir Hugh Trenchard inspecting the First Entry at Halton, 1922.

RAF Museum Collection.

Secretary of state for air,
Lord Weir of Eastwood.

RAF Museum Collection.

Secretary of state for air,
Lt. Col. Samuel J. G. Hoare,
ca. 1920s.

RAF Museum Collection.

Hawker Hurricane I of 111 Squadron with two-bladed wooden propellers as sent to France in 1939–1940.

Charles Brown Collection, RAF Museum.

A Hurricane on loan to the USAAF test center at Wright Field, Ohio, in September 1941.

USAF photo.

Franco-British Staff Talks

As important as the air forces themselves, the aircraft industry and the special parts of the infrastructure such as airfields, guns, and RDF were the development of staff talks between the two air forces. They were essential in the creation of a unified front under a cohesive command. As the records of the Anglo-French staff talks show, this was where various practical matters had to be agreed upon. Both sides were reluctant to be frank and it is quite obvious that their approaches and readiness differed considerably.

In 1937 the British Air Attaché in Paris had consulted the Deuxième Bureau as to the Luftwaffe and suitable targets. In February 1938 the Cabinet authorized secret technical talks between the air forces on aerodromes and other facilities in France. But there was considerable reluctance on both sides to talk. Attempts to widen Anglo-French talks during 1936–1939 to military and naval staffs were quashed by the British chiefs of staff because no BEF was then contemplated, for "we could deal adequately with Germany by ourselves."[28]

One important legacy of World War I was the need for Home air defense. The 1918 system of meeting raids was perfected through paper and real air exercises on which the new monoplane fighters, RDF, and sector control could be grafted in time for a successful air defense in the summer of 1940.[29] Conversations proceeded in early 1938, therefore, not regarding a BEF, but rather regarding a German "knock-out blow" against industrial Britain. The chiefs of staff restricted the talks because of Britain's numerical weakness that would preclude any help to France except that which would also aid British defense. So talks focused on the movement of Bomber Command's AASF to France and its protection there, and on the coordination of air-defense systems.

The Cabinet ultimately accepted the consideration of a BEF and of naval talks limited to attaché level. By the end of December 1938, plans to dispatch two divisions to France were almost complete, as were those for the AASF, which would have twenty squadrons with an initial establishment of sixteen aircraft each, to be based on ten main and ten satellite airfields. The AASF was not promised as an aid to the Armée de Terre, but rather was to be sent as a matter of range. Once Bomber Command received the new "ideal" heavies, it would not need the AASF in France to hit Germany.

The Chamberlain visit to Paris in November 1938 made it obvious that longer talks were needed. There were as yet no Anglo-French plans for command or operations in war to fulfill the obligations under the Locarno peace treaties to aid France against German aggression.[30] Paris assured London that if the main blow fell upon England, French aerodromes would still be available. On 2 February 1939 the Cabinet endorsed the assessment that in view of likely Italian hostility, wider talks should take place not only with France, but also with Belgium and if possible the Netherlands.

Arrangements were now made by the chiefs of staff from which there could be no pulling back. The 1939 conversations dealt with grand strategy. As to command management, detailed administrative arrangements for the move to France were put in 1938 in close touch with War Office 3 (the Liaison) at the Air Ministry.[31] Thus all arrangements were well advanced by the 1939 conversations regarding routing, recognition, supply and storage, maintenance, signals, air defense coordination, and ancillary services. The final administrative plan was *SD107*. Communications links were established, especially to Fighter Command and Bomber Command, and a new cross-Channel cable was to be laid via the British Jersey Island, off the coast of Normandy.

Anglo-French staff conversations in the spring of 1939 were in general terms and based on the idea of the war they thought they would face.[32] They had their origin in the joint talks inspired by the German occupation of the Rhineland in March 1936, but these had been circumscribed by Whitehall's instructions to make no commitments. Information about the strengths of the air forces and the availability of aerodromes was exchanged.

The British were represented by the Joint Planning Committee in lieu of the chiefs of staff themselves. Group Capt. J. C. Slessor, director of Plans, and his deputy, together with the air attaché in Paris, faced the two French GSAF delegates. The British were instructed that if Germany attacked France, Britain would dispatch the ACBEF. Britain would not initiate attacks on the enemy civilian population, and, finally, RDF could be revealed to the French, but any components would be manufactured in Great Britain.

Grand strategies being very similar, it was quickly agreed—defensive against a short war, protective of industry and sea-lanes, and a search for allies, especially the United States. The second phase would be to eliminate Italy first in Africa and to build the British land forces on the Continent while bombing industrial and economic objectives in Germany. Last, there would be the tough struggle to eliminate Germany.[33]

At this time the stated strengths were 488 RAF bombers of more than three hundred miles operational radius at Home, 496 fighters, and 222 reconnaissance (84 Army Cooperation), for a total in Great Britain of 1,290 machines, as opposed to the French 336 "long-range" bombers, 466 *chasse*, 324 *aviation d'assaut*, and 324 reconnaissance, for a total of 1,450, easily supplemented by aircraft in North Africa. To these the RAF added 100 percent reserves of bombers, but none of fighters. Yet the Armée de l'Air figures were misleading, as almost all of their 336 bombers were obsolescent, and of the 466 *chasse*, 106 were for "local defense."

In May 1939 two stocks of British bombs and pyrotechnics were in the Reims area, and a translated copy of the French air staff note regarding the establishment of the AASF in France was ready on 1 May 1939. But the Allied first-line totals of 824 bombers, 856 fighters/*chasse*, and 954 *aviation d'assaut* and reconnaissance were opposed to the 2,344 bombers, 1,450 fighters, and 1,299 *aviation d'assaut* and reconnaissance German and Italian aircraft, backed, it was believed, by 100 percent reserves. The French could not claim to have been deceived.

In the course of the Anglo-French staff talks on 27 February 1939 it was agreed that the RAF would visit on 1 March the proposed air stores park site at the Château de Romont near the Rilly railhead in the Reims area. As part of a move to France, the RAF expected to fly fifty civil planes each day for five weeks, refueling at Reims. French works could not fill RAF oxygen bottles to 3,800 pounds per square inch (U.S.), and so the British would only send those to be filled to 1,800 pounds per square inch, and a sample bottle would be sent (in a diplomatic bag!) so the French could make the needed connections.

The salvage section would move with the advanced party of five hundred (agreed on 9 September 1938) and be supplied at Reims with four light trucks to have a two thousand–kilogram useful load, one liaison car, together with ropes, chains, planks, tarpaulins, and hoisting tackle. The *gendarmerie* would guard broken-down British airplanes the same as they would guard French machines. The British asked for trenches to be dug within two weeks after the opening of hostilities to protect the five hundred advanced party airmen, and for the casualty clearing stations. The French said they would see. There was also to be an exchange of Met information in time of war. As to auxiliary aerodromes, one for each main base, the French told the British that it was not possible to supply these as they were only selected in times of peace and had neither personnel nor matériel, nor had the ground been claimed. On the other hand, once rough-and-ready work had been done, airplanes could land there if their main aerodrome had been damaged by bombing.[34]

Already Hitler had laid Munich in ruins by seizing Prague. The British had responded on 29 March, the day the conversations opened, by doubling the size of the Territorial Army, and two days later, in April, with the guarantee to Poland following the Military Service Act. The situation called for renewed Anglo-French consultations, which took place from 24 April until 3 May. It also heralded acrimonious debate between the War Office and the Air Ministry over the number of Army Cooperation squadrons to be sent with the newly expanded BEF.

While it was hoped Poland could occupy the Germans for some time and that potential Polish air force attacks on Berlin and other places would fix both flak and fighter forces, a lot depended on Soviet aid because the Western Allies could help neither Poland nor Romania directly. The British placed less faith than did the French in the Russians, who were recuperating from their involvement in Spain.

The air discussions dealt with British bombers collaborating with both the Armée de l'Air and the Allied armies to delay a German advance through the Low Countries. This was agreed to be the RAF's primary role, to create bottlenecks under French direction. The French argued for attacks on the rail network, but the RAF asserted that even using 80 percent of the force available and with 15 percent hits not enough damage would befall enemy railways to slow traffic.[35] Moreover, a minimum of six medium or three heavy bombers would be needed to make a breach on an open line, and such a breach could be repaired in four hours. The French plan involved making ninety-nine cuts, far beyond the bomber force's capacity, and vitiated by the dense rail network in northwest Germany and the Low Countries. The British argued (and Slessor in his 1936 *Air Power and Armies* had studied the World War I results) that better rail targets were defiles and embankments.[36] Village defiles would involve civilian casualties.

After considering desiderata such as rapidity of communication, central field intelligence, and maps covering coded targets selected to block motorized columns, the talks turned to action against the Luftwaffe and its infrastructure to reduce the scale of attack on France and Britain. But an attack on aerodromes was not likely to be profitable and would be costly due to the high state of German aerodrome defenses, large numbers of such potential targets, and the disparity between the air forces. If necessity demanded it, the French would attack south and the British north of the Saarbrucken-Wiesbaden-Frankfurt-Eisenach line. The Armée de l'Air argued for general attacks on aerodrome surfaces due to enemy airfield defenses. The RAF held that these would be of little use; only aircraft and hangars were useful targets. (In fact in the Battle of Britain, as long as British Army manpower was available, grass airfields were quickly repairable.) The AIR (Air Ministry and RAF Records) 41/21 report states, "In general it was clear that the allies pinned no great faith in attacks on aerodromes, though the French were more optimistic than the British."[37]

Bombing German war industry was the subject simply of general discussion and was left to the air staffs to work out. The British proposed only to attack "military" targets in the first phase of the war, leaving oil and synthetics to the second phase. In general, discussion of this topic was in its infancy. The conference then went on to consider selected "military" objectives if the Germans did not start with "unrestricted air attack." The RAF said that these should be chosen by the air staffs in conjunction with the general staffs. The Hague Conventions of 1899 and 1907 existed—the international treaties dealing with the moral and human conduct of war and in theory limited attacks on civilians.[38] But a fair proportion of the population in a modern war is engaged in the armaments industry or support activities.

After air aid to Poland, the only such wartime aid possible had been ruled out; when neutral opinion was considered, the air staff considered oil to be the best target.[39] Then late in April Gamelin reneged on the 1938 promise to protect the BEF disembarking and assembling and asked London to do it. Britain would eventually supply four fighter squadrons and three heavy AA regiments (seventy-two guns), three light batteries (thirty-six guns), and two light AA regiments, plus one searchlight battalion to handle this. At this time only one fighter squadron was mobile, and thus the British would not be able to implement the 1940 program to protect British forces in France. In April the French pressed for more British fighters for northern France in order to launch an air attack against Italy from Tunisia. London said it could not do it then, but in war it would reconsider. And regarding gas attacks, the French were more apprehensive than the British and were less well-prepared.[40]

An exchange of missions was agreed, with No. 1 Air Mission to go to Vuillemin's HQ and No. 2 to Mouchard's. Z day was to be that on which British mobilization orders would be issued.[41] The quantities of petrol (gasoline), oil, and lubricants (POL) that the AASF required to be attained by Z + 19 totaled 40,000 hectolitres (105,600 U.S. gallons), with 2,000 hectolitres of oil. The French needed to know at which aerodromes and at what times of day fuel would be needed.

Since the ACBEF arrived later, due to a subsequent government decision, its arrival would not be nearly as tough to serve as it would be within the normal framework of the army supply and communications system. Within twenty-six days of mobilization, twenty bomber squadrons of the AASF together with two bomber-reconnaissance, six Army Cooperation, and four fighter squadrons of the ACBEF would be in France.[42]

During 28–31 August there was a third round of Anglo-French air staff talks in the face of the Polish crisis. Slessor was replaced by Air Vice Marshal D. C. S. Evill, followed by "more regular methods of wartime liaison and coordination."[43] By late August the Air Ministry in London had instructed the Allied commander as a matter of expediency and not legality to limit bombing to purely military objectives in the narrowest sense of that word (to aid Poland, the French attacked enemy aerodromes). In general, the commanders accepted facts and "adopted a policy that was natural and sensible in the circumstances."[44] But there was little stress on the urgency to make a great national effort in production to make use of time. London resolved that, without Soviet backing, the Poles would be destroyed, so the Allies pledged to restore their territory after the war.[45] And there was doubt that the air menace was as great as some had thought.[46] During these August conversations it was decided to make three more RAF squadrons mobile, as their rigidity was a handicap and a hazard. The divergence in views on this led to the Air Council being brought into the conversations.

Munich

Daladier let the British lead at Munich and was willing to take all steps to avoid a war for which France was not prepared. He was joined in his pro-Munich stand by the Appeasers, but did his abandonment of Czechoslovakian strength pay? As Winston Churchill said later of Chamberlain, he had a choice between war and dishonor, chose dishonor, and got war.[47] Though in 1939 Daladier had become a man readying France for war with new tanks and aircraft, the new confidence crumbled before the blitzkrieg in May 1940. After decades of debate, by the twenty-first century the cause of the French defeat was neither simply German military prowess nor French political betrayal. Among the complex causes, pacifism was strong throughout France, and in the Western democracies in general. The French government, in addition, failed to counter German propaganda, in part because public relations still was not a normal tool at the time, and the German embassy was paying Parisian newspapers to use his country's propaganda.[48]

On 29 September 1938 the French had 1.221 million men under arms when Hitler, Chamberlain, Daladier, and Mussolini met to settle the six-month old Czech crisis started by Hitler's Austrian Anschluss of March. During the critical days of 10–13 March 1938, France had no government. And when Daladier came in on 14 March he refused to advocate Foreign Minister Paul-Boncour's policy of supporting Poland and Czechoslovakia with their French-trained armies. Daladier needed the Front Populaire to stay in power and so could not act in France's best interests to get a rapprochement with Mussolini's Fascist Italy. The new French foreign minister was the devious Georges Bonnet, who deceived Whitehall as well as the Poles and the Czechs. Bonnet was a defeatist who thought British policy both wise and intelligent; he did not expect England to support his country.

Anglo-French talks between Daladier, Bonnet, and the Chamberlain government lacked the backing of a viable military pact, the Locarno peace treaties being, in effect, dead. France's effectiveness versus Germany was limited by the need to face Italy along the Alps and in North Africa, and uncertainty both as to what the Little Entente could do as well as to how the British Empire would react in the circumstances. The Soviet Union was thought to be unreliable, sapped by the Stalinist purges. Chamberlain would not go beyond British public opinion and saw an Anglo-French preventive war as only a last resort. Bonnet then said France would honor its pledges if Czechoslovakia lost Teschen to Poland and Slovakia to Hungary.

Meanwhile, President Edvard Beneš in Prague did not trust the Little Entente and thought the Poles would not help. The Russian ambassador in London suggested that the French try to persuade Warsaw to let Russian troops cross Poland. The alternative was a route across Romania, which Bucharest feared. French journalist Henri Nogueres' view, in *Munich: Peace in Our Time,* was that London had engaged in May 1938 in "the hesitation waltz." But after Foreign Secretary Lord Halifax's pledge to aid France if Hitler attacked, the German dictator backed off on 23 May.[49]

On 8 August 1938 the chief of the French GSAF, Vuillemin, visited Germany, where Goering put on displays that dismayed the French general. Vuillemin told his ambassador as he left the Luftwaffe chief's Karin Hall hunting lodge that if war came at the end of September there would not be a single French plane left after a fortnight, a prediction he repeated in Paris again on 24 August before going to spend summer vacation with the Bonnet family.[50]

Chamberlain seized the initiative by visiting Hitler, and on his return briefed Daladier and Bonnet in London. In the end there was to be no plebiscite, but the Czechs would cede the 1 million Deutsch people in the Sudentenland to Germany. The French were pleased they had managed to engage the British.

In Paris, both Gamelin and Vuillemin opposed war; the Soviet position was unclear, and Paris persuaded Prague not to mobilize. Military inadequacies there were a result of French failures, and Bonnet was unaware that the Czechs and Germans had a 1,250-mile frontier. French policy was based on awareness (only on the part of Daladier and Bonnet) of the Czech military. Now faced with an ultimatum not from Berlin but from Paris and London, the Hobson's choice was either war or oblivion. On 21 September Churchill was in Paris and believed that Beneš should have manned his fortress line so as to make France come to his aid and Britain to go to France's. After Munich, a divided France greeted Daladier with relief.

The result of the Munich Agreement was that France lost face in central Europe and that its safety, said Nogueres, largely depended on Britain. Nogueres called Munich "the phoney peace."[51] The Poles realized that the Anglo-French guarantee of the spring of 1939 was valueless. In Paris there was euphoria as the "war party" had been overcome, but with the relief there was uneasiness. By not taking a firm stand, France sacrificed both peace and security. Chamberlain in London, however, was unashamed, having declared "peace in our time." But Parliament opposed his appeasement. The public told Daladier in Paris that because for three years he had been war minister, he could not blame Munich for France's impotence. Beneš resigned in October just as Hitler began plans to destroy the rump of his state. By late February Germany declared that Eastern Europe was no longer an Anglo-French but a German concern. And on 15 March 1939 the Germans occupied Prague.

Hitler had been the realist. The Anglo-French dreamers had sacrificed some thirty Czech divisions and a 1,500-aircraft Czech air force, as well as forty-five motorized Soviet divisions of uncertain quality. The Czechs had one thousand pilots versus the Armée de l'Air's perhaps eight hundred. In the end, it was a German psychological and propaganda victory over the West, whose leaders did not see eye to eye, did not like each other, and still lacked the faith to be able to stand firm. Munich fitted in the old European diplomatic pattern of sacrificing the pawns to save the kings.[52]

What is noticeable in the two roads to war is that the French took a different route than did the British, not because of their continental position but because of their culture and perceptions, so that they initiated ideas but did not follow them with orders. In contrast, the British used their committee-mindedness to seek evidence and solutions followed by action as far as fiscal limits would allow.

Other Developments and Staff Talks

In much of this work we have been concerned with the air forces and their supporting aircraft industry, as well as with the omnipresent diplomatic, political, and economic background. Of equal importance, and also consumers of manpower, money, and materials, were four interlinked ground-bound aspects of airpower—airfields, POL, early warning systems, and AA/DCA. The difference between the French and the British approach to war is reflected in their cultural and organizational approaches to defense.

Airfields, 1918–1940

Airfields are one other very important matter that has to be examined in this comparison and contrast of the French and British air forces on the road to 1940. France had five major air bases in 1934, one with a 1,100-yard concrete runway and the others with grass runways; the RAF in Britain had fifty-two permanent stations.[53]

With rainfall in northeast France at only twenty-five inches per acre annually, and most aircraft still able to operate from small fields, the pressure of finances precluded the concrete revolution that the RAF embarked on in the late 1930s. Like the Luftwaffe's aircraft, French machines were designed to operate from grass. When the ACBEF landed in France in September 1939, it complained that in many cases it was allotted former World War I airfields, many nothing more than pastures, lacking even the most primitive necessities such as cookhouses, toilets, and communications. Moreover, on the one hand, both the ACBEF and the AASF lacked motor transport (MT), RDF, and Fighter Command cover. On the other hand, the RAF was not very bothered by the above as it assumed, as did the French, that the war would resume in 1918 fashion.[54]

One of the Armée de l'Air difficulties during the Battle of France was that there were more than two hundred "airfields" in northeast France with many different types of aircraft, making the whole a logistical nightmare. Moreover, C$_3$ broke down rapidly as the communications net was the public telephone system, about which the British complained that a priority call took four hours to be connected.[55] Even Gamelin did not have a wireless set in his HQ. This failure to provide the basic needs of a fighting force has to be laid on the shoulders of Armée de l'Air leaders and staff, as well as on the Ministère des Finances.

There was the need to expand and harden airfields for the rapidly rising weight and speeds of aircraft taxiing and taking off (they landed much lightened); in addition, hardstands and hangarage were needed, as well as dispersals and airfield defenses. DCA also increased in weight and rate of fire, and all services as well as aircraft had to be supplied. Very rapidly aviation became a large and complicated business that made serious demands on manpower. As will be seen, the French did a lot of solid experimental work, but though there were numbers of AA guns on both sides, and the French had predictor equipment, the British had the more unified approach and in the end had the significant link to RDF.

In the fall of 1939 the destruction of the Polish air force caused the dispersal of the RAF in France. As of May 1940 the RAF had 59 new airfields under construction in France, but they were not expected to be ready until July 1940. After the end of World War I in 1918 the RAF had 27 airfields at Home. By the start of the new war in 1939 it had 112, the majority of which were the more expensive permanent stations. By September 1939 costs were also rising as concrete runways were installed.[56]

In 1939 the Emergency War Powers (Defence) Act allowed immediate possession of land, with claims deferred until after war's completion. Up to 1935 the Air Ministry Lands Branch had seen each airfield as an individual challenge, and thus there was no effective planning. Expansion coincided with increased demands to keep up with technical developments and domestic requirements including, among others, reserves and RDF.

The sixty new aerodromes of the 1934 program in Britain started out as permanent stations, but after Munich, shortcuts were taken to be able to house and service as many aircraft as possible. Building these new fields proved to be more complex than anticipated. For one thing, they were contemporaries of the Technological Revolution, which brought higher wing loadings, quadrupled maximum aircraft weight, and made greater demands for POL, as well as armaments, and the corresponding needs for specialist shops and skilled workers. And just as in the competing aircraft industry, shortages of manpower had to be overcome and mechanization introduced to save labor. To economize on transportation, the British laid down a major pipeline and storage system for fuel. Such inflammable facilities had to be sited where, if they were bombed, they would damage the airfield as little as possible.

Estimates of POL needs in the mid-1930s turned out to be well below the basic necessity of daily wartime operations. By 1938 the Air Ministry needed storage for 800,000 tons of aviation spirit (gasoline) and 50,000 tons of oil. And demand kept rising, to 2,096,000 tons in September 1943. Estimates were outdated by increasing numbers of aircraft and MT, and the rise in engine horsepower.

One of the keys to rapid expansion was standardization during the early part of the airfield revolution. Not only were buildings and hangars built from standard designs, but the three-runway layout was as well. Still, a significant change had to be made: clustered peacetime layout designs with marching in mind had to be dispersed at the newer airfields because of their vulnerability to bombing. The move coincided with greater availability of MT, but bicycles also played an important role.

Expansion called for durable, but not permanent, buildings that were less expensive to construct than the regular stations and used as few strategic materials as possible. The Air Ministry Design Branch thus became a drawings factory. Its work was complicated by the need to protect against air attack with both active and passive defenses according to the Air Staff's estimates. One basic problem was the lack of bomb-damage data, none having been gathered in World War I. Only in April 1939 did the RAF test its own 500-pound bombs, and these and other trials led to the conclusion that just the key posts at any station could be protected. After a visit to Germany, it was decided that slit trenches outside protected buildings would not do in the British climate and thus proper shelters were developed. Expansion also included, from 1936, new schools and training facilities, aircraft storage units, repair depots, and hospitals.

In other words, the RAF was preparing for war, probably a long one. All in all, in the period from 1934 to 1940 the Air Ministry built or began work on some 123 new or modernized airfields, added accommodations at 207 new sites, and began work on 109 bombing and gunnery ranges. All of this was hardly muddling through, compared to the rational French effort that apparently paid little attention to facilities at all.

Fuel, 1930–1940

It was not until the years of 1930–1937 that the ministries developed major plans to supply the Armée de Terre and the air force with POL in case of war.[57] A reserve of 450,000 tons versus a civil stock of 20,000 tons was to be built up in cooperation with civil companies and placed in protected storage holding 600,000 tons of POL. At the same time, the Armée de l'Air equipped a large number of airfields with refueling facilities. Numerous little depots were established throughout the northeast of France to ease the 1939–1940 deployment of the army, with major depots in North Africa. Also established in France was a pool of railway tank wagons. A 285-mile pipeline from Donges to Amilly was started in 1939, but never completed.

The Comité Permanente de la Défense Nationale decided in November 1937 that the Service des Essences des Armées (military fuel service) should become the Service Interministériel (interministerial service) under the armaments minister. The Service des Essences des Armées since 1928 had served both the Ministère de la Guerre and Ministère de l'Air, and from 1936 had also served the Ministère de la Marine Nationale. From late 1937, commanded by a naval specialist, it embarked on a major expansion. By 10 May 1940 France had its supplies in protective storage and, thanks to the Phoney War, had managed to accumulate sufficient stocks in eleven magazines with 387,000 cubic meters (roughly 280,700 long tons), able to supply sixty-six rail trains or 2.8 million imperial gallons daily.

At the beginning of May 1940 the artillery service could supply 700,000 imperial gallons monthly. Unfortunately here, as in other fields, mobilization deprived the oil companies of exactly those specialists needed to make the system work. Much of the Phoney War was spent trying to get these workers released to the *services de l'essence*.[58]

Across the Channel serious efforts were being made to provide British aerodromes with POL. In spite of starting work on a fueling system in 1936, in the winter of 1939–1940 the Air Ministry was forced to requisition coastal steamers to move aviation spirit. A scheme to use the copious network of canals left from the eighteenth and nineteenth centuries was vetoed when it was realized that the trucks to deliver and recover gasoline from barges would themselves consume too much fuel.[59]

In July 1936 the Air Ministry decided to hold a three-month stock at war consumption rates. While the Air Staff Memorandum No. 50, *SD98*, "Calculations of Wastage and Consumption in War," was used from 1936 on as a basis for planning, it proved to have much underestimated consumption because increased horsepower alone required larger amounts of gasoline.

In 1938 the railways moved 250,000 tons of POL monthly. By September 1939 the Air Ministry owned 350 tank cars. Civilian firms were used to haul POL from distribution points to airfields, the necessity being to schedule drivers to the maximum. Thus it was that both the French and the British had anticipated wartime needs, but French demand fell off dramatically after June 1940 whereas British requirements rose slowly until the ground and air offensives in 1944.

The Problem of Antiaircraft Defense in France

DCA weapons were distinctly different from the more conventional stores sought at a leisurely pace by the director of artillery. Air attack was the most widely viewed concern of the interwar years. The focus was clearly the bomber, and that was a public matter. Bombing was likely not to be limited to military areas, but to spill over onto civilians.[60] AA/DCA was thus a common concern, but preparations were not complete by 10 May 1940.

In 1939 France air defense was nonexistent. In 1931 the army position of inspector general of the DAT had been created; in 1935 it was shifted to the Ministère de l'Air, and in 1938 to the inspector general fighters, which had no funds. The DCA guns remained as passive defense under the Ministère de l'Intérieur (ministry of the interior), within the Ministère de la Guerre, and communications under the Postes, Télégraphes, et Téléphones (French post office). In spite of the fact that there had been awareness of an aerochemical threat since 1928, nothing had been done regarding air defense—no aircraft, no DCA, and no air-raid-precautions organization. The French had talked about it, but had taken no action. Therefore French DCA defense was not a problem for the German attackers in May 1940.

DCA was first started by the naval architect Dupuy de Lôme in the 1860s. Shortly thereafter Deville was made inspector general of autocannon as well as inspector general of the army's artillery.[61]

By then the technical problem had arisen of increased aircraft speeds, so that there was no longer time to correct a first shot. Work began in 1915 to measure heights by theodolites linked by telephone; this was haphazard when the front was being bombarded, but the French soon could measure the ground speed and direction as well as the altitude of approaching enemy aircraft. By 1918 all autocannon sections had an improved apparatus, but indirect fire, as opposed to that aimed at the estimated future position of the target, was not pursued.

Searchlights were produced unsuccessfully to oppose the zeppelin attacks of early 1916; only in 1917, however, were listening devices developed. By the end of the war, DCA consisted mostly of the 75-mm guns aimed optically. Success had risen from 85 enemies shot down in 1916 to 260 in 1918. After the 1914–1918 war it was necessary to form a DCA gunnery school. This practical course for DCA was established at Metz, where, since the War of 1870–1871, there had been a school of application for artillery. It functioned until the 1939 war.[62]

Due to the Treaty of Versailles, not until 1925 was DCA work renewed. The 1917 rapid-firing Hotchkiss machine gun was then taken up, and the 13.5-mm adapted as the Model 1930 with a *connecteur* (link to a machine) that could predict the route and speed of the target. It was tested and adopted in 1934 and series production was ordered that same year. The Hotchkiss 25-mm did not satisfactorily pass its tests until 1938–1939 and was then adopted as Model 1940, but series production began only at the

1940 Armistice dénouement. The 1925 commission had found its 20-mm superseded by the Oerlikon 20-mm from Switzerland and the Bofors 40-mm from Sweden. The Bofors had a 130-rounds-per-minute rate of fire and a sensitive fuse. However, as the laying system was judged poorer, it was replaced with the French 40CA Model 1939, though due to the lateness of the placing of orders, none had been delivered before the Armistice of June 1940. The 1925 Commission also looked into heavy DCA guns.

Evolution of the light gun was slow and it was only adopted as *matériel de 75 CA sur remarque model* (75-mm DCA gun revised) 1917–1934 with production beginning in 1935 at Puteaux. The modern 75 was similarly adapted on a trailer as Model 1930, and the Ministère de la Guerre ordered batteries of thirty-three guns each. Concurrently the authorities ordered a semimobile 75 for thirty-five batteries in 1931, and two years later fifty batteries of a Schneider model. Only this latter was to go into production on mobilization and would be issued to higher commands. In 1939 production was started, but only thirty to forty guns per month were being delivered at the time of the Armistice of 24 June 1940. The 1935 Schneider mobile DCA gun was not adopted until April 1940, too late for production. In the meantime, Schneider had developed a naval 90-mm DCA for coastal defense, but of the 120 batteries ordered, only 7 had been delivered by late June 1940.

The French, however, had made great progress in directors, with optical range finding perfected in 1919–1924. Several electrical and mechanical means were suggested, the winner being a small set tested at Toulon in 1931 and adopted in 1934 as the *poste central de tir direct* (center for direct fire) Model 1934; 150 were issued to the army in 1937. In a parallel development, one of General Pagezy's 1916 ideas was refined to use "tele transmissions" for long-distance ranging. This was approved in 1932; thirty-four sets were produced for mobile, and the next year eighty-five sets were issued for semimobile batteries.

In 1935 it was found that a single day-and-night director could be fitted to most guns up to 90-mm, and 190 sets were ordered without a prototype stage. Nevertheless, deliveries were stopped by the Armistice. New 1938-design searchlights also had not been delivered by then. Sound locators were ordered during 1933–1934, and others studied up to 1940.

In April 1939 a French mission visited the British RDF establishment at Bawdsey and saw for the first time the new RDF system. The idea had been known in France as early as 1927 and studied on the basis of emission from aircraft-engine magnetos. In 1935 the military wireless service undertook a new series of investigations of emissions and reflections from the new all-metal aircraft. However, the significance was not understood in France, and it was only in March 1940 that serious work began in that country. Joyau in his 1950 article makes no reference either to doctrine or to the basis of the numbers ordered.[63] The army's failure to order the excellent DCA guns developed in 1922 and its neglect of the training of its troops to resist air attack cost it dearly in 1940.

Ack-Ack in Britain

The development of antiaircraft (AA, or ack-ack) guns, detection, and direction in Britain remained in the charge of the Royal Artillery. Gun making was under the master general of the ordnance with manufacturing at the Woolwich Arsenal, the depot at which gunners and sappers (engineers) were trained, officers who played a significant role in the British Army.[64]

In the mid-1930s the British Army was still equipped with 1918 guns and attitudes, though the interest was there for better material, with guns effective above a 17,000-foot ceiling of the 1918 3-inch 20-hundred-weight gun. For heavy guns the new caliber would be 4.7 inches. This emphasis on Home defense overshadowed the need for mobile AA power for the BEF, yet the latter needed guns to defend bases and lines of communication. Mobility was needed at Home, also, to allow flexibility in the defenses. The anxieties of 1934 and of Rearmament forced the Army Council to make decisions, and both the multiplying needs of the Field Force and of the ADGB stimulated the two sides of air defense.

The fundamental assumption in London was that Germany would launch the whole of its air fleet against Britain to cripple it, and thus to plan for anything else would be foolish. The Air Ministry in 1937 believed the only effective way to prevent the Luftwaffe from dropping two thousand tons daily from 1939 was by air attack on the enemy, by fighters on his bombers, and by bombers on his immediate aircraft reserves, parks (aircraft storage), and aircraft factories. The Luftwaffe's effectiveness could be blunted by protection of the community and the supply system through such passive measures as dispersion, elasticity, and air raid precautions. The army and AA played a secondary role, to divert and render harmless enemy attacks with the guns and fighters linked under the operational control of AOC-in-C Fighter Command. Gun development followed both the need for a rapid-fire weapon for up to 12,000 feet and a heavy gun for the 20,000–30,000-foot levels. Time being of the essence, the Swedish Bofors mobile 40-mm, firing 120 two-pound shells per minute, was adopted, and then its ammunition modified. But the British model weighed 2.4 tons compared to the German 1.7.

The 4.7-inch gun had been tested in 1933 and 1934 and found, at twenty-two tons, to be virtually immobile. In the meantime, the 3.7-inch had been designed and tenders called for. Concurrently the Admiralty wanted the 4.7-inch both for mounting on ships and for the defense of ports. So as to simplify ammunition supply, the War Office accepted this request and took some 4.7-inch guns, but modernized 3-inch guns were also in army hands by the outbreak of war.

Still well before the war, AA was readied, and the research continued on flashless powder and on tracer ammunition. Work also was done on unrotated projectiles—rockets. By 1936 these were seen as useful in war, and thus a Ballistic Research Department was created with focus toward the ADGB, controlled by the ministerial Air Defence Research Committee of the CID. By the end of 1938 both the Admiralty and the War Office were pushing manufacture ahead, but development proceeded slowly until after Dunkirk in June 1940.

In the meantime, predictor accuracy was being revolutionized by RDF. A primitive form of this method of fire control was available in September 1939; when put to the test in July and August 1940 the deficiencies were found to be almost completely quantitative and not qualitative.

During the years after Versailles, minute budgets and political disinterest meant that little attention was paid to AA defense other than that associated with the ADGB and the persistent work of Maj. Gen. E. B. Ashmore on the early-warning system. Not only the Ten Year Rule, but also the view that there would be no continental commitment and thus no BEF severely limited the War Office. As a result, in 1935 Britain lacked AA guns capable of dealing with either high- or low-flying modern aircraft. Nevertheless, from this year on the rapidly expanding Territorial Army was charged with ack-ack defense. National manpower requirements, however, had not been sorted out after the 1925 Steel-Bartholomew Committee report on needs. Yet by 1939, in theory the AA component of the Territorial Army was a corps of five divisions. The Munich mobilization exposed all these weaknesses.

On the tactical planning side, London had built on the 1918 establishment of air defenses with the 1923 Steel-Bartholomew Committee proposals to defend the capital with fighters and guns, the latter in both inner and outer artillery zones. Such a scheme was also to be applied to the major ports. Steel-Bartholomew reckoned that 264 guns and 672 searchlights would be needed. Plenty of guns were in store, but the necessary brigades were unmanned. The fifty-two-squadron HDAF agreed in 1923, and the wide-ranging Romer Committee report, together with the creation of ADGB and the recruiting of a new Observer Corps, were not fully implemented.

Complicating defense problems was the speed of the modern bomber. Acoustic mirrors did not provide the hoped-for increase in early warning of approaching raiders, and all-metal aircraft were not lethally damaged by the four-gun fighter. Before RDF was known, Prime Minister Baldwin was correct in stating, after French visitors in 1931 had evaded their greeting escort, that the bomber would always get through. The only defensive solution would have to be standing patrols, which would soon ground squadrons due to high flying hours leading to unserviceability. Thus the defense of Great Britain had to combine a strong bomber deterrent with diplomatic appeasement. It proved internationally impossible to ban bombers, and the Disarmament Conference, 1932–1934, caused a lull in other action.

In the fall of 1933 the government appointed the Defence Requirements Committee–Treasury, Foreign Office, and the three chiefs of staff. The committee quickly concluded that Germany was likely to be a formidable air menace and recommended that the BEF should have two AA brigades. Once it was clear that Germany was the likely enemy, the Reorientation

Committee under the AOC-in-C, ADGB, reported early in 1935 and upheld the continuous defense-zone concept. The War Office intended to allot 88 guns and 174 searchlights to the air defense of Manchester, Sheffield, Leeds, and Birmingham. The new plan increased the Romer figures from 218 to 456 guns and from 624 to 2,100 searchlights. Though the Observer Corps was expanded, the real problem remained early warning. Faced as always with fiscal restraints, the Reorientation Committee proposed a three-stage approach to be completed by 1942. However, the government limited it to completion of Stage 1 in 1940. At the same time, by cutting the Defence Requirements Committee's recommendations for the army, the Cabinet deprived the War Office of the means to provide the Territorial Army to man the needed air defenses. But at least definitive objectives had been set. At this point, the Air Staff was willing to separate fighters and guns from the ultimate bomber deterrent, whose commander would be freed to choose offensive objectives. And so the 1936 functional commands came into being, with Fighter Command having operational control of fighters, guns, and lights. From 14 July 1936 Air Marshal Sir High Dowding led the change from experimental to active preparation for an emergency.

Meanwhile in 1935, on the recommendation of ADGB, the Anti-Aircraft Research Committee had been revived and resulted in both the CSSAD and the ADGB committee. On 26 February R. A. Watson-Watt of the National Physical Laboratory demonstrated to Dowding, then AMSR, the feasibilities of detecting aircraft by radio waves. As noted in the RDF section below, progress was rapid.

In the fall of 1935, the crisis with Italy caused almost all the AA ammunition in Britain to be shipped to the Mediterranean, leaving Home air defense in a perilous state. At the same time, the secret knowledge of RDF made it clear that the Steel-Bartholomew and Romer plans would have to be modified, and therefore an artillery zone was no longer needed and was abolished in 1936. The guns saved were rapidly absorbed elsewhere. Concurrently, 450 balloons were sanctioned for the defense of London against low-flying aircraft. This led to an analysis and list of British targets to determine those that were vital, that needed protection against air attack. Of the two hundred or so listed, twenty-five were inspected and recommendations made. In addition, the requirements for heavy AA guns were raised to 648, with 2,547 searchlights in the 1936 review. At that moment, however, there were in fact roughly 60 useable guns and 120 searchlights in Britain.

Intelligence of the growth of the Luftwaffe soon clearly indicated the RAF's inferior position. The appointment of Sir Thomas Inskip as minister for the Co-ordination of Defence led to his request to Dowding, head of Fighter Command, for an "ideal scheme" for the air defense of Britain regardless of cost. The response called for 45 fighter squadrons, 1,264 guns, and 4,700 searchlights. This had enormously far-reaching implications. In the summer of 1937 the CID gave approval in principle to the ideal scheme. Shortly thereafter the Air Ministry introduced Scheme L for 12,000 aircraft by the spring of 1940 to fight in the face of odds. Business as usual was no longer the watchword.

In 1936 the War Office warned the government that there would be a long delay before the new 3.7- and 4.7-inch AA guns would be available. These were just beginning to appear early in 1938, but production was slow due to shortages of skilled labor and materials. Refurbished 3-inch guns were scarce and incapable of dealing with modern aircraft.

In the Munich deployment of the fall of 1938, only 142 barrage balloons of the 450 for London were in place, and only one-third of the guns and lights demanded in 1937 were ready, though 50,000 men of the Territorial Army responded. Some guns would not work and others lacked suitable ammunition or equipment. Only roughly fifty 3.7- and 4.7-inch modern guns were operational.

The lesson of Munich for the air defenses was that a knockout blow would preempt a bomber offensive. The secretary of state for air at once promulgated Scheme M, in which priority went to having fifty fighter squadrons ready in the spring of 1939 and with full reserves a year later. Fighter Command also received Auxiliary Air Force squadrons from Bomber Command. Salvage and repair of damaged aircraft was organized, and Group Pools (later operational training units) relieved squadrons of schooling new intakes in the spring of 1939. By that summer there were two hundred modern fighters in reserve giving hope that the gap between resources and wastage would be closed. Also by the spring of 1939, 570 heavy AA guns and 2,000 searchlights were ready for deployment, but only 60 percent of the planned RDF stations and Observer Corps, for there was a severe shortage of trained operators for both RDF and balloons.

On the outbreak of war the newly reorganized Anti-Aircraft Command had only one-third of the heavy guns and one-eighth of the light guns needed. For eons the master general of the ordnance had been in charge of guns, and in the twentieth century had a seat on the army council and was directly responsible to the CIGS. The continuity of development was reflected in stability of personnel; the same gunner carried out the wishes of the master general of the ordnance during 1938–1945, tacking previous competence to wartime mastery.[65]

Radio Direction Finding

The Canadian David Zimmerman has studied the development of radar (then known as radio direction finding, or RDF) in Britain, including RAF command and control.[66] Moreover, as John Ferris has recorded, the air defense system was developed by Maj. Gen. E. B. Ashmore from 1917 to 1929 so that when RDF began suddenly to become available, Dowding as AOC-in-C Fighter Command from 1936 was able to integrate it into an already existing system in which warnings were given by the Royal Observer Corps.[67] Dowding then proved the system with a series of annual air exercises in 1938 and 1939.[68] In the 1914–1918 war, scientists had been introduced to the problems of air defense and had developed sound locators.[69]

In February 1923 Air Cdre. J. M. Steel and Col. W. H. Bartholomew rendered their joint Air Ministry–War Office report. This followed closely Ashmore's 1918 London Air Defence Area approach and remained the basic schema into which RDF would be fitted. Owing to the time defending fighters needed to reach the bombers' altitude, the Steel-Bartholomew scheme had an outer observer belt, an outer artillery zone, an aerial fighting zone, and an inner artillery zone. The aerial fighting zone was thirty-five miles from the coast to allow fighters time to climb to 14,000 feet.[70]

In 1924 the ADGB Command was created and the CID appointed the Antiaircraft Research Subcommittee. From 1925 to 1935 large two hundred–foot acoustical mirrors were tested, but these were abandoned as soon as the first tests showed that RDF was feasible.

In 1932 the new TR-9 R/T set was introduced, which allowed fighters to talk between aircraft up to five miles distant and to a ground station up to thirty-five miles away. However, the air exercises of the early 1930s were unrealistic because bombers flew with their lights on and even gave wireless position reports; in addition, the exercises were cancelled if the weather was murky.[71]

Senior RAF officers knew that high-speed bombers were in the specification stages. In 1935 most of Britain began to come within range of 250 miles per hour German bombers flying at 20,000 feet, which meant that the defending fighter needed seventy miles' notice. Meanwhile, in 1934 the Air Ministry formed the CSSAD, chaired by Henry Tizard, who had had long experience in aeronautical research and was also an expert chairman. In January 1935 the AOC-in-C of the ADGB called for a committee to examine the whole of British, not just London's, air defenses. Shortly thereafter Baldwin appointed the Air Defence Research Committee, a CID subcommittee.

On 14 August 1935 the Air Ministry formally adopted RDF as their solution to air defense. Robert Watson-Watt, the young scientist who had proved the idea workable just shortly before, had already sketched out the RDF stations, code-named Chain Home (CH), along England's coasts, for which the Air Defence Research Committee approved £62,000 together with the purchase of the 168-acre Bawdsey Manor, ten miles south of Orfordness, for the Bawdsey Research Station. The first six CH stations were to be ready for the June 1936 air exercises.

Like many other innovations at the time, RDF was delayed by bureaucrats, contractors, unrealistic schedules, the general demand for specialists, and the machinations of one of Tizard's earlier colleagues at Farnborough, the Oxford don Professor F. A. Lindemann, Churchill's protégé on the Tizard Committee. Baldwin refused to let Churchill off the Air Defence Research Committee and thus effectively muzzled him.[72] Tizard very soon made his major contribution of linking RDF to the air-defense system with senior RAF approval. It helped that the AOC-in-C Fighter Command, Dowding, had from 1929 been on the R&D side of the Air Council and understood what was becoming available.[73]

New tactics were now needed, as closing rates were rising to six hundred miles per hour or more. Work on location of lost aircraft led to three linked direction-finding sets, which gave a triangulated position that could be used with either wireless or R/T transmissions. At the same time, Biggin Hill was fitted with a fully staffed operations room and began to develop the crucial, and in the end simple, "Tizzy Angle" vectoring tactics essential later for the Battle of Britain.

On 12 August 1937 the Treasury approved £1 million for the CH stations plus £160,000 per annum for operating expenses. Training of the CH RAF operators had started at Bawdsey in February 1937. In March an RDF set had been airborne—airborne interception—and in September Royal Navy ships were detected at sea by an air-to-surface-vessel set. In August the air exercises justified the faith in RDF. Daylight interceptions were now being solved with War Office help, but night missions had to await the further development of airborne interception and the arrival of the Beaufighter in 1940.

An offshoot of the development of RDF was the switch in Labour Party tactics in early 1938 from support for collective security to attacking the government for not doing more for air defense now that Scheme L had switched priorities from bombers to fighters. RDF, however, was still secret. Clement Attlee, the Labour leader, was informed of RDF and so muzzled. The media was admonished not to mention the CH towers then being erected on the eastern and southern coasts, as that would be against the national interest and the Defence of the Realm Acts would be applied.

Domestic politics even at the time of Munich saw Churchill foist Lindemann back on the Tizard Committee, which shifted power from the CID's Air Defence Research Committee to the Air Ministry's CSSAD under Tizard. By early 1939 Watson-Watt's hands-off administrative manner was no longer feasible as development, integration, and production had all to be coordinated with training and readiness of the CH system. The Air Ministry needed a new senior policy-making and planning staff, which would have to do far more than handle the Bawdsey Research Station as wireless, RDF, and information management were also involved. With Treasury approval, Watson-Watt became director of Communications Development under the new Air Ministry director of Scientific Research. By the summer of 1939 Watson-Watt was the scientific adviser to both the Air Staff and to the Commands, as well as to both the Admiralty and the War Office regarding communications. He was also the director of RDF production, chief design engineer, and finally head of RDF maintenance at home and abroad. It was too much.

At the same time, the RAF was developing a special vocabulary for interceptions. Fighters could now be directed from the RDF plotting rooms. Concurrently, operations researchers began to examine all results and discuss these with Bawdsey, to be sure no lessons were missed.

In April 1938 the General Post Office asked for clearly defined policies with regard to air operations, including the locations of all control rooms and lines of communications so that technological, tactical, and strategic issues could be addressed. This led to a GPO questionnaire to all the Home Commands, which included a query as to what they expected in wartime.

In 1938 Dowding held the first realistic maneuvers since 1918, and shortly thereafter it was concluded that, because of an overload of information, the Biggin Hill interception method would have to be replaced by standing patrols. This also made plain the need for operational research. Four weeks after Munich the system was mobilized, with the highest priority being given to the completion of the CH stations and an underground block at Fighter Command HQ at Bentley Priory, to include a filter (information) room. The Treasury authorized the Air Ministry to go to direct, noncompetitive contracts. The emergency impacted Bawdsey, as the staff had to help erect the CH stations. The Air Ministry gave Tizard permission to contact professors of science and to receive their students for the summer of 1939, and to spread the word as to scientific careers.

By late 1938 calculations were being introduced that could convert information into a single line of data, electrified in the fall of 1939. In June 1939 RAF RDF personnel were trained at a new facility at Tangmere, as by then the RAF realized it needed 1,800 operators and mechanics. Thus the idea of using women was instituted in late 1938. This was successful, but raised the question of separate bathroom and sleeping facilities. When in January 1939 the number of fighter squadrons was raised to fifty, it was decided to give RDF coverage to the whole of the United Kingdom, and six more CH stations were approved.

Yet still to be solved, in addition to refining the system, were IFF (identification, friend or foe) and the RAF defense against low-flying enemy aircraft. In the case of IFF, a fresh start was made and a simple set devised. By the end of February 1940, 258 aircraft were fitted, but the signal was effective only 50 percent of the time due to crew error and faulty settings. By October 1940 virtually all RAF aircraft had IFF, and thanks to the arrival of new low frequencies, low-flying enemy aircraft could be detected when CH antennae were lowered.

By May 1940 Dowding had had an extra ten months to complete the RDF system. The Air Defence Research Committee and the CSSAD quietly disappeared, and Churchill, having been made First Lord of the Admiralty in September 1939, was muzzled. Tizard had been an excellent committee chair, but not a good manager.

Part of the especially inadequate filtering since March 1939 had been due to using poorly trained NCOs, in themselves not suitable for conversion of present reports into estimated targets. Thus it was that early in 1940 the Treasury approved assigning pilot officers and flying officers to filter rooms, and they reported on 10 June 1940.

On 15 May Dowding had asked operations research to help him stop the drain of fighters to France, and in two hours he received a graph that persuaded the Cabinet not to accede to French pleas. A necessary link in this C_3 system was a reliable radio set. Only 240 of the new TR 1130 VHF sets were available in May 1940.[74] Especially critical also was the lack of height-finding RDF.

Once war started, Dowding, a micromanager, was overwhelmed. The issue of centralization became a prime concern between Dowding and the Air Staff. But mid-July 1940 was not the time to demand Dowding's resignation, as the Battle of Britain had begun with 700 Hurricanes and Spitfires facing, according to Zimmerman, 760 Me-109s. Moreover, the RDF system faced a strategic and tactical dilemma for which it had never been designed—

the Luftwaffe bases were located in northern France, and Britain's Fighter Command personnel were not yet well trained. Then there was the surprise that enemy bombers would be escorted by modern fighters.[75]

David Zimmerman concluded that the RDF system worked admirably and showed that the bomber would not always get through without unacceptable losses. Moreover, the men and women running the system of CH and sector stations were as much responsible for saving Britain as were the fighter pilots. It was only the August attacks on the CH sites and the sector control rooms that gave Dowding and Park cause for alarm. The disagreement over decentralization of filter rooms led the Air Ministry to force Dowding finally to agree on 27 September to changes, and only after all RAF aircraft received IFF sets. Churchill doubted the efficacy of this move, but by November the failure to stop the night blitz enabled the secretary of state for air to inform Dowding that he was to head a mission to the United States.[76]

That the French really did not know anything about RDF and the relationship of RDF to RAF Fighter Command's control of interceptors in the Air Defence of Great Britain had a positive side—the secret was not disclosed to the Germans in the summer of 1940, giving the British a better chance of winning the coming air battle. C_3 and intelligence needed to be synthesized for a modern, three-dimensional war. In 1939 this was only beginning to be realized, even theoretically, while the apparatus, mental and physical, was only just evolving.

In most things the French had looked ahead and even developed equipment, but they had not made purchases on the scale necessary. The British had planned, procured, and financed better, but were still far short of both the needed perceptions and of the necessary equipment by the time of the Battle of Britain.

PART IV
WAR, 1938–1940

7

MUNICH AND THE PHONEY WAR, SEPTEMBER 1938–10 MAY 1940

War Again

Hitler invaded Poland on 1 September 1939 with the Poles valiantly resisting, believing that the Franco-British Guarantee of the past spring would help them. They had, however, just been disheartened by the German-Soviet Pact of 23 August 1939. They had earlier refused to allow the passage of their archenemy, the Russians, to aid Czechoslovakia, and their stubbornness had played into Hitler's hands.

Franco-British aid was not forthcoming, as Hitler gambled it would not be. The French had no intention of attacking Germans from the west, for the Armée de Terre was a 1918 cadre composed of ill-trained reservists. The Armée de l'Air was almost impotent. It had accepted half-completed aircraft and lacked a war establishment of pilots and mechanics as well as a clear doctrine, a streamlined command structure, and a communications net. Nor did it have sustainability. It could not bomb Germany because the civilians in Paris feared retaliation, and in any case it had only eighteen heavy bombers to do the job.

Across the Channel the generals still thought at 1918 speed, but the BEF was motorized and had a small armored force. Moreover, it had been training—though half the Territorial Army, which made up its reserves, was assigned to ack-ack duties as part of the defense against a German air attack on London. The BEF did have time to move to the Continent and dig in for an active defense and to train. It was at its core an élite professional force commanded at the second level by officers experienced in the 1914–1918 war and aware of the teachings of British theorists J. F. C. Fuller and B. H. Liddell Hart.[1]

The RAF had long been prepared for Home defense and was by September 1939 beginning to be able to launch an effective force of modern fighters warned by RDF and directed by sector-controllers. The long delay of the Phoney War (3 September 1939–10 May 1940) enabled Fighter Command to win—but only just—the Battle of Britain in the summer of 1940. The RAF had pilots and mechanics, thanks to both the foresight of Trenchard and the decisions made by Dowding and his colleagues, backed by the politicians from 1934 onward. Also crucial was Minister for the Co-ordination of Defence Sir Thomas Inskip's switch of emphasis to fighters to defend Great Britain, as opposed to the deterrent HDAF (from 1936 Bomber Command), which was incapable of reaching beyond the Ruhr, let alone hitting anything in Germany it could find. So in September 1939 Britain could not aid Poland because its offensive arm would not have the needed heavy bombers until 1942 and would not weld them into an effective strike force until 1944.

In the meantime, the incompatible Allies still had to work out an alliance. Paris wanted London to send Fighter Command to defend the French capital city as their DAT was impotent, but London saw the air defense of London and British industry as more vital. Ironically both sets of leaders saw the "air menace" as their biggest danger. Both were wrong. Moreover, the Deuxième Bureau had a more accurate assessment up to July 1940 of the Luftwaffe than did Air Intelligence in London, including evaluation of the German passive defenses.[2]

Hitler had no intention of bombing Britain; his aim was conquest of France and that was what the Wehrmacht and the Luftwaffe were trained to do in a coordinated blitzkrieg—a modern war.[3] At sea the Royal Navy would once again face U-boats, which it detested, yet neither blitzkrieg nor submarine warfare had been properly appreciated by Paris and London because their prejudices and inability to believe that the enemy did not think as they did blinded them. From May 1940, however, they would get a clear message.

In the meantime, Poland fell and a few of its servicemen escaped to the West first to join the French and then, after France fell, to be accepted into British service along with their exiled government. The Phoney War (*Drôle de Guerre*), which ensued from September 1939 to April and May 1940, gave the Allies time.[4] That precious commodity was wasted in France because the Haut Commandement was complacent in its belief that it could sit on the defensive, though it planned a forward encounter in Belgium. It never really shifted France to a war basis, because at heart the country was losing its nationalism. French people were no longer willing to train for another Verdun, and the cadre army lacked unity, cohesion, and the officers and NCOs necessary to make it function. Though machinery was put into place to manage armaments, the conveyor belt of war production was not accelerated under quality control. In aviation this resulted in the products of Plan V being delivered to the Armée de l'Air and accepted, though by no means *bon de guerre*. A bad statistical and fiscal system gave the impression that the Armée de l'Air could actually launch a force well above reality. On top of these failings, many of the Armée de l'Air's obsolescent machines had to be withdrawn from operations so as not uselessly to sacrifice the crews. And on the ground the command and control apparatus was not a system suited to modern war because all orders had to be approved at the top and then transmitted over the civil telephone Postes, Télégraphes, et Téléphones system or by dispatch rider.

The months of the Phoney War were squandered. Training bases were closed and unfinished aircraft hangared or parked in the open, not worked on. There was no sense of wartime urgency. Marc Bloch, in *Strange Defeat*, believed that many French people were little concerned, compared to those across the Channel who viewed the scene quite differently, thanks to planning.[5] Ironically, for the first six months of World War II the Daladier government enjoyed what appeared to be a renewed self-confidence in France itself. However, there was journalistic, photographic, and immigrant evidence that morale of the *poilus* was low.

Julian Jackson, in his *The Fall of France*, notes that the reasons for this most humiliating defeat in French history were still puzzling, in 2003. But the debate is now more serene and devoid of the earlier polemics and accusations, though still protective. As to the army, Jackson notes that by the end of the Phoney War the *poilus* were bored, ill led, ill fed, and ill housed, and morale was low. But on 10 May those who were well led and properly armed acquitted themselves well, though the performance at the Battle of Sedan was exceptionally poor in part because of the lack of radios; from 23 May the chaos of defeats encouraged panic.[6]

Paul Reynaud, the minister of finance slated to lead France in April–June 1940, tells in his memoirs, *In the Thick of the Fight, 1930–1945*, how he assessed the campaign as it proceeded.[7] Gamelin's Dyle-Breda plan thrust the Armée de Terre into the sort of fighting for which it was totally unprepared. The soldiers were trained for methodical battle. Yet blame may be laid on the political culture, which distrusted the ambitions of the army; the democratic society wanted a conscript army. Julian Jackson believes that, because of World War I and the circumstances of the 1930s, only about half of the French people were convinced that the new war was theirs too. And the Phoney War killed enthusiasm, if any, for the war—the years of decadence lingered on. The politics of the 1930s help explain the defeat, but not its causes. There was a legacy of errors. Gen. Charles de Gaulle, a Reynaud man, supported this view.[8]

Raoul Dautry, the minister of armaments, only appointed in late August 1939, protested to Daladier that his factories were 250,000 workers short. Daladier did not act. As the Phoney War progressed, Dautry told his son that the war was already lost. His pessimism and the prime minister's refusal to supply soldiers to manufacture armaments led Dautry to resign in March 1940 so as not to be blamed for the defeat he could see coming.[9]

When in March 1940 Reynaud and his mistress, Countess Hélène de Portes, succeeded Daladier and his mistress—both ladies like moths fluttering around the candle of power—time was not on the French side. Gamelin was afraid Reynaud, his friend, would change strategic direction. Reynaud wanted action in Norway, the Black Sea, and the Caucasus, as a reaction to a multifaceted internal crisis. British help, never enough, was welcomed, but France wanted an Eastern Front to which Weygand, then governor general of Syria, tried in December to get Wavell, the British general officer commanding-in-chief of the Middle East, to agree; however, the British government, with memories of Salonika in 1916–1918, refused. While Daladier, the Quai d'Orsay (foreign office), and some army officers supported the idea, others noted the ease with which the Germans, moving on interior Danubian lines, could counter it, and that it would do little damage to their Nazi war economy. Still, Weygand again met the British Middle East Command in the spring of 1940. According to Martin Thomas, the Balkans was still under discussion in January 1940, with an Anglo-French conference held at Aleppo, in Syria. The idea of a Salonika expedition was not finally shelved until after the Germans invaded Norway in early April 1940.[10] Moreover, not then an entity, Poland and Romania could only be useful allies if supported by the Soviet Union. The Armée de l'Air engaged in wishful thinking in supposing that the Red Air Force could bomb Germany from Polish airfields, vitiated by the Nazi-Soviet Pact.

France entered the war lacking a coherent strategy that involved a balance of power. In October both London and Paris overestimated the Luftwaffe as having about 14,000 planes of all types. Concurrently French aircraft production was still lagging and had acceptance problems. (In January 1940 only 198 of 340 produced were taken on charge, fewer than the 248 in September 1939.) Yet across the Rhine the Germans were producing close to 2,000 modern machines (though the French had gone to war with only 400!).[11] Both in Paris and London the rapid expansion of the Luftwaffe was regarded as creating a weak force. At the same time, French manpower limits had been reached with eighty-four divisions in the line and twenty-three in fortresses. The British in 1939 were realists. In the spring of 1939 they had just adopted a fifty-five-division continental policy, and though in 1914–1918 had eventually fielded ninety, the French doubted their abilities to do this again.[12] In addition, in 1939, owing to the needs of Home Defence, the RAF could only offer limited help in the form of basing the ACBEF and the AASF of Bomber Command in France.

Beginning in the spring of 1940, the holes in the blockade, French inability to supply its Balkan allies, and the economic exchanges between Germany and the Soviet Union all sapped French confidence in the long-war strategy. Robert Young notes that at this same time the top French decision-makers were increasingly hypnotized by hope.[13] Fear of Communism negated any relations with the Soviet Union, and Daladier's attempt to revive the *union sacrée* of 1914 failed, as owners and labor went off in opposite directions, leading to strikes and reduced production in spite of the revocation of the forty-hour workweek. Daladier failed to reconcile with Mussolini, and, in the French mind, the Soviet attack on Finland put the Russians in the same bed as the Nazis and aroused sympathy for aid to the Finns. But the failure to aid Helsinki before the Finns sued for peace led to Daladier's fall. Reynaud succeeded, but without a stable majority in Parlement, and so was squeezed between the political factions.

In London, First Lord of the Admiralty Winston Churchill, always anxious for action, had launched in April the disastrous Norwegian campaign, preempted by the daring German first strike. Bad intelligence, lack of knowledge of Scandinavia, and the arrogance of ignorance resulted in failure and the hasty evacuation of both French and British forces.[14] In the meantime the laissez-faire attitude to introducing and enforcing a war economy meant that France was not geared up for the war it had declared but was not waging.[15] After the war started, there was no system of priorities for supplies, leading to an inefficient and incoherent economy without the strains of recalling the 40 percent of skilled workers from the army and disruptions in the metalworking industries. The economy only finally began to produce in the spring of 1940—too late.

By September 1939 the *patronats* were strong enough to be divided between those who foresaw a short war and those who accepted the long-war strategy, and so aligned with the government for a policy of business as usual in order to benefit in the postwar world. The *patronats* were hostile to wartime controls, not to the war itself. War brought benefits and profits to the heavies and to the "sheltered" industries, but the small businessperson had been buried by new paperwork following the Matignon Accords of 1936.

At the same time, Reynaud as finance minister feared that France would be bankrupt in 1941, and thus he opposed ordering further planes from America. By the spring of 1940, employers and government officials saw the workers as sullen, suffering low morale, and unwilling to boost war production. Official use of surveillance only acerbated the situation. France was—on the surface at least—decadent and defeatist before 10 May 1940.

After the September 1938 Munich Agreements, Britain—at least the Foreign Office—tried to conciliate and stiffen the French.[16] But these moves subsequently were marred by the French refusal to declare war on 1 September 1939 when Hitler invaded Poland. And while by December 1939 there were ten Anglo-French economic committees, there was no overriding ministerial body to vet overseas purchases nor an economic super-body to show the public the unanimity of purpose of the two governments. Yet the French were hard-pressed economically and, in spite of their declared grand strategy, were not prepared to wait the three years until Britain was fully mobilized, militarily and industrially, for the grand strategy.[17]

In Britain there was a conflict between the Foreign Office's need to reassure French public opinion that the BEF and the RAF were moving swiftly to France's aid, and the War Office's desire for secrecy to protect surprise. By mid-October the BEF in France numbered 158,000 versus the 3.5 million French under arms. The need was to boost French morale to offset German propaganda. Conversely, the few British newspaper articles on France were likely to offend the French. Statements of war and peace aims were another point of contention, the British believing such pieces of paper were worthless. And the French were suspicious that London would make peace with a Germany without Hitler and the Nazis.

In the Foreign Office a senior official noted that this suspicion was the difference between the Anglo-Saxon and the Latin mentality, though ultimately both were fighting for their own security. Any territorial settlement had to await the defeat of Germany. But Britain then wanted Germany back in the European system, while France wished to crush her. By mid-December the British had come to agree on a joint declaration of no separate peace. On 21 March 1940 the War Cabinet in London approved a new wider draft, but to the Foreign Office's dismay, Reynaud succeeded Daladier the same day and on 28 March signed it.

In parallel, trade and fiscal issues rose due to the British ban on the importation of luxury goods to conserve foreign exchange, which hit French exports, while French import license restrictions made it difficult for the BEF to find the francs needed. When concessions were made in late November, the French were still not fully satisfied. Eventually both sides agreed to liberalize finances, not to hinder trade between them either to protect home industries or foreign exchange. And finally on 16 February 1940 both sides agreed to keep in place only a few trade restrictions. But there remained the issue of tension, as the locals were complaining that John Bull had dropped Marianne into a war that made paupers out of the French. An agreement was not ready for signature until 22 May—again, too late.

Late in 1939 some inside the Foreign Office began to tout the idea of a union with France. By March it was urged on the grounds that high French morale might collapse if the Phoney War continued much longer. In late winter Hankey headed an intergovernmental committee on the subject, and on 28 March the Allied Supreme War Council agreed to meet regularly and create its own permanent secretariat. Concurrently the Chatham House study group in London produced a draft for a perpetual Anglo-French association. This Zimmern memorandum was not accepted by all, but did place the highest priority on teaching each other's languages in the schools to achieve bilingualism. However, issues of sovereignty, customs, a common currency, and a military alliance created further difficulties. The project then fell with France. Churchill's 16 June offer of union to France was made without consulting the Hankey Committee.[18]

Michael Dockerill, the British diplomatic historian, has concluded that while military assistance was negligible, in economic and political spheres the collaboration had borne fruit. However, suspicions also lingered.[19] The switch on 10 May from Chamberlain to Churchill as prime minister and war leader was, as David Dilkes has noted, most cordial and gentlemanly.[20]

The Armée de l'Air, 1939–1940

On 22 August 1939 the Armée de l'Air mobilized the "A" echelons of pursuit, bombing, and reconnaissance. On 26 August the general cover—the protection of mobilization—took place, and on 27 August the reserve echelons of *chasse* and reconnaissance groups were in their turn activated, followed on 1 September by the bomber reserves and finally on 3 September by general mobilization after the German attack on Poland. By then most Armée de l'Air units had left their peacetime bases for their operational airfields and landing strips. At 1700 on 3 September, France went to war. Contrary to expectations, there was no German attack.

At the time there were thirty-seven different types of aircraft based on 205 aerodromes in Metropolitan France, with a serviceability of 67 percent. The Armée de l'Air deployed 115 *groupes* (wings of two *escadrilles*) and 17 flights consisting of 23 *groupes* and 9 regional flights of fighters, 33 of bombers, 14 of reconnaissance, and 47 of observation *groupes*.[21]

The Armée de l'Air made use of the Phoney War to obtain more modern aircraft and to improve its situation. However, training facilities in North Africa were closed, and at stations in France the approach was pleasure before training. Experienced Czech pilots were shuttled around instead of being mounted on combat airplanes, until too late.[22] From his new Grand Quartier-Général Aérien (GQGA; the HQ of the Armée de l'Air in wartime) at Saint-Jean-les-Deux-Jumeaux, Gen. Joseph Vuillemin commanded three air armies adapted to the organization of the ground command, with one *chasse groupe* and one reconnaissance *groupe* per army, with one observation *groupe*, and one or two balloon companies per corps, cavalry, light mechanized or armored division, as well as reserve air forces. In the northeast, General Mouchard's Première Armée de l'Air (first air army) had fifteen fighter *groupes* (two of night fighters) and four regional fighters *groupes*, fifteen bomber *groupes*, eleven reconnaissance *groupes*, and thirty-one observation *groupes*. Gen. Jean-Paul Houdemon commanded the Troisième Armée de l'Air (third air army) along the Neus River, and Gen. René Bouscat's Cinquième Armée de l'Air (fifth air army) covered North Africa.

As land army groups were created, this cumbersome and overcentralized organization was divided and simplified. The Premiere Armée de l'Air was split into two, to go with the two lead army groups. On 1 October Gen. François d'Astier de La Vigerie took command of ZOAN (Zone d'Opérations Nord; air zone of operations north), with General Pennes having ZOAE (Zone d'Opérations Est; air zone of operations east). Each reported to Mouchard, whose responsibility was to put the reserves into operations, but he was only the technical adviser regarding army use of ground-support air. Farther south, ZOAS (Zone d'Opérations Sud; air zone of operations south) came into being. However, the system quickly proved unwieldy, and thus the intermediate commands were eliminated and ground-support air forces and DAT were placed directly under Gen. Alphonse Georges, general officer commanding of the northeast, who received three air operational areas commanded by Gen. Marcel Tétu with similar arrangements for North Africa and for Syria.

Vuillemin also established on 11 October 1939 six inspectorates at GQGA to keep him informed of the employment of his forces and the modernization of the planes in service. On 17 February 1940 the bomber brigades and squadrons were made subordinate to the air divisions, and then on 15 April the chief of the GSAF laid down the organization of the assault bomber groups, all of which were to be equipped with the Breguet 693. These Phoney War changes were not perfect, and the campaign from 10 May revealed more weaknesses.

On the outbreak of war the Premiere Armée de l'Air had only 138 MS 406s, 94 Curtiss Hawks, and 37 Potez 630s and 631s, with an additional 39 Potezes assigned to the Paris area. The remaining forty-three fighters were a ragbag of obsolete Dewoitine 501s and 510s, Spad 510s, and Nieuport 622s. The rest of the fighter forces had but 120 single-seaters and 35 multiseaters.

The bomber forces had only eighteen modern bombers, all the rest being obsolescent. Much of the material was decrepit and highly dangerous in action to their crews. Plan V had not yet borne fruit. The most desirable policy was to accelerate production in order to reequip units and train crews. On the outbreak of war the production goal was increased from 335 planes per month to 780, and resulted in the wartime Plan II of 14 September. GQGA and the Ministère de l'Air asked for 1,600 planes monthly, of which 30 percent of the 1,314 fighters would be reserves, 23 percent of the bombers, and similar set-sides to the other categories, adding up to a total of which 23 percent would be in reserve.[23] Manpower was increased while heavy bombers were eliminated in favor of a doubling of the ground-support aircraft.

The fighter forces were to be equipped with the new, untested Dewoitine D-520, Bloch 152s, and Arsenal VG-33s, while bomber units would also receive nine different new types. But this whole plan was based on overly optimistic production forecasts that did not take into account the difficulties of bringing new types to operations. In February 1940 GQGA realized this and urged the minister to adjust the goal to what the domestic industry could produce, together with what could be bought abroad—nor should the difference be expected to be made up by RAF Fighter Command. Vuillemin thus asked for 1,500 single-seat and 200 multiseat fighters, with the addition of assault aircraft, in a new Plan V(a) published on 25 April 1940 as Plan VI. This would give the Armée de l'Air 3,534 first-line planes on 1 May 1941, or with reserves a total of 9,186. This program, of course, was preempted by events.

For the period of the Phoney War, plans called for the October 1939 through May 1940 production of 8,055 planes, though only 2,629 were actually delivered, and about 30 percent of these were not operationally war ready—*bon de guerre*.[24] As a result, Guy La Chambre had asked to purchase 3,300 U.S.-made planes; but this was easier said than done, as the United States had instituted an embargo on the export of arms on the outbreak of war. Only in November 1939 was the "cash-and-carry" law passed. Soon the French combined with the British to ask for 4,700 planes, most of which were only in the prototype stage. In May 1940 the French did agree to buy a group of modern planes, but none reached France before 24 June 1940, most going instead to the British.[25]

In mid-September 1939 the bomber units withdrew to safer rear bases, and on 3 December Vuillemin began a vast modernization of his forces, based on predicted production. The MS 406 and Curtiss Hawks had proven adequate against the German Me-109D, but would not be so against the newer E models and Me-110s. Losses of MS 406s made it clear that reequipment was essential. GQGA's plan was to have expanded and modernized fighter forces by the end of April 1940—fourteen *groupes* of MS 406s, ten of Bloch 152s, eight of Dewoitine 520s, four of Hawks, and one of VG-33s. But there was both a shortage of trained personnel and reduced output of D-520s and VG-33s that delayed withdrawal of the MS 406s. On 10 May the Armée de l'Air had only twenty-eight fighter *groupes* (fifteen of 406s, eight of Blochs, four with Hawks, and only one with D-520s) instead of the planned thirty-eight. According to the testimony of the Czech pilot who later flew Spitfires in the RAF, training was lethargic or inappropriate.[26] In addition, at Tours alone in the spring of 1940, 150 new Bloch 151/152 were hangared for lack of personnel.[27] And Tours was not unique. Faris Kirkland has noted that aircraft were stored throughout on French air bases because of a shortage of pilots and mechanics.[28]

Meanwhile, in December the bombers had been sent to the south of France to set up a bomber-training group to convert crews to the new LeO 45s, Amiot 350s, and Breguet 691s as they became available. A smaller group in North Africa began to train crews for the Martin 167 and Douglas DB-7s arriving from the United States. Nevertheless, "the inferiority of the French bomber force on 10 May 1940 was crushing."[29] GQGA's plans did not call for more bombers until May.

The new heavy bombers were delayed in delivery and then had to be used for training; and the Breguet 691s had continual engine problems and weak undercarriages. All suffered from the shortage of wireless-operator aircrew. On 10 May most of the bomber groups were still forming, but none had crews trained for night work nor for work on modern aircraft. The reconnaissance groups were almost ready, but the arrival of the superior Me-109E early in 1940 had severely limited their activities. The newer Bloch 175s and the Martin 167s were only available in very small quantities. Because older aircraft had to be withdrawn as too vulnerable, reconnaissance was desperately short of its needed strength. Observation was even worse off. It was to have been reequipped with the Potez 63-11s, but although three training bases were opened, the instruction was sketchy, consisting of only a few hours in the air before units were rushed to the armies. But at least on 10 May thirty-five Armée de l'Air observation groups had the new Potez 63-11.[30]

When war came in 1939, the Armée de l'Air was in the midst of a personnel crisis. While the HQs were overstaffed, the units had serious shortages— 60 percent in NCOs and radio operators, 31 percent of air gunners, and 77 percent of NCO lighter-than-air mechanics. To meet the output of Plan V the Armée de l'Air between January 1940 and April 1941 would be short 1,800 pilots, 3,200 observers under the Ministère de l'Air, and 1,800 observers under the Ministère de la Guerre. All of this meant a demand for training facilities and one thousand instructors. The plan to produce all of this showed it could not be completed until the end of 1940 rather than the original date of April 1940. Noting that the losses in the early Phoney War were well below estimates—sixty-three aircraft shot down, eighteen damaged, for a claimed eighty Luftwaffe shot down and thirty-four probables—the planners assumed that the 3,200 Plan V machines could be manned in time by May 1940. Though extra schools were opened, the results by the spring of 1940 were well below the optimistic predictions due to bottlenecks in training and bad winter weather. Plan VI simply added to the deficit, which was already caused by near-zero output from the schools. By mid-April it was obvious to the commanding general of ZOAE that in a crisis he would not be able to sustain a continuous effort. By the Armistice on 24 June 1940 only 4,742 newly commissioned aircrew and 3,348 noncommissioned officer aircrew (a total of only 8,090) had been trained out of the 12,000 planned, or 67.5 percent, and few, if any, had reached operational units.

Air operations to support the ground attack, promised to aid the Poles on 7–9 September, fizzled. By 13 September all was quiet again on the Saar Front. By the end of the second week of September, the Luftwaffe controlled the air. With the ground war seemingly becoming static, Vuillemin decided to oppose all Luftwaffe incursions into French air space, yet to economize as much as possible on men and matériel so as to build up a modern air force. Reconnaissance flights were limited to only eleven kilometers (6.8 miles) into enemy air space, and in 1940 the GQGA ordered the Armée de l'Air to avoid major air battles. Otherwise offensive ideas anywhere were on hold until the means were available.

Early encounters with the new German Me-109E saw the MS 406 and the Curtiss H-75s outclassed, though French pilots did not take this seriously. The demand for better French aircraft was only just being met as the Dewoitine D-520, Bloch 152, and VG 33 were readied for service. All together 736 Armée de l'Air fighters were spread over five hundred miles, from the North Sea coast to Switzerland. The main *chasse* was distributed within the ZOANE (Zone d'Opérations Nord-Est; air zone of operations northeast) of the four northern armies where there were six and a half fighter *groupes* (123.5 aircraft) on four air bases to the rear of the armies. Another four *groupes* (92 aircraft) were in ZOAE. All these fighters could reinforce each other. There were also 36 aircraft of mixed types to defend

Paris, 9 at Lyon, and another 20 under the *Admiral du Nord* at Calais. Of the 736 Armée de l'Air fighters, 80 percent were in the northeast, in addition to 160 reinforcing the RAF. All of these fighters had many tasks for which they had few reserves. However, the reality test of Armée de l'Air planes, organization, and doctrine would be from 10 May.

The RAF in France, September 1939–May 1940

When the RAF went to France after the declaration of war against Germany on 3 September 1939, its move was paradoxical.[31] The Air Staff had thought it either would immediately be engaged with the "air menace" blow against London or that it would be facing a German ground campaign, which Anglo-French forces would have to hold. The other possibility was that it would be a long war, as the Allies were planning, in which case the two British air forces in France—the ACBEF and the AASF of Bomber Command—would have plenty of time to perfect their administration, organization, and tactics. Once neither of the immediate possibilities occurred and Hitler failed to attack in November, the British Air Ministry, especially, began more to follow the French view that time was not of the essence.

On the outbreak of war, the AASF moved first to preselected aerodromes in eastern France, preceded by servicing flights and essential personnel sent by air to receive the Fairey Battle squadrons of No. 1 Group and its HQ under "The Quick Dispatch Scheme." The new AASF airfields had already supposedly in peacetime been supplied with stocks of bombs, ammunition, and POL; and there also were French air companies to provide essentials until the RAF administrative and supply organization was complete.

This first echelon of ten Fairey Battles (commonly called the Battles) was expected to be ready for action within twenty-four hours of leaving England. The rest of the squadrons and their personnel were to be dispatched by sea within three weeks. The army in France supplied RAF needs to the railhead, from whence the RAF had to collect its stores. Once the first echelon was settled in, the second of ten Blenheim squadrons was to follow. However, this latter force was retained in Britain. As no active operations emerged until 10 May 1940, the Battles undertook reconnaissance duties, and in the spring of 1940 actually did night-flying practice over Germany to avoid restrictive French instructions.

Almost all the aerodromes and their satellites assigned lacked accommodations, or were in remote locations by tiny villages, making tracking MT a major difficulty and billeting arrangements embarrassing. And the French air companies were generally overwhelmed, for they had expected an advance party, for instance, of 5 officers and 30 other ranks, but instead received on the first day 29 officers, 53 senior NCOs, and 143 airmen. Only one tent had been provided, and POL facilities were nonexistent. The French air companies had no idea what to do and had received no orders from above. Thus it was that for the first six days RAF officers worked hard to feed and shelter their men, as supply and operations had been separated from each other.

Those dislocations were in part due to the shift from peace to war levels and in part due to service movements control. The delay in the arrival of rations was because the requisition had to go to accounts in Saint-Nazaire three hundred miles to the west, and because the unloading of MT was slow. In addition, the MT were delayed en route by the lack of guides, maps, refueling arrangements, staging posts, and billeting on the more than three-day journey. The lesson was plain that a move should not be ordered without adequate organization. By the end of October, the AASF was at last drawing British rations as opposed to the unfamiliar and unpalatable French supply.

The Armée de l'Air had not guaranteed in prewar conversations that the satellite landing grounds would be ready, and they were not. This led to the revised decision not to move the second echelon of ten Blenheim squadrons to France. The satellites were not expected to be ready until the spring of 1940, when they would be under plow and the weather would be wet. Meanwhile, the campaign in Poland had shown that the Germans would open their offensive with an attack on airfields, and thus the Battles were dispersed as widely as possible over the second echelon's five main aerodromes, with each having a Battle squadron by 12 September. This dispersal caused the wing organization to be revamped from two to three squadrons to a wing.

The ACBEF, however, had followed the schedule linking its movement to that of the BEF, the first necessity being to protect the port of debarkation and the move of the BEF from there to its assembly area. Four days after the ground and wing echelons had been sent over, the first four fighter squadrons of sixteen aircraft each flew over to two aerodromes, and the main parties followed during 17–27 September. Unexpected delays were caused by No. 1 Squadron's vehicles being off-loaded at Brest and having a three and a half–day drive to Le Havre to pick up personnel.

ACBEF HQ was established colocated at Le Mans with BEF HQ, and then both moved in October to Arras. By 30 September the ACBEF was set up with Air Marshal A. S. Barratt promoted to AOC-in-C. Barratt did not have to administer the AASF and the ACBEF as such services had already been established. The AASF was detached from Bomber Command and paired with the ACBEF to support the armies in France. High Wycombe, Bomber Command HQ, was still responsible for AASF training such as night-flying in the spring of 1940 for Battle squadrons to mine the Rhine. Though this was blocked by the French because of possible retaliation, it did save the Battles when their casualties during 10–15 May caused their use temporarily only at night from 16 May onward.

In case of conflicting demands for the overall bomber force, General Georges of ZOAN would decide. Thus on 21 January Barratt, by then the AOC-in-C, British Air Forces France (BAFF), suggested that to streamline the operational process generals George and Vuillemin should assign French liaison officers to BAFF HQ with a British officer representing himself, at each of the two French HQs, with another at HQ Premiere Armée de l'Air (General Mouchard). These were accepted, along with the exchange of intelligence, and the renaming of the Allied central air bureaus as advanced HQ BAFF (North) with the AASF HQ becoming advanced HQ AASF (East). Barratt also told Vuillemin that when the battle opened he would move his HQ to whichever place would be best suited to work with the French general officer commanding. In addition to two British air missions sent in September to Armée de Terre and Armée de l'Air HQs, the No. 3 Air Mission was formed in November and became operational in February 1940 as a fully mobile unit to move up to the Dyle and join Belgian GQG, while a detached party would do reconnaissance and report by dispatch rider.

In the meantime, General Gamelin had pushed again in September for six more RAF fighter squadrons at a time when CAS Newall denied them because the defense of Britain needed fifty and had only thirty-one. Britain could not afford to make the whole of the RAF mobile, but the Air Staff was also worried by the inefficiencies of the French air-raid-reporting system. This was never satisfactory because there was neither enough time nor resources required. The solution needed close cooperation with the French, overcoming the backwardness of the French air-defense system, and the difficulty of sparing the essential personnel and equipment from Britain (even though Secretary of State Kingsley Wood had offered it in April 1939). To be of value, the system needed reliable reporting, a defensive filter apparatus, AA, searchlights, balloons, and fighters. But there were not enough of these for an effective organization. The Corps d'Observation Français (French observer corps) was sparse, reporting over the public telephone system, and its posts were allotted along the coasts and eastern frontier with a second line fifty miles to the rear. There could be no continuous tracking, and reports took not twenty seconds, as in the BEF, but several minutes to reach centers. The Armée de Terre, too, had a Corps d'Observation connected directly to the fighter groups serving each army, but the results were variable in part because of lack of standardization, in part because—for one example—there were too few gasoline generators to keep wireless transmitter–set batteries charged. French DCA, in spite of technical advances, was negligible. Fighters in one army group could not receive reports from another. This made, on 10 May, for ineffectiveness, with no link to the Field Force's mobile wireless intelligence screen (WIS). From April 1940 the WIS had been set up across the likely paths of Luftwaffe attacks when they were concentrated along the Franco-Belgian border, and they were reporting directly to No. 14 Fighter Group, ACBEF. At the same time, WIS East was passed to the AASF. The weakness of the WIS was in the training of its army spotters and its inability to estimate the height of raids.

In June 1939 approval had been granted for six French officers to be trained at Bawdsey, England. The French had planned a national triservice RDF network of forty stations, but the details had not been settled by May 1940, and such a network was, anyway, beyond British supply capacity. Of the gun-laying RDF sets desired by the French, only thirteen were available to the BEF by 10 May. Two filter rooms were designed: the one at Reims never opened and the one at Arras did not live up to the designer's hopes. A further problem was sorting the movements of friendly aircraft from those of the enemy. A system linking Bentley Priory, Stanmore, and Fighter Command HQ in the United Kingdom, to Rouen, Lille, Dunkirk, and Versailles in France failed because the connecting circuits became overloaded with additional intelligence. Shortage of cross-Channel phone lines also hindered the usefulness of the system. On 10 May Barratt complained that the RDF system was so weak that enemy aircraft had flown right over the Lille and Arras centers without being detected, though Stanmore was tracking them at 20,000 feet.[32] One of the arguments made was that fighters based in Britain could be operated far more efficiently than those relying on the inefficient French reporting system and so suffering much heavier wastage.

In the fall of 1939 Nos. 1 and 73 Hurricane squadrons were moved to a position between the Maginot Line and the AASF airfields. However, due to rains and the chronic shortage of airfields, some of which the French had taken back, these two squadrons ended up at Lille-Seclin, controlled after 20 January 1940 by No. 14 Group, too close to the Belgian border to intercept Luftwaffe photoreconnaissance unit flights coming in over the northern coast. Meanwhile some of the flexibility of squadron locations was due to the formation of fighter wing servicing units, which also acted on occasion as wing HQs. By March 1940 enough of these were in France to allow the potential fighter force to rise from six to ten squadrons, and possibly more, as happened during the Battle of France. Part of the problem with the RAF fighters was that the Hurricane, designed as an interceptor at Home, had a short fifty-five-minute endurance and thus was limited in operating from England, along whose south coast there was a shortage of airfields. As a result, to protect the left flank of the advancing French Septième Armée de Terre (7th army) after 10 May, Hurricanes and Blenheims patrolled on France's seaward side. During the "Norwegian emergency" (10–27 April), with the German invasion, the RAF squadrons in France were dispersed, but then returned to their bases. When the Battle of France began on 10

May, the RAF fulfilled its pledge with ten fighter squadrons in France as well as patrols from Home.

Meanwhile, farther south the position of the AASF bombers during the Phoney War was changing. The Blenheims of the Second Echelon never moved to France. When Vuillemin suggested stockpiling spares, CAS Newall pointed out that there was none at all in the training establishment. Gamelin agreed that the Blenheims could operate as effectively from Britain against their "permanent" targets in the Netherlands and Belgium, while the Battles could attack the "fleeting" targets between Liège and Namur on the Meuse. The Blenheims in England would be secure from attack while the Battles could be well dispersed in the province of Champagne in northeast France. If the Germans attacked through Luxembourg, then the Blenheims could refuel from supplies already in place in France. These remained the plans from October 1939 to 10 May 1940, because suitable aerodromes and protection were hard to obtain in France. At the same time, from September 1939 to 10 May 1940, arrangements were made so that six additional squadrons could operate from AASF airfields. However, these plans were complicated by the proposal to refuel heavy bombers in Champagne, which caused headaches. This plan required five more new airfields with night-flying facilities, and these could not be available until mid-1940. Fortunately, the Germans erased these ideas on 10 May.

At the same time, the Battle squadrons needed reequipping, as these aircraft, according to the Air Historical Branch (AHB) history, were "obsolescent and of little redeeming operational value."[33] Both Slessor and the pundit B. H. Liddell Hart, however, thought the underpowered Fairey Battle the best aircraft for short-range low-level attacks. This was a complete misconception, as May 1940 would show, owing to operational instructions to fly at 12,000 feet.[34] The Battle crews had been trained to strike the heads of Wehrmacht columns in low-level daylight attacks. But the plan to replace them was scotched by the need to convert the Blenheim I to night fighters at Home, and to reequip the ACBEF with Blenheim IVs for long-range strategic reconnaissance. Though started in November 1939, the Battle reequipment was soon postponed to the fall of 1940. The ten squadrons did get a revised MT plan to give them more efficiency with their widely separated airfields, and thus spring plans worked until the 16 May retreat westward, when the RAF had to borrow MT from the French to allow the squadrons to escape the advancing enemy.

In the early stages of the Phoney War there was a sometimes acrimonious Air Ministry–War Office debate over the air needs of the army, a matter first raised in the 1920s. The 1939 decision to create a field force of thirty-two divisions would have required thirty-nine Army Cooperation squadrons, and in June 1939 the CIGS asked for another thirty-four, plus artillery spotters as well as fighter and transport squadrons. Such a demand would have seriously weakened Home Defence but also the proposed grand-strategic bomber force. By the time war started, the War Office wanted the motor industry to mass-produce Brabazon dive-bombers à la Stuka, under direct British Army control, as in the Wehrmacht. The Cabinet put a stop to this attempt to re-create the RFC. To provide the BEF with bomber support was another reason the BAFF was created with reconnaissance squadrons as the prewar joint Army Cooperation subcommittee had agreed. Allocations were to be based on BEF armies that, however, had not been brought into being before 29 May 1940. In the meantime, by 10 May there were ninety short takeoff and landing Lysanders in France compared to the original forty-eight.

Another topic basic to the success of the RAF in France was aerodromes.[35] When the RAF moved to France it understood that it would take over a suitable number of Armée de l'Air facilities. What it found was that many of the fields allotted had no accommodations and were badly in need of work, as were their satellites, to bring them up to operational standards. Few had even primitive runways, so that these had to be constructed or sown with durable grass seed. The Royal Engineers program eventually grew from twenty-five main and twenty-five satellite fields, to fifty-nine landing grounds alone. These new and refurbished fields would begin to be available in March and July, but some not until the end of 1940. Delays were due to the difficulty of locating suitable sites, and then persuading the French to release them. The process of site selection had not been completed by the time the RAF evacuated in June 1940. It was especially difficult to obtain fields in the Verdun-Metz and Orléans areas where the Armée de l'Air was thick and the country difficult. Then, too, airfield building was limited by scarcity of labor since so much of the French pool had been called up; the British labor pool was even leaner. Also affecting airfield building were shortages of raw materials and machinery—essential equipment, including tipping trucks and mechanical diggers, which had to be imported from the scarce available stock in England. And not until late March 1940 were British airfield construction companies available. Still, after the very hard winter, the work was plagued with a shortage of materials— 1,500 long tons being received daily out of the 10,000 long tons needed. Improved British railway wagons designed to help relieve the shortage were not allowed to operate on French railways until fitted with air brakes, and trucks were needed to build access roads to sites that often were remote. In places, runways had to be built in deeply muddied soil. The new airfields were divided between those that could handle any aircraft and those only useable by the short takeoff and landing Lysander. The British official historian commented on airfields as on other delayed projects, noting "the whole work went for nothing" because it was abandoned to the Germans, as were ten airfields built for the ACBEF.[36]

Although the French had agreed prewar to RAF occupation of named fields, many of these needed quite a lot of work and some were totally unsuitable even for the "first generation" of modern RAF aircraft. Moreover, there was an Anglo-French confusion over the term "satellite" (*bâtiment annexe d'une aérogare*). In Britain it meant a fully equipped aerodrome administratively under another station; in France it meant a landing ground with an access road. The misunderstanding caused both disorder and delay, so that some AASF aerodromes would not have been ready until June 1941. Of the ten AASF satellites on 10 May, only one was rated usable and safe. Of these ten only three had been on the September 1939 list and eight had had to be resown in the spring of 1940; these eight thus would not have been available until July, though some were used in emergencies after 10 May.

The Ministère de l'Air was directly responsible for the five new airfields and satellites in the Orléans–Le Mans area, together with sites for training schools. Twenty-five sites were needed, but by January 1940 only eight had been selected. By the end of March fifteen flying-training school sites had been agreed to by the French, though they had refused to allow selections to be made in Beauce and the Vendôme because of agricultural needs. In May the RAF abandoned the heavy bomber airfield sites. Of the eleven flying fields being developed, the RAF occupied all during the second retreat of 2–14 June, and these enabled the ground organization to withdraw from southern Champagne.

The Air Ministry historian viewed the original proposals for fifty-four airfields as "an act of faith," as no organization existed to build them, but writes that after the Royal Engineers took hold in March, remarkable progress was made so that although the program was "not an unqualified success, neither was it an unrelieved disaster."[37]

The effectiveness against Luftwaffe raids, which could choose their time and place, combined with the inefficiency of the French air-raid-detection system, which lacked RDF, was limited. In the Battle of Britain the enemy was restricted because of his escorts' endurance to 250 miles of British coastline. In addition, the French DCA was limited to medium altitude and was nonexistent against low-flying aircraft. On 3 September the British believed that the French had 369 DCA guns of 75-mm and 105-mm; the new 90-mm DCA gun had never reached the armies, and only 2,500 of the new 25-mm light gun had been issued by 10 May. (Daladier at Riom asserted there were another 1,200 available, however.) There was also a shortage of trained gunners and of tracer ammunition. All of the above had to protect eight armies and forty important defended areas (*zones importantes défendues*) in the interior. The Neuvième Armée de Terre (ninth army) had only three of its required forty-five batteries of light guns. This inherent weakness of the French made them demand more of the British.

In September 1939 Home Defence in Britain had only 800 of the 2,872 heavy guns authorized and only 279 light guns of the 3,000 authorized. The War Office estimated that the Germans at that time had 6,000 heavies, 3,000 Bofors 40-mm, and 5,400 other guns. While the BEF provided its own AA defenses, the AASF in southern Champagne was dependent on the French until London believed it could release enough guns. Still, Gamelin at once pressed for British AA for the AASF fields. London promised to send seventy-two heavy guns by 1940. Even so, the War Office ordered forty-eight 3-inch guns to the AASF area in October 1939. This relieved the

French, but not the AASF, which was widely scattered around Reims with many airfields, satellites, railheads, and stores parks to protect. In December the Royal Artillery Brigade Commander, supported by the Air Officer Commanding, AA, requested forty heavy 3.7-inch and seventy-two Bofors. By 10 May he had only eight 3.7-inch and twelve Bofors to protect twelve airfields. Lack of 3.7s meant that the Luftwaffe could easily overfly the AASF aerodromes. To the north, the ACBEF had 224 heavy guns and 204 light guns protecting eight main airfields. However, the general scale, or allotment, while very insufficient, was far better than that of the French. The ACBEF also had eight RAF-manned machine guns on each airfield, while the AASF had sixteen each, though some were of an airborne type that overheated without a slipstream. There were no Scarff machine-gun mounting rings for truck cabs, and thus guns there were on improvised attachments.

The French had a searchlight system to illuminate intruders against clouds (*la chasse observée*), but it had only been used against aircraft capable of flying 135 miles per hour. French important defended area gunners fired at everyone outright, thus limiting the BEF's proposed lighted area in which their night fighters could operate, but this had not been set up by 10 May. In addition, the British had begun to raise balloon barrages in April and a Ground Observer Corps BEF post every 3,500 yards. Early in May an Anglo-French Air Defence Committee was being set up, as was an Air Defence Signals Board, but both were overtaken by events. Effective air defense in France was still, according to the London AHB BAFF historian, "an enormous unfinished business."[38]

For the BAFF to be effective it could not function without an efficient maintenance organization—a very complicated and controversial subject.[39] The story has been made the more difficult, as noted in AIR, because, "Moreover, there is a national tendency for commands in the field to regard the Ministry at home as an instrument of unwitting obstruction."[40] Basically the Air Staff transferred to France the maintenance system that was in use in settled Britain. Squadrons did all routine inspections of their aircraft and MT and carried out limited repairs in permanent station facilities. But in France there was a lack of skilled personnel and of equipment to set up the normal infrastructure, let alone hangars.[41]

The amount of repair and salvage to be accomplished rose as aircraft flew more and operated off primitive fields, frozen in winter. No. 21 Aircraft Depot was not in a position to handle salvage until six months after it was established. It was evident that No. 21 could not cope with a major campaign while the forward air stores parks were so loaded as to be immobile. These circumstances led to the formation of Maintenance Control in December 1939 under the newly created post of maintenance officer in charge at BAFF HQ, with a proper staff to replace the small QRAF (quartermaster, known in the British forces as "Q") which had been overwhelmed with the major tasks of coordinating the demands of the ACBEF and AASF and liaison with the Armée de Terre and the French railways. The officer in charge worked directly with both the Air Ministry and Maintenance Command at Home on technical matters.[42]

Because the French did not vacate Château-Bougon, No. 21 Aircraft Depot was not able to unpack and store its inventory. Aircraft Depot personnel had to be used to erect Bessoneau hangars and tentage, and to build roads, while trying to stay warm and healthy. In January 1940 personnel were still in tents in a very hard winter. At the same time, the Equipment Holding Unit came into being to keep six weeks of supplies for the BAFF; it moved into new Bellman hangars shipped out from England, which the Equipment Holding Unit had to erect. It was thus March before the first stocks were moved in.[43] As No. 21's units came on line, the air stores parks reduced their inventories and stopped ordering direct from England. By the end of April, No. 21 was ready to receive all the Vocabulary—the list by name of all stores—up to a six-month stock, and to issue in France clothing, barracks stores, and MT spares. By 14 May it could issue from all sections of the Vocabulary.[44]

The solution to the repair and salvage unit's difficulties dragged on from fall until spring when on 27 March the Air Ministry announced a new arrangement and further delays to fill establishments. The Engineering Section of No. 21 Aircraft Depot was not expected for similar reasons to be up and running until 27 May, and that deadline was missed because of the tardiness in connecting it to the French power-and-light mains. The repair and salvage units were to operate independently after 27 March in the vital role of reducing wastage and in increasing serviceability by both aiding squadrons with major repairs and reducing to scrap what could not be reused. These scrap shipments went to an Army Salvage Center in the United Kingdom.

The fact that by no means all of the 27 March changes were in place by 10 May was due to Air Ministry–approved delays and a constant shortage of equipment, as well as AASF resistance to some policies, and lack of coordination between London, BAFF HQ, and the AASF.

Air Marshal Barratt later concluded that in the future maintenance units should be dispatched concurrently with the squadrons and with the maintenance officer in charge being not on the air officer commanding's staff, but in executive control guided by Maintenance Command at Home in technical matters. A key block in building up the BAFF was MT for mobility, "the need to be able to carry out a general simultaneous movement over a limited land area without reliance upon external means of conveyance."[45]

But on 10 May BAFF was suddenly thrust into a mobile war—not a holding war of two or three years. All that it appeared to be able to do was to move up to the Dyle-Breda Front. But the RAF had in May no picture of the pathetic state of the French equipment, as later emerged. The Air Staff had taken on faith the French defensive plan, the quality of the Armée de Terre, and the strength of the Maginot Line, with the corollary that the Germans would have to fight very hard indeed to win. No one had given any thought to the ACBEF being forced to evacuate within days of the start of serious fighting, and the AASF being forced out in five weeks.

The ACBEF was supposedly mobile, but its ancillaries were not, and the AASF was only semimobile. With only one squadron per airfield, the AASF needed more MT. The Air Ministry subcommittee saw the AASF as serving behind the Maginot Line. The subcommittee noted that the RAF in France had by 10 May actually become less mobile. Thus the proposal was that no more than four AASF squadrons should become mobile with just half an air stores park. The AASF response was that the Air Ministry's idea was based on "surmise." The problem was "to combine maximum economy with sufficient mobility."[46]

While the Air Ministry appeared to accept Barratt's views of his expanded need on 5 February, the approval was granted on 25 February for MT but not for personnel, until 8 April, and then it lacked establishments for HQ MT companies in the AASF. The aim, Barratt stressed, was to make all ACBEF squadrons able to make a three-day move using only their own transport, with MT pools moving the air stores parks. On 15 April the AOC-in-C pointed out that he had total deficiencies of 771 vehicles. The Air Ministry reckoned he was more than 7,000 short. On 11 May the director of organization at the Air Ministry said the delay was due to the slow production of three-tonners, the newness of the need for vans, and the diversions to the Norwegian campaign. Establishments had now been issued and vehicles were on their way. However, on 16 May BAFF needed all the vehicles it could get. The AASF was forced to reduce its bomber squadrons from ten to six and to borrow transport from the French.

While the training of the RAF sent to France was generally good, when it was thrust into unfamiliar roles it proved to have had little or no instruction. The AASF Fairey Battle crews were unfamiliar with Army Cooperation, and in January 1940 it was discovered that most of the pilots had done no night-flying and that the Battle was unsuitable for that role. The result was a series of accidents. A great deal of training was needed, but there was a shortage of equipment such as blind-flying hoods. In the three months of December 1939 through February 1940, airfields were snowbound, engines would not start, and aircraft were damaged on the frozen ground. It took up to six weeks to get replacement parts for this sort of breakage, so training was cut to preserve machines for active operations. Aircrew was cold and rusty. French routing and lighting did not help navigation practice. Only the threat to return whole units to Britain for training alleviated the situation, though hard-and-fast rules to benefit the French air defenses were tough to alter. These restrictions tended, then, to limit crews' night flying to "circuits and bumps" at their own airfields. The other expedient was to send the Battles over Germany to practice night navigation. Fatal accidents were ascribed to inexperience. However, there was a silver lining. When during 10–15 May it was proved that Battles could not operate in daylight because of fatalities, the crews had just enough experience to switch over to night work.

The former chief of SHAA, General Lucien Robineau, in the June 2008 *Letters of the Air and Space Academy* pointed to both the matériel and tactical weaknesses of the Armée de l'Air on the eve of the Battle of France.[47] It had 1,872 aircraft in metropolitan France to face the 3,300 of the Luftwaffe involved in the Battle. On the French side, twenty-three of twenty-eight *groupes* had MS 406 or Bloch 152 fighters, which had difficulty catching the equally fast Luftwaffe bombers. Of the planned sixty bomber squadrons, only thirty-three were partially available. The supply side was bogged down in bureaucracy and transport. Despite industry's workings at last to full capacity by June, fewer than 30 percent of the Armée de l'Air could be dispatched on operations. And the communication system was archaic, as there was no liaison between troops and the aircraft that were to support them. In addition to lack of DCA (the Wehrmacht had highly effective flak), the Armée de l'Air lacked RDF and its control system, as well as mobility. Martin Alexander has noted that Gamelin's HQ at Château Vincennes lacked even a wireless transmission set.[48]

According to I. B. Holley Jr., of every 1,000 aircraft produced in the United States during World War II, 380 remained in the United States and 620 reached operational theaters, 279 of which were under repair. Of the 341 aircraft that took off on sorties, only 275 reached the target. Thus, in terms of effectives fewer than 28 percent took off on an effective operational sortie. In France, this would have been a much smaller percentage, for the reasons General Robineau cited, and a much smaller force altogether.[49]

CONCLUSIONS

It is important to realize that the Armée de l'Air's failure contributed to the French military defeat of 1940, but it was not the primary cause. A more immediate blame must fall on the Haut Commandement of the Armée de Terre and then on the state. The grand strategy was faulty and France's assessment and its view of the world of the late 1930s were skewed. The story of the Armée de l'Air is symptomatic of the larger catastrophe.

After studying the French and British air arms, it seems clear that France between the wars was not so much decadent as it was unable to meet the challenge of the post-Victorian world in the most important field of national defense. Broadly speaking, France's failure was its inability to create an administrative and fiscal machinery compatible with the needs of modernization. One then has to wonder why the French were surprised by the disastrous events of 1940, including that at the Dyle-Breda Front, for perhaps the ingrained characteristic cultural and organizational attitudes were still similar to those of 1914, with the execution of Plan XVII by General Joffre. Plan XVII failed and the French learned that a strategy centered on the national *élan*—the spirit of a people—was not enough in the face of large, organized, enemy armies.

Britain, in contrast, being a much more commercialized nation with a broader base of entrepreneurs heavily involved with industry and commerce, fared somewhat better during the interwar years of transition from the old staple export industries of textiles, steel, and shipping, to the new areas of electrical components and aviation. The RAF was far ahead of the Armée de l'Air in its defensive preparations, not only with RDF and sector control, but also with plans for emergency backup operations rooms and communications. Although the latter proved not to be good enough when serious attacks took place on airfields and their sector control rooms on 24 August–7

September, these strikes stimulated the removal of operations and filter rooms from airfields, often in above-ground facilities, to new rooms within five miles of the station. The French, in contrast, had done no such work.[1]

In Britain the directors, owners, and managers of businesses did visit the shop floor and relations with workers and their unions were adversarial and not antagonistic. In Britain, aeroengine development was pursued by the Air Ministry by means of cost-plus-10-percent contracts. Notably these bore fruit in the Rolls-Royce Merlin and the Bristol Hercules; when the Rolls-Royce Vulture failed, the Napier Sabre was the backup, followed by the Rolls-Royce Griffon. Progress was also made by capital grants and the shadow-factory schemes for production capacity.

In France, as with their aeroengines, so too it was with DCA—designs were developed but never thoroughly tested, and only sometimes ordered, not in quantity and too late. This was symptomatic of what ailed France in the 1930s: not so much a lack of money, but of will, direction, and a sense of urgency to put the country in order for a modern war. France and Britain had emerged from the Pyrrhic victory of World War I with different foci. The French saw themselves as a great power, but with a continental concentration that ignored their Empire, except as a well of manpower in the case of another war against a resurgent Germany. Exhausted, rebuilding, depressed by the casualties of the 1914–1918 conflict, France focused on conscription and a 1918-style defense. But Paris had neither the will nor the skills to prepare for the next war. The inertia solidified into the 1930s, saw near revolution during 1934–1936, delayed Rearmament, and led France to its nadir in 1940.

Across the Channel, morale and perception were different. World War I had been won without honor and without paralyzing mutinies. The Empire was held in high esteem, and Britain, nationally, remained a great power. There was no interwar conscription until the spring of 1939, no continental commitment. Then there was a long depression and a general strike, but never the danger of a revolutionary collapse. What happened on either side of the Channel in many ways followed historical precedent.

Perhaps to the French workers and petite bourgeoisie the conspicuous consumption of the upper classes, especially in Paris, appeared self-indulgent and decadent, often seen as a process of decay that included a decline in art and literature. Yet it was more than that. As the generation of strong leaders passed on by the end of the 1920s, they were succeeded by individuals beset, it is true, by problems for whose solutions they could not see precedents. Added to this, the structure of French government contained flaws. The major problems were in the industrial northeast, while Parlement was being dominated by the senators and deputies from the agrarian south. Moreover, the leaders who emerged were *avocats* (lawyers), or petite bourgeosie, but not the wealthy *patronats* who boycotted politics and had a disdain for democracy.

On the other hand, many of the élites were graduates of the *écoles polytechniques* and formed a technically oriented "old-boy" network. Yet, in spite of this, a great weakness in the interwar years was in the administrative machinery, starting in the Comités d'Aviation (aviation committees) of the Sénat and Chambre des Députés. They seized the role in World War I of browbeating the short-lived ministers in charge of aviation, in effect dictating not only policy, but also procurement. Moreover, the committees grilled the ministers almost daily, wasting time that would have been far better spent on developing both an appropriate government policy and an administration.

The hatred of the bourgeoisie for the working class was strong in the 1930s, and the ruling class after 1936 thirsted for revenge for the fight they had gone through. Therefore it was either naïve or cynical to ask them in 1939 to die for France. The Right did not understand that decay could be combated by social reform. They simply hated the Front Populaire. The real reason for the failure of the Troisième République was social and moral— hatred of workers, Jews, Communists, and Socialists. Political rifts became chasms, and on the Left there was a split over whether to oppose or appease Fascism. Survival of both Left and Right depended on an outmoded political system.[2] There was no man on horseback.

What France needed was a new style of capitalism. The problem, as Marc Bloch saw it, was that there was a ruling government that did not now know how to wield power at a time of political lethargy.[3] It was an incurable state of degeneracy. The defeat was rendered inevitable by the loud chaos in the economy, society, and politics. The Front Populaire frightened the aging ruling class, but inspired the post-Vichy regeneration by the young.[4]

The state of hostility between the French *métallos* and the *patronats* became very evident at the 10 June 1936 Matignon meetings. There the workers' representatives could argue from intimate knowledge of piece rates, hours, and wages, whereas the *patronats*' representative had no idea of that end of their business, for they never went down on the shop floor. Complicating the process was the characteristic of gesticulating garrulity rather than gentlemanly discourse. As Stanley Hoffman noted, the French had difficulty talking face to face, and as a result walls were erected between opponents rather than compromises being adopted.[5] This was to be seen also in the relations of *patronats* and managers to labor. Rather than recognize that World War I had forced management and workers to come to some arrangements about skills, hours, and the employment of women, the *patronats* distanced themselves from the fray and failed to see the pernicious impact of the Russian and other revolutions, as well as the rise of democracy around the world.

However, if there were the traditions of the French Revolution of 1789 and of the Communard of 1871, there was also the precedent of being able to rule by decree to overcome stonewalling the national interest or of necessity. Thus in 1933, Pierre Cot, the Radical Socialist air minister, created with a stroke of his pen the independent Armée de l'Air. The French Right leaned toward authoritarianism and Fascism. An aviation dictator would have helped, provided he had sound advice and helpful supervision, but Cot's successor, Gen. Victor Denain, was a military autocrat with a narrow mind. He knew nothing of the technology and dismissed the civilian technical staff and the experienced Albert Caquot, the developer of the prototype policy of 1928–1933. The result was that Denain thrust on the manufacturers large orders for the BCR aircraft, which they had not the ability to produce in quantity and which was soon obsolescent, and this at a time when they needed to be learning how to build the all-metal aircraft of the Technological Revolution. If it is acceptable to see the 1940–1944 Quatrième République (fourth republic) of the Vichy regime as the end of the Troisième République, then some of the rancor, detestable themes, and political, social, and economic worries and hostilities continued, perhaps typified by both the Riom *procès* and by the imprisonment of the former Front Populaire prime minister Léon Blum. The 1965 colloquium on his 1936 government raised the questions as to whether or not there had been circumstances, that June, close to revolution, for it had a touch at least of that phenomenon. Blum personified the problems of the Troisième République.[6]

This work started out by wondering why the world's two greatest air arms of 1918 came to such different ends in 1940. It now seems plain that the answer lay deep in their national histories and apparent beliefs. The two roads to 1940 actually originated before the dawn of the air age in the natural conflict of focus between the continental power south of the Channel and the insular-imperial nation to its north.

By the outbreak of the Great War—World War I, as remembered in the 1920s and 1930s—change was taking place. In France the provincial bourgeoisie were reaching Paris as deputies, whereas in Britain members of Parliament were still selected by the central party committees and adopted, and then, hopefully, elected by the constituency voters. Unlike in France, representatives did not have to reside in the locale to be eligible for election. What then happened during the 1914–1918 war was that in France Parlement created committees to control aviation as well as finance. With forty-four members apiece, these unwieldy bodies ruled, rather than the ministers and their cabinets. Professional airmen were placed in office by politicians and forced out by politics. Across the Channel, however, where the British government had access to businesspeople, Parliament merely oversaw the public accounts after having passed the annual Estimates presented by the minister with Cabinet approval.

Yet in spite of these differences, the French did manage to produce the larger share of aviation matériel. However, in the course of converting their economy to the necessities of war, minus the German-occupied industrial northeast and the lost province of Alsace-Lorraine, the French were forced more and more into an Anglo-French business matrix, which they, as Europe's prime power (in their own view), resented.

After the war, national policies diverged and antagonisms arose such that in 1923 the RAF HDAF was created as a deterrent versus Paris. At the same time divergences of view as to Germany created tensions as well. The legacy of World War I's casualties hung as a pall over both countries. France desperately needed assurances of British help in its defense, but Britain was determined not again to have a continental commitment.

The impact of the Great Depression showed the difference between bourgeoisie talk and concern for the value of the franc based on gold and the British willingness to abandon the gold standard and engage in deficit financing while beginning to plan for another German war.

Ironically it was the earlier French menace that caused Britain to retain fighters in the HDAF, the lesson being learned from the German attacks of 1917–1918. Thus while the French argued interminably about the nature and responsibilities of an air arm, the British steadily developed the fighters, gun defenses, and intelligence early-warning system that would make them effective in 1940. In contrast, the French lacked a viable grand-strategic vision of a coming war, seeing instead another 1918-style stalemate. As a result, the French fell behind as the Technological Revolution concurrently brought radical changes in aircraft. Moreover, when Britain and others were moving into Expansion schemes in the factories and on the airfields, the French were standing pat. By May 1940 the Armée de l'Air had only 96,000 officers and men and 637 *chasseurs,* while across the Channel the RAF dedicated to Home air defense had close to 300,000 officers and men, and Fighter Command had roughly 600 modern fighters and 1,200 pilots.

Moreover, the acquisition systems north and south of the Channel were as different as the business climates. In France, aircraft that were nowhere near war-ready were accepted at the depot, whereas in Britain they had to have been Aeronautical Inspection Department accepted, test-flown, and delivered to aircraft storage units using a pool of ferry pilots and be ready to be issued in a few days. In back of the system in Britain were private constructors and engine firms distributed in 1936 in both parent and shadow factories that were turning out sufficient machines to keep ahead of wastage in the Battle of Britain in spite of the loss of nearly 1,000 aircraft in France. In addition, from 1930 on the RAF also had the advantage of an Air Staff Operational Requirements Branch, which specified with the CAS' approval what types were required and the performance they needed to reach. A somewhat similar conception in France did not lead to such clear-cut results. And in Britain the air officers commanding could estimate their needs from 1936 through the secret *SD98* on consumption and wastage. One other key area was in budgetary support. Because in France the Armée de Terre received the bulk of the credits, the Armée de l'Air was restrained until 1938. Even then, in standard pounds sterling in mid-1938 the ratio was £63 million to £212 million, with the RAF also being two years ahead in aircraft design.

It is true that following Chief of the GSAF Joseph Vuillemin's visit to Germany, just weeks before the 1938 Munich Agreement, he had predicted his French force would only last two weeks against a German threat; it actually lasted forty-six days, from 10 May to 24 June. In contrast, Air Chief Marshal Sir Hugh Dowding of Fighter Command, by refusing to send more squadrons to France in May 1940, saved his twenty-nine squadrons of fighters and built them up to fifty-five and more, well-backed logistically, and so prevented British defeat in the Battle of Britain in late summer 1940.

Many new aircraft, especially at times of technological change, are delayed, often for technical reasons. The lag in production is not understood by politicians, higher military leaders, or the public. Once "teething troubles" are overcome, many such aircraft have proved successful. All three French fighters of 1940—the MS 406, the Bloch 151/152, and the D-520—were involved. A combination of troubles caused the demise in February 1940 of Marcel Bloch's enterprises. British fighters, similarly, were not immune to delay, and the Air Ministry in the spring of 1939 had wanted to cancel the Spitfire for that reason.

A further contrast between the two allies was that the Armée de Terre was prepared for a 1918-style war and not for blitzkrieg, whereas the British Army did have mechanized divisions, but they were wasted by the faulty French plan to fight the opening battle outside France, thus allowing the BEF to be cut off by the German thrust through the Ardennes and across the Meuse at Sedan. From there the blitzkrieg moved rapidly to the Channel and past Paris. Contributing also to the debacle was the lack of a modern communications system using wireless. The rigidity of the French higher direction and lack of ability to use initiative was in sharp contrast to the British use of R/T and RDF to control the Battle of Britain.

An important question remains: Why could not France pay for the Armée de l'Air it needed? Apart from the matter of doctrine and rules, military mentality and dominance of General Gamelin, does the answer lie in its adherence to orthodox finance and a refusal to go in for Keynesian deficit funding, as in Britain?

As has been explained in *Why Air Forces Fail: The Anatomy of Defeat*, the origins of the "two roads to war" go back several generations and along different national routes.[7] The defeat of the Armée de l'Air was accelerated by its ill-equipped air bases. The faulty French strategy of assuming a 1918-style war with the great frontier battle being in Belgium had resulted in the Armée de l'Air being located in the northeast and thus vulnerable to the German blitzkrieg. And, most important, an air force is only as good as its airfields, even if its aircraft are designed to operate off grass or other surfaces to have the range, the warning, and the command structure to support their being sited farther back from the front. They still had to have the infrastructure to sustain them at least at 75 percent serviceable.

The two roads to war were parallel, but quite different for the two countries that had fought Germany in 1918 and were destined to do so again in 1940. In the post–World War I and interwar years, differences of geography, national culture, and grand strategies, as well as perceptions of self-interest and business, would determine the routes traveled. The French were concerned—or at least Paris was—about great power status, while London was confident that the British Empire was still a reality. Paris clung to collective security and the gold standard for the franc; and London eschewed alliances, especially a continental commitment, while letting the pound sterling float.

Militarily both inherited the legacies of 1918. The French interpreted that as a return to the need for a trench system manned by reservists and supported by artillery, with the additional strategy of protecting its northeast industrial area by a forward defense in Belgium. Despite the lesson of the Duval Division of 1918, the French Haut Commandement insisted on meager "penny-packet" air support for each army unit—that was "cooperation." Across the Channel, however, the view was that Britain and the Empire could not afford more trench warfare and thus army cooperation was relegated to the fringes—an attitude helped by the misreading in the 1930s of the purpose and scope of the Luftwaffe. Instead, fortunately, London followed the 1918 path of air defense, which after 1923 gave the RAF the counterstrike deterrent role as part of ADGB. That led to both perfection of fighter defense and to a clear doctrine. In France there was always confusion as to the allocation of priorities and francs to the three air force roles of army cooperation, defense of the territories, and an independent strike force; in Britain there was not. As a result, thanks to Dowding, there was after 1936 Fighter Command with RDF and sector control. Two-thirds of ADGB was devoted to the offensive; Bomber Command from 1936, however, did not have the technical development of Fighter Command. Ironically it was the latter's prowess that eventually enabled Bomber Command to forge a war-winning weapon, but it was six years too late.

The political systems also resulted in different results. When Hitler dismantled French collective security, it was too late for Paris to develop its fallback position, partly because Parlement was only as strong as the weakest needs linking coalitions together, and partly because pouring inflated money into the recently created Armée de l'Air in 1938 had not the same immediate effect as in London where in 1934 Chamberlain bought the grand strategy of deterrence as part of Appeasement.

Coupled to this was the 1918 founding of the Air Ministry and the RAF, and consistency of vision and purpose, even if Trenchard's belligerence versus the Admiralty was harmful. The result was that the RAF had the pilots and mechanics in cadre and expandable as crises arose in the 1930s, and it had the technical developments, especially in engines, that Paris did not have. Moreover, as a legacy of 1918 was the procurement system that ensured that aircraft delivered were almost fit to be issued rather than, as across the Channel, incomplete airframes.

A significant difference on the two sides of the Channel was the decision-making machinery. In Paris the "Haut Direction" (higher direction) was a jumble of committees or councils in which the army dominated so that the airmen could never work out clear doctrine and policy and have them approved until too late. In Britain the stability of Cabinet membership, the proven structure of the Cabinet Office and the CID, together with the organizational strength and minutes of Sir Maurice Hankey from 1912 to 1938, provided an orderliness and consistency to grand strategy. Whereas the Luftwaffe had concentrated its resources into ten air fleets under a single commander, the Armée de l'Air was spread out and not concentrated, due to the linear front concept and subject to the orders of the zone commander, as well as to those of Generals Tétu and Vuillemin. Benoist-Méchin notes, "France was no more capable than any other country of forming an army that did not resemble its system of government"—that is, a system that was lax and uncoordinated. "The Government," he adds, "must take final responsibility for the tragedy; it had allowed France to stagnate."[8] French plans were constantly outpaced by events.

By May 1940 when France was surprised fatally by the misreading of the Deuxième Bureau's reports on Germany that revealed blitzkrieg, Britain's distrust of France allowed it to pull off the Dunkirk evacuation, avoid the Breton redoubt, and have Fighter Command just able to meet the German air menace, even when the latter rose from French airfields and was escorted. The margin of victory was narrow, but it was enough to avoid defeat.

At the bottom of the causal analysis are cultural traits. As others including Adamthwaite have noted, the French thought that if they had talked about something, they had solved it, whereas the British were much less concerned with words than with deeds. In France the Cabinet was a coalition vulnerable always to the committees of Parlement and rarely in office long enough to get a policy accepted, let alone funded. In Britain the Cabinet formulated policy and often had five or more years in which to focus it with the annual parliamentary backing of the Estimates, thus ensuring a supply of money that matched policy. Civil servants impartially served their masters, and were part of the picture as they rose in rank.

The story of the French and Britain air arms between the wars is one of management of technology. It is also a study in transitions from the late nineteenth to the mid-twentieth centuries. While in the end it involved many individuals, most of the crucial decisions—whether of political economy or of technology—were made by a very few: on the French side, by people like Daladier and Gamelin; Cot and La Chambre, Potez, and Breguet; and Bloch (Dassault), Albert Caquot, and Dewoitine; on the British side, by Churchill and Chamberlain; Hoare (1st Viscount Templewood), Swinton, and Weir; Mitchell, Camm, F. B. Halford, and Fedden; and the designers and engineers at Rolls-Royce, together with Trenchard, Ashmore, and Dowding of the RAF.

What France needed in the 1930s—at least during 1936–1940—was that "man on horseback" who had periodically come to the rescue in its time of crisis. The country found one too late, on 17 June 1940, in the figure of the savior of Verdun, Pétain. His Vichy administration gave the Fascist *patrie,* some say, what it had needed from before 1936.[9] At the same time, a week earlier in May, the British received their parliamentary, constitutional hero in Winston Churchill, who successfully combined the offices of prime minister and defense minister, as Daladier had failed to do. The politics that had stopped Churchill becoming defense minister in 1936 could no longer be tolerated on 10 May 1940.

It is not correct to say that the military alone was to blame for the defeat of France in June 1940. Both economic and political historians have noted how internal problems preoccupied the French leaders of industry and labor as well as the politicians. Too little was done on grand-strategic matters, the sort of planning that had to start with concern for national security and proceed from the prime policy to prepare the country for the future. Certainly Germany rose phoenix-like and suddenly during 1933–1935. While the German economic and diplomatic threat had always been present since 1872, the rise of Hitler—the strong leader France lacked—already by 1936 put France behind the eight ball.

Too little fresh thought had taken place in Paris regarding what another war might be like, how it might be waged, and what might be needed to do so. This was exemplified by the clinging to the franc until 1937, and to adherence to orthodox financing in a gold mentality. As a result, Paris and the Ministère des Finances put France three to four years behind Britain in terms of paying for Rearmament. The Armée de l'Air, consequently, did not begin to receive most of the monies it needed until 1938 and Paul Reynaud's Keynesian deficit financing. By then, of course, the Armée de l'Air should have had up-to-date designs, but what it got was poorly engineered and inadequately tested aircraft, in May 1940, unsuccessful in facing the new German enemy. Moreover, thanks to General Gamelin's pervasive influence and stubbornness in preparing a 1918 army for a 1940 war, and the airmen's bitterness at their own frustration, no suitable doctrine had been worked out. Nor had anyone really done the sums to see what was needed and at about what cost, and how priorities should be allocated. The refusal to pay for Rearmament may be seen also as an inability to meet the challenges of modernization in the post-Victorian world with suitable administrative machinery. The strong leaders of the 1920s were succeeded by lesser lights who were unable to see, or to devote time to comprehend and provide solutions to the problems that beset them, especially in national defense.

That the Armée de l'Air would be ready early in 1941, as its leaders optimistically stated, was not proof that it was ready for war in 1939, or even May 1940. In fact, the opposite was true. The French were slow to put the pieces of power together. Their first modern aircraft of the Technological Revolution were not up to par, unequal to either enemy or Allied machines. They were replacing the MS 406 in early 1940 by the D-520, itself not a thoroughly tested design. And the third *chasse* fighter, the MB-151/152, like the MS 406, was inadequate, with both lack of design experience and horsepower. Furthermore, the French had only forty-nine modern bombers. For reconnaissance they had the twin-engine Potez 63 and the high-speed Bloch 174, but only the Bloch was fast enough to evade the German Me-109. French airframes were not thoroughly tested, and instead of refining types by modifications derived from continuous testing and squadron service, production runs were terminated in favor of a new type that also was not definitively ready for combat.

A further great weakness was the production of the recently nationalized (1936) aircraft industry with the horrible system of accounting for machines on charge versus those actually *bon de guerre*, as well as the absence of ferry pilots and of spares. The airfields and the logistics system were still in a 1918 mode and unsuited in the face of mobile war, and the numbers of aircrew and mechanics were inadequate. In May 1940 the Armée de l'Air had perhaps 97,000 on duty, but after the Armistice the Armée de l'Air generals

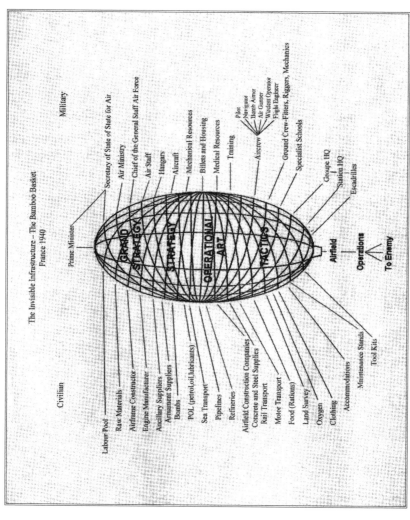

The Invisible Infrastructure—
The Bamboo Basket.
France 1940
(© Robin Higham)

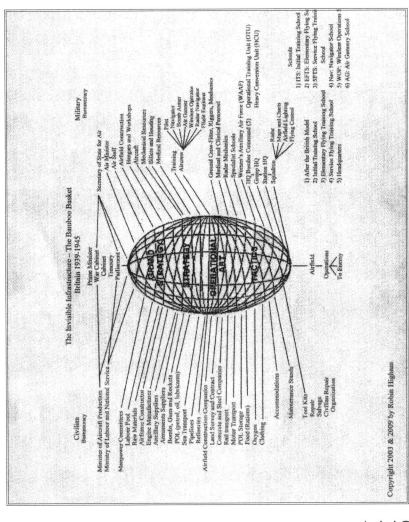

The Invisible Infrastructure—
The Bamboo Basket.
Britain 1939–1945.
(© Robin Higham)

concluded that they had needed 500,000 personnel. And both the Armée de l'Air and the Armée de Terre were sadly lacking in DCA. Moreover, the spring of 1941 date for readiness is not to be trusted, for as the "Bamboo Basket" graphic shows, an immense amount of organization, administration, training, and readiness had yet to be achieved to be able to field a force viable in war. In addition, behind all of this was the lack of money, or credits, which in 1938 were but 20 percent of what the British Air Ministry and the RAF were receiving. By the start of the Battle of Britain, RAF Fighter Command had 54 squadrons and almost 1,400 pilots, versus the perhaps 637 pilots of the Armée de l'Air with no replacements.

Yet it was not just those concerns that were responsible for the debacle. There also had been a failure since 1934, and really well before, to develop an engine program with its ancillaries, notably propellers. The problems in France cascaded from the general disinterest of the bourgeoisie in politics because the legislators only sought their votes at elections and ignored them the rest of the time. The collapse was also the responsibility of the *patronats*, who were haughtily detached from affairs in their Parisian *sièges* and knew little or nothing about the shop floors of their factories. They were surprised when in the spring of 1936 the workers unexpectedly occupied the factories as long-pent-up grievances, with Communist help, bubbled up.

The Matignon Accords were a wake-up call, but once they had redone their business organization to defeat the Front Populaire in the battle with the strikes and return to discipline on the shop floor and productivity, the *patronats*' disinterest in France made them lukewarm patriots when the war came. Capitalist-labor relations in France were never healthy, and that went deep to the French inability to talk to each other. If it was the Matignon Accords that killed the small businesspeople with paperwork and inspections, it then was the governing élite, the ministers, who lacked the focus to plan and implement grand strategy: they held office for too few months at a time, they had to train their own personal cabinets, they had to appear constantly before parliamentary committees, they had an endless battle to obtain legislation needed, they had to play politics and campaign for reelection, and they almost never had time to consider policy papers or to discuss them. French Cabinet meetings, like the meetings of French business directors, were gesticulating sessions without recorded minutes of their proceedings. To paraphrase the Texas cowboy when asked what he thought about a head-on crash on a single-line railroad, he responded, "It was a helluva way to run one." France thought it was a great power, but it did not know how to act and be run like one.

As evident in the "Bamboo Basket," everything has to start at the top and then follow an orderly multipath to the airfield before any action can be launched. In 1939, France was not a cohesive nation but rather was clumps of people divided by *département*, locale, class, religion, and politics. Paris was at the head and heart, but without a magnetic individual it could not provide a unifying leadership. Charles de Gaulle had to separate from Pétain to be that guiding persona, and yet as had England's earlier Cromwell, de Gaulle would later have trouble getting the French to govern themselves.

Basically, the reasons for the French defeat in May–June 1940 and for the British success in August–September were the different systems, organizations, and cultures of government and society that were rooted in the Victorian age and World War I. A modern state has to anticipate, plan, and finance defense at all levels, and in the end, analysis of the French and British situations in 1940 may conclude that culture and geography were certainly fundamental, if subtle, determinants.

EPILOGUE

The Germans struck at dawn on 10 May 1940. By 12 May they had the Allies beaten because the Breda-Dyle plan of France's Gen. Maurice Gamelin saw the French and British armies charging forward to fight in Belgium while in reality the Germans cut through the Ardennes and crossed the Meuse into France behind them. Gamelin, having committed all to the northeastern threat, had no strategic reserve.

By late May the encircled BEF and some French troops were being evacuated from Dunkirk under cover of Spitfires from England. The BAFF was withdrawn to Britain or fled southwest.

The Armée de l'Air reaped the seeds it had been sowing since 1928. There was no French grand strategy and no air doctrine to cover the army, the defense of France, and grand-strategic attacks on the enemy's industry. By 10 June the hapless Armée de l'Air was impotent, yet after fighting stopped on 24 June its leaders would assert that it had never been defeated and that it had more modern aircraft than on 3 September 1939.

The RAF was part of a conscious British grand strategy and had the doctrine to cover its two main roles—defense of the United Kingdom from the German air menace and a still ineffective bomber deterrent force. Britain was saved in the summer of 1940 by Fighter Command, which was technically proficient, by the logistics system in place, and by competent leadership. Above all, on 10 May Britain acquired an experienced, determined, and spirited leader in Winston Churchill, such as France did not have. The story of the French Troisième République's self-deception is to be found in the sequel to this work, which examines the air battles of 1940 over France and Britain.

—Robin Higham

PRESIDENTS, MINISTERS, CHIEFS OF STAFF, FRANCE (1914–1940)

Presidents of the Republic

Raymond Poincaré	January 1913–January 1920
Paul Deschanel	February–September 1920
Alexandre Millerand	September 1920–June 1924
Gaston Doumergue	June 1924–June 1931
Paul Doumer	June 1931–May 1932 (assassinated)
Albert Lebrun	May 1932–July 1940

Prime Ministers

René Viviani	June 1914–October 1915
Aristide Briand	October 1915–March 1917
Alexandre Ribot	March 1917–September 1917
Paul Painlevé	September–November 1917
Georges Clemenceau	November 1917–January 1920
Alexandre Millerand	January–September 1920
Georges Leygues	September 1920–January 1921
Aristide Briand	January 1921–January 1922
Raymond Poincaré	January 1922–June 1924
François Marsal	9–13 June 1924
Edouard Herriot	June 1924–April 1925
Paul Painlevé	April–November 1925
Aristide Briand	November 1925–July 1926
Edouard Herriot	July 1926–July 1929
Aristide Briand	July–November 1929
André Tardieu	November 1929–February 1930
Camille Chautemps	February–March 1930
André Tardieu	March–December 1930
Theodore Steeg	December 1930–January 1931

Pierre Laval	January 1931–February 1932
André Tardieu	February–June 1932
Edouard Herriot	June–December 1932
Joseph Paul-Boncour	December 1932–January 1933
Edouard Daladier	January–October 1933
Albert Sarraut	October–November 1933
Camille Chautemps	November 1933–January 1934
Edouard Daladier	January–February 1934
Gaston Doumergue	February–November 1934
Pierre-Etienne Flandin	November 1934–May 1935
Fernand Bouisson	June 1935
Pierre Laval	June 1935–January 1936
Albert Sarraut	January–June 1936
Léon Blum	June 1936–June 1937
Camille Chautemps	June 1937–March 1938
Léon Blum	March–April 1938
Edouard Daladier	April 1938–March 1940
Paul Reynaud	March–June 1940
Philippe Pétain	June–July 1940

Foreign Ministers

René Viviani	June 1914–August 1914
Théophile Delcassé	August 1914–October 1915
Aristide Briand	October 1915–March 1917
Alexandre Ribot	March–November 1917
Stephen Pichon	November 1917–January 1920
Alexandre Millerand	January–September 1920
Georges Leygues	September 1920–January 1921
Aristide Briand	January 1921–January 1922
Raymond Poincaré	January 1922–June 1924
Edouard Herriot	June 1925–April 1925
Aristide Briand	April 1925–January 1932
Pierre Laval	January–February 1932
André Tardieu	February–May 1932
Edouard Herriot	June–December 1932
Joseph Paul-Boncour	December 1932–January 1934
Edouard Daladier	January–February 1934

Louis Barthou	February–October 1934
Pierre Laval	October 1934–January 1936
Pierre-Etienne Flandin	January–June 1936
Yvon Delbos	June 1936–March 1938
Joseph Paul-Boncour	March–April 1938
Georges Bonnet	April 1938–September 1939
Edouard Daladier	September 1939–March 1940
Paul Reynaud	March–May 1940
Edouard Daladier	May–June 1940
Paul Reynaud	5–16 June 1940

Air Ministers (1928–1940)

André Laurent-Eynac	14 September 1928–13 December 1930
Paul Painlevé	13 December 1930–26 January 1931
J. L. Dumesnil	27 January 1931–21 February 1932
None	22 February 1932–2 June 1932
Paul Painlevé	3 June 1932–31 January 1933
Pierre Cot	31 January 1933–7 February 1934
General Victor Denain	9 February 1934–22 January 1936
Marcel Déat	24 January 1936–4 June 1936
Pierre Cot	4 January 1936–18 January 1938
Guy La Chambre	18 January 1938–21 March 1940
André Laurent-Eynac	21 March 1940–16 June 1940
General Bertrand Pujo	16 June 1940–12 July 1940

Chiefs of Staff (1930–1940)

General René Michaud	5 Oct. 1930–3 Jan. 1931 (Chief of General Staff Air Force)
General Joseph Barès	4 Jan. 1931–26 Aug. 1931 (Chief of General Staff Air Force)
General Emile Hergault	27 Aug. 1931–15 Jan. 1933 (Chief of General Staff Air Force)
General Joseph Barès	16 Jan. 1933–1 Apr. 1933 (Chief of General Staff Air Force)
General Victor Denain	1 Apr. 1933–8 Feb. 1934 (Chief of General Staff Air Force)

General Joseph Barès	15 Feb. 1934–2 Sept. 1934 (Chief of General Staff Air Force)
General Picard	3 Sept. 1934–25 Dec. 1935 (Deputy Chief of General Staff Air Force)
General Bertrand Pujo	26 Dec. 1935–14 Oct. 1936 (Chief of General Staff Air Force)
General Philippe Féquant	15 Oct. 1936–21 Feb. 1938 (Chief of General Staff Air Force)
General Joseph Vuillemin	22 Feb. 1938–2 Sept. 1939(Chief of General Staff Air Force)
General Joseph Vuillemin	2 Sept. 1939–4 July 1940 (Commanding General, Armée de l'Air)

PRIME MINISTERS, FOREIGN SECRETARIES, AND AIR MINISTERS OF GREAT BRITAIN (1914–1940)

Prime Ministers

H. H. Asquith	5 August 1914–May 1915
H. H. Asquith	May 1915–December 1916
David Lloyd George	December 1916–January 1919
David Lloyd George	December 1916–October 1919 (War Cabinet without portfolio)
David Lloyd George	January 1919–October 1922
Andrew Bonar-Law	October 1922–May 1923
Stanley Baldwin	May 1923–January 1924
J. Ramsay MacDonald	January–November 1924
Stanley Baldwin	November 1924–June 1929
J. Ramsay MacDonald	June 1929–August 1931
J. Ramsay MacDonald	August–November 1931
J. Ramsay MacDonald	November 1931–June 1935
Stanley Baldwin	June 1935–May 1937
Neville Chamberlain	May 1937–May 1940 (War Cabinet from September 1939)
Winston Churchill	May 1940–1945

Foreign Secretaries

Sir Edward Grey	[December 1905]–December 1916
Arthur J. Balfour	December 1916–October 1919
Lord Curzon	October 1919–January 1924
J. Ramsay MacDonald	January–November 1924
Austen Chamberlain	November 1924–June 1929
Arthur Henderson	June 1929–August 1931
Marquis of Reading	August–November 1931
Sir John Simon	November 1931–June 1935

Sir Samuel Hoare	June–December 1935
Anthony Eden	December 1935–February 1938
Lord Halifax	March 1938–December 1940
Anthony Eden	December 1940–[July 1945]

Air Ministers (Secretaries of State for Air)

Winston Churchill	January 1919–April 1921 and Secretary of War, Jan. 1919–Feb. 1921
Capt. Frederick Guest	April 1921–October 1922
Sir Samuel Hoare	October 1922–January 1924
Christopher Birdwood [Lord] Thomson	January–November 1924
Sir Samuel Hoare	November 1924–June 1929
Christopher Birdwood [Lord] Thomson	June 1929–October 1930
William Warrender Mackenzie, Lord Amulree	October 1930–November 1931
Charles Vane-Tempest-Stewart, Marquis of Londonderry	November 1931–June 1935
Sir Philip Cunliffe Lister	June 1935–May 1938 [Created Viscount Swinton]
Sir Kingsley Wood	May 1938–April 1940
Sir Samuel Hoare	April–May 1940
Sir Archibald Sinclair	May 1940–[May 1945]

STRUCTURES DE L'ARMÉE DE L'AIR
AU 1ER JUILLET 1934 (5 RÉGIONS AÉRIENNES)

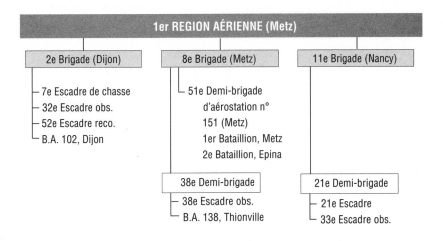

1er REGION AÉRIENNE (Metz)

2e Brigade (Dijon)
- 7e Escadre de chasse
- 32e Escadre obs.
- 52e Escadre reco.
- B.A. 102, Dijon

8e Brigade (Metz)
- 51e Demi-brigade
  d'aérostation n°
  151 (Metz)
  1er Bataillion, Metz
  2e Bataillion, Epina

38e Demi-brigade
- 38e Escadre obs.
- B.A. 138, Thionville

11e Brigade (Nancy)

21e Demi-brigade
- 21e Escadre
- 33e Escadre obs.

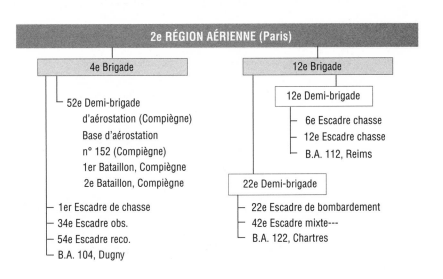

2e RÉGION AÉRIENNE (Paris)

4e Brigade
- 52e Demi-brigade
  d'aérostation (Compiègne)
  Base d'aérostation
  n° 152 (Compiègne)
  1er Bataillon, Compiègne
  2e Bataillon, Compiègne
- 1er Escadre de chasse
- 34e Escadre obs.
- 54e Escadre reco.
- B.A. 104, Dugny

12e Brigade

12e Demi-brigade
- 6e Escadre chasse
- 12e Escadre chasse
- B.A. 112, Reims

22e Demi-brigade
- 22e Escadre de bombardement
- 42e Escadre mixte---
- B.A. 122, Chartres

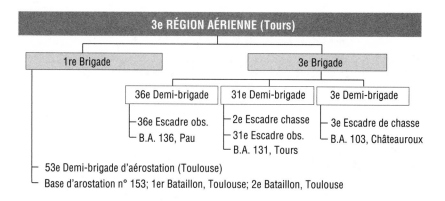

3e RÉGION AÉRIENNE (Tours)

1re Brigade

3e Brigade

36e Demi-brigade

31e Demi-brigade

3e Demi-brigade

- 36e Escadre obs.
- B.A. 136, Pau

- 2e Escadre chasse
- 31e Escadre obs.
- B.A. 131, Tours

- 3e Escadre de chasse
- B.A. 103, Châteauroux

- 53e Demi-brigade d'aérostation (Toulouse)
- Base d'arostation n° 153; 1er Bataillon, Toulouse; 2e Bataillon, Toulouse

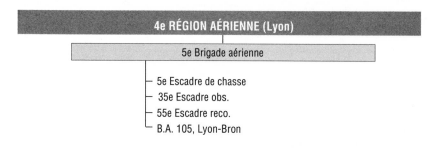

4e RÉGION AÉRIENNE (Lyon)

5e Brigade aérienne

- 5e Escadre de chasse
- 35e Escadre obs.
- 55e Escadre reco.
- B.A. 105, Lyon-Bron

5e RÉGION AÉRIENNE (Alger)

37e Régiment d'aviation, Rabat (Maroc)

- 1er Groupe d'aviation d'Afrique. Blida, Sétif (Algérie)
- 2e Groupe d'aviation d'Afrique. La Sénia, Colomb-Béchard (Algérie)
- 4e Escadre d'aviation d'Afrique. El Aouina, Sidi-Ahmed (Tunisie)

LEVANT

39e Régiment d'aviation. Rayack (Liban)

AÉRONAUTIQUE COLONIALE

Indochine : 4 escadrilles. Madagascare : 1 escadrille A.E.F. : 1 escadrille
A.O.F. : 3 escadrilles. Côte française des Somalis : 1 demi-escadrille

ORGANISATION GÉNÉRALE DE L'ARMÉE DE L'AIR EN TEMPS DE PAIX

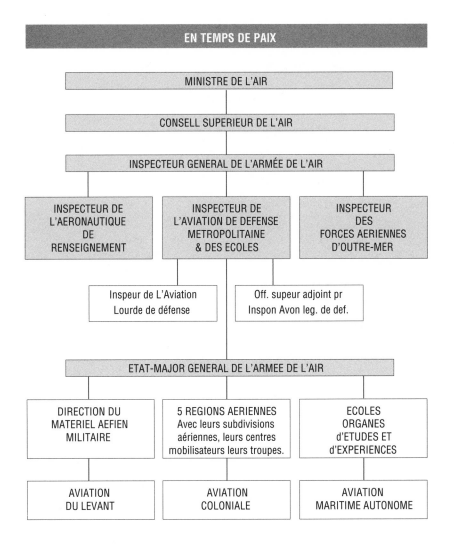

EN TEMPS DE PAIX

MINISTRE DE L'AIR

CONSELL SUPERIEUR DE L'AIR

INSPECTEUR GENERAL DE L'ARMÉE DE L'AIR

INSPECTEUR DE L'AERONAUTIQUE DE RENSEIGNEMENT	INSPECTEUR DE L'AVIATION DE DEFENSE METROPOLITAINE & DES ECOLES	INSPECTEUR DES FORCES AERIENNES D'OUTRE-MER

Inspeur de L'Aviation Lourde de défense	Off. supeur adjoint pr Inspon Avon leg. de def.

ETAT-MAJOR GENERAL DE L'ARMEE DE L'AIR

DIRECTION DU MATERIEL AEFIEN MILITAIRE	5 REGIONS AERIENNES Avec leurs subdivisions aériennes, leurs centres mobilisateurs leurs troupes.	ECOLES ORGANES d'ETUDES ET d'EXPERIENCES
AVIATION DU LEVANT	AVIATION COLONIALE	AVIATION MARITIME AUTONOME

ORGANISATION TERRITORIALE

I – ORGANISATION TERRITORIALE –

A la date du 15 Octobre 1939, l'organisation territorial de l'Armée de l'Air sera celle définie par les tableaux A et B ciaprès:

A – Tracé des Régions Aériennes –

Régions Aériennes		Correspondance avec l'organisation territorial de l'Armée de Terre
Ière Région Aérienne,	DIJON	5°, 7°, 8°, 10°, 20° Régions Militaires
comprenant:		
la 1° Subdivis. Aérienne	ORLEANS	
2° - -	DIJON	
3° - -	NANCY	
2ème Région Aérienne,	PARIS	1, 2, 6, 12 Régions Milit.,
comprenant:		Region de Paris,
la 4° Subdivis. Aérienne,	REIMS	1° et 2° Subdivisions de la 3° Region Militaire,
5° - -	AMIENS	4° Subdivis.de la 4° Reg.Milit.
6° - -	PARIS	
7° - -	ROUEN	
3ème Région Aérienne,	TOURS	9°, 11°, 17°, 18° Régions Milit.
comprenant:		
la 8° Subdivis. Aérienne,	RENNES	4° Rég. Milit. mons sa 4° Subdivis.
9° - -	TOURS	3° et 4° Subdiv. de la 3° Région Militaire
10° - -	TOULOUSE	
4ème Région Aérienne,	AIX-en-PROVENCE	13°, 14°, 15°, 16° Régions Militaires, y compris la Corse.
comprenant:		
la 11° subdivis. Aérienne,	MARSEILLE	
12° - -	LYON	
5ème Région Aérienne,	ALGER	Territoire de la Tunisie, 19ème Corps d Armée, Territoire du Maroc.
comprenant:		
les Commandements de l'Air:		
- de Tunisie	TUNIS	
- d'Algérie	ALGER	
- du Maroc	RABAT	

B – ....

ORGANISATION DE L'ARMÉE DE L'AIR
AU 1ER JUILLET 1939

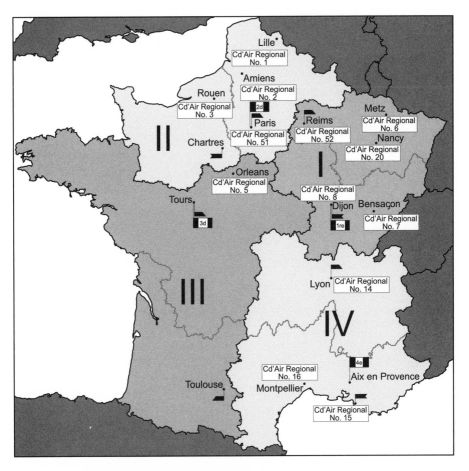

Cd'Air Regional is the Air Regional Command
Headquarters.

I - IV indicate divisions of the l'Armée de l'Air

NOTES

Preface

1. As background reading on France, see Rod Kedward, *France and the French: A Modern History* (New York: Overlook Press, 2006); Robert Magraw, *A History of the French Working Class*, vol. 1, *The Age of Artisanal Revolution, 1815–1871*, and vol. 2, *Workers and the Bourgeois Republic, 1871–1939* (Oxford: Blackwell, 1992); Pierre Nora, ed., *Rethinking France: Les Lieux de Memoire*, vol. 1, *The State*; vol. 2, *Space* (Chicago: University of Chicago Press, 1999, 2006); Shanny Peer, *France on Display: Peasants, Provincials, and Folklore in the 1937 Paris World's Fair* (Albany: State University of New York, 1998); Graham Robb, *The Discovery of France: A Historical Geography from the Revolution to the First World War* (New York: W. W. Norton, 2007).

2. Robert B. Bruce, *Pétain: Verdun to Victory* (Washington, DC: Potomac Books, 2008); Robert Frankenstein, *Le prix du réarmement français, 1935–1939* (Paris: Sorbonne, 1982); Albert Sauvy, *Histoire économique de la France entre les deux guerres, 1939–1939*, vol. 1, *De L'amistice à la dévaluation de la livre*, vol. 2, *De Pierre Laval à Paul Reynaud* (Paris: Fayard, 1965, 1967); Charles Williams, *Pétain: How the Hero of France Became a Convicted Traitor and Changed the Course of History* (New York: Macmillan, 2005).

3. The Riom *procès* during 1942–1943 was the Vichy effort to prove that Troisième République leaders were responsible for the 1940 French defeat by the Germans. It enabled historians to compare prewar statements and actions with those of 1942.

4. Marc Bloch, *Strange Defeat: A Statement of Evidence Written in 1940* (New York: W. W. Norton, 1968); André Géraud (under the pseudonym Pertinax), *Les fossoyeurs* [*The Gravediggers of France*] (Paris: Editions du Sagittaire, 1944; Garden City, NY: Doubleday, Doran & Co., 1944).

5. The "man on horseback" is a dynamic military leader.

6. Jean-Baptiste Duroselle, *La décadence (1932–1939): Politique extérieure de la France* (Paris: Imprimerie Nationale, 1979).

7. William L. Shirer, *The Collapse of the Third Republic* (New York: Simon & Schuster, 1969).

8. Robert B. Young, *In Command of France* (Cambridge, MA: Harvard University Press, 1978).

9. "The Indomitable de Gaulle," *The Economist* (29 June 2010): 52; and "France's Noble Exasperating Icon," review of Jonathan Fenby's *The General: Charles de Gaulle and the France He Saved* (New York: Simon and Schuster, 2010), in *The Economist* (17 June 2010): 85–86. Matt Parry has commented in *French History* 16, no. 4 (2002): 41–468, on neglect of the archives since 1980. See also *The Economist* (20 Mar. 2010): 58, review of the 2010 film *La rafle* about the police round-up of Parisian Jews in 1942.

10. Robert Gildea, *Marianne in Chains: Daily Life in the Heart of France During the German Occupation* (New York: Metropolitan Books, 2002), 4–13. Marianne is the national emblem of France and an allegory of Liberty and Reason.

11. "*La France profonde*" refers to the profoundly "French" aspects of French towns, villages, and rural life, and excludes the life of Paris.

12. Allan R. Millett, Williamson Murray, and Kenneth H. Watman, "The Effectiveness of Military Organization," *International Security* 11, no. 1 (Summer 1986): 37–71.

13. Robin Higham and Stephen J. Harris, eds., *Why Air Forces Fail: The Anatomy of Defeat* (Lexington: University of Kentucky Press, 2006, enlarged 2012).

14. See Patrick Fridenson and other French writers on aeronautical construction; and Philip Jarrett, ed., *Biplane to Monoplane: Aircraft Development 1919–1939* (London: Putnam; Herndon, VA: Brassey's, 1997). In recent years there have been a number of studies that have addressed innovation, change, and modernization. See, for instance, Eugenia Kiesling, "Resting Uncomfortably on Its Laurels: The Army of Interwar France," in *The Challenge of Change: Military Institutions and the New Realities, 1918–1941*, ed. Harold R. Winton and David Mets (Lincoln: University of Nebraska Press, 2000), 1–34; Dennis E. Showalter, "Military Innovations and the Whig Perspective of History," in *The Challenge of Change*, ed. Winton and Mets, 220–236; Harold R. Winton and David Mets, eds., *The Challenge of Change: Military Institutions and the New Realities, 1918–1941* (Lincoln: University of Nebraska Press, 2000). See also the following in Allan R. Millett and Williamson Murray, eds., *Military Effectiveness* (London: LSE/Routledge, 1988), 1–30; Millett, Murray, and Watman, "The Effectiveness of Military Organization"; Williamson Murray, "Armored Warfare: The British, French, and German Experiences," in *Military Innovation in the Interwar Period*, ed. Williamson Murray and Allan R. Millett (New York: Cambridge University Press, 1996), 6–49; Williamson Murray and Allan R. Millett, eds., *Military Innovation in the Interwar Period* (New York: Cambridge University Press, 1996), "Introduction," 1–5; Barry Watts and Wiliamson Murray, "Military Innovation in Peacetime," 369–415.

Also see Anon., "Decision Superiority: An Air Force Concept Paper," no. 28 (Nov. 2008) (Canberra, Aus.: [RAAF] Air Power Development Centre, 2008). Also, see Jonathan Dewald, "Lost Worlds: French Historians and the Construction of Modernity," *French History* 14, no. 4 (Dec. 2000): 424–442; and Williamson Murray and Richard Hart Sinnreich, *The Past Is Prologue: The Impact of History to the Military Profession* (New York: Cambridge University Press, 2006).

15. Elizabeth Kier, *Imagining War: French and British Military Doctrine Between the Wars* (Princeton, NJ: Princeton University Press, 1997).

16. Patrick Fridenson and Jean Lecuir, *La France et la Grande-Bretagne face aux problèmes aériens, 1935–Mai 1940* (Vincennes: SHAA, 1976).

17. Fernand Braudel, *The Identity of France* [*L'identité de la France*], vol. 2, *People and Production*, trans. Sian Reynolds (New York: Harper Collins, 1990).

18. Harold Larnder, "The Origin of Operational Research," *Operations Research* 32, no. 2 (Mar.–Apr. 1984): 471.

19. Ibid., 474.

20. Talbot C. Imlay and Monica Duffy Toft, eds., *The Fog of Peace and War Planning: Military and Strategic Planning Under Uncertainty* (London: Routledge, 2006).

21. The reader may wish to reference the following: Emanuel Chadeau, *L'industrie aéronautique en France, 1900–1950: De Blériot à Dassault* (Paris: Fayard, 1987); Patrick Facon, "The High Command of the French Air Force and the Problem of Rearmament, 1938–1939: A Technical and Industrial Approach," in *The Conduct of the Second World War: An International Comparison*, ed. Horst Boog (Oxford: Berg, 1988, 1992), 148–168; and Thierry Vivier, *La Politique aéronautique militaire de France Janvier 1933–Septembre 1939* (Paris: Editions l'Harmattan, 1997). For the technical side here I have followed Colin Sinnott, *The Royal Air Force and Aircraft Design, 1923–1939: Air Staff Operational Requirements* (London: Frank Cass, 2001). See also Richard Bonney, "Twenty Years On: A View of the Study of French History from Its Co-Founders," *French History* 21, no. 2 (2007): 231–236; Chadeau, *L'industrie aéronautique en France*; Charles Christienne and Pierre Lissarrague, *A History of French Military Aviation* [*Histoire de l'aviation militaire française*] (Washington, DC: Smithsonian Institution Press, 1986); Jean-Louis Crémieux-Brilhac, *Les français de l'an 40*, vol. 1, *La guerre oui ou non?* and vol. 2, *Ouvriers et soldats* (Paris: Gallimard, 1990); Donna Evleth, "The Ordre Des Medecins in Vichy France, 1940–1946," *French History* 20, no. 2 (June 2006): 204–224; Stanley Hoffmann, "Paradoxes of the French Political Community," in *In Search of France: The Economy, Society, and Political System in the Twentieth Century*, ed. Stanley Hoffmann, Charles P. Kindleberger, Laurence Wylie, Jesse R. Pitts, Jean-Baptiste Duroselle, and François Goguel (Cambridge, MA: Harvard University Press, 1963 and New York: Harper & Row, 1965), 1–117; Kedward, *France and the French*; Paul Lawrence, "Un flot d'agitateurs politique, de fauteurs de désordre et de criminels: Adverse Perceptions of Immigrants in France Between the Wars," *French History* 14, no. 2 (June 2000): 201–221.

Introduction: France to 1940

1. Karine Varley, "Under the Shadow of Defeat: The State and the Commemoration of the Franco-Prussian War, 1871–1914," *French History* 16, no. 3 (2002): 323–344.

2. Rachel Chrastil, *Organizing for War: France, 1870–1914* (Baton Rouge: Louisiana State University Press, 2010); and John H. Morrow Jr., "Review Article:

Refighting the First World War," *International History Review* 28, no. 3 (Sept. 2006): 561–565.

3. Arthur Fontaine, *French Industry During the War* (New Haven, CT: Yale University Press, 1926), App. II., 403–405.

4. For Léon Blum and the Comintern, see Léon Blum, *Chef de gouvernement, 1936–1937*, a Colloquia held at the National Political Science Foundation, 17–26 Mar. 1965 (Paris: Presses de la Fondation Nationale des Sciences Politique, 1967).

5. Philippe Bernard and Henri Dubief, *The Decline of the Third Republic, 1914–1938*, transl. Anthony Forster (London: Cambridge University Press, 1985), 169–170.

6. Ibid., 191.

7. Peter Hart, *The Somme: The Darkest Hour on the Western Front* (New York: Pegasus Books, 2008). According to Hart, total British casualties in World War I were 908,371 dead for the Empire, of whom 131,000 were killed on the Somme in 1916 of 419,654 casualties there (p. 328).

8. Roy Hattersley, *Borrowed Time: The Story of Britain Between the Wars* (London: Little Brown, 2007); see the review in *BBC History* (Dec. 2007): 60.

9. Ronald Hyam, *Britain's Declining Empire: The Road to Decolonization, 1918–1968* (New York: Cambridge University Press, 2006).

10. Syndicalism is a radical political movement that advocates bringing industry and government under the control of federations of labor unions.

Chapter 1. Britain and France

1. Irving B. Holley Jr., *Ideas and Weapons* (New Haven, CT: Yale University Press, 1953); and Timothy Moy, "Structure Ascendant: I. B. Holley, *Ideas and Weapons*," *Technology and Culture* (Oct. 2005): 797–804.

2. Air Cdre. Neville Parton, "The Development of Early RAF Doctrine," *Journal of Military History* 72, no. 4 (Oct. 2008): 1153–1177; and Wesley K. Wark, "The Air Defence Gap: British Air Doctrine and Intelligence Warnings in the 1930s," in *The Conduct of the Air War in the Second World War: An International Comparison*, ed. Horst Boog (Conference 1988) (Oxford: Berg, 1992), 512.

3. Edward Carlos Carter, Robert Forster, and John N. Moody, *Enterprise and Entrepreneurs in Nineteenth and Twentieth Century France* (Baltimore: Johns Hopkins University Press, 1976).

4. John Ferris, "The Greatest Power on Earth: Great Britain in the 1920's," *International History Review* (Can.) 13, no. 4 (1991): 726–750; Robin Higham, *Official Histories* (Manhattan: Kansas State University Library, 1970); and Robin Higham, ed., with Dennis Showalter, *Researching World War I: A Handbook* (Westport, CT: Greenwood, 2003).

5. Christienne and Lissarrague, *A History of French Military Aviation*; and A. J. P. Taylor, *English History, 1914–1945* (Oxford: Clarendon Press, 1965), 73–111.

6. Carl von Clausewitz, *On War* (1833), several modern editions; S. E. Finer, *The Man on Horseback: The Role of the Military in Politics* (London: Pall Mall Press, 1962); Jere Clemens King, *Generals and Politicians: Conflict Between France's High Command, Parliament and the Government, 1914–1918* (Berkeley: University of California Press, 1951).

7. Cyril Falls, *The First World War* (London: Longman's, 1960).

8. Bloch, *Strange Defeat*; Hoffman et al., *In Search of France.*

9. King, *Generals and Politicians.*

10. Georges Wormser, *La république de Clemenceau* (Paris: Presses Universitaire de France, 1961).

11. Hoffman et al., *In Search of France.* Hoffman's 1959 essay was reprinted therein.

12. Michael Howard, *The Continental Commitment: The Dilemma of British Defence Policy in the Era of the Two World Wars* (London: Temple Smith, 1972).

13. Gerd Hardach, "Industrial Mobilization in 1914–1918: Production, Planning, and Ideology," in *The French Home Front 1914–1918*, ed. Patrick Friedenson (Oxford: Berg, 1992), 57–88.

14. Hardach, "Industrial Mobilization in 1914–1918."

15. John F. Godfrey, *Capitalism at War: Industrial Policy and Bureaucracy in France, 1914–1919* (Lexington Spa, UK: Berg, 1987); and Richard F. Kuisel, *Capitalism and the State in Modern France, Renovation and Economic Management in the Twentieth Century* (London: Cambridge University Press, 1981).

16. Charles S. Maier, *Recasting Bourgeois Europe: Stabilization in France, Germany, and Italy in the Decade After the World War* (Princeton, NJ: Princeton University Press, 1975).

17. Godfrey, *Capitalism at War.*

18. Mary Lynn Stewart, *Women, Work, and the French State: Labour Protection and Social Patriarchy, 1879–1919* (Kingston, Ontario, Can.: McGill-Queen's University Press, 1989), 191.

19. Godfrey, *Capitalism at War*, 37 ff.

20. Bernard Gonon, "Les moteurs d'avion et l'evolution de l'armée aérienne, 1914–1940," *Proceedings*, Colloque International, Paris, École militaire (4–7 Sept. 1984): 251–255.

21. John H. Morrow, *The Great War in the Air: Military Aviation from 1909 to 1921* (Washington, DC: Smithsonian Institution Press, 1993).

22. Hoffman et al., *In Search of France.*

23. Magraw, *A History of the French Working Class*, vol. 1, *The Age of Artisan Revolution, 1815–1871*, vol. 2, *Workers and the Bourgeois Republic, 1871–1939*, 148.

24. Laura Lee Downs, *Manufacturing Inequality: Gender Division in the French and British Metalworking Industries, 1914–1939* (Ithaca, NY: Cornell University Press, 1995); Hoffman et al., *In Search of France.*

25. The number of British casualties depends on whether or not the imperial contingents are counted. See www.google.com, "Casualties of the First World War."

26. Taylor, *English History, 1914–1945.*

27. J. M. Bruce, *British Aeroplanes, 1914–1918* (London: Putnam, 1957); Air Cdre. Peter J. Dye, "France and the Development of British Military Aviation," *Royal Air Force Air Power Review* 12, no. 1 (Spring 2009): 1–13; and Peter Fearon, "The Formative Years of the British Aircraft Industry, 1913–1924," *Business History Review* 43, no. 4 (Winter 1969): 476–495.

28. J. M. Bruce, *Aircraft of the Royal Flying Corps [Military Wing]* (London: Putnam, 1982); Robin Higham, *The British Rigid Airship, 1908–1931: A Study in Weapons Policy* (London: G. T. Foulis, 1961); Morrow, *The Great War in the Air*; Owen Thetford, *British Naval Aircraft Since 1912* (London: Putnam, 1977).

29. Morrow, *The Great War in the Air*; Sir Walter Raleigh and W. A. Jones, *The War in the Air*, 6 vols. (London: HMSO, 1922–1937); Hilary St. George Saunders, *Per Ardua: The Rise of British Air Power, 1911–1939* (London: Oxford University Press, 1944); and Sydney F. Wise, *The Official History of the Royal Canadian Air Force*, vol. 1, *Canadian Airmen and the First World War* (Toronto, Can.: University of Toronto Press, 1980).

30. George Kent Williams, *Biplanes and Bombsights: British Bombing in World War I* (Maxwell AFB, AL: Air University Press, 1999).

31. Morrow, *The Great War in the Air.*

Chapter 2. Postwar, 1918–1932

1. Salvador de Madariaga, *Englishmen, Frenchmen, and Spaniards* (New York: Hill & Wang, 1989 [orig. 1928]). See also Sharon Begley, "West Brain, East Brain: What a Difference Culture Makes," *Newsweek* (1 Mar. 2010): 22; Sisley Huddleston, *France and the French* (New York: Charles Scribner's, 1925); Sisley Huddleston, *France—The Tragic Years 1939–1947: An Eyewitness Account of War, Occupation, and Liberation* (New York: Devin-Adair, 1955); and Ivor Richard, *We, the British: An Inside Look at Foibles, Customs, and Institutions* (New York: Doubleday, 1983).

2. Martin S. Alexander, ed., *Knowing Your Friends: Intelligence Inside Alliances and Coalitions from 1914 to the Cold War* (London: Frank Cass, 1998), 14; Robb, *The Discovery of France*; Robert Gildea, *Children of the Revolution: The French, 1799–1914* (London: Allen Lane, 1008), the third volume in the Penguin trilogy replacing Albert Cobban's classic volumes, *History of Modern France*, which cover 1715–1962. See also J. P. Daughton, *An Empire Divided: Religion, Republicanism, and the Making of French Colonialism, 1880–1914* (New York: Oxford University Press, 2006).

For the ongoing French volatility in politics and the man-on-horseback syndrome, see *Time*, 26 September 1969, 34–35; and "Manifesto Takes Air Out of Racism in France," *USA Today*, 11 Nov. 2008, regarding the French president's wife. See also the Bodleian Library, ed., *Instructions for British Servicemen in France, 1944* (Oxford, UK: Bodleian Library, University of Oxford, 2006); Emma Griffin, *Blood Sport: Hunting in Britain Since 1066* (New Haven, CT: Yale University Press, 2007); Peter Mandler, *The English Character: The History in Idea from Edmun Burke to Tony Blair* (New Haven, CT: Yale University Press, 2006); W. D. Rubinstein, "British Millionaires, 1809–1949," *Bulletin of the Institute of Historical Research* (Nov. 1974): 202–223; and *"The English": The Times Literary Supplement*, 7 Aug. 1948 [off-print].

3. William B. Cohen, "The Lure of Empire: Why Frenchmen Entered the Colonial Service," *Journal of Contemporary History* 4, no. 1 (Jan. 1969): 103–116.

4. Royal Air Force Historical Society, *Royal Air Force Reserve and Auxiliary Air Forces* (2003).

5. Braudel, *The Identity of France*, vol. 2, *People and Production*, 543–556, 674–679; and Huddleston, *France and the French*.

6. Adrian Gregory, *The Last Great War: British Society and the First World War* (New York: Cambridge University Press, 2008); Catherine Hall and Sonya A. Rose, *At Home with the Empire: Metropolitan Culture and the Imperial World* (New York: Cambridge University Press, 2007); and Juliet Nicolson, *The Great Silence, 1918–1920: Living in the Shadow of the Great War* (London: BBC History Books, 2009).

7. Sir Ian Jacob, "Principles of British Military Thought," *Foreign Affairs* 29, no. 2 (Jan. 1951): 219–229; and Christopher Lee, "Evolution of the Nation," *BBC History* (Dec. 2007): 33–35.

8. Peter Dennis, *Decision by Default: Peacetime Conscription and British Defence, 1919–1939* (London: Routledge, 1972); and Robin Higham, *Armed Forces in Peacetime: Britain, 1918–1939* (London: Foulis, 1962), 244–245.

9. M. Kirby and R. Capey, "The Air Defence of Great Britain, 1920–1940: An Operational Research Perspective," *Journal of the Operational Research Society*, 48 (May 1997): 555–568; and United Kingdom, National Archives, AIR 20/32, *Review of Air Defence Policy, 1923–1935*.

10. On the evolution of grand-strategic bombing see Robin Higham, *The Military Intellectuals in Britain, 1918–1939* (New Brunswick, NJ: Rutgers University Press, 1966), 160–234; Neville Jones, *The Origins of Strategic Bombing* (London: Kimber, 1973); Barry P. Powers, *Strategy Without Slide Rule* (London: Croom Helm, 1976); and Air Cdre. Henry Probert, *"Bomber Harris": His Life and Times* (London: Greenhill Books, 2001).

11. The essential work is Sir Charles Webster and Noble Frankland, *The Strategic Air Offensive Against Germany, 1939–1945*, 4 vols. (London: HMSO, 1961). For a recent reassessment of Bomber Command see Stephen J. Harris, "RAF Bomber Command as Phoenix," in *Why Air Forces Fail: The Anatomy of Defeat*, 2nd ed., ed. Robin Higham and Stephen J. Harris (Lexington: University Press

of Kentucky, 2012). For an overview of the recent controversies see Tami Davis Biddle, "Dresden 1945: Reality, History, and Myth," *Journal of Military History* 72 (Apr. 2008): 413–449.

12. Taylor, *English History, 1914–1945*, vol. 15, 240–243.

13. Ibid., 248.

14. Ibid., 249.

15. Martin Horn and Talbot Imlay, "Money in Wartime: France's Financial Preparations for the Two World Wars," *International History Review* 27, no. 4 (Dec. 2005): 709–753.

16. Higham and Harris, *Why Air Forces Fail*.

17. Roger Beaumont, *Right Backed by Might—The International Air Force Concept* (Westport, CT: Greenwood, 2002).

18. Ibid.; Franklyn Arthur Johnson, *Defence by Committee: The British Committee of Imperial Defence, 1885–1959* (London: Oxford University Press, 1960); Nicholas d'Ombrain, *War Machinery and High Policy: Defence Administration in Peacetime Britain, 1902–1914* (London: Oxford University Press, 1973).

19. Stephen W. Roskill, *Hankey: Man of Secrets*, vol. 1, *1919–1931* (London: Collins 1972).

20. Anthony Adamthwaite, *Grandeur and Misery: France's Bid for Power in Europe, 1914–1940* (London: Arnold, 1995).

21. Claude d'Abzac-Epézy, *L'Armée de l'Air de Vichy, 1940–1944* (Vincennes: SHAA, 1997), 33–91.

22. Richard Vinen, *The Politics of French Business 1936–1945* (London: Cambridge University Press, 1991), 22.

23. Gen. Lucien Robineau, "French Air Policy in the Inter-war Period and the Conduct of the Air War Against Germany from September 1939 to June 1940," in *The Conduct of the Air War in the Second World War: An International Comparison*, ed. Horst Boog (Oxford: Berg, 1992), 650–657. See also Robert W. Krauskopf, "French Air Power Policy, 1919–1939," Ph.D. Dissertation, Georgetown University, Washington, DC, 1965.

24. See Julian Jackson, *The Fall of France: The Nazi Invasion of 1940* (Oxford: Oxford University Press, 2003), 104–141; and William Wiser, *The Twilight Years: Paris in the 1930s* (London: Robson Books, 2001), 228 ff.

25. S/Ldr. Peter Brown, *Honour Restored: The Battle of Britain, Dowding, and the Fight for Freedom* (Staplehurst, UK: Spellmount, 2005); Winston S. Churchill, *History of the Second World War*, vol. 2, *Their Finest Hour* (Boston: Houghton Mifflin, 1948); Martin Gilbert, *Winston S. Churchill*, vol. 4 and vol. 6 (London: Heinemann, 1975–1983); T. C. G. James, *Air Defence of Great Britain*, vol. 1, *The Growth of Fighter Command, 1936–1940*, ed. with an introduction by Sebastian Cox (London: Frank Cass, 2002); and Robert Wright, *The Man Who Won the Battle of Britain* (New York: Scribner's, 1969).

26. See Charles Christienne, Patrick Facon, Patrice Buffotot, and Lee Kennett, *French Military Aviation: A Bibliographical Guide* (New York: Garland, 1989); and Robin Higham, *100 Years of Air Power and Aviation* (College Station: Texas A&M University Press, 2003). Of 825 entries on the interwar years, only three deal with maneuvers: "Histoire de l'Armament Française," special issue of *Revue Historique de l'Armée* (1984); Phillip S. Meilinger, *Airmen and Air Theory* (Maxwell AFB, AL: Air University Press, 2001) [limited essentially to U.S. airmen]; and Winton and Mets, *The Challenge of Change*.

27. Karl Gundelach, "Commentary," *The Conduct of the Air War in the Second World War: An International Comparison* [1988 Conference, *The Conduct of the Air War in the Second World War*], ed. Horst Boog (Oxford: Berg, 1992), 496–507; and John Terraine, "The Theory and Practice of the Air War: The Royal Air Force," in *The Conduct of the Air War in the Second World War*, ed. Boog, 467–495.

28. Horn and Imlay, "Money in Wartime"; Faris R. Kirkland, "Planes, Pilots, and Politics: French Military Aviation, 1919–1940," *Proceedings of the 1988 National Aerospace Conference* (Dayton, OH: Wright State University, 1999), 285–293. The story is complex and wanting as to that south of the Channel by lack of research in France. To the north of the Channel, we are much better served by several relatively recent detailed studies of the hidden processes that bound the Air Ministry to the manufacturers. Not only are there the Putnam volumes, but also Sinnott, *The Royal Air Force and Aircraft Design*.

29. Robert J. Young, "Preparation for Defeat: French War Doctrine in the Interwar Period," *Journal of European Studies* 2, no. 2 (June 1972): 155–172; and Robert J. Young, "The Strategic Dream: French Air Doctrine in the Inter-war Period," *Journal of Contemporary History* 9, no. 4 (Oct. 1974): 57–76.

30. Christienne and Lissarrague, *A History of French Military Aviation*, 205–216 ff, on which this chapter is based.

31. Martin Alexander, *The Republic in Danger: General Maurice Gamelin and the Politics of French Defence, 1933–1940* (London: Cambridge University Press, 1992); Bernard Destremau, *Weygand* (Paris: Perrin, 1959); Gen. Maurice Gamelin, *Servir: Le prologue du drame (1930–août 1929)*, 3 vols. (Paris: Librairie Plon, 1946–1947); and Gen. Maxime Weygand, *Recalled to Service: The Memoirs of General Maxime Weygand of the Academie Français*, transl. E. W. Dickes, 3 vols. (Paris: 1950–1951).

32. Barnett Singer, *Maxime Weygand: A Bibliography of the French General of the Two World Wars* (Jefferson, NC: McFarland, 2008). On the Italian airpower theories see A. Curami and G. Rochat, eds., *Guilio Douhet Scritti, 1901–1915* (Rome: State Maggiore Aeronautica, Ufficio Storico, 1993); and Amadeo Mecozzi, *Scritti Scelti sul potere aereo e l'aviazione d'assalto (1920–1970)*, vol. 1, *Il periodo tra le due guerre e la 2a Guerra Mondiale (1920–1943)* and vol. 2, *Il dopoguerra e la guerra fredda (1945–1970)* (Rome: Aeronautica Militarie Ufficio Storica, 2006).

33. James S. Corum, *The Luftwaffe: Creating the Operational Air War 1918–1940* (Lawrence: University Press of Kansas, 1997).

34. Anon., "Juin le Morocain," *Revue Historique de l'Armée* 8, no. 2 (1952): 8–10; Nicole Cooper, *France in Indo-China: Colonial Encounters* (Oxford: Berg, 2000); Alf Andrew Heggoy and John M. Haar, *The Military in Imperial History: The French Connection* (New York: Garland, 1984); *Icare* 2, no. 121 (1987): 52–105; Rémy Le Clerc, "Les ailes française en Tunisie," *Revue Historique de l'Armée* 11, no. 1 (1955): 97–110; David E. Omissi, *Air Power and Colonial Control: The Royal Air Force 1919–1939* (Manchester, UK: Manchester University Press, 1990), 184–209; Capitaine de Montalembert, "Le front sud-tunisien 1915–1918," *Revue Historique de l'Armée* 11, no. 1 (1955); Peter A. Shamod, *French Imperialism in Syria, 1927–1936* (Reading, PA: Ithaca Press, 1998), 149–168.

35. See Martin Thomas on French colonial warfare, "At the Heart of Things? French Imperial Defense Planning in the Late 1930s," *French Historical Studies* 21, no. 2 (Spring 1981): 325–361; also Joyce Laverty Miller, "The Syrian Revolt of 1925," *International Journal of Middle East Studies* 8, no. 4 (Oct. 1977): 545–565.

36. Robert Allan Doughty, *The Seeds of Disaster: The Development of French Army Doctrine, 1919–1939* (Hamden, CT: Archon Books, 1985).

37. On the Royale, see Chalmers Hood, "The French Navy and Parliament Between the Wars," *International History Review* 6 (Aug. 1984): 386–403. See also Alexander, *The Republic in Danger*; George H. Cassar, *The French in the Dardenelles: A Study in the Failure of the Conduct of the War* (London: George Allen & Unwin, 1971); E. H. Jenkins, *A History of the French Navy from the Beginnings to the Present Day* (London: Macdonald and Jane's, 1973); Philippe Masson, *Historie de la Marine*, vol. 1, *L'ere de la voile*, vol. 2, *De la vapeur à l'atome* (Paris: Lavauzelle, 1981, 1983); Guy Pedroncini, *Pétain: General en chef, 1917–1918* (Paris: Presses Universitaire de France, 1974); and Owen Thetford, *British Naval Aircraft Since 1912* (London: Putnam, 1977).

38. For the DCA story, see Chapters 6 and 7 herein.

39. Eugenia C. Kiesling, *Arming Against Hitler: France and the Limits of Military Planning* (Lawrence: University Press of Kansas, 1996); and Eugenia C. Kiesling, "'If It Ain't Broke, Don't Fix It': French Military Doctrine Between the World Wars," *War in History* 3, no. 2 (1996): 208–223.

40. E-mail to the author, 13 April 2004.

41. André Beaufré, "Liddell Hart and the French Army, 1919–1939," in *The Theory and Practice of War: Essays Presented to Captain B. H. Liddell Hart*, ed. Michael Howard (London: Cassell, 1965); Brian Bond and Martin Alexander, "Liddell Hart and DeGaulle: The Doctrines of Limited Liability and Mobile Defence," in *Makers of Modern Strategy from Machiavelli to the Nuclear Age*, ed. Peter Paret (Princeton, NJ: Princeton University Press, 1986), 598–623; Brig. Gen. Charles Christienne, "Le haut commandement français face au progress technique entre les deux guerres," *ICMH Acta* 5, Bucharest, 10–17 Aug. 1980 (Bucharest, 1981): 398–412; Guilio Douhet, *Il dominio dell'aria* [*The Command of the Air*], trans. by Dino Ferrari (New York: Coward-McCann, 1942); Patrick Facon, "Douhet et sa doctrine à travers la literature militaire et aéronautique française de l'entre-deux-guerres: Une etude de perception," Congresso internazionale di Studi *La figura*

e l'opera di Guilio Douhet (Caserte: Società di Storia di Terra di Lavoro con la collaborazione dello Stato Maggiore dell'Aeronautica Militare), 12–14 Apr. 1987, *Actes* l (Società di Storia Patria di Lavoro, 1988): 109–127, reprinted in *Revue Historique des Armées* 1 (1988): 94–103; Irving M. Gibson, "Maginot and Liddell Hart: The Doctrine of Defence," in *Makers of Modern Strategy: Military Thought from Machiavelli to Hitler*, ed. E. M. Earle (Princeton, NJ: Princeton University Press, 1943); Marcellin Hodeir, "La chambre bleu horizon et la commission de l'armée face aux problemes de l'aviation militaire," *Colloque International* (Paris: École Militaire du 4 au 7 Sept. 1984): 341–352; Giorgio Rochat, "Douhet and the Italian Military Thought, 1919–1930," *Colloque International* (Paris: École militaire du 4 au 7 Sept.1984): 19–30; and Maurice Vaisse, "Le procès de l'aviation de bombardement," *Revue Historique des Armées* 2 (1977): 41–61.

42. Maj. René Prioux [Articles on armored warfare, 1922–1924; unable to locate source]. See also Jeffrey Clarke, "Military Technology in Republican France: The Evolution of the French Armored Force 1917–1940," Ph.D. Dissertation, Duke University, Durham, NC, 1968 (University microfilms 47 and 990); Faris R. Kirkland, "The Aristocratic Tradition and Adaptation to Change in the French Cavalry, 1920–1940," *European Studies Journal* 4, no. 2 (Fall 1987): 1–17; Col. François-André Paoli, *L'armée française de 1919 à 1939: La reconversion* (Vincennes: Service Historique de l'Armée de Terre, n.d.) [containing both chronology and text].

43. Kirkland, "The Aristocratic Tradition and Adaptation to Change in the French Cavalry."

44. Pierre Cot, *L'Armée de l'Air 1936–1938* (Paris: Edition Bernard Grasset, 1939); Paoli, *L'Armée française de 1919 à* 1939; Marcel Spivak, "Les problèmes posées à l'armée de l'air, et les perspectives d'independence de l'Armée de l'Air (1918–1934)," *Colloque International*, Paris (4–7 Sept. 1984): 177–189; Pascal Vennesson, "Institution and Air Power: The Making of the French Air Force," *Journal of Strategic Studies* 18 (1995): 36–67.

45. Paul-Marie de la Gorce, *The French Army: A Military-Political History* (New York: Brazillier, 1963). For much that follows, see Alexander, *The Republic in Danger.*

46. Jean Kerisel, *Albert Caquot, 1881–1976: Createur et precurseur* (Paris: Editions Eyrolles, 1978).

47. His Majesty's Dockyard cases. William Ashworth, *Contracts and Finances* (London: HMSO, 1953).

48. Chadeau, *L'industrie aéronautique en France.*

49. Claude Carlier, *Marcel Dassault: La légende d'un siècle* (Paris: Perrin, 1992); and Herrick Chapman, *State Capitalism and Working-Class Radicalism in the French Aircraft Industry* (Berkeley: University of California Press, 1991).

50. Ian V. Hogg, *Anti-Aircraft Artillery* (Ramsbury, Wilts., UK: Crowood Press, 2002), notably in France, 76–78, and in Britain, 66–75; and Mecozzi, *Scritti scelti sul poere areo e l'amazlone d'assalto*, vol. 1.

51. Gen. Maurice-Henri Gauché, *Le deuxième bureau au travail, 1935–1940* (Paris: Amiot-Dumont, 1953); and Julian Jackson, *France: The Dark Years, 1940–1944* (London: Oxford University Press, 2001).

52. Eric Ash, *Sir Frederick Sykes and the Air Revolution, 1912–1918* (London: Frank Cass, 1999); Andrew Boyle, *Trenchard: Man of Vision* (London: Cassell, 1956); Higham, *Armed Forces in Peacetime*; H. Montgomery Hyde, *British Air Policy Between the Wars, 1918–1939* (London: Heinemann, 1976); and Sir Frederick Sykes, *From Many Angles* (London: Harrap, 1942).

53. Air Marshal Sir Hugh M. Trenchard, *Permanent Organisation of the Royal Air Force: Note by the Secretary of State for Air on a Scheme Outlined by the Chief of the Air Staff* (Dec. 1919) (*Cmd.467*).

54. Stephen W. Roskill, *Naval Policy Between the Wars*, vol. 1 (New York: Walker and Co. 1968), 234–268, 356–420, 461–497, 512 ff.

55. Hyde, *British Air Policy Between the Wars*.

56. John Ferris, "Treasury Control: The Ten Year Rule and British Service Policies, 1919–1924," *Historical Journal* [UK] 30, no. 4 (Dec. 1987): 859–883; G/Cpt. E. B. Haslam, *The History of Royal Air Force Cranwell*, Air Historical Branch (RAF) (London: HMSO, 1982); Stephen W. Roskill, "The Ten Year Rule," *Journal of the Royal United Services Institute for Defence and Security Studies* 665 (Mar. 1972): 64–68; and Bill Taylor, *Halton and the Apprentice Scheme* (n.p.: Midland Publishing, n.d. [ca. 1995]).

57. For the history of the RAF, see Terraine, "The Theory and Practice of the Air War," 467 ff. See also Hyde, *British Air Policy Between the Wars*; and the older work by Saunders, *Per Ardua*. The Treasury's power over budgets did not really take effect until 1924 and especially after 1928 when it was placed on a rolling basis. Christopher M. Bell, "Winston Churchill and the Ten Year Rule," *The Journal of Military History* 74 (Oct. 2010): 1097–1128.

58. Joan Bradbrooke, *The Centenary History of the Royal Aeronautical Society* (London: Royal Aeronautical Society [RAeS], 1966); and on Cardington and Howden, see Higham, *The British Rigid Airship, 1908–1931*; and Gordon Kinsey, *Martlesham Heath* (Lavenham, UK: Terence Dalton, 1975).

59. Diana Urquhart, *The Ladies of Londonderry: Women and Political Patronage* (London: J. B. Taurus, 2007).

60. On Groves see John Ferris, "The Theory of a 'French Air Menace,' Anglo-French Relations and the British Home Defence Air Force Programmes of 1921–25," *Journal of Strategic Studies* 10, no. 1 (1987): 62–83; and Higham, *The Military Intellectuals in Britain*, 159–176.

61. Robin Higham, *Britain's Imperial Air Routes: 1918–1939*. (London: G. T. Foulis, 1960). See also United Kingdom, National Archives, CAB 3/3, CID, *Note on the Comparative Cost of the British and French Air Services*, CID 106-A, July 1922; and United Kingdom, National Archives, AIR 5/564 of 17 January 1921.

62. Stephen W. Roskill, *Admiral of the Fleet Earl Beatty* (New York: Athenaeum, 1981).

63. *Icare* 189, no. 2 (2004); Derek N. James, *Schneider Trophy Aircraft, 1913–1931* (London: Putnam, 1981).

64. Memorandum, CAS Hugh Trenchard, "The War Object of an Air Force," 1928, United Kingdom, National Archives, [formerly Public Record Office (PRO)] AIR 9/8.

65. A. D. English, "The RAF Staff College," *Journal of Strategic Studies* 16 (Sept. 1993): 408–431; John Ferris, "Fighter Defence Before Fighter Command: The Rise of Strategic Air Defence in Great Britain, 1917–1934," *Journal of Military History* 63, no. 4 (Oct. 1989): 854–884; W/Cdr L. L. MacLean, "Air Exercises 1935," *Journal of the Royal United Service Institution* (Jan. 1936): 50 ff.; G/Capt. F. C. "Dickie" Richardson, *Man Is Not Lost: The Log of a Pioneer RAF Pilot/ Navigator, 1933–1946* (Shrewsbury, UK: Airlife, 1997); Scot Robertson, *The Development of RAF Strategic Bombing Doctrine, 1919–1939* (Westport, CT: Praeger, 1995); Sinnott, *The Royal Air Force and Aircraft Design*; and United Kingdom, National Archives, AIR 10/1659, *SD98*.

66. Sir Charles Callwell, *Small Wars: Their Principles and Practice* (London: HMSO, 1896); Sir Julian Corbett, *Some Principles of Maritime Strategy* (London: Longmans, 1911); and United Kingdom, National Archives [PRO], Air Historical Branch, AIR 5/299, Air Publications (AP) 882, *CD 22 [Confidential Document], Operations Manual for the Royal Air Force* (July 1922).

67. Webster and Frankland, *The Strategic Air Offensive Against Germany,* vol. 4, 71–87, and vol. 1, 138–139, 190–201.

68. "Squadron Leader" (pseudonym), *Basic Principles of Air Warfare: The Influence of Air Power on Sea and Land Strategy* (Aldershot: Gale & Polden, 1927).

69. Robertson, *The Development of RAF Strategic Bombing.*

70. C. G. Jefford, *Observers and Navigators and Other Non-Pilot Aircrew in the RFC, RNAS, and RAF* (Shrewsbury, UK: Airlife, 2001).

71. Sinnott, *The Royal Air Force and Aircraft Design*, 224.

72. Ibid.

73. Richardson, *Man Is Not Lost.*

Chapter 3. French and British Aircraft Industries, 1918–1934

1. On the Technological Revolution see Ronald Miller and David Sawyers, *The Technical Development of Modern Aviation* (New York: Praeger, 1970). John Pannebecker's review of Bruno Belhoste, *La formation d'une technocratie: L'école polytechnique et ses élèves de la révolution au second empire* (Paris: Berlin, 2003), in *Technology and Culture* 46, no. 3 (July 2005): 618–622, provides a useful introduction to the French *écoles*. See also Jarrett, *Biplane to Monoplane*; and Robert Schlaifer and S. D. Heron, *The Development of Aircraft Engines and Aviation Fuels: Two Studies of the Relations Between Government and Industry* (Boston: Harvard University, Graduate School of Business Administration, 1950).

2. Michael Stephen Smith, *The Emergence of Modern Business Enterprise in France, 1800–1930* (Cambridge, MA: Harvard University Press, 2006), 416–420 on the aircraft industry, more generally 461–484. The author, however, skips the 1930s and concludes with the "golden" thirty years of 1960–1990.

3. This section is based on Christienne and Lissarrague, *A History of French Military Aviation*; and on Chadeau, *L'industrie aéronautique en France*; as well as on Chadeau's article, "Government, Industry, and Nation: The Growth of Aeronautical Technology in France (1900–1950)," *Aerospace Historian* (Mar. 1988): 26–44; and on Christienne, "Le haut commandement français face au progrès technique entre les deux guerres," *ICMH Acta 5*, Bucharest, 10–17 Aug. 1980 (Bucharest, 1981): 161–177, reprinted in *Recueil d'articles et d'études, 1979–1981* (Vincennes: SHAA, 1986), 398–412. For background, see Robert Fox and Anna Guagnini, eds., *Education, Technology, and Industrial Performance in Europe, 1850–1939* (London: Cambridge University Press, 1993); and Smith, *The Emergence of Modern Business Enterprise in France*. See also *Histoire de la France industrielle*, under the direction of Maurice Levy-Leboyer (Paris: Larousse, 1996).

4. Herschel Smith, *A History of Aircraft Piston Engines* (Manhattan, KS: Sunflower University Press, 1998).

5. Colonel Delaye and A. Dumas, "Les conquêtes de l'aluminium et des metaux légers," *Revue Historique de l'Armée* 16, no. 2 (1960): 121–140; R. L. [sic], "Le service des essences jusqua au en 1942," *Revue Historique de l'Armée* 12, no. 1 (1956): 123–130. See also S. D. Heron on aviation fuels in Schlaifer and Heron, *The Development of Aircraft Engines and Aviation Fuels*.

6. François Pernot, "Les missions aéronautiques françaises en Amérique du Sud dans les années vingt," *Revue Historique des Armées*, no. 185 (Dec. 1991): 97–107.

7. Crémieux-Brilhac, *Les français de l'an 40*, vol. 2, *Ouvriers et soldats*, 204–211.

8. Ibid.

9. Ibid., 197.

10. Christienne and Lissarrague, *A History of French Military Aviation*, 222.

11. Ibid.

12. Clarke, "Military Technology in Republican France."

13. Chadeau, *L'industrie aéronautique en France*, 149.

14. Ibid., 160.

15. Kerisel, *Albert Caquot*.

16. Ibid., 460.

17. Ibid., 180.

18. Ibid., 184.

19. Ibid., 196.

20. Ibid., 204.

21. Ibid., 212.

22. Ibid., 216.

23. Ibid., 222–223.

24. Sinnott, *The Royal Air Force and Aircraft Design*, 48–75. See also Ferris, "Fighter Defence Before Fighter Command"; Raymond Fredette, *The Sky on Fire: The First Battle of Britain, 1917–1918, and the Birth of the Royal Air Force* (New York: Holt, Rinehart & Winston, 1966, and Washington, DC: Smithsonian Institution Press, 1991); Robin Higham, "British Air Exercises of the 1930s," *Proceedings, National Aerospace Conference* (Dayton, OH: Wright State University, 1999): 303–312; H. F. King, *The Armament of British Aircraft, 1909–1939* (London: Putnam, 1971); and G. F. Wallace, *The Guns of the Royal Air Force 1939–1945* (London: Kimber, 1972).

25. M. M. Postan, D. Hay, and J. D. Scott, *The Design and Development of Weapons: Studies in Government and Industrial Organization* (London: HMSO, 1964). At this time in the Cold War there was much concern that the Soviets might learn something useful.

26. Sebastian Ritchie, *Industry and Air Power: The Expansion of British Aircraft Production, 1935–1941* (London: Frank Cass, 1997). See also Ritchie, "Aircraft Production Between the Wars," in *Biplane to Monoplane*, ed. Jarrett, 214–240; and Sebastian Ritchie, "The Price of Air Power: Technological Change, Industrial Policy, and Military Aircraft Contracts in the Era of British Rearmament, 1935–1939," *Business History Review* 71, no. 1 (1997): 82–111. See also Alec Harvey-Bailey, *The Merlin in Perspective—The Combat Years* (Derby, UK: Rolls-Royce Heritage Trust, 1981, 1995); Peter Fearon, "Aircraft Manufacturing," in *British Industry Between the Wars: Instability and Industrial Development, 1919–1939*, ed. Neil K. Burton and Derek H. Aldcroft (London: Scolar Press, 1979), 216–239; Ian Lloyd, *Rolls-Royce*, 3 vols. (London: Macmillan 1978) (vol. 1, *The Growth of a Firm*, vol. 2, *The Years of Endeavour*, vol. 3, *The Merlin at War*); Paul L. Robertson, "Technical Education in the British Shipbuilding and Marine Engineering Industries, 1863–1914," *Economic History Review*, 2nd series, 26, no. 2 (May 1974): 236–251. See also, Robin Higham, "Governments, Companies and National Defence: British Aeronautical Experience, 1918–1945 as the Basis of a Broad Hypothesis," *Business History Review* 39, no. 3 (Fall 1963): 325–344; and Robin Higham, "Quantity vs. Quality: The Impact of Changing Demand on the British Aircraft Industry 1900–1960," *Business History Review* 42, no. 4 (Winter 1968): 443–466.

27. Higham, *The Military Intellectuals in Britain*.

28. Ritchie, *Industry and Air Power*, 10.

29. Higham, *Britain's Imperial Air Routes, 1918–1939*; and Ritchie, *Industry and Air Power*, 29.

30. Higham, "Governments, Companies, and National Defence"; and Higham, "Quantity vs. Quality." [See note 26 herein, this chapter.]

31. Peter Brooks, *The Modern Airliner* (Manhattan, KS: Sunflower University Press, 1982); United Kingdom, National Archives, AIR 10/906, "Schedule of Fittings and Accessories for Aircraft Engines" (1923) and "Airframes" (1917).

32. Peter Fearon, "The British Airframe Industry and the State, 1918–1935," *Economic History Review* 27, no. 7 (May 1974): 236–251.

33. Darrel Stilton, "The Structural Revolution," in *Biplane to Monoplane*, ed. Jarrett, 127–140.

34. United Kingdom, Public Record Office, Ministry of Aircraft Production [PRO AVIA] 46/228, "Aircraft: The Spares Problem—Narrative." See also Robin Higham, "Royal Air Force Spares Forecasting in World War II," *[U.S.] Air Force Journal of Logistics* (Spring 1996): 23–26.

35. United Kingdom, National Archives, PRO AIR 10/1442 (1928), 1445 (1928), 1447, 1448 (1929), 1458 (1929), 1459 (1930), 1470 (1930), 1471 (1931), 1479 (1931), 1480 (1932), 1492 (1932), 1493 (1933), 1560 (1934), 1561 (1934), 1586 (1934), 1587 (1935), 1588 (1936), 1589 (1936), 1590 (1937), 1591 (1937), 1592 (1938), and 1593 (1938). For flying accidents, for instance, see United Kingdom, National Archives, AIR 10/1573 (1932, 1933), and 1574 for wastage and consumption of aircraft by types. United Kingdom, National Archives, AIR 50/1564 is the *20th Report on Flying Accidents During July–December 1933 (SD90 [2])* (Apr. 1934). United Kingdom, National Archives, AIR 10/1594 is the 1934 edition of Air Staff Memorandum, no. 50, *Data for the Calculation of Wastage and Consumption in War*, of which *SD98* of 1936 was the definitive document revised as newer aircraft entered the inventory. *SD98*, 4th edition (1941–43), is in United Kingdom, National Archives, AIR 10/3916.

36. C. F. Andrews, *Vickers Aircraft Since 1918* (London: Putnam 1969); Eric Lund, "The Industrial History of Strategy: Reevaluating the Wartime Record of the British Aviation Industry in Comparative Perspective, 1919–1945," *Journal of Military History* 62, no. 1 (Jan. 1998): 75–99; and J. E. Morpurgo, *Barnes Wallis: A Biography* (London: Longman, 1972).

37. Higham, *Britain's Imperial Air Routes*; and Richard K. Smith, "The Intercontinental Airliner and the Essence of Airplane Performance, 1929–1939," *Technology and Culture* 24, no. 3 (July 1983): 428–449.

38. Ritchie, *Industry and Air Power*.

39. Bill Gunston, *By Jupiter: The Life of Sir Roy Fedden* (London: Royal Aeronautical Society, 1978).

40. See Douglas R. Taylor, *Boxkite to Jet: The Remarkable Career of Frank B. Halford* (Derby, UK: Rolls-Royce Heritage Trust, 1999), 96–105.

41. Schlaifer and Heron, The *Development of Aircraft Engines and Aviation Fuels*; and Smith, *A History of Aircraft Piston Engines*.

42. *Icare* 189, no. 2 (2004); and James, *Schneider Trophy Aircraft*.

43. Facon, "The High Command of the French Air Force," 148–168. See also Anthony Christopher Cain, *The Forgotten Air Force: French Air Doctrine in the 1930s* (Washington, DC: Smithsonian Institution Press, 2002).

44. Facon, "The High Command of the French Air Force."

45. Chadeau, *L'industrie aéronautique en France*.

46. Facon, "The High Command of the French Air Force," 148–168, esp. 166.

47. United Kingdom, National Archives, [PRO] AIR 10/3916, *SD98, Calculations of Wastage and Consumption in War*, 4th ed. (1941–1943).

48. As far as I know, there is no French equivalent to *SD98*.

49. Sinnott, *The Royal Air Force and Aircraft Design*.

50. Francis K. Mason, *Battle Over Britain: A History of German Air Assaults on Great Britain, 1917–18 and July–December 1940, and of the Development of Britain's Air Defences Between the World Wars* (Turnbridge Wells, UK: McWhirter Twins, 1969).

51. Christienne and Lissarrague, *A History of French Military Aviation*, 394–416; Facon, "The High Command of the French Air Force," 148–168.

52. See W. J. Reader, *Architect of British Air Power: The Life of the First Viscount Weir* (London: Collins, 1968); and the British Official Histories of the Second World War.

Chapter 4. From the Advent of Hitler to War, 1933–1940

1. See Patrick Fridenson, "Automobile Workers in France and Their Work, 1914–1983," in *Work in France: Representations, Meaning, Organization, and Practice*, ed. Steven L. Kaplan and Cynthia J. Koepp (Ithaca, NY: Cornell University Press, 1986), 514–547.

2. Eugen J. Weber, *The Hollow Years: France in the 1930s* (New York: W. W. Norton & Company, 1994). See also Gayle K. Brunelle and Annette Finley Croswhite, *Murder in the Metro: Laetitia Toureaux and the Cagoule in 1930s France* (Baton Rouge: Louisiana State University Press, 2010); Greg Burgess, "France and the German Refugee Crisis of 1933," *French History* 16, no. 2 (2002): 203–229; Brian Jenkins, "Historiographical Essay: The Six Fevrier 1934 and the 'Survival' of the French Republic," *French History* 20, no. 3 (2006): 333–351; and Matt Perry, "Unemployment Revolutionizes the Working Class: *Les cri des chômeurs*. French Communists and the Birth of the Movement of the Unemployed in France 1931–1932," *French History* 16, no. 4 (2002): 441–468.

3. Weber, *The Hollow Years*, 241.

4. Field Marshal Lord Alanbrooke, *The War Diaries, 1939–1945*, ed. Alex Danchev and Daniel Todman (Berkeley: University of California Press, 2001); Doughty, *The Seeds of Disaster*; and Kiesling, *Arming Against Hitler*.

5. For a country-by-country overview see Higham and Harris, *Why Air Forces Fail*. *The Times* of London briefly covered the annual French army maneuvers from mid-1934 to the end of 1939. The first mention of air cooperation as such was not until the 8 September 1936 issue in which several squadrons including one of autogyros took part, as did heavy bombers, also present in 1935 (7 Sept.), at which time motorized troops were involved (5 Sept.). The British secretary for war, Hore-Belisha, and the CIGS, Field Marshal Sir Cyril Deverell, were present

in Normandy in 1937 (14 Sept.) at which it was noted that there were supply difficulties—36,000 gallons of petrol for two days of war. Hore-Belisha was taken in by what he saw (18 Sept. 1937). See United Kingdom, Public Record Office, War Office, *Notes on the French Army, Prepared by the General Staff of the War Office*, July 1936, as amended November 1937 (PRO WO 287/17). See also E. Angot and R. de Lavergne, *Le Général Vuillemin, figure légendaire de l'aviation française de 1914 à 1940: Le combatant, le pioneer de Sahar, le chef* (Paris: Palatine, 1965); Cain's chapter "L'Armée de l'Air, 1933–1940: Drifting Toward Defeat," in *Why Air Forces Fail*, ed. Higham and Harris; John Connell, *Wavell: Scholar and Soldier* (New York: Harcourt Brace, 1964), 171–173, on the three-week visit to Paris and Versailles, for his 1940 appraisal of their moral disintegration; and Doughty, *The Seeds of Disaster*. See also Cain, *The Forgotten Air Force*; Sir Edward Spears, *Prelude to Victory* (London: Jonathan Cape, 1939); and Arnaud Teyssier, "Le général Vuillemin: Un haut responsible militaire face du danger allemande (1938–1939)," *Revue Historique des Armées* 2 (1987): 104–113. On the German side of Vuillemin's visit to Germany in August 1938 and the elaborate grand bluff pulled on him, see Charles Christienne, "L'armée de l'air française de mars 1936 à septembre 1939," *Proceedings of the 15th Franco-German Colloquium* (Bonn, 26–29 Sept. 1978): 171–211; Christienne and Lissarrague, *A History of French Military Aviation*, 335 ff; Edward L. Homze, *Arming the Luftwaffe: The Reich Air Ministry and the German Aircraft Industry, 1919–1939* (Lincoln: University of Nebraska Press, 1976), 247; Peter Jackson, "La perception de la puissance aérienne allemande et son influence sur la politique extérieure de la France pendant les crises internationals de 1938 à 1939," *Revue Historique des Armées* 4, no. 94 (1990): 76–78; Arnaud Teyssier, "L'armée de l'air et l'aviation d'assaut, 1933–1939: Histoire del'un malentendu," *Revue Historique des Armées* 1 (1989): 98–109; Arnaud Teyssier, "L'appui aux forces de surface: L'armée de l'air à la recherché d'une doctrine (1933–1939)," *Colloque International—Histoire de la Guerre Aérienne, Hommage au Capitaine Guynemer* (Paris: ENSTA, SHAA, IHCC, CEAS, 10–11 Sept. 1987), *Actes* (Vincennes, SHAA, 1988): 247–272; and Vaisse, "Le procès de l'aviation de bombardement." See also *Actes, France et Allemagne* (*1932–1936*) (Paris: CHRS, 1980), 315–331; Charles Christienne and Patrice Buffotot, "L'Armée de l'Air française et la crise du 7 mars 1936," *Recueil d'articles et d'études*, 1976–1978 (Vincennes, SHAA, 1984): 315–331; XIVe Colloque historique franco-allemand *La France et l'Allemagne 1932–1936* (Paris: Palais du Luxembourg, Salle Médicis), Comité d'histoire de la Seconde Guerre mondiale, 10–12 Mar. 1977. See also Larry Addington, *The Blitzkrieg Era and the German General Staff, 1865–1941* (New Brunswick, NJ: Rutgers University Press, 1971); Alexander, *The Republic in Danger*; James S. Corum, *The Roots of Blitzkrieg: Hans von Seeckt and German Military Reform* (Lawrence: University Press of Kansas, 1992); and Kiesling, "'If It Ain't Broke, Don't Fix It.'"

6. Robert J. Young, "The Use and Abuse of Fear: France and the Air Menace in the 1930s," *Intelligence and National Security* 4, no. 2 (Oct. 1987): 88–109. See also Young, "The Strategic Dream."

7. Irving B. Holley Jr., *Buying Aircraft: Matériel Procurement for the Army Air Forces* (Washington, DC: Office of the Chief of Military History, 1966), 246.

8. Bernard and Dubief, *The Decline of the Third Republic*.

9. Christienne and Buffotot, "L'armée de l'air francaise et la crise du 7 mars 1936"; and France, Ètat-major, *Exercise de combat de la courtine* 1, 2, 3 August 1933 (Staff Report, English section only). Also see Maurice Baumont, "The Rhineland Crisis, 7 March 1936," in *Troubled Neighbours: Franco-British Relations in the Twentieth Century*, ed. Neville Waites (London: Weidenfeld and Nicolson, 1971); and Stephen A. Schuker, "France and the Penetration of the Rhineland," *French Historical Review* 14, no. 3 (Spring 1980): 299–338.

10. Angot and de Lavergne, *Le général Vuillemin*.

11. Ibid.

12. Patrice Buffotot, "Le rearmament aérien allemande et l'approche de la guerre vue par le 2e bureau français," XVe Colloque historique franco-allemand *Deutschland und Frankreich 1936–1939*, Bonn, Institut historique allemande de Paris, Comité français d'histoire de la Seconde Guerre mondiale, Oct. 1978, *Actes* (Munich, Zurich: Artemis, 1982), 249–289. See also John C. Cairns, "A Nation of Shopkeepers in Search of a Suitable France, 1919–1940," *American Historical Review* 79, no. 3 (June 1974): 710–743; John C. Cairns, "Along the Road Back to France, 1940," *American Historical Review* 64, no. 3 (April 1959): 583–603; and Col. Paul Paillole, *Fighting the Nazis: French Military Intelligence and Counterintelligence 1935–1945* (New York: Enigma Books, 2003).

13. Pierre Cot, *Triumph of Treason* [*Contre nous de la tyrannie*], trans. Sybille and Milton Crane (Chicago: Ziff-Davis 1944); Thierry Vivier, "Pierre Cot et la naissance de l'armée de l'air (1933–1934)," *Revue Historique des Armées*, no. 4 (1990): 108–115. For more on Cot, see Christopher Andrew and Oleg Gordievsky, *KGB: The Inside Story* (New York: Harper Collins, 1990), 446–447; Christopher Andrew and Vasili Mitrokhin, *The Mitrokhin Archive. The KGB in Europe and the West* (London and New York: Penguin, 2000), 143, 162–163; John Earl Haynes and Harvey Klehr, *Venona: Decoding Soviet Espionage in America* (New Haven, CT: Yale University Press, 1999), 211–212, 221; Harvey Klehr, John Earl Hynes, and Fridrikh Igorevich Firsov, *The Secret World of American Communism* (New Haven, CT: Yale University Press, 1995), 234, 236–237; and Herbert Romerstein and Eric Breindel, *The Venona Secrets: Exposing Soviet Espionage and America's Traitors* (Washington, DC: Regnery, 2000), 303–304.

14. Thierry Vivier, "Le général Denain, bâtisseur de l'armée de l'air (1933–1936)," *Revue Historique des Armées*, no. 3 (1993): 21–31.

15. Ibid.

16. Ibid.

17. Dominique Breffort and André Jouineau, *French Aircraft from 1939 to 1942: Fighters, Bombers, and Observation Types*, vol. 1 (Paris: Histoire et Collections, 2004), 12–17; Général Guerin, "Les transmissions de 1919 à 1939," *Revue Historique des Armées* 23, no. 1 (1967): 51–56; and Jane's, *All the World's Aircraft, 1938* (London, published annually), 119c.

18. Vivier, *La politique aeronautique militaire de la France*, 88.

19. Ibid., 89.

20. James S. Corum, "The Spanish Civil War: Lessons Learned and Not Learned by the Great Powers," *Journal of Military History* 62, no. 2 (Apr. 1998): 313–334. See also Madeline Astorkia, "Les leçons aériennes de la guerre d'Espagne," *Revue Historique des Armées* 2, (1977): 145–173; and Gen. Maurice Duval, *Les leçons de la guerre d'Espagne* (Paris: Plon, 1938).

21. Teyssier, "Le général Vuillemin"; and Patrick Facon, "Le Plan V (1938–1939)," *Recueil d'articles et d' études, 1979–1981* (Vincennes: SHAA, 1985): 51–80.

22. Alexander, *The Republic in Danger*, 123–141.

23. François Pernot, "L'Armée de l'Air face aux crises des années trente: une étude du moral," *Revue Historique des Armées* no. 4 (1990): 116–127.

24. *Actes*, 1 (Società di Storia Patria di Lavoro, 1988); Facon, "Douhet et sa doctrine à travers la literature militaire et aéronautique française"; and *Revue Historique des Armées* 1 (1988): 94–103.

25. Patrick Facon, "L'aviation populaire: entre les mythes et la réalité," *Revue Historique des Armées* 2, no. 82 (1994): 54–59. See also Vital Verry, *L'aviation populaire* (Paris: Editions du Genfaut, 2007).

26. Royal Air Force Historical Society, *Royal Air Force Reserve and Auxiliary Air Forces*.

27. Christienne and Lissarrague, *A History of French Military Aviation*, 301–310.

28. See Hyde, *British Air Policy Between the Wars*, 414 ff; and Marshal of the Royal Air Force Sir John Slessor, *The Central Blue* (London: Cassell, 1956), 152 ff.

29. Air Cdre. Peter Dye, "Logistics and Airpower—A Failure in Doctrine?" [*U.S.*] *Air Force Journal of Logistics* 23, no. 3 (Fall 1999): 26–28, 41.

30. Young, "The Strategic Dream."

31. Christienne and Lissarrague, *A History of French Military Aviation*; Martin Thomas, "France in British Signals Intelligence, 1939–1945," *French History* 14, no. 1 (2000): 41–66; and Wark, "The Air Defence Gap," 511–526.

32. On the Nye Committee see Wayne S. Cole, *Senator Gerald P. Nye and American Foreign Relations* (Minneapolis: University of Minnesota Press, 1962).

33. Malcolm Smith, *British Air Strategy Between the Wars* (Oxford: Clarendon Press, 1984); and Malcolm Smith, "The RAF and Counter-Force Strategy Before World War II," *Journal of the Royal United Services Institute for Defence and Security Studies* 121, no. 2 (1976): 68–77.

34. J. W. R. Taylor, *C.F.S.: Birthplace of Air Power* (London: Putnam, 1958).

35. Sinnott, *The Royal Air Force and Aircraft Design*, 224.

36. Basil Collier, *The Defence of the United Kingdom* (London: HMSO, 1957), 31–37; and Wright, *The Man Who Won the Battle of Britain*.

37. Collier, *The Defence of the United Kingdom*, 31–77; and Johnson, *Defence by Committee*.

38. Great Britain Home Office, *Air Raid Precautions* (London: HMSO, 1938; Stroud, UK: Tempus, 2007).

39. Hyde, *British Air Policy Between the Wars.*

40. Collier, *The Defence of the United Kingdom*, 36; and Sinnott, *The Royal Air Force and Aircraft Design*, 76–107.

41. C. H. Barnes, *Handley Page Aircraft Since 1907* (London: Putnam, 1976); and H. A. Taylor, *Fairey Aircraft Since 1915* (London: Putnam, 1974).

42. Derek N. James, *Gloster Aircraft Since 1917* (London: Putnam, 1971).

43. Ronald W. Clark, *Tizard* (London: Methuen, and Cambridge, MA: MIT Press, 1965).

44. F. W. Winterbotham, *Secret and Personal* [U.S. title: *The Nazi Connection*] (London: Kimber, 1969).

45. Frederick Winston Furneaux Smith, Earl of Birkenhead, *The Professor and the Prime Minister: The Official Life of Professor F. A. Lindemann, Viscount Cherwell* (Boston: Houghton Mifflin, 1962) [English title: *The Prof in Two Worlds: The Official Life of Professor F. A. Lindemann, Viscount Cherwell* (London: Collins, 1961)]; and C. P. Snow, *Science and Government* (London: Oxford, 1961, app. rev. 1962).

46. The best modern account is David Zimmerman, *Britain's Shield: Radar and the Defeat of the Luftwaffe* (Stroud, UK: Sutton, 2001).

47. See Lothar Hilbert, "Les attachés militaire françaises: Leur statut de l'entre-deux guerres," typescript of paper presented to the International Commission of Military History (ICMH), Bucharest, Aug. 1980, reprinted in *ACTA* (1981); F. H. Hinsley, E. E. Thomas, C. F. G. Ransome, and R. C. Knight, *British Intelligence in the Second World War: Its Influence on Strategy and Operations*, vol. 1 (London: HMSO, 1979), 1–88; and Winterbotham, *Secret and Personal.* See also Norman Henry Gibbs, *Grand Strategy*, vol. 1, *Rearmament Policy* (London: HMSO, 1976).

48. Hinsley et al., *British Intelligence in the Second World War*, vol. 1, 20–30; and Winterbotham, *Secret and Personal.*

49. Hinsley, *British Intelligence in the Second World War*, vol. 1, 487–493; and Winterbotham, *Secret and Personal.*

50. J. A. Cross, *Lord Swinton* (Oxford: Clarendon Press, 1982); and Reader, *Architect of British Air Power.*

51. Hyde, *British Air Policy Between the Wars.*

52. Leslie Hunt, *Twenty-One Squadrons: The History of the Royal Auxiliary Air Force, 1925–1957* (London: Garnstone Press, 1972); Jefford, *Observers, Navigators and Other Non-Pilot Aircrew in the RFC*; and Royal Air Force Historical Society, *Royal Air Force Reserve and Auxiliary Air Forces; Royal Air Force Volunteer Reserve Memories* (n.p.: RAF Historical Society, 1997), various authors.

53. C. F. Andrews and E. B. Morgan, *Supermarine Aircraft Since 1914* (London: Putnam, 1981); Francis K. Mason, *Hawker Aircraft Since 1920* (London: Putnam, 1961).

54. Wallace, *The Guns of the Royal Air Force.*

55. Much like Roman Emperor Caligula's horse, which he admired to the extent that he made the animal a senator.

56. Neil K. Buxton and Derek H. Aldcroft, *British Industry Between the Wars: Instability and Industrial Development, 1919–1939* (London: Scota Press, 1979); Fearon, "Aircraft Manufacturing"; Fearon, "The British Airframe Industry and the State"; Alex Henshaw [test pilot at Castle Bromwich], *Sigh for a Merlin: Testing the Spitfire* (London: John Murray Publishers Ltd., 1979); William Hornby, *Factories and Plant* (London: HMSO, 1958); and M. Miller and R. A. Church, "Motor Manufacturing," in *British Industry Between the Wars*, ed. Buxton and Aldcroft, 179–215.

57. Lloyd, *Rolls-Royce*, 3 vols.; Peter Pugh, *The Magic of a Name: The Rolls-Royce Story*, 3 vols. (Duxford, UK: Icon Books, 2000).

58. Richardson, *Man Is Not Lost*, 130–135.

59. Sinnott, *The Royal Air Force and Aircraft Design*, 178–216.

60. Higham, *Armed Forces in Peacetime.*

61. Corum, *The Luftwaffe*; Homze, *Arming the Luftwaffe*; and Williamson Murray, *Strategy for Defeat: The Luftwaffe 1933–1945* (Maxwell AFB, AL: Air University Press, 1983; Baltimore: The Nautical and Aeronautical Publishing Co., 1986).

62. David Irving, *The Rise and Fall of the Luftwaffe: The Life of Field Marshal Erhard Milch* (Boston: Little Brown, 1974).

63. Slessor, *The Central Blue*, 144–185.

64. Hyde, *British Air Policy Between the Wars.*

65. Ritchie, *Industry and Air Power.*

66. Hyde, *British Air Policy Between the Wars.*

67. H. Duncan Hall, *North American Supply*, vol. 1 (London: HMSO, 1955).

68. Ritchie, *Industry and Air Power*, 90.

69. Collier, *The Defence of the United Kingdom.*

70. Cross, *Lord Swinton*; Reader, *Architect of British Air Power*; and Hyde, *British Air Policy Between the Wars*, 422–423.

71. Hyde, *British Air Policy Between the Wars.*

72. Anthony Furse, *Wilfrid Freeman: The Genius Behind Allied Survival and Air Supremacy, 1939–1945* (Staplehurst, UK: Spellmount Ltd., 2000).

73. Vincent Orange, *Tedder* (London: Frank Cass, 2004).

74. Collier, *The Defence of the United Kingdom*, 67.

75. Hyde, *British Air Policy Between the Wars*, 500.

76. Harold Balfour, *Wings Over Westminster* (London: Hutchinson, 1973).

77. Robin Higham, *The Bases of Air Strategy: Building Airfields for the RAF, 1914–1945* (Shrewsbury, UK: Airlife, 1998). The French were opposed to concrete runways. Also see Christienne and Lissarrague, *A History of French Military Aviation*, 309–310.

78. Higham, "Royal Air Force Spares Forecasting in World War II," 81.

79. Zimmerman, *Britain's Shield.*

80. Derek Wood, *Attack Warning Red: The Royal Observer Corps and the Defence of Britain, 1925–1975* (London: Macdonald and Jane's, 1976).

81. United Kingdom, Air Historical Branch, National Archives, AIR 9/105, AFC 14, *Anglo-French Staff Conversations: Preparations of Joint Plans for Action for Franco-British Air Force,* and AFC 30, *Anglo-French Staff Conversations, 1939: Summarized History of the Conversations*; and Webster and Frankland, *The Strategic Air Offensive Against Germany,* vol. 1, *Preparation.*

82. J. C. Slessor, *Air Power and Armies* (London: Oxford, 1936).

83. Webster and Frankland, *The Strategic Air Offensive Against Germany,* vol. 1.

84. See Chapter 5 herein regarding Armée de l'Air credits; and Christienne and Lissarrague, *A History of French Military Aviation,* 304–305.

85. Curtis Lettice, *The Forgotten Pilots* (Henley-on-Thames, UK: Foulis & Co., 1971); and Royal Air Force Historical Society, *Royal Air Force Reserve and Auxiliary Air Forces.*

86. Fred Hatch, *The Aerodrome of Democracy: Canada and the British Commonwealth Air Training Plan, 1939–1945* (Ottawa, Can.: Department of National Defence, 1994).

87. The Territorial Army is the part-time volunteer force of the British Army.

88. Hyde, *British Air Policy Between the Wars,* 486.

89. Sinnott, *The Royal Air Force and Aircraft Design,* 178–216; and *The Royal Air Force Builds for War: A History of Design and Construction in the RAF 1935–1945,* originally Air Publications (AP) 3236 *Works,* AM (Air Historical Branch) 1956 (London: HMSO, 1997).

Chapter 5. Technical Infrastructure, 1928–1940

1. For the state of French economic, business, and labor relations, consult the following: Herrick Eaton Chapman, "Reshaping French Industrial Politics: Workers, Employers, State Officials, and the Struggle for Control of the Aircraft Industry 1928–1950," Berkeley, University of California, Ph.D. Dissertation, 1983, published in revised form as Chapman, *State Capitalism and Working-Class Radicalism*; Michael Crozier, *The Bureaucratic Phenomenon* (Chicago: University of Chicago Press, 1964); Downs, *Manufacturing Inequality*; Fridenson, "Automobile Workers in France," 514–547; Maurice Levy-Leboyer, "Innovation and Business Strategies in Nineteenth and Twentieth Century France," in Carter et al., *Enterprise and Entrepreneurs in Nineteenth and Twentieth Century France,* 87–135; Richard Hamilton, *Affluence and the French Workers in the Fourth Republic* (Princeton, NJ: Princeton University Press, 1967); Talbot Imlay, "Strategic and Military Planning, 1919–1939," in Imlay and Toft, eds., *The Fog of Peace and War Planning*; Anne Kriegel, "The French Communist Party and the

Problems of Power, 1920–1933," in John C. Cairns, ed., *Contemporary France: Illusion, Conflict, and Regeneration* (New York: New Viewpoint, 1978); Kuisel, *Capitalism and the State in Modern France*; Michael Torigian, *Every Factory a Fortress: The French Labor Movement in the Age of Ford and Hitler* (Athens, OH: Ohio University Press, 1999); Vinen, *The Politics of French Business*; Vivier, *La politique aéronautique militaire de la France*; and Weber, *The Hollow Years*. See also Robert Jacomet, *L'armament de la France 1936–1939* (Paris: Les Editions La Jeunesse, 1945). Jacomet was comptroller general at the Ministère de la Guerre and tried by Vichy for not having armed France adequately after, in the 1920s, it had been Europe's most heavily armed, then declined, especially relative to Germany from 1933 on. The testimony of the ministers and generals is in *Témoignes et-documents recueillés par la commision d'enquière parlementerie . . . .* 9 vols. (Paris, 1947–1950). For further reading, consult the following: Alexander, *Knowing Your Friends*; Jean-Pierre Azema, *From Munich to the Liberation, 1938–1944* (Paris: Le Seuil, 1949, and London: Cambridge University Press, 1984); Bernard and Dubief, *The Decline of the Third Republic*; Air Cdre. Peter Dye, "Logistics Doctrine and the Impact of War: The Royal Air Force Experience in the Second World War," in Sebastian Cox and Peter Gray, eds., *Air Power History: Turning Points from Kitty Hawk to Kosovo* (London: Frank Cass, 2002), 207–223; John Ferris, "Catching the Wave: The RAF Pursues the RMA [Revolution in Military Affairs], 1918–1939," 159–178; Kier, *Imagining War*; Kiesling, *Arming Against Hitler*; Charles P. Kindleberger, *Economic Growth in France and Britain, 1851–1950* (Cambridge: Harvard University Press, 1964); Malcolm MacLennan, Murray Forsyth, and Geoffrey Denton, *Economic Planning and Policies in Britain, France, and Germany* (New York: Praeger, 1968), essentially a post-1945 book with a theoretical introduction; Sir Peter Masefield, "La royal air force et la production d'avions de guerre en Grand-Bretagne, 1934–1940," in *Colloque International* (1975–1979): 410–452; Williamson Murray, "The Influences of Pre-War Anglo-American Doctrine on the Air Campaigns of the Second World War," in Boog, *The Conduct of the Air War in the Second World War*, 235; William Philpot and Martin S. Alexander, "The French and the British Field Force: Moral Support or Material Contribution?" *Journal of Military History* 71, no. 3 (July 2007): 743–772; Guy Rossi-Landi, "Le pacifism en France (1939–1940)," Comité de la 2e Guerre Mondiale, *Française et Britanniques dans la Drôle de Guerre, Actes du colloque franco-britannique tenu à Paris du 8–12 decembre 1975* (Paris: Editions de Centre National de la Recherche Scientifique, 1979), 123–153 (includes panel discussion); Thomas, "At the Heart of Things?"; and Piotr S. Wandycz, *The Twilight of French Eastern Alliances, 1926–1936: French-Czechoslovak-Polish Relations from Locarno to the Remilitarization of the Rhineland* (Princeton, NJ: Princeton University Press, 1988). On the British industry, employers, and labor, also see Niall Barr, *The Lion and the Poppy: British Veterans, Politics, and Society, 1921–1939* (Westport, CT: Praeger, 2005); Miriam Glucksmann, *Women Assemble: Women Workers and the New Industries in Interwar Britain* (London: Routledge, 1990); David Greasley and Les Oxley, "Discontinuities in Competitiveness: The Impact of the First World War on British Industry," *Economic History Review*, new ser. 49, no. 1 (Feb. 1996):

82–100; Hornby, *Factories and Plant*; Peggy Inman, *Labour in the Munitions Industries*, History of the Second World War: United Kingdom Civil Series, War Production Series (London: HMSO, 1957); Sidney Pollard, *The Development of the British Economy, 1914–1967*, 2nd ed. (London: Edward Arnold, 1969); Ritchie, *Industry and Air Power*; and David Silbey, *The British Working Class and Enthusiasm for War, 1914–1916* (London: Frank Cass, 2005).

2. Chapman, *State Capitalism and Workingclass Radicalism*; Edward Shorter and Charles Tilley, *Strikes in France, 1830–1968* (London: Cambridge University Press, 1974), 127; and Torigian, *Every Factory a Fortress*. See also Frankenstein, *Le prix du réarmament français 1935–1939*, 289, as quoted in Robert A. Doughty, "The French Armed Forces, 1918–1940," in Millett and Murray, *Military Effectiveness*, 50. Looking at Frankenstein's figures for the division of French budgetary credits, the Armée de l'Air's share grew steadily from 1935's 18.8 percent of the defense budget, then slipped in 1936 to 18 percent, and rose in 1937 to 19 percent. In 1938 it reached 22.8 percent and, finally, in 1939 totaled 27 percent—or, in terms of the real budgets in French francs, from FF27.6818 million in 1936 to FF41.002 million in 1937, to FF6,646.88 million in 1938, to FF25,295.47 million in 1939. The credits in 1938 were more than double those of 1936, but inflation had reduced them by one-third, and those of 1939 even further. Until 1938 the Ministère de l'Air money was going into infrastructure rather than production, as in Britain, but the results were more meager.

3. Fridenson, "Automobile Workers in France," 514–530.

4. James McVicar Haight, *American Aid to France 1938–1940* (New York: Atheneum, 1970).

5. Christienne, "Le haut commandement français"; Delaye and Dumas, "Les conquêtes de l'aluminum et des metaux legers"; and Vivier,"Le général Denain." For the percentages of the credits the French services shared, see Robert Frankenstein's table as quoted in Doughty, "The French Armed Forces," 50. See also Chapman, "Reshaping French Industrial Politics"; Geoffrey Dorman, *Fifty Years Fly Past* (London: Forbes Robertson, 1951); Ritchie, *Industry and Air Power*, 57–59 ff; and Owen Thetford, *Aircraft of the Royal Air Force* (London: Putnam, 1988).

6. F. R. Banks, *I Kept No Diary: 60 Years with Marine Diesels, Automobile and Aero Engines* (Shrewsbury, UK: Airlife, 1978); S. D. Heron, "Development of Aviation Fuels," in Schlaiffer and Heron, *The Development of Aircraft Engines and Aviation Fuels*; and Ian Lloyd, *Rolls-Royce*, vol. 3, *The Merlin at War*; Pugh, *The Magic of a Name*.

7. Schlaifer and Heron, *The Development of Aircraft Engines and Aviation Fuels*.

8. Smith, *A History of Aircraft Piston Engines*, 230.

9. Chadeau, *L'industrie aéronautique en France*, 299.

10. Smith, *A History of Aircraft Piston Engines*, 130–132.

11. On the *écoles polytechniques*, see David Granick, *The European Executive* (New York: Doubleday, 1962), 60–72, 140–145, 186–202, 257–266.

12. Chadeau, *L'industrie aéronautique en France*, 412–416.

13. Clarke, "Military Technology in Republican France."

14. Christienne and Lissarrague, *A History of French Military Aviation*; Hall, *North American Supply*; and Higham, *Armed Forces in Peacetime*, 326–327.

15. Charles Christienne, "L'industrie aéronautique française de septembre 1939 à mai 1940," Comité d'histoire de la 2e Guerre Mondiale, *Français et Britanniques dans la Drôle de Guerre* (Paris: Editions du Centre National de la Recherche Scientifique, 1979), 359–410, esp. 404; and *Colloque International* (Paris, 1975), 404. There was also a severe lag in acceptance versus production, a gap due to bad weather in January 1940 that saw only 178 accepted out of the 358 produced. Pursuit aircraft production totaled 209 in September 1939, but only 79 in February 1940, rising to 164 in May. The MS 406 rolled off production lines at the rate of 125 in September 1939, but then dropped steadily down to eight in March, seven in April, and six in May 1940. See also Christienne, "Le haut commandement français" (note 5 herein).

16. Corum, *The Luftwaffe*; R. J. Overy, *The Battle of Britain: The Myth and Reality* (New York: W. W. Norton, 2000). Unfortunately, studies of the French specifications and industry relations are lacking in detail despite the excellent work of Emmanuel Chadeau, thus the emphasis has to be on how the British proceeded.

17. d'Abzac-Epézy, *L'Armée de l'Air de Vichy*, especially 289–304; and Chadeau, *L'industrie aéronautique en France*, 347–359. See also Chapter 8. See also "La Coupe Schneider, 1913–1931," *Icare* 189 (2004) [whole issue].

18. United Kingdom, National Archives, [PRO] AIR 41/21, First Draft of the Air Historical Branch (AM), *The War in France-Flanders* (n.d.); The Air Historical Branch Narrative of the Battle of France [*The Campaign in France 10 May–18 June 1940, The Campaign in France and the Low Countries*, Sept. 1939–June 1940, esp. pp. 1–32, 273–285, 425]. For a summary of the discussions between Sir Kingsley Wood and Guy LaChambre in London on 25 July 1939, see United Kingdom, National Archives, AIR 41/21 and AIR 9/78. On AVM Barratt's visit to France, 18–20 April 1939, see United Kingdom, National Archives, AIR 9/78. Also for a record of the Anglo-French Air Staff's discussions in Paris on 27 February 1939, see United Kingdom, National Archives, AIR 40/2032. See also United Kingdom, National Archives, AIR 9/105, AFC 14, *Anglo-French Staff Conversations: Preparations of Joint Plans for Action for Franco-British Air Force*, and AFC 30, *Anglo-French Staff Conversations, 1939: Summarized History of the Conversations*.

19. Lloyd, *Rolls-Royce*, vol. 3, *The Merlin at War*, 11–19.

20. Ibid.

21. Alexandre P. de Seversky, *Victory Through Air Power* (New York: Simon and Schuster, 1942), 184–201.

22. Vinen, *The Politics of French Business*, 23.

23. Torigian, *Every Factory a Fortress*, 14–15.

24. Chapman, *State Capitalism and Working-Class Radicalism*, 222.

25. Frankenstein, *Le prix du réarmement français*, 282–303, 526–529.

26. Vicki Caron, "The Missed Opportunity: French Refugee Policy in Wartime, 1939–40," *Historical Reflections [Reflexions historiques]* 22, no. 1 (Winter 1996): 117–157.

27. Downs, *Manufacturing Inequality.*

28. Charles P. Kindleberger, "Technical Education and the French Entrepreneur," in Edward C. Carter et al., *Enterprise and Entrepreneurs in Nineteenth and Twentieth Century France*, 3–39.

29. See Tables 3, 6, and 7. The Armée de Terre's failure to order the excellent antiair-craft guns developed in 1922, and its neglect of the training of its troops to resist air attack, cost it dearly in 1940.

30. The Air Staff in London in 1931 pointed out that the wastage in testing, ferrying, and lost at sea was estimated as 20 percent, or roughly half of the ready reserves. "Lost at sea" can be equated in mobile war with the rapid changes of location of units after 14 May 1940.

31. Christienne and Lissarrague, *A History of French Military Aviation*, 300.

32. Charles Christienne, Patrick Facon, Patrice Buffotot, and Lee Kennett, *French Military Aviation: A Bibliographical Guide*. See also Daniel Hucker, "French Public Attitudes Towards the Prospect of War in 1938–1939: 'Pacifism' or 'War Anxiety'?" *Journal of French History* 21 no. 4 (Dec. 2007): 431–449. (Hucker argues that pacificism was but one element that brought on war after Munich. More powerful was the "war anxiety" that demanded France prepare for war.)

33. Christienne and Lissarrague, *A History of French Military Aviation*, 277; Jeffrey J. Clarke, "The Nationalization of War Industries in France, 1936–1937: A Case Study," *Journal of Modern History* 49, no. 3 (Sept. 1977): 411–430; and Janes's, *All The World's Aircraft 1938*, 103 ff. On the nationalization see Chadeau, *L'industrie aéronautique en France*, 224–270; on the late 1930s to 1960, 308–346; and on engines, 296–307. In addition, see Carlier, *Marcel Dassault*, 86 ff.

34. Kenneth Mouré, "'Une eventualité absolument excluée,' French Reluctance to Devaluation, 1933–1936," *French Historical Studies* 15, no. 3 (Spring 1988): 479–505.

35. Christienne and Lissarrague, *A History of French Military Aviation*, 290; and Teyssier, "Le général Vuillemin." See also Patrick Facon, "Le haut commande-ment aérien français et la crise de Munich," also published in *Recueil d'articles et d'etudes 1981–1983* (Vincennes: SHAA, 1987): 171–195; and in *Revue Historique des Armées* 3, no. 83 (1987): 10–18.

36. Elisabeth du Réau, *Édouard Daladier, 1884–1970* (Paris: Fayard, 1993).

37. Ibid.

38. Hervé Artzet, "Le general Jean-Henri Jauneaud: Une personalité áeronautique de l'entre-deux-guerres," *Revue Historique des Armées* [photocopy, ca. 1998]; and Jean-Henri Jauneaud, *De Verdun à Dien-Bien-Phu* (Paris: Collections Alternance, Editions de Scorpion, 1960).

39. Young, "Preparation for Defeat"; and Young, "The Strategic Dream."

40. Jenkins, *A History of the French Navy*; Masson, *Historie de la Marine*, vol. 2, *De la vapeur à l'atome*; and Chalmers Wood, "The French Navy and Parliament Between the Wars," *International History Review* 6 no. 3 (Aug. 1983): 386–403. Jonathan R. Dull, *The Age of the Ship of the Line: The British and French Navies, 1650–1815* (Lincoln: University of Nebraska Press, 2009) shows that the Royale, as the second French armed service, was often short of ships, supplies, money, and manpower in the 165 years of Ango-French wars due to military demands and inadequate national financing.

41. Chadeau, *L'industrie aéronautique en France*, 319–320.

42. Carlier, *Marcel Dassault*, 87.

43. Ibid., 99.

44. Cairns, "A Nation of Shopkeepers."

45. See Fridenson and Lecuir, *La France et la Grande-Bretagne*.

46. Ritchie, *Industry and Air Power*; Sinnott, *The Royal Air Force and Aircraft Design*. Sinnott provides the latest details, but see also Sir Geoffrey de Havilland, *Sky Fever* (London: Hamish Hamilton, 1961); Peter Fearon, "A Reply" [to A. J. Robertson, "The British Airframe Industry and the State, 1918-1935: A Comment"], *Economic History Review* 28, no. 4 (Nov. 1975): 658–662; Fearon, "The British Airframe Industry and the State"; Furse, *Wilfrid Freeman*; A. J. Jackson, *De Havilland Aircraft Since 1904* (London: Putnum, 1962); A. J. Robertson, "The British Airframe Industry and the State, 1918–1935: A Comment," *Economic History Review* 28 no. 4 (Nov. 1975): 650–658; C. Martin Sharp, *DH: A History of De Havilland* (London: Faber and Faber, Ltd., 1960; and rev. ed., Shrewsbury, UK: Airlife, 1982).

47. Sinnott, *The Royal Air Force and Aircraft Design*. See also Ritchie, *Industry and Air Power*, 57–59 ff.

48. Jarrett, *Biplane to Monoplane*.

49. Ibid.

50. Ferris, "Treasury Control"; and Roskill, "The Ten Year Rule."

51. Pollard, *The Development of the British Economy*, 197.

52. John Maynard Keynes, *General Theory of Employment, Interest and Money* (London: Macmillan, and New York: St. Martin's Press, 1936).

53. Hornby, *Factories and Plant*.

54. Ibid., 195. Hornby offers a useful short historical introduction to the British ministries of war production, which includes the World War I aircraft industry: pp. 135, 195–295, 362–403. See also J. D. Scott and Richard Hughes, *The Administration of War Production* (London: HMSO, 1955), 33–49, 291 ff.

55. Inman, *Labour in the Munitions Industries*, 1–35.

56. Sandra Dawson, "Working-Class Consumers and the Campaign for Holidays with Pay," *20th Century British History* 18, no. 3 (2007): 277–305.

57. Glucksmann, *Women Assemble*.

58. Ibid., 81.

59. Ibid., 155–159.

60. Lund, "The Industrial History of Strategy."

61. Ritchie, "The Price of Air Power."

62. Higham, *The Bases of Air Strategy*.

63. Robin Higham, "The Perils of Patriotism" [in process].

64. Ritchie, *Industry and Air Power*.

65. Ibid., 59–60.

66. Lloyd, *Rolls-Royce*, vol. 3, *The Merlin at War*.

67. Gunston, *By Jupiter*. See also Lloyd, *Rolls-Royce*, vol. 3, *The Merlin at War*; and C. M. Wilson and W. J. Reader, *Men & Machines: D. Napier & Son, 1808–1958* (London: Weidenfeld and Nicolson, 1958).

68. Ritchie, *Industry and Air Power*, 127 ff.

69. Correlli Barnett, *Audit of War* (London: Macmillan, 1986).

70. Ibid.; Ferris, "The Greatest Power on Earth," 726–750; and Sebastian Ritchie, "A New Audit of War," *War and Society* 12 (May 1994): 125–147.

Chapter 6. On the Road to War, 1933–1940

1. Doughty, *The Seeds of Disaster*.

2. See Chapter 5 herein, note 2.

3. Azema, *From Munich to the Liberation*; Silbey, *The British Working Class and Enthusiasm for War*; Leonard V. Smith, *The Embattled Self: French Soldiers' Testimony of the Great War* (Ithaca, NY: Cornell University Press, 2007); and Thomas, "At the Heart of Things?"

4. Martin Thomas, "European Crisis, Colonial Crisis? Signs of Fracture in the French Empire from Munich to the Outbreak of War," *International History Review* 32, no. 3 (September 2010): 389–413.

5. Alexander, *The Republic in Danger*; and esp. Martin S. Alexander, "Force de Frappe ou Feu de Paille? Maurice Gamelin's Appraisal of Military Aviation Before the Blitzkrieg of 1940," *Colloque Internationale* (Paris, 1984): 65–80.

6. Higham, *The British Rigid Airship, 1908–1931*.

7. Christienne and Lissarrague, *A History of French Military Aviation*, 273–276.

8. Regarding nationalization, see Chapter 5 herein.

9. Alexander, *The Republic in Danger*, 85 ff.

10. Gauché, *Le deuxième bureau au travail*.

11. Alexander, *The Republic in Danger*, 130 ff.

12. Ibid.

13. Julian Jackson, *The Popular Front in France: Defending Democracy, 1934–38* (New York: Cambridge University Press, 1988). See also Torigian, *Every Factory à Fortress.*

14. Kerisel, *Albert Caquot.*

15. Kirkland, "Planes, Pilots, and Politics," 285–291. [His figures do not agree with the SHAA archives, per General Robineau, Jan. 17, 2012.]

16. Faris R. Kirkland, "Anti-military Group-Fantasies and the Destruction of the French Air Force, 1928–1940," *Journal of Psychohistory* 14, no. 1 (Summer 1986): 25–42.

17. Kirkland, "Planes, Pilots, and Politics," 285–291.

18. Breffort and Joineau, *French Aircraft from 1939 to 1942.*

19. Angot and de Lavergne, *Le Général Vuillemin.*

20. Christienne and Lissarrague, *A History of French Military Aviation,* 301–316.

21. Facon, "The High Command of the French Air Force," 148–168.

22. d'Abzac-Epézy, *L'armée de l'air de Vichy,* 80.

23. Facon, "The High Command of the French Air Force," 161.

24. Ibid., 163.

25. Cairns, *Contemporary France.*

26. See Domnic Sundbrook, "Opinion: Chamberlain Deserves Our Admiration, Not Our Ridicule," *BBC History* (June 2008): 21; and Will Swift, *The Kennedys Amidst the Gathering Storm: A Thousand Days in London 1938–1940* (London: Collins, 2008).

27. Martin S. Alexander and William J. Philpott, "The Entente Cordiale and the Next War: Anglo-French Views on Future Military Co-operation, 1928–1939," in Alexander, *Knowing Your Friends,* 53–84.

28. United Kingdom, National Archives, AIR 41/21, First Draft of the Air Historical Branch (AM), *The War in France-Flanders* (n.d.), 3.

29. Peter Neville, *Hitler and Appeasement: The British Attempt to Prevent the Second World War* (London/New York: Hambledon Continuum, 2006).

30. United Kingdom, National Archives, [PRO] AIR 9/105, AFC 30, *Anglo-French Staff Conversations, 1939: Summarized History of the Conversations;* and Gibbs, *Grand Strategy.*

31. United Kingdom, National Archives, [PRO] AIR 9/105, 22.

32. United Kingdom, National Archives, AIR 41/21, for a summary of the discussions between Sir Kingsley Wood and Guy La Chambre in London on 25 July 1939. On Air Vice Marshal Barratt's visit to France, 18–20 April 1939, see United Kingdom, National Archives, AIR 9/78. For a record of the Anglo-French air staff's discussions in Paris on 27 February 1939, see United Kingdom, National Archives, AIR 40/2032; AIR 9/105; AFC 14, *Anglo-French Staff Conversations: Preparations of Joint Plans for Action for Franco-British Air Force;* and AFC 30, *Anglo-French Staff Conversations, 1939: Summarized History of the Conversations.*

33. As Jon Sumida pointed out in his fall 2009 *Army History* article, the French long-war strategy had its roots intellectually in Jomini's observation that the Spanish and Russians had successfully dragged out the Napoleonic war so as to bring the French emperor down. And Clausewitz reinforced that by noting that even a well-defeated country could carry on only guerrilla warfare. See Jon T. Sumida, "The Clausewitz Problem," *Army History* (Fall 2009): 17–21.

34. United Kingdom, National Archives, [PRO] AIR 40/2032. See also note 32 herein.

35. United Kingdom, National Archives [PRO] AIR 40/2032; United Kingdom, National Archives, AIR 41/21, 13.

36. Slessor, *Air Power and Armies.*

37. United Kingdom, National Archives, AIR 41/21, 16. See also Webster and Frankland, *The Strategic Air Offensive Against Germany*, vol. 1, for AOC-in-C Bomber Command's opinion.

38. United Kingdom, National Archives, AIR 41/21, 17.

39. Ibid., 18.

40. Ibid., 21.

41. United Kingdom, National Archives, [PRO] AIR 40/2032.

42. United Kingdom, National Archives, AIR 41/21, 24–25.

43. Ibid., 26.

44. Ibid., 29.

45. Ibid., 30.

46. Ibid., 310.

47. Azema, *From Munich to the Liberation*, 6–7.

48. Scott M. Cutlip, Allen H. Center, and Glen M. Broom, *Effective Public Relations* (New York: Prentice Hall, 1999).

49. Henri Nogueres, *Munich: Peace for Our Time* (New York: McGraw-Hill, 1965), 66.

50. Angot and de Lavergne, *Le Général Vuillemin*, 88–89.

51. Nogueres, *Munich*, 356.

52. Ibid.

53. Here, again, we face the problem that no scholarly work has been done on French aerodromes as compared to what is now available on the British. Thus we must apologize for the unbalanced nature of this account. Nevertheless, we can maintain that airfields being the very basis of airpower, the subject cannot be neglected, and we can argue further that there are useful lessons to be exposed and that airfields are also a further answer to the question as to why France fell.

54. Philip Birtles, *World War II Airfields* (London: Ian Allen, 1999); Higham, *The Bases of Air Strategy*; and David J. Smith, *Britain's Military Airfields, 1939–1945* (Wellingborough, UK: Patrick Stephens Ltd., 1989). See also the Action Stations series: Chris Ashworth, *Military Airfields of the Central South and South-East*

(Wellingborough, UK: Patrick Stephens Ltd., 1985); Chris Ashworth, *Military Airfields of the South-West* (Wellingborough, UK: Patrick Stephens Ltd., 1982); Michael J. F. Bowyer, *Military Airfields of the Cotswolds and the Central Midlands* (Wellingborough, UK: Patrick Stephens Ltd., 1983); Michael J. F. Bowyer, *Wartime Military Airfields of East Anglia 1939–1945* (Wellingborough, UK: Patrick Stephens Ltd., 1979); Bruce Barrymore Halpenny, *Military Airfields of Greater London* (Wellingborough, UK: Patrick Stephens Ltd., 1984, 1993); Bruce Barrymore Halpenney, *Military Airfields of Lincolnshire and the East Midlands* (Wellingborough, UK: Patrick Stephens Ltd., 1981); Bruce Barrymore Halpenny, *Military Airfields of Yorkshire* (Wellingborough, UK: Patrick Stephens Ltd., 1982); Bruce Quarrie, *Action Stations: Supplement and Index* (Wellingborough, UK: Patrick Stephens Ltd., 1987); David J. Smith, *Military Airfields of Scotland, the North-East, and Northern Ireland* (Wellingborough, UK: Patrick Stephens Ltd., 1983, 1989); David J. Smith, *Military Airfields of Wales and the North-West* (Wellingborough, UK: Patrick Stephens Ltd., 1981).

55. According to Patrick Facon at SHAA, there is no work on French airfields (e-mail, 23 April 2004). Though the Armée de l'Air was small and had only 738 pilots in France in May 1940, it had many aircraft types in service. Breffort and Jouineau, *French Aircraft from 1939 to 1942*.

56. Air Historical Branch, *The Second World War, 1939–45, Royal Air Force Works* (AP.3236, in [PRO] AIR 10/5559, 1956), 29–76; Higham, *The Bases of Air Strategy*; Major General R. P. Pakenham-Walsh, *The History of the Corps of Royal Engineers*, vol. 8, *1938–1945, Campaigns in France and Belgium, 1939–40, Norway, Middle East, East Africa, Western Desert, North West Africa, and Activities in the U.K.* (Chatham, UK: Institution of Royal Engineers, 1958).

57. R. L., "Le service des essences," 123–130.

58. Ibid.

59. Two of the official histories of the United Kingdom in World War II contain aspects of the British story of POL: D. J. Peyton-Smith, *Oil: A Study of Wartime Policy and Administration* (London: HMSO, 1971); and C. I. Savage, *Inland Transport* (London: HMSO, 1957).

60. Collier, *The Defence of the United Kingdom*, 41–48, 88–95; James Steiner, *Hitler's Wehrmacht: German Armed Forces Support of the Fuhrer* (Jefferson, NC: McFarland, 2008); and Edward B. Westermann, *Flak: German Anti-Aircraft Defense, 1914–1945* (Kansas: University Press of Kansas, 2001).

61. *Ingénieur militaire en chef des fabrications d'armements Joyau*, "La défénse contre avions," *Revue Historique de l'Armée* 12, no. 4 (1950): 141–154; and Edward B. Westermann, "Fighting for the Heavens from the Ground: German Ground-Based Air Defenses in the Great War, 1914–1918," *Journal of Military History* 65 (Apr. 2001): 641–670.

62. Remi Baudoui, *Raoul Dautry, 1880–1951: Le technocrate de la république* (Paris: Editions Balland, 1992), 201; and *Ingénieur militaire en chef des fabrications d'armements Joyau*, note 9. Essentially beyond the scope of this work, the French interest in atomic bombs was stimulated by Frédéric Joliot-Curie, who

in February 1940 persuaded Daladier to dispatch a mission to Norway to collect samples of heavy water, found in the Earth's oceans and containing a greater than usual amount of an isotope of value to nuclear weapons programs. This mission evaded German counterespionage and the sample packet was safely in the wine cellars of the Collège de France in Paris by 16 March.

63. Baudoui, *Raoul Dautry*; and *Ingénieur militaire en chef des fabrications d'armements Joyau*. See also James D. Crabtree, *On Air Defense* (Westport, CT: Praeger, 1994), 21–46.

64. Gen. Sir Frederick A. Pile, *Ack-Ack: Britain's Defence Against Air Attack During the Second World War* (London: Harrap, 1949, and Panther, 1956).

65. Christienne, "Le haut commandement français"; Hogg, *Anti-Aircraft Artillery*; O. F. G. Hogg, *The Royal Arsenal [Woolwich]*, vol. 2, *The Background Origin and Subsequent History* (London: Oxford University Press, 1963); Postan et al., *The Design and Development of Weapons*, 252–284; and Vivier,"Le général Denain."

66. Zimmerman, *Britain's Shield*.

67. Maj. Gen. E. B. Ashmore, *Air Defence* (London: Longmans Green, 1929).

68. Ferris, "Fighter Defence Before Fighter Command."

69. Collier, *The Defence of the United Kingdom*.

70. Time to climb to *x*-thousand feet became established as a basic datum.

71. Ferris, "Fighter Defence Before Fighter Command."

72. Gilbert, *Winston S. Churchill*, vol. 6, 479; Smith, *The Prof in Two Worlds*; and Snow, *Science and Government*.

73. Clark, *Tizard*.

74. United Kingdom, National Archives, [PRO] AIR 10/5520, *The Second World War, 1939–1945*, Royal Air Force, *Signals*, vol. 5 *Fighter Control and Interception* (*CD116*, 1952), 42–45.

75. See Colin Sinnott's exposition above of RAF views in the late 1930s. See also Vincent Orange, *Sir Keith Park* (London: Methuen, 1984); and Sinnott, *The Royal Air Force and Aircraft Design*.

76. Brown, *Honour Restored*; E. B. Haslam, "How Lord Dowding Came to Leave Higher Command," *Journal of Strategic Studies* 4, no. 2 (1981): 175–186; Brian Johnson, *The Secret War* (London: BBC, 1978), 63 ff; and United Kingdom, National Archives, [PRO] AIR 19/572.

Chapter 7. Munich and the Phoney War, September 1938–10 May 1940

1. See Higham, *The Military Intellectuals in Britain*.

2. Sebastian Cox, "The Sources and Organization of RAF Intelligence and Its Influence on Operations," in Boog, *The Conduct of the Air War in the Second World War*, 553–579; Facon, "The High Command of the French Air Force,"

148–168; Murray, "The Influences of Pre-War Anglo-American Doctrine on the Air Campaigns of the Second World War," 235–253; Terraine, "The Theory and Practice of the Air War," 467–495; and Wark, "The Air Defence Gap," 511–526. On planning for war in the 1930s in the United States, see Constance M. Green, Harry C. Thomson, and Peter C. Roots, "The Ordnance Department: Planning Munitions for War," in *The United States Army in World War II, The Technical Services* (Washington, DC: U.S. Army Center for Military History, 1955, reprint 1990); and Harry C. Thomson and Lida A. Mayo, "The Ordnance Department, Procurement and Supply," in *The United States Army in World War II: The Technical Services* (Washington, DC: Office of the Chief of Military History, Department of the Army, 1960), 9–11. See also Alexander, *Knowing Your Friends*, esp. "Introduction," 1–17; Alexander and Philpott, "The Entente Cordiale and the Next War"; Gen. André Beaufré, *Le drame de 1940* (Paris: Plon, 1965) [English translation, *1940: The Fall of France* (London: Cassell, 1967)]; Patrice Buffotot, "Le moral dans l'armée de l'air française (de septembre 1939 à juin 1940)," *Colloque International* (Paris, 1975): 173–197; Christienne, "L'industrie aéronautique française de septembre 1939 à juin 1940"; E. B. Haslam, "La préparation à la guerre: Étude de quelques éléments de l'efficacité opérationalle des forces aériennes sur le front du nord-est (de septembre 1939 à mai 1940)," *Colloque International* (Paris, 1975): 517–553; J. F. V. Keiger, "'Perfidious Albion?' French Perceptions of Britain as an Ally after the First World War," in Alexander, *Knowing Your Friends*, 37–52; Col. W. B. R. Neave-Hill, "L'évolution de la stratégie Franco-Anglaise (1939–1940)," *Colloque International* (Paris, 1975): 333–358; Rossi-Landi, "Le pacifism in France (1939–1940)"; and Mark S. Watson, *Chief of Staff: Prewar Plans and Preparations* (Washington, DC: Historical Division, Department of the Army, 1950). In addition, see Michael Jabara Carley, *1939: The Alliance That Never Was and the Coming of World War II* (Chicago: Ivan R. Dee, 1999); Cutlip et al., *Effective Public Relations*; Holley Jr., *Buying Aircraft*, 246 ff; Imlay, "Strategic and Military Planning," 139–158; Jacomet, *L'armement de la France*; Neville, *Hitler and Appeasement*; Mona L. Siegal, *The Moral Disarmament of France: Education, Pacifism, and Patriotism, 1914–1940* (London: Cambridge University Press 2004); and Thomas, "At the Heart of Things?"

3. See Karl-Heinz Frieser, with John T. Greenwood, *The Blitzkrieg Legend: The 1940 Campaign in the West* (Annapolis, MD: Naval Institute Press, 2005).

4. Talbot Imlay, "France and the Phoney War, 1939–1940," in Robert Boyce, ed., *French Foreign and Defence Policy, 1918–1940: The Decline and Fall of a Great Power* (London: LSE/Routledge, 1998), 261–282; and Czech pilot M. A. Liskutin, *Challenge in the Air: A Spitfire Pilot Remembers* (London: Kimber, 1988), 38–66.

5. Bloch, *Strange Defeat.*

6. Jackson, *The Fall of France*, 2–4, 152, 154, 157, 161, 165, 167.

7. Paul Reynaud, *In the Thick of the Fight, 1930–1945*, trans. James P. Lambert (New York: Simon and Schuster, 1955), esp. Ch. 17, "The Disaster," 288 ff. See also Crémieux-Brilhac, *Les français de l'an 1940*, vol. 2; and Fontaine, *French Industry During the War.*

8. Gen. Charles de Gaulle, *The Complete War Memoirs of Charles de Gaulle, 1940–1946* (New York: Simon and Schuster, 1964; and Cambridge, MA: Da Capo Press [abridged of 1955, 1956, and 1959], 1984), 53–54, 79–80; and Jackson, *The Fall of France*, 220–249.

9. Baudoui, *Raoul Dautry.*

10. Thomas, "At the Heart of Things?" 351.

11. On French aircraft production see the charts in Christienne and Lissarrague, *A History of French Military Aviation*, 307–308, 327, 330–331.

12. Brian Bond, ed., *Chief of Staff: The Diaries of Lieutenant-General Sir Henry Pownall*, vol. 1, *1933–1940* (Hamden, CT: Archon Books, 1973); Higham, *Armed Forces in Peacetime*, 233–242; Howard, *The Continental Commitment*; and Col. R. Macleod and Dennis Kelly, eds., *Time Unguarded: The Ironside Diaries* (London: Constable, 1962).

13. Robert Young, *France and the Origins of the Second World War* (London: Macmillan, and New York: St. Martin's Press, 1966).

14. United States, War Department, *The German Campaigns in Norway and Denmark 1940—Operation Weserübung* (Derbyshire, UK: Military Library Research Service, Ltd. [MLRS], reprint 2005).

15. John Lukacs: "Although Britain and France declared war, they stopped short of waging war, except slightly in the air and more at sea." "The Coming of the Second World War," *Foreign Affairs* (Fall 1989): 167.

16. Michael Dockrill, "The Foreign Office and France During the Phoney War, September 1939–May 1940," in Michael Dockrill and Brian McKercher, eds., *Diplomacy and World Power: Studies in British Foreign Policy, 1890–1951* (London: Cambridge University Press, 1996), 171–196, upon which what follows is based.

17. Dockrill and McKercher, *Diplomacy and World Power.*

18. Byron Hollinshead and Theodore K. Rabb, eds., *I Wish I Had Been There*, vol. 2, *European History* (London: Doubleday, 2008). See also Margaret MacMillan, "Tunnels, Territory, and Broken Promises: France Betrayed by the Anglo-Saxons?" in Hollinshead and Rabb, *I Wish I Had Been There*, 248–267. See also Raymond Callahan, *Churchill and the Generals* (Lawrence: University Press of Kansas, 2007); Carlo d'Este, *Warlord: A Life of Winston Churchill at War, 1874–1945* (New York: Harper Collins, 2008); and Margaret MacMillan, *Paris 1919: Six Months That Changed the World* (New York: Random House, 2002).

19. Dockrill and McKercher, *Diplomacy and World Power*; Max Egremont, *Under Two Flags: The Life of Major-General Sir Edward Spears* (London: Weidenfeld and Nicolson, 1997); D. W. J. Johnson, "Britain and France in 1940," *Transactions of the Royal Historical Society* 11 (1972): 141–157; Avi Shlaim, "The British Offer of Union to France, June 1940," *Journal of Contemporary History* 9 no. 3 (July 1974): 27–63; and Nick Smart, *British Strategy and Politics During the Phoney War: Before the Balloon Went Up* (Westport, CT: Praeger, 2003).

20. David Dilks, "The Twilight War and the Fall of France: Chamberlain and Churchill in 1940," *Transactions of the Royal Historical Society* 28 (1978): 61–86. On the change of government of May 1940 in London, see Winston Churchill's own account in his *History of the Second World War*, vol. 1, *The Gathering Storm* (London: Cassel, 1948). Also see John Lukacs, *Five Days in May* (Yale University Press, 1999), on how Churchill grasped the reins and staved off defeat.

21. For details, see Christienne and Lissarrague, *A History of French Military Aviation*, 340–343.

22. Liskutin, *Challenge in the Air.*

23. See Christienne and Lissarrague, *A History of French Military Aviation*, 326–327.

24. Ibid., 325–327, 330–331.

25. See Hall, *North American Supply*; and Haight, *American Aid to France.*

26. Liskutin, *Challenge in the Air.*

27. See note 8 herein.

28. Kirkland, "Planes, Pilots, and Politics," 285–293.

29. Christienne and Lissarrague, *A History of French Military Aviation*, 332.

30. Ibid., 340–343, deployment of Armée de l'Air on 3 September 1939.

31. United Kingdom, National Archives, AIR 41/21, the Air Historical Branch narrative of the Battle of France.

32. For the French air-defense system, see United Kingdom, National Archives, AIR 41/21, 102; Jane's, *All the World's Aircraft* (annual); and Wood, *Attack Warning Red.*

33. United Kingdom, National Archives, AIR 41/21.

34. Ibid., 113.

35. Ibid., especially 78 ff; Higham, *The Bases of Air Strategy*, 89–116; and Pakenham-Walsh, *The History of the Corps of Royal Engineers*, vol. 8.

36. United Kingdom, National Archives, AIR 41/21, First Draft of the Air Historical Branch (AM), *The War in France-Flanders* (n.d.), The Air Historical Branch Narrative of the Battle of France, 93. [*The Campaign in France 10 May–18 June 1940; The Campaign in France and the Low Countries*, Sept. 1939–June 1940, especially pp. 1–32, 273–285, 425].

37. United Kingdom, National Archives, AIR 41/21, First Draft of the Air Historical Branch (AM), *The War in France-Flanders* (n.d.), The Air Historical Branch Narrative of the Battle of France, 94. [*The Campaign in France 10 May–18 June 1940; The Campaign in France and the Low Countries*, Sept. 1939–June 1940, esp. 1–32, 273–285, 425.]

38. United Kingdom, National Archives, AIR 41/21.

39. Here, as in many other aspects of the BAFF, reconstructing the story has been hampered by the loss of records during the retreat and evacuation. Only those of the maintenance officer in chief at BAAF HQs reached the Air Historical Branch; neither the engineering and equipment staff's papers, nor those of No. 21 Aircraft Depot, reached the Air Historical Branch.

40. United Kingdom, National Archives, AIR 41/21, 114.

41. For the history of the subject, see F. J. Adkin, *From the Ground Up: A History of RAF Ground Crew* (Shrewsbury, UK: Airlife, 1983); and United Kingdom, National Archives, [PRO] AIR 10/5559, *CD 1131, Maintenance* (1954) and AP3236 *Works* (1956).

42. Air Cdre. Peter J. Dye, "Logistics and the Battle of Britain, Fighting Wastage in the RAF and the Luftwaffe," *[U.S.] Air Force Journal of Logistics* 24, no. 4 (Winter 2000): 31–40.

43. On the RAF's hangars, see Bruce Robertson, *Aviation Archaeology*, 2nd ed. (Cambridge: Patrick Stephens, 1983).

44. See United Kingdom, National Archives, AP [Air Publication] 113, *Vocabulary of Stores for the Royal Air Force (prices)*, AP 1086 and 1086A.

45. AP 113, *Vocabulary of Stores for the Royal Air Force (prices)*; United Kingdom, National Archives, AIR 41/21, 125.

46. AP 113, *Vocabulary of Stores for the Royal Air Force (prices)*; United Kingdom, National Archives, AIR 44/27, 129.

47. Gen. Lucien Robineau, *Letters of the Air and Space Academy* (June 2008), 2–3.

48. Martin S. Alexander, "The Fall of France, 1940," *Journal of Strategic Studies* 13, no. 1 (1990): 34.

49. Holley Jr., *Buying Aircraft*, 246.

Conclusions

1. United Kingdom, National Archives, AIR 10/5520, *The Second World War, 1939–1945*, Royal Air Force, *Signals*, vol. 5, *Fighter Control and Interception* (*CD116*, 1952), 47–48.

2. Bernard and Dubief, *The Decline of the Third Republic*, 334–335.

3. Bloch, *Strange Defeat*.

4. Ibid., 336–337.

5. Hoffman, "Paradoxes of the French Political Community."

6. Blum, *Chef de governement*.

7. Higham and Harris, *Why Air Forces Fail*.

8. Jacques Benoist-Méchin, *Sixty Days That Shook the West: The Fall of France, 1940* (New York: Putnam, 1963), 536.

9. See Jackson, *The Fall of France*; and Philippe Burrin, *France Under the Germans: Collaboration and Compromise* (New York: New Press, 1996); and Robert O. Paxton, *Parades and Politics at Vichy: The French Officer Corps Under Marshal Pétain* (Princeton, NJ: Princeton University Press, 1966). The history of Vichy has been distorted by the barrage of memoirs and moral judgments, and what has been written concentrates on the army. See d'Abzac-Epézy, *L'Armée de l'Air de Vichy*; Daniel Gaxie, "Morphologie de l'armée de l'air: Les officiers (1924–

1974)," in "Service Historique de l'Armée de l'Air," *Recueil d'articles et d'Études* (Vincennes: SHAA, 1975); Hervé Lucereau, *L'armée nouvelle issue de l'armistice, 1940–1942*, mémoire de maîtrise (Paris: Institut Catholique de Paris, Oct. 1995); Paxton, *Parades and Politics at Vichy*; and Arnaud Teyssier, "La crise en pied de l'armée de l'air . . . . Dec. 1940," *Colloque de FEDN and IHCC* (Paris, 1985): 323–337. See also Philippe Burrin, *France Under the Germans: Collaboration and Compromise* (New York: New Press, 1996); Michael Curtis, *Verdict on Vichy: Power and Prejudice in the Vichy France Regime* (London: Phoenix Press, 2004), for the story of the Jews in France, of which the French are now ashamed; Kirrily Freeman, *Bronze to Bullets: Vichy and the Destruction of French Public Statuary, 1941–1944* (Palo Alto, CA: Stanford University Press, 2009); Frederick Spotts, *The Shameful Peace: How French Artists and Intellectuals Survived the Nazi Occupation* (New Haven, CT: Yale University Press, 2009); and Richard Vinen, *The Unfree French: Life Under the Occupation* (New Haven, CT: Yale University Press, 2006).

GLOSSARY

Aéro-Club de France: air club of France (Fr.)

Aéronautique Militaire: military aeronautics (Fr.)

Aéronavale: naval air arm (Fr.)

Aéroport de Paris–Le Bourget: Le Bourget airport (Fr.)

Arme Aéronautique: French air arm (Fr.)

Armée de Terre: French army (Fr.)

Arsenal de l'Aéronautique: aviation arsenal (Fr.)

atelier: workshop (Fr.)

aviation d'assaut: army cooperation (Fr.)

aviation populaire: popular aviation (Fr.)

bourgeois: mercantile middle class (Fr.)

Centre d'Aéronautique: center for aeronautics (Fr.)

Centre d'Aéronautique Militaire Expérimental: military air experimental
centre (Fr.)

Centre d'Essais en Vol: experimental test center (Fr.)

Centre d'Études Tactiques: center for tactical studies (Fr.)

Centre d'Instruction Avancé: advanced training center (Fr.)

Centre de Réception d'Avions de Série: center of reception of airplanes
of a series (Fr.)

Centre des Hautes Études Militaires: center for high military studies (Fr.)

College des Hautes Études de la Défense Nationale: college of high studies
of national defense (Fr.)

Comité Aéronautique de la Chambre des Députés: the aeronautical
committee of the chamber of deputies (Fr.)

Comité Aviation Militaire: military air matériel department (Fr.)

Comité d'Équipement et Matériel: equipment and matériel committee (Fr.)

Comité d'Essais en Vol: flight test commission (Fr.)

Comité de la Guerre: war committee (Fr.)

Comité de Technique et Industriel: technical and industrial department (Fr.)

Comité des Finances: finance commission of the Sénat (Fr.)

Comité des Forges: committee of the ironworks proprietors, a group of steel industry leaders (Fr.)

Comité du Budget: budget commission of the Chambre (Fr.)

Comité du Matériel: matériel committee (Fr.)

Comité Permanente de la Défense Nationale: standing committee on national defense (Fr.)

Comités d'aéronautiques: aeronautics committees (Fr.)

Comités d'Aviation: aviation committees of the Sénat and Chambre des Députés (Fr.)

Commandement de Région Aéronautique: regional air command (Fr.)

Commission Aéronautique de la Chambre: chamber air commission (Fr.)

Commission Militaire: chamber army commission (Fr.)

Conférence Permanente de Défense Nationale: permanent conference on national defense (Fr.)

Conseil d'Administration: directorate of military aerial matériel (Fr.)

Conseil de Contrôle de Travail: labor control board (Fr.)

Département d'aéronautique: aeronautical department (Fr.)

Deuxième Bureau: French military intelligence agency pre-1940 dealing with foreign armed forces; the second of two intelligence bureaus (Fr.)

Direction Technique: technical directorate (Fr.)

Directoire de l'Ingénieur: directorate of engineering (Fr.)

Directorates de l'Arme Aéronautique de la Terre et de la Mer: land and sea air arms (Fr.)

Division Aérienne: air division (Fr.)

Division Légères Mécanisées: cavalry-armored divisions (Fr.)

droit: the right to do something (Fr.)

École de Guerre: war college (Fr.)

École de l'Air: air school (Fr.)

École des Surintendantes d'Usine: school of factory superintendents (Fr.)

École Libre des Sciences Politiques: free school of political science (Fr.)

École Militaire et Application de l'Aéronautique: military school of air application (Fr.)

École Nationale Supérieure de l'Aéronautique: superior school of aeronautics (Fr.)

École Supérieure de Guerre: high war school (Fr.)

École Supérieure de Guerre Aérienne: advanced military aviation school (Fr.)

Écoles de Mineurs et Génie: schools of miners and engineers (Fr.)

écoles polytechniques: engineering schools (Fr.)

escadre: wing (Fr.)

escadrille: squadron (Fr.)

Front Populaire: Socialist Popular Front (Fr.)

gendarmerie: the police (Fr.)

gendarmes: police officers (Fr.)

Haut Commandement: High Command (Fr.)

Judicaire: judicial chamber (Fr.)

Luftwaffe: German air force

main-d'oeuvre: manpower (Fr.)

métallos: metalworkers (Fr.)

Ministère de l'Agriculture: ministry of agriculture (Fr.)

Ministère de l'Armée de Terre: ministry of the army (Fr.)

Ministère de l'Armement: ministry of armaments (Fr.)

Ministère de l'Intérieur: ministry of the interior (Fr.)

Ministère de la Défense Nationale: ministry of national defense (Fr.)

Ministère de la Guerre: war ministry (Fr.)

Ministère de la Marine: navy ministry (Fr.)

Ministre de Commerce: commerce minister (Fr.)

Ministre de l'Air: air minister (Fr.)

Ministre de la Guerre: war minister (Fr.)

Musée de l'Air et de l'Espace: air and space museum (Fr.)

offensive à outrance: offensive to excess (Fr.)

Organisme de Coordination Générale pour l'Aéronautique: office of general coordination of aeronautics (Fr.)

Parlement: parliament (Fr.)

patrie: the homeland (Fr.)

patronats: the wealthy capitalist French class (Fr.)

Plan de Défense Nationale: national defense plan (Fr.)

poilus: infantrymen; literally hairy ones (Fr.)

Service Aéronautique de l' Orient: aeronautic service of the East (Fr.)

Service de Société Aéronautique Centrale: central safety service (Fr.)

Service Interministériel: interministerial service (Fr.)

Service Technique d'Inspection Aéronautique: aeronautical technical inspection service (Fr.)

Sociéte pour la Liquidation des Stocks de l'Aviation: air liquidation company (Fr.)

Troisième République: Third Republic; the republican government of France from 1870 to 1940 (Fr.)

union sacrée: the World War I bonding of labor and capital (Fr.)

Vocabulary: the list by name of all stores (Br.)

BIBLIOGRAPHY

Note: Regarding United Kingdom documents cited (up to World War II known as Great Britain): Command Papers were published by Parliament, but copies are also to be found in the files of what until 1972 was the Public Record Office (PRO), now the National Archives (TNA). The records are filed by ministry, usually self-explanatory, i.e., WO (War Office) and AIR (Air Ministry); but the Ministry of Aircraft production (MAP) is AVIA. The CAB (Cabinet) files contain in CAB 106/262 the 1945 Luftwaffe *Abteilung* postwar summary files.

Abzac-Epézy, Claude. *See* d'Abzac-Epézy.

Actes, France et Allemagne (1932–1936). Paris: CHRS, 1980.

Adamthwaite, Anthony. *Grandeur and Misery: France's Bid for Power in Europe, 1914–1940*. London: Arnold, 1995.

Addington, Larry. *The Blitzkrieg Era and the German General Staff, 1865–1941*. New Brunswick, NJ: Rutgers University Press, 1971.

Addison, Paul. *Churchill: TheUnexpected Hero*. New York: Oxford University Press, 2004.

Addison, Paul, and Jeremy A. Craig, eds. *The Burning Blue: A New History of the Battle of Britain*. London: Pimlico, 2000.

Adkin, F. J. *From the Ground Up: A History of RAF Ground Crew*. Shrewsbury, UK: Airlife, 1983.

Aero Journal. 38 (Dec. 2004), complete issue; Christian–Jacques Ehrengardt, "La chasse française, 1939–1945." 34 (Dec. 2003–Jan. 2004): 68–71; *Les avions français au combat—le Dewoitine D-520*. Paris: Aéro-Editions, 2004.

After the Battle. The Battle of Britain (*Mark II*). London: Battle of Britain Books International, 1980.

———. *The Blitz: Then and Now*. 2 vols. London: Battle of Britain Prints International, 1987–1988.

Air Historical Branch [AHB]. *See* United Kingdom.

Alanbrooke, Field Marshal Lord. *The War Diaries, 1939–1945*. Edited by Alex Danchev and Daniel Todman. Berkeley: University of California Press, 2001.

Alexander, Bevin. *How Great Generals Win*. New York: Avon, 1993, 1995.

Alexander, Martin S. "The Fall of France, 1940." *Journal of Strategic Studies* 13, no. 1 (1990): 10–44.

———. "Fighting to the Last Frenchman: Reflections on the BEF Deployment to France and the Strains in the Franco-British Alliance, 1939–1940." *Historical*

Reflections [Reflexions Historique] 22, no. 1 (Winter 1996): 235–262; see also Alexander, Martin S. "Fighting to the Last Frenchman . . . " In *The French Defeat of 1940—Reassessments*, edited by Joel Blatt. New York: Berghahn, 1997.

———. "Force de Frappe ou Feu de Paille? Maurice Gamelin's Appraisal of Military Aviation Before the Blitzkrieg of 1940." *Colloque International.* (Paris, 1984): 65–80.

———. "In Defense of the Maginot Line: Security Policy, Domestic Politics, and the Economic Depression in France." In *French Foreign and Defence Policy, 1918–1940: The Decline and Fall of a Great Power*, edited by Robert Boyce. London: LSE/Routledge, 1998, 164–194.

———. "In Lieu of Alliance: The French General Staff's Secret Cooperation with Neutral Belgium 1936–1940." *Journal of Strategic Studies* 14, no. 4 (1991): 413–427.

———. ed. *Knowing Your Friends: Intelligence Inside Alliances and Coalitions from 1914 to the Cold War.* London: Frank Cass, 1998, including Martin S. Alexander, "Introduction: Knowing Your Friends, Assessing Your Allies—Perspectives on Intra-Alliance Intelligence," 1–17.

———. "La faillite de la mechanization dans les armées françaises et britanniques entre 1935 et 1940—une étude comparative." Sorbonne *Colloque*, May 1978; Ph.D. thesis, Paris, ca. 1980.

———. *The Republic in Danger: General Maurice Gamelin and the Politics of French Defence, 1933–1940.* New York: Cambridge University Press, 1992.

Alexander, Martin S., and Helen Graham, eds. *The French and Spanish Popular Fronts: Comparative Perspectives.* London: Cambridge University Press, 1989.

Alexander, Martin S., and William Philpott. "The Entente Cordiale and the Next War: Anglo-French Views on Future Military Co-operation, 1928–1939." In *Knowing Your Friends: Intelligence Inside Alliances and Coalitions from 1914 to the Cold War*, edited by Martin S. Alexander. London: Frank Cass, 1998, 53–84.

Allen, S/Ldr. H. R. "Dizzy." *The Battle of Britain: Recollectons of H. R. "Dizzy" Allen.* London: Arthur Barker, 1973.

———. *The Legacy of Lord Trenchard.* London: Cassell, 1972.

Andrew, Christopher, and Oleg Gordievsky. *KGB. The Inside Story.* New York: Harper Collins, 1990.

Andrew, Christopher, and Vasili Mitrokhin. *The Mitrokhin Archive: The KGB in Europe and the West.* London and New York: Penguin, 2000.

Andrews, C. F. *Vickers Aircraft Since 1918.* London: Putnam 1969.

Andrews, C. F., and E. B. Morgan. *Supermarine Aircraft Since 1914.* London: Putnam, 1981.

Angelucci, Enzio. *Illustrated Encyclopedia of Military Aircraft 1914 to the Present.* Edison, NJ: Chartwell Books 2001, plate 7.

Angot, E., and R. de Lavergne. *Le Général Vuillemin, figure légendaire de l'aviation française de 1914 à 1940: Le combatant, le pioneer de Sahar, le chef.* Paris: Palatine, 1965.

Anon. "Decision Superiority: An Air Force Concept Paper." No. 28 (Nov. 2008). Canberra, Aus.: [RAAF] Air Power Development Centre, 2008.

———. *The Diary of a Staff Officer (Air Intelligence Liaison Officer at Advanced Headquarters, North BAFF, 1940)*. London: Methuen & Co., 1941.

———. "Juin le morocain." *Revue Historique de l'Armée* 8, no. 2 (1952): 8–10.

Armengaud, Général. *Batailles politiques et militaries sur l'Europe témoignages (1932–1940)*. Paris: Collection pour comprendre l'historie, Editions du Mynte, 1948.

Artaud, Denise. "Reparations and War Debts: The Restoration of French Financial Power, 1919–1929." In *French Foreign and Defence Policy, 1918–1940*, edited by Robert W. D. Boyce. London: LSE/Routledge, 1998, 89–106.

Artzet, Hervé. "Le général Jean-Henri Jauneaud: Une personalité áeronautique de l'entre-deux-guerres." *Revue Historique des Armées* [photocopy, ca. 1998].

Ash, Eric. *Sir Frederick Sykes and the Air Revolution, 1912–1918*. London: Frank Cass, 1999.

Ashford, Douglas E. *Policy and Politics in France: Living with Uncertainty*. Philadelphia: Temple University Press, 1982.

Ashmore, Maj. Gen. E. B. *Air Defence*. London: Longmans Green, 1929.

Ashworth, Chris. *Military Airfields of the Central South and South-East*. Action Stations Series. Wellingborough, UK: Patrick Stephens, 1985.

———. *Military Airfields of the South-West*. Action Stations Series. Wellingborough, UK: Patrick Stephens, 1982.

Ashworth, William. *Contracts and Finances*. London: HMSO, 1953.

Astorkia, Madeline. "Les leçons aériennes de la guerre d'Espagne." *Revue Historique des Armées* 2 (1977): 145–173.

Atkin, Nicholas. *The French at War, 1934 to 1944*. London: Longmans, 2001.

Azema, Jean-Pierre. *From Munich to the Liberation, 1938–1944*. Paris: Le Seuil, 1949; London: Cambridge University Press, 1984.

Baker, David. *Adolf Galland—The Authorized Biography*. London: Windrow & Greene, 1996.

Balderston, T. "War Finance and Inflation in Britain and Germany, 1914–1918." *Economic History Review*, 2nd ser., 42, no. 2 (1989): 222–244.

Balfour, Harold. *Wings Over Westminster*. London: Hutchinson, 1973.

Balke, Ulf. *Zusammengestellt nach unterlagen aus RL 2 III/707/einstazbereitschaft der fliegenden verbände*. (Tables). Bundesarchiv-Militarchiv, Freiburg, Germany.

Banks, F. R. *I Kept No Diary: 60 Years with Marine Diesels, Automobile and Aero Engines*. Shrewsbury, UK: Airlife, 1978.

Bankwitz, Philip, C. F. *Maxime Weygand and Civil Military Relations in Modern France*. Cambridge, MA: Harvard University Press, 1967.

Barnes, C. H. *Fairey Aircraft Since 1915*. London: Putnam, 1974.

———. *Handley Page Aircraft Since 1907*. London: Putnam, 1976.

———. *Short's Aircraft Since 1900*. London: Putnam, 1967.

Barnett, Corelli. *Audit of War*. London: Macmillan, 1986.

———. "The Education of Military Elites." *Journal of Contemporary History* 2, no. 23 (July 1967): 15–35.

Barr, Niall. *The Lion and the Poppy: British Veterans, Politics, and Society, 1921–1939*. Westport, CT: Praeger, 2005.

Bartov, Omer. *Hitler's Army: Soldiers, Nazis, and War in the Third Reich*. New York and Oxford: Oxford University Press, 1991.

———. "Martyrs' Vengeance: Memory, Trauma, and Fear of War in France, 1918–1940." *Historical Reflections [Reflexions Historique]* 22, no. 21 (Winter 1996): 47–76; also in *The French Defeat of 1940: Reassessments*, edited by Joel Blatt. Providence, RI: Berghahn Books, 1998, 54–84.

Batchelor, John, and Ian Hogg. *Artillery*. New York: Charles Scribner's Sons, 1972.

Baudoui, Remi. *Raoul Dautry, 1880–1951: Le technocrate de la république*. Paris: Balland, 1992.

Baum, Warren C. *The French Economy and the State*. Princeton, NJ: Princeton University Press, 1958.

Baumont, Maurice. "The Rhineland Crisis, 7 March 1936." In *Troubled Neighbours: Franco-British Relations in the Twentieth Century*, edited by Neville Waites. London: Weidenfeld and Nicolson, 1971.

Baxter, Ian. *Images of War: Blitzkrieg in the West—Rare Photographs from Wartime Archives*. Barnsley, UK: Pen and Sword Military, 2010.

Beamont, Roland. *My Part of the Sky: A Fighter Pilot's Firsthand Experiences, 1939–1945*. Wellingborough, UK: Patrick Stephens, 1989.

Beaufré, André. *Le drame de 1940*. Paris: Plon, 1965 [English translation, *1940: The Fall of France*. London: Cassell, 1967].

———. "Liddell Hart and the French Army, 1919–1939." In *The Theory and Practice of War: Essays Presented to Captain B. H. Liddell Hart*, edited by Michael Howard. London: Cassell, 1965.

———. *1940: The Fall of France*. New York: Alfred A. Knopf, 1968.

Beaumont, Roger. *Right Backed by Might—The International Air Force Concept*. Westport, CT: Greenwood Press, 2002.

Becker, Annette. *War and Faith: The Religious Imagination in France, 1914–1930 (Legacy of the Great War)*. Oxford/New York: Berg, 1998.

Becker, Jean-Jacques. "That's the Death Knell of Our Boys . . . " In *The French Home Front, 1914–1918*, edited by Patrick Fridenson. Oxford: Berg, 1992, 17–36.

Beckett, Ian. *The First World War: The Essential Guide to Sources in the UK National Archives*. Richmond, UK: National Archives/Public Record Office, 2002.

Beckett, Ian F. W., and Keith Simpson, eds. *A Nation in Arms: A Social Study of the British Army in the First World War*. Manchester, UK: Manchester University Press, 1985.

Begley, Louis. *Why the Dreyfus Affair Matters*. New Haven, CT: Yale University Press, 2009.

Begley, Sharon. "West Brain, East Brain. What a Difference Culture Makes." *Newsweek* (1 Mar. 2010): 22.

Bekker, Cajus. *The Luftwaffe War Diaries*. New York: Doubleday, 1968.

Bell, Christopher M. "Winston Churchill and the Ten Year Rule." *Journal of Military History* 74 (Oct. 2010): 1097–1128.

Bell, P. M. H. "The Breakdown of the Alliance in 1940." In *Troubled Neighbors: Franco-British Relations in the Twentieth Century*, edited by Neville Waites. London: Weidenfeld and Nicolson, 1971.

———. *France and Britain 1900–1940: Entente and Estrangement*. London: Longman, 1996.

Bennett, Gill. *Churchill's Man of Mystery: Desmond Morton and the World of Intelligence*. New York: Routledge, 2007.

Benoist-Méchin, Jacques. *Sixty Days That Shook the West: The Fall of France, 1940*. New York: Putnam, 1963.

Berkwitz, Philip C. F. "Maxime Weygand and the Fall of France: A Study in Civil-Military Relations." *Journal of Military History* 31, no. 3 (Sept. 1959): 225–242.

Bernard, Philippe, and Henri Dubief. *The Decline of the Third Republic, 1914–1938*. Translated by Anthony Forster. London: Cambridge University Press, 1985.

Betts, Raymond F. *France and Decolonization, 1900–1960*. New York: St. Martin's Press, 1991.

Beyerchen, Alan. "From Radio to Radar: Interwar Military Adaptation to Technological Change in Germany, the United Kingdom, and the United States." In *Military Innovation in the Interwar Period*, edited by Williamson Murray and Allan R. Millett. New York: Cambridge University Press, 1996, 265–299.

Bialer, Uri. "Elite Opinion and Defence Policy: Air Power Advocacy and British Rearmament in the 1930s." [*British*] *Journal of International Studies* 6 (1980): 32–51.

Bickers, Richard Townshend, Gordon Swanborough, William Green, Bill Gunston, Air Vice Marshal J. E. Johnson, Mike Spick, and G/C Sir High Dundas. *The Battle of Britain: The Greatest Battle in the History of Air Warfare*. New York: Prentice Hall, 1990; London: Salamander, 1999.

Biddle, Tami Davis. "Dresden 1945: Reality, History, and Myth." *Journal of Military History* 72 (Apr. 2008): 413–449.

Bingham, Victor F. *Blitzed: The Battle of France May–June 1940*. New Maldon, UK: Air Research Publications, 1990.

Birtles, Philip. *World War II Airfields*. London: Ian Allen, 1999.

Black, Jeremy. "Frontiers and Military History." *Journal of Military History* 72, no. 4 (October 2008): 1047–1060.

Blake, Robert, and William Roger Louis, eds. *Churchill*. London: Oxford University Press, 1993.

Blatt, Joel. "The French Defeat of 1940: Introduction." *Historical Reflections [Reflexions Historique]* 22, no. 1 (Winter 1996): 1–10.

———, ed. *The French Defeat of 1940: Reassessments*. Providence, RI: Berghahn, 1998.

Bloch, Marc. *Strange Defeat: A Statement of Evidence Written in 1940*. New York: W. W. Norton, 1968.

Blum, Léon. *Chef de gouvernement, 1936–1937*. A colloquia held at the National Political Science Foundation, 17–26 Mar. 1965. Paris: Presses de la Fondation Nationale des Sciences Politique, 1967.

Bodleian Library, The, ed. *Instructions for British Servicemen in France, 1944*. Oxford, UK: The Bodleian Library, University of Oxford, 2006.

Bond, Brian, ed. *Chief of Staff: The Diaries of Lieutenant-General Sir Henry Pownall*. Vol. 1, *1933–1940*. Hamden, CT: Archon Books, 1973.

Bond, Brian, and Martin Alexander. "Liddell Hart and DeGaulle: The Doctrines of
    Limited Liability and Mobile Defence." In *Makers of Modern Strategy from
    Machiavelli to the Nuclear Age*, edited by Peter Paret. Princeton, NJ: Princeton
    University Press, 1986, 598–623.

Bondil, Général. "Le chemin de fer, 1871–1914 et la guerre 1914–1918." *Revue
    Historique de l'Armée* 5, no. 1 (1959): 117–132.

Bonney, Richard. "Twenty Years On: A View of the Study of French History from Its
    Co-Founders." *French History* 21, no. 2 (2007): 231–236.

Boog, Horst, ed. *The Conduct of the Air War in the Second World War: An International
    Comparison* [1988]. Oxford: Berg, 1988, 1992.

———. "Luftwaffe and Logistics in the Second World War." *Aerospace Historian*
    (Summer/June 1988): 103–110.

———. "The Policy, Command, and Direction of the Lufwaffe in World War II." *Royal
    Air Force Historical Society Journal* 41 (2008): 67–85.

Boog, Horst, Gerhard Krebs, and Detlef Vogel. *Germany and the Second World War*.
    Vol. 7, *The Strategic Air War in Europe and the War in the West and East Asia
    1943–1944/5*. Oxford: Oxford University Press, 2006.

Bosworth, R. J. B. "Benito Mussolini: Dictator." *Historically Speaking* (June 2003): 7–9.

Botts, Colonel Ferruccio. "Amadeo Mecozzi." *Colloque International* (Paris, 8 Oct.
    1990): 131–150.

Boussard, Dominique. *Un problème de défense nationale: L'aéronautique militaire au
    parlement (1928–1940)*. Vincennes: SHAA. (1983).

Bowers, Peter M. *Curtiss Aircraft 1907–1947*. London: Putnam, 1979.

Bowyer, Michael J. F. *Military Airfields of the Cotswolds and the Central Midlands*.
    Action Stations Series. Wellingborough, UK: Patrick Stephens, 1983.

———. *No. 2 Group RAF: A Complete History, 1936–1945*. London: Faber & Faber,
    1974.

———. *Wartime Military Airfields of East Anglia 1939–1945*. Action Stations Series.
    Wellingborough, UK: Patrick Stephens, 1979.

Boyce, Robert. "Business as Usual: The Limits of French Economic Diplomacy,
    1926–1933." In *French Foreign and Defence Policy, 1918–1940: The Decline and
    Fall of a Great Power*, edited by Robert Boyce. London: LSE/Routledge, 1998,
    107–131.

———, ed. *French Foreign and Defence Policy, 1918–1940: The Decline and Fall of a
    Great Power*. London: LSE/Routledge, 1998.

Boyle, Andrew. *Trenchard: Man of Vision*. London: Cassell, 1956.

Bradbrooke, Joan. *The Centenary History of the Royal Aeronautical Society*. London:
    Royal Aeronautical Society [RAeS], 1966.

Braudel, Fernand. *The Identity of France [L'Identité de la France]*. Vol. 2, *People and
    Production*. Translated by Sian Reynolds. New York: Harper Collins, 1990.

Breche, Yves, "Les officiers de l'armée de l'air à travers la littéraire militaire." *Revue
    Historiques des Armées* 2 (1977): 113–144.

Breffort, Dominique, and André Jouineau. *French Aircraft from 1939 to 1942—Fighters,
    Bombers, and Observation Types*. 2 vols. Paris: Histoire et Collections, 2004.

Broadberry, Stephen, and Mark Harrison. *The Economics of World War*. Vol. 1. London: Cambridge University Press, 2005.

Brogan, D.W. *France Under the Republic: The Development of Modern France (1870–1939)*. New York: Harper, 1940.

Brooks, Peter. *The Modern Airliner*. Manhattan, KS: Sunflower University Press, 1982.

Brooks, Tim. *British Propaganda to France, 1940–1944: Machinery, Methods and Message*. Edinburgh, UK: Edinburgh University Press, 2007.

Brown, Frederick. *For the Soul of France: Culture Wars in the Age of Dreyfus*. New York: Alfred A. Knopf, 2010.

Brown, S/Ldr. Peter. *Honour Restored: The Battle of Britain, Dowding, and the Fight for Freedom*. Staplehurst, UK: Spellmount, 2005.

Bruce, J. M. *Aircraft of the Royal Flying Corps [Military Wing]*. London: Putnam, 1982.

———. *British Aeroplanes, 1914–1918*. London: Putnam, 1957.

Bruce, Robert B. *Pétain: Verdun to Victory*. Washington, DC: Potomac Books, 2008.

Brunelle, Gayle K., and Annette Finley Croswhite. *Murder in the Metro: Laetitia Toureaux and the Cagoule in 1930s France*. Baton Rouge: Louisiana State University Press, 2010.

Bryson, Bill. *The Mother Tongue: English and How It Got That Way*. New York: W. Morrow, 1990.

Buckley, John. "Contradictions in British Defence Policy 1937–39: The RAF and the Defence of Trade." *Twentieth Century British History* 5, no. 1 (1994): 100–113.

———. *The RAF and Trade Defence, 1919–1945*. Keele, UK: Keele University Press, 1995.

Buffotot, Patrice. "L'armée de l'air dans la bataille de France." *Recueil d'Articles et Études*. Vincennes: SHAA. (1991): 183–200.

———. "L'Armée de l'Air française et la crise du 7 mars 1936." Also published in *Recueil d'Articles et Études 1976–1978*. Vincennes: SHAA. (1984): 47–68; XIVe Colloque historique franco-allemand *La France et l'Allegamne 1932–1936*. Paris: Palais du Luxembourg, Salle Médicis; Comité d'Histoire de la Deuxieme Guerre mondiale, 10–12 Mar. 1977, *Actes, France et Allemagne (1932–1936)*. Paris: CHRS, 1980, 315–331.

———. "Le moral dans l'armée de l'air française (de septembre 1939 à juin 1940)." Comité de la 2e Guerre Mondiale, *Français et Britannique dans la drôle de guerre, actes du colloque franco-britannique tenu à Paris du 8 au 12 décembre 1975*. Paris: Editions de Centre National de la Recherche Scientifique, 1979; *Colloque International* (Paris, 1975): 173–197.

———. "Le rearmament aérien allemande et l'approche de la guerre vue par le 2e bureau français." XVe Colloque historique franco-allemand *Deutschland und Frankreich 1936–1939*, Bonn, Institut historique allemande de Paris, Comité français d'histoire de la Seconde Guerre mondiale, Oct. 1978, *Actes* (Munich and Zurich: Artemis, 1982): 249–289.

Buffotot, Patrice, and J. Ogier, "L'armée de l'air français pendant la bataille de France du 10 mai 1940 à l'armistice: Essai de bilan numerique d'une bataille aérienne." *Revue Historique des Armées* 3 (1975): 88–117; reprinted in *Recueil d'Articles et Études, 1974–1975*. Vincennes: SHAA. (1977): 197–226.

Bullitt, William C. *For the President*. Boston: Houghton Mifflin, 1972.

Burgess, Greg. "France and the German Refugee Crisis of 1933." *French History* 16, no. 2 (June 2002): 203–229.

Burk, Kathleen, ed. *War and the State: The Transformation of British Government, 1914–1919*. London: George Allen & Unwin, 1982.

Burrin, Philippe. *France Under the Germans: Collaboration and Compromise*. New York: New Press, 1996.

Buxton, Neil K., and Derek H. Aldcroft. *British Industry Between the Wars: Instability and Industrial Development, 1919–1939*. London: Scota Press, 1979.

Byford, G/Cpt. Alistair. "The Battle of France, May 1940: Enduring, Combined, and Joint Lessons." *Royal Air Force Air Power Review* 11 (Summer 2008): 60–73.

Cain, Anthony Christopher. *The Forgotten Air Force: French Air Doctrine in the 1930s*. Washington, DC: Smithsonian Institution Press, 2002.

———. "L'Armée de l'Air, 1933–1940: Drifting Toward Defeat." In *Why Air Forces Fail: The Anatomy of Defeat*, edited by Robin Higham and Stephen J. Harris. Lexington: University Press of Kentucky, 2006, 41–70.

Cairns, John C. "Along the Road Back to France, 1940." *American Historical Review* 64, no. 3 (Apr. 1959): 583–603.

———, ed. *Contemporary France: Illusion, Conflict, and Regeneration*. New York: New Viewpoint, 1978.

———. "Great Britain and the Fall of France: A Study in Allied Disunity." *Journal of Modern History* 27, no. 4 (Dec. 1955): 365–409.

———. "A Nation of Shopkeepers in Search of a Suitable France, 1919–1940." *American Historical Review* 79, no. 3 (June 1974): 710–743.

———. "Some Recent Histories and the 'Strange Defeat' of 1940." *Journal of Modern History* 46, no. 1 (Mar. 1974): 60–85.

Callahan, Raymond. *Churchill and the Generals*. Lawrence: University Press of Kansas, 2007.

Callwell, Sir Charles. *Small Wars: Their Principles and Practice*. London: HMSO, 1896.

Caloire, Maurice. "La direction des services de l'armistice à Vichy." *Comité d'histoire de la deuxième guerre mondiale* 14 (1954); 17 (1955).

Camelio, Paul, and Christopher Shores. *Armée de l'Air: A Pictorial History of the French Air Force, 1937–1945*. Warren, MI: Squadron/Signal, 1978.

Cannadine, David. *Ornamentalism: How the British Saw Their Empire*. London: Oxford University Press, 2001.

Cardoza, Thomas. *Intrepid Women: Cantinières and Vivandières of the French Army*. Bloomington, IN: Indiana University Press, 2010.

Carley, Michael Jabara. *1939: The Alliance That Never Was and the Coming of World War II*. Chicago: Ivan R. Dee, 1999.

———. "The Origins of the French Intervention in the Russian Civil War, January–May 1918: A Reappraisal." *Journal of Modern History* 48, no. 3 (Sept. 1970): 413–439.

Carlier, Claude. *Marcel Dassault: La légende d'un siècle*. Paris: Perrin, 1992.

Caron, Vicki. "The Missed Opportunity: French Refugee Policy in Wartime 1939–40." *Historical Reflections [Reflexions Historique]* 22, no. 1 (Winter 1996): 117–157.

Carter, Edward Carlos, Robert Forster, and John N. Moody. *Enterprise and Entrepreneurs in Nineteenth and Twentieth Century France*. Baltimore: Johns Hopkins University Press, 1976.

Cassar, George H. *The French in the Dardenelles: A Study of Failure in the Conduct of War*. London: George Allen & Unwin, 1971.

———. *Kitchener's War: British Strategy from 1914–1916*. Washington, DC: Potomac Books, 2004.

Castellan, G. "La Wehrmacht vue de France, Septembre 1939." *Revue Historique de l'Armée* 5 no. 2 (1949): 35–48.

Centennial Journal—Journal of the Royal Aeronautical Society (1966). (*See* Joan Bradbrooke.)

Chadeau, Emmanuel. "Government, Industry and Nation: The Growth of Aeronautical Technology in France (1900–1950)." *Aerospace Historian* (Mar. 1988): 26–44.

———. *L'industrie aéronautique en France, 1900–1950. De Blériot à Dassault*. Paris: Fayard, 1987.

———. "Réalisation des programmes aéronautiques français (1938–1940)," in *L'industrie aéronautique en France, 1900–1950. De Blériot à Dassault*. Paris: Fayard, 1987.

Challener, Richard D. *The French Theory of the Nation in Arms, 1866–1939*. New York: Columbia University Press, 1955.

Chambe, René. *Histoire de l'aviation des origines à nos jours*. Paris: Flammarian, 1958.

Chamier, Air Cdre. John Adrian. *The Birth of the Royal Air Force: The Early Historical Experiences of the Flying Services*. London: Sir Isaac Pitman, 1943.

———. "Strategy and Air Strategy." *Journal of the Royal United Service Institution* (1921): 641–661.

Chandos, John. *Boys Together: English Public Schools, 1800–1864*. New Haven: Yale University Press, 1984.

Chapman, Guy. *Why France Collapsed*. New York: Holt, Rinehart & Winston, 1968.

Chapman, Herrick Eaton. "Reshaping French Industrial Politics: Workers, Employers and State Officials and the Struggle for Control of the Aircraft Industry, 1928–1950." Ph.D. Dissertation, University of California, Berkeley, 1983.

———. *State Capitalism and Working-Class Radicalism in the French Aircraft Industry*. Berkeley: University of California Press, 1991.

Chrastil, Rachel. *Organizing for War: France, 1870–1914*. Baton Rouge: Louisiana State University Press, 2010.

Christienne, Charles [Gen.]. "L'armée de l'air française de mars 1936 à septembre 1939." *Proceedings of the 15th Franco-German Colloquium* (Bonn, 26–29 Sept. 1978): 171–211.

———. "L'industrè aéronautique française de septembre 1939 à juin 1940." *Recueil d'Articles et Études, 1974–1975*. Vincennes: SHAA. (1974): 141–163

———. "L'industrie aéronautique française de septembre 1939 à mai 1940." Comité d'histoire de la 2e Guerre Mondiale. *Français et Britannique dans la drôle de guerre, actes du colloque franco-britannique tenu à Paris du 8 au 12 décembre 1975*. Paris: Editions de Centre National de la Recherche Scientifique, 1979, 359–410.

———. "La RAF dans la bataille de france au travers des raports de vuillemin de juillet, 1940." *Recueil d'Articles et d'Études, 1981–1983*. Vincennes: SHAA. (1987): 313–333.

———. "Le haut commandement français face au progrès technique entre les deux guerres." *ICMH Acta*, 5 (Bucharest, 10–17 Aug. 1980; 1981): 161–177. Reprinted in *Recueil d'Articles et d'Études, 1979–1981*. Vincennes: SHAA. (1986): 398–412.

Christienne, Charles, and Patrice Buffotot. "L'armée de l'air française et le crise du 7 mars 1936."*Recueil d'articles et d'Études, 1976–1978*. Vincennes: SHAA. (1984): 47–68; XIVe Colloque historique franco-allemand *La France et l'Allemagne 1932–1936*. Paris: Palais du Luxembourg, Salle Médicis, Comité d'histoire de la Seconde Guerre mondiale, 10–12 Mar. 1977; *Actes, France et Allemagne (1932–1936)*. Paris: CHRS, 1980: 315–331.

Christienne, Charles, Patrick Facon, Patrice Buffotot, and Lee Kennett. *French Military Aviation: A Bibliographical Guide*. New York: Garland, 1989.

Christienne, Charles, and Pierre Lissarrague. *A History of French Military Aviation* [*Histoire de l'aviation militaire française*]. Paris: Charles-Lavauzelle, 1980; English edition, *A History of French Military Aviation*. Washington, DC: Smithsonian Institution Press, 1986.

Christofferson, Thomas R., and Michael S. Christofferson. *France During World War II: From Defeat to Liberation*. New York: Fordham University Press, 2006.

Churchill, Winston S. *History of the Second World War*. Vol. 1, *The Gathering Storm*. London: Cassell, 1948.

———. *History of the Second World War*. Vol. 2, *Their Finest Hour*. Boston: Houghton Mifflin, 1948.

Clark, Ronald W. *Rise of the Boffins*. London: Phoenix House, 1962.

———. *Tizard*. London: Methuen; Cambridge, MA: MIT Press, 1965.

Clarke, Jeffrey J. "Military Technology in Republican France: The Evolution of the French Armored Force, 1917–1940." Ph.D. Dissertation, Duke University, Durham, NC, 1968. (University microfilms 47 and 990).

———. "The Nationalization of War Industries in France, 1936–1937: A Case Study." *Journal of Modern History* 49, no. 3 (Sept. 1977): 411–430.

Clément, Jean-Louis. "The Birth of a Myth: Maurras and the Vichy Regime." *French History* 17, no. 4 (Dec. 2003): 440–454.

Cobb, Richard. *French and Germans: Germans and French. A Personal Interpretation of France Under Two Occupations, 1914–1919/1940–1944*. Hanover, NH: University Press of New England, 1993.

Cohen, William B. "The Lure of Empire: Why Frenchmen Entered the Colonial Service." *Journal of Contemporary History* 4, no. 1 (Jan. 1969): 103–116.

Cohrs, Patrick O. *The Unfinished Peace After World War I: America, Britain, and the Stabilization of Europe, 1919–1932*. London: Cambridge University Press, 2006.

Cole, Wayne S. *Senator Gerald P. Nye and American Foreign Relations*. Minneapolis: University of Minnesota Press, 1962.

Collier, Basil. *The Defence of the United Kingdom*. London: HMSO, 1957.

———. *Leader of the Few*. London: Jarrolds, 1957.

Colloque International. (Paris, 1975).

Comité d'Histoire de la 2e Guerre Mondiale. *Français et Britannique dans la drôle de guerre, actes du colloque franco-britannique ténu à Paris du 8 au 12 décembre 1975.* Paris: Editions du Centre Nationale de la Recherche Scientifique, 1979.

Connell, John. *Wavell: Scholar and Soldier.* New York: Harcourt Brace, 1964.

Cooling, B. F., ed. *Case Studies in the Achievement of Air Superiority.* Washington, DC: Office of Air Force History, 1994, 115–174.

Cooper, Nicole. *France in Indo-China: Colonial Encounters.* Oxford: Berg, 2000.

Corbett, Sir Julian. *Some Principles of Maritime Strategy.* London: Longmans, 1911.

Cornelius, John C. *Military Forces of France.* U.S. Army Military History Institute, Special Bibliographic Series No. 15. Carlisle Barracks, PA: USAMHI, 1977.

Cornwell, Peter D. *The Battle of France Then and Now.* Old Harlow, Essex, UK: Battle of Britain International, 2007 [2008].

Corum, James S. *The Luftwaffe: Creating the Operational Air War 1918–1940.* Lawrence: University Press of Kansas, 1997.

———. *The Roots of Blitzkrieg: Hans von Seeckt and German Military Reform.* Lawrence: University Press of Kansas, 1992.

———. "The Spanish Civil War: Lessons Learned and Not Learned by the Great Powers." *Journal of Military History* 62, no. 2 (Apr. 1998): 313–334.

———. *Wolfram von Richthofen: Master of the German Air War.* Lawrence: University Press of Kansas, 2008.

Cot, Pierre. "En 1940 où ont nos avions? La preparation, la doctrine, l'emploi de l'armée de l'air avant et pendant la bataille de France." *Icare* 57 (1971): 34–57.

———. *L'Armée de l'Air 1936–1938.* Paris: Edition Bernard Grasset, 1939.

———. *Triumph of Treason (Contre nous de la tyrannie).* Chicago: Ziff-Davis, 1944.

Cox, Sebastian. "The Sources and Organization of RAF Intelligence and Its Influence on Operations." In *The Conduct of the Air War in the Second World War: An International Comparison,* edited by Horst Boog. Oxford: Berg, 1988, 1992, 553–579.

Cox, Sebastian, and Peter Gray, eds. *Air Power History: Turning Points from Kitty Hawk to Kosovo.* London: Frank Cass, 2002.

Crabtree, James D. *On Air Defense.* Westport, CT: Praeger, 1994.

Crémieux-Brilhac, Jean-Louis. "*La France libre.*" In *La France des années noires.* Vol. 1, *De la défaite à Vichy,* edited by Jean-Pierre Azéma and François Bédarida. Paris: Editions de Seuil, 2000, 191–242.

———. *Les français de l'an 40.* Vol. 1, *La guerre oui ou non?* Vol. 2, *Ouvriers et soldats.* Paris: Gallimard, 1990.

Cromwell, Valerie. "'A World Apart': Gentlemen Amateurs to Professional Generalists." In *Diplomacy and World Power: Studies in British Foreign Policy, 1895–1950,* edited by Michael Dockrill and Brian McKercher. London: Cambridge University Press 1996.

Cross, J. A. *Lord Swinton.* Oxford: Clarendon Press, 1982.

———. *Sir Samuel Hoare: A Political Biography.* London: Jonathon Cape, 1977.

Crowell, Benedict. *America's Munitions.* Washington, DC: USGPO, 1919.

Crozier, Michael. *The Bureaucratic Phenomenon*. Chicago: University of Chicago Press, 1964.

Cull, Brian, Bruce Lander, and Heinrich Weiss. *Twelve Days in May* [RAF Hurricanes in France 1940]. London: Grub Street, 1995.

Cumming, Anthony J. "Ready or Not? The RAF in the Battle of Britain." *BBC History* 8, no. 11 (Nov. 2007): 22–24.

Curami, A., and G. Rochat, eds. *Guilio Douhet Scritti, 1901–1915*. Rome: State Maggiore Aeronautica, Ufficio Storico, 1993.

Curtis, Michael. *Verdict on Vichy: Power and Prejudice in the Vichy France Regime*. London: Phoenix Press, 2004.

Cutlip, Scott M., Allen H. Center, and Glen M. Broom. *Effective Public Relations*. 8th ed. New York: Prentice Hall, 1999.

"'Cyclops,' The Air Defence of Great Britain Command Exercise, 1933." *Journal of the Royal United Service Institution* 78 (Nov. 1933): 739–745.

Cynk, Jerszy. *The Polish Air Force at War*. 2 vols., 1939–1943, 1943–1945. Atglen, PA: Schiffer Publishing, 2010.

d'Abzac-Epézy, Claude. "Camille Rougeron, stratège de l'aviation et de la guerre totale." *Revue Historique des Armées* 91, no. 4 (1998): 117–125.

———. *L'Armée de l'Air de Vichy, 1940–1944*. Vincennes: SHAA. (1997).

d'Este, Carlo. *Warlord: A Life of Winston Churchill at War, 1874–1945*. New York: Harper Collins, 2008.

d'Ombrain, Nicholas. *War Machinery and High Policy: Defence Administration in Peacetime Britain, 1902–1914*. London: Oxford University Press, 1973.

Daughton, J. P. *An Empire Divided: Religion, Republicanism, and the Making of French Colonialism, 1880–1914*. New York: Oxford University Press, 2006.

Dawson, Sandra. "Working-Class Consumers and the Campaign for Holidays with Pay." *20th Century British History* 18, no. 3 (2007): 277–305.

de Cosse-Brisac, LTC Charles. "Combien d' avions allemands contre combien d'avions français le 10 mai 1940?" *Revue de Défense Nationale* 4 (1948): 741–759.

———. "L'Allemagne et son armée, 1919–1939." *Revue Historique de l'Armée* 5, no. 2 (1949).

de Gaulle, Charles. *The Complete War Memoirs of Charles de Gaulle, 1940–1946*. New York: Simon and Schuster, 1964; Da Capo Press, reprint, 1984.

De Groot, Gerard J. *The First World War*. New York: Palgrave Macmillan, 2000.

de Havilland, Sir Geoffrey. *Sky Fever*. London: Hamish Hamilton, 1961.

de la Gorce, Paul-Marie. *The French Army: A Military-Political History*. New York: Brazillier, 1963.

de Lorris, Roland Maurice. *La politique economique et industriel du ministre de l'air*. *The French Aerospace Industry*. Vol. 1, 1970–1947. Paris: GIFAS, 1984.

de Madariaga, Salvador. *Englishmen, Frenchmen, Spaniards*. New York: Hill and Wang, 1969 [1928].

de Montalembert, Capitaine. "Le front sud-tunisien 1915–1918." *Revue Historique de l'Armée* 11, no. 1 (1955).

de Seversky, Alexandre P. *Victory Through Air Power*. New York: Simon and Schuster, 1942.

Delaye, Colonel, and A. Dumas. "Les conquêtes de l'aluminum et des metaux légers." *Revue Historique de l'Armée* 16, no. 2 (1960): 121–140.

Denfeld, D. Colt. "Marston Mat: American Military Mobility." *Journal of America's Military Past* (Fall 2005): 43–56.

Dennis, Peter. *Decision by Default: Peacetime Conscription and British Defence, 1919–1939*. London: Routledge, 1972.

Denton, Geoffrey. *Economic Planning and Policies in Britain, France, and Germany*. New York, Praeger, 1968.

Destrenou, Bernard. *Weygand*. Paris: Perrin, 1959.

Dewald, Jonathan. "Lost Worlds: French Historians and the Construction of Modernity." *French History* 14, no. 4 (Dec. 2000): 424–442.

Dewerpe, Alain. *Le monde du travail en France, 1800–1950*. Paris: Armand Colin, 1989.

Diamond, Hanna. *Fleeing Hitler: France, 1940*. London: Oxford University Press, 2007.

Diamond, John. *Collapse: How Societies Choose to Fail or Succeed*. New York: Viking 2005.

Dilks, David. "The Twilight War and the Fall of France: Chamberlain and Churchill in 1940." *Transactions of the Royal Historical Society* 28 (1978): 61–86.

Dockrill, Michael. *British Establishment Perspectives on France, 1936–40*. New York: St. Martin's Press, 1999.

———. "The Foreign Office and France During the Phoney War, September 1939–May 1940." In *Diplomacy and World Power: Studies in British Foreign Policy, 1890–1951*, edited by Michael Dockrill and Brian McKercher. London: Cambridge University Press, 1996, 171–196.

Dockrill, Michael, and Brian McKercher, eds. *Diplomacy and World Power: Studies in British Foreign Policy, 1890–1951*. London: Cambridge University Press, 1996.

Dombrowski, Nicole. "Beyond the Battlefield: The French Civilian Exodus of May–June 1940." Ph. D. Dissertation, New York University, New York, 1995.

Dorman, Geoffrey. *Fifty Years Fly Past*. London: Forbes Robertson, 1951.

Dormois, Jean-Pierre. *The French Economy in the Twentieth Century*. New York: Cambridge University Press, 2003.

Doughty, Robert A. "Almost a Minute." In *No End Save Victory: Perspectives on World War II*, edited by Robert Cowley. New York: Putnam, 2001, 22–39.

———. *The Breaking Point: Sedan and the Fall of France, 1940*. Hamden, CT: Archon Books, 1990.

———. "The French Armed Forces, 1918–1940." In *Military Effectiveness*. Vol. 2, *The Interwar Period*, edited by Allan R. Millett and Williamson Murray. Winchester, MA: Allen & Unwin, 1988, 50.

———. "French Strategy in 1914: Joffre's Own." *Journal of Military History* 63 (Apr. 2003): 427–454.

———. *The Seeds of Disaster: The Development of French Army Doctrine, 1919–1939*. Hamden, CT: Archon Books, 1985.

Douglas, Roy. "Chamberlain and Eden, 1937–38." *Journal of Contemporary History* 13 (1978): 97–116.

Douglas, W. A. B. *The Official History of the Royal Canadian Air Force*. Vol. 2, *The Creation of a National Air Force*. Toronto: University of Toronto Press, 1986.

Douglas, Lord [William S.] of Kirtleside. *Combat and Command*. New York: Simon and Schuster, 1963, 1966.

Douhet, Guilio. *Il dominio dell'aria* [*The Command of the Air*]. Translated by Dino Ferrari. New York: Coward-McCann, 1942.

Downs, Laura Lee. *Manufacturing Inequality: Gender Division in the French and British Metalworking Industries, 1914–1939*. Ithaca, NY: Cornell University Press, 1995.

du Réau, Elisabeth. *Édouard Daladier, 1884–1970*. Paris: Fayard, 1993.

Dull, Jonathan R. *The Age of the Ship of the Line: The British and French Navies, 1650–1815*. Lincoln: University of Nebraska Press, 2009.

Duroselle, Jean-Baptiste. *La Décadence, 1932–1939: Politique extérieure de la France*. Paris: Imprimerie Nationale, 1979.

Duval, Gen. Maurice. *Les leçons de la guerre d'Espagne*. Paris: Plon, 1938.

Dye, Air Cdre. Peter J. "The Aviator as Super Hero: The Individual and the First War in the Air." *Royal Air Force Air Power Review* 7, no. 3 (Fall 2004): 64–74.

———. "France and the Development of British Military Aviation." *Royal Air Force Air Power Review* 12, no. 1 (Spring 2009): 1–13.

———. "Logistics and Airpower—A Failure in Doctrine?" [*U.S.*] *Air Force Journal of Logistics* 23, no. 3 (Fall 1999): 26–28, 41.

———. "Logistics and the Battle of Britain: Fighting Wastage in the RAF and the Luftwaffe." [*U.S.*] *Air Force Journal of Logistics* 24, no. 4 (Winter 2000): 31–40.

———. "Logistics Doctrine and the Impact of War: The Royal Air Force Experience in the Second World War." In *Air Power History: Turning Points from Kitty Hawk to Kosovo*, edited by Sebastian Cox and Peter Gray. London: Frank Cass, 2002, 207–223.

———. "Royal Flying Corps Logistical Organization." *Royal Air Force Air Power Review* 1 (2000): 42–59; reprinted in [*U.S.*] *Air Force Journal of Logistics* 14, no. 4 (Winter 2000): 60–73.

———. "Sustaining Air Power: The Influence of Logistics on RAF Doctrine." [*U.S.*] *Air Force Journal of Logistics* 30, no. 4; 31, no. 1 (Jan. 2005): 69–77.

———. "Sustaining Air Power: The Influence of Logistics on Royal Air Force Doctrine." *Royal Air Force Air Power Review* 9, no. 2 (Fall 2006): 40–51.

"École de specialization de l'artillerie anti-aérienne." *Revue Historique de l'Armée* 10, no. 3 (1954): 208–221.

The Economist (10 Mar. 2010): 58; (29 June 2010): 52, 85–86.

Edgerton, David. *England and the Aeroplane: An Essay on a Militant and Technological Nation*. Basingstoke, UK: Macmillan, 1991.

———. *The Warfare State: Britain, 1920–1970*. New York: Cambridge University Press, 2006.

Egremont, Max. *Under Two Flags: The Life of Major-General Sir Edward Spears*. London: Weidenfeld and Nicolson, 1997.

Ehrengardt, Christian-Jacques. " . . . *La couronne t'attend: Les écoles de l'armée de l'air, 1939–40*." *Aero Journal* 37 (June–July 2004): 40–46.

———. "Le chasseur à la francaise: La famille Dewoitine D.500-D.510." *Aero Journal* 40 (Dec. 2004–Jan. 2005): 8–37.

Ehrmann, Henry W. *Organized Business in France*. Princeton, NJ: Princeton University Press, 1957.

Ellis, L. F. *The War in France and Flanders, 1939–1940*. History of the Second World War, United Kingdom Military Series. London: HMSO, 1953.

Elton, Geoffrey. *The English*. Oxford: Blackwell, 1993.

"The English." *The Times Literary Supplement* (7 Aug. 1948) [off-print].

English, A. D. "The RAF Staff College." *Journal of Strategic Studies* 16 (Sept. 1993): 408–431.

Evleth, Donna. "The Ordre Des Medecins in Vichy France, 1940–1946." *French History* 20, no. 2 (June 2006): 204–224. [French medical discrimination against Jews during Vichy was not acknowledged by the Ordre until 1997 (p. 224).]

Facon, Patrick. "Aperçus sur la doctrine d'emploi de l'aeronautiques de militaire français, 1914–1918." *Recueil d'Articles et Études, 1984–1985*. Vincennes: SHAA (1991).

———. "C'était hier—logistique—un impératif? Approvisionner l'armée de l'air." *Air Actu* 534 (Aug.–Sept. 2000): 44–45.

———. "Douhet et sa doctrine à travers la littérature militaire et aéronautique française de l'entre-deux-guerres: Une étude de perception." Congresso internazionale di Studi *La Figura e l'Opera di Guilio Douhet* (Caserte: Società di Storia di Terra di Lavoro con la collaborazione dello Stato Maggiore dell'Aeronautica Militare). (12–14 Apr. 1987): 109–127; *Actes* l (Società di Storia Patria di Lavoro, 1988); reprinted in *Revue Historique des Armées* 1 (1988): 94–103.

———. "The High Command of the French Air Force and the Problem of Rearmament, 1938–1939: A Technical and Industrial Approach." In *The Conduct of the Second World War: An International Comparison*, edited by Horst Boog. Oxford: Berg, 1988, 1992, 148–168.

———. *L'armée de l'air dans la tourmente: La bataille de France, 1939–1940*. Paris: Economica, 1997.

———. "L'aviation populaire: Entre les mythes et la réalité." *Revue Historique des Armées*, no. 2 (1982): 55–59.

———. "L'image des aviateurs à travers l'oeuvre de Jacques Mortane." *Revue Historique des Armées* 2, no. 91 (1987): 93–102.

———. "Le haut commandement aérien français et la crise de Munich." Also published in *Recueil d'Articles et Études 1981–1983*. Vincennes: SHAA. (1987): 171–195, and in *Revue Historique des Armées* 3, no. 83 (1987): 10–18.

———. "Le Plan V (1938–1939)." *Recueil d'Articles et Études, 1979–1981*. Vincennes: SHAA. (1985): 51–80.

———. "Les mille victoires de l'armée de l'air en 1939–1940: Autopsie d'une mythe." *Revue Historique des Armées* 4 (1997): 79–97.

Fair, John. "The Norwegian Campaign and Winston Churchill's Rise to Power in 1940: A Study of Perception and Attribution." *International History Review* 9 (1987): 410–437.

Falls, Cyril. *The First World War*. London: Longman's, 1960.

Fearon, Peter. "Aircraft Manufacturing." In *British Industry Between the Wars: Instability and Industrial Development, 1919–1939,* edited by Neil K. Buxton and Derek H. Aldcroft. London: Scolar Press, 1979, 216–240.

———. "The British Airframe Industry and the State, 1918–1935." *Economic History Review* 27, no. 7 (May 1974): 236–251.

———. "The Formative Years of the British Aircraft Industry, 1913–1924." *Business History Review* 43, no. 4 (Winter 1969): 476–495.

———. " . . . A Reply" [to A. J. Robertson, "The British Airframe Industry and the State, 1918–1935: A Comment"]. *Economic History Review* 28, no. 4 (Nov. 1975): 658–662.

Fenby, Jonathan. *Sinking of the* Lancastrian. New York: Carroll & Graff, 2005.

Ferris, John [Robert]. "Before 'Room 40': The British Empire and Signals Intelligence, 1898–1914." *Journal of Strategic Studies* 12, no. 4 (1989): 431–457.

———. "Catching the Wave: The RAF Pursues the RMA [Revolution in Military Affairs], 1918–1939." In *The Fog of Peace and War Planning: Military and Strategic Planning Under Uncertainty,* edited by Talbot C. Imlay and Monica Duffy Toft. London: Routledge, 2006, 159–178.

———. *The Evolution of British Strategic Policy 1919–26.* Basingstoke, UK: Macmillan, 1988.

———. "Fighter Defence Before Fighter Command: The Rise of Strategic Air Defence in Great Britain, 1917–1934." *Journal of Military History* 63, no. 4 (Oct. 1999): 854–884.

———. "The Greatest Power on Earth: Great Britain in the 1920's." *International History Review* (Can.) 13, no. 4 (1991): 726–750.

———. "The Theory of a 'French Air Menace', Anglo-French Relations and the British Home Defence Air Force Programmes of 1921–25." *Journal of Strategic Studies* 10, no. 1 (1987): 62–83.

———. "Treasury Control: The Ten Year Rule and British Service Policies, 1919–1924." *Historical Journal* [UK] 30, no. 4 (Dec. 1987): 859–883.

Ferro, Marc. *Pétain.* Paris: Fayard, 1987.

Ferry, Vital. *L'aviation populaire.* Paris: Editions du Genfaut, 2007.

Finer, S. E. *The Man on Horseback: The Role of the Military in Politics.* London: Pall Mall Press, 1962.

Fink, Carole. "Marc Bloch and the Drôle de Guerre: Prelude to the 'Strange Defeat.'" *Historical Reflections [Reflexions Historiques]* 22, no. 1 (Winter 1996): 33–46; also in *The French Defeat of 1940: Reassessments,* edited by Joel Blatt. Providence, RI: Berghahn, 1998, 34–46.

Fischer, Lt. Fritz. *Comment dura la guerre: Souvenirs et réflexion sur l'entretién des armies francaises au moyend des chemin de fer de 1914 á 1918.* Paris: Charles-Lavauzelle & Cie, 1965.

Fontaine, Arthur. *French Industry During the War.* New Haven, CT: Yale University Press, 1926.

Forçade, Olivier, Éric Duhamel, and Philippe Vial. *Militaires en république, 1870–1962: Les officiers, le pouvoir et la vie publique en France.* Paris: Publications de la Sorbonne, 1999.

Foreman, John. *Battle of Britain: The Forgotten Months*. New Malden Surrey, UK: Air
    Research Publications, 1988.
Fowler, Will. *Poland and Scandinavia 1939–1940*. Vol. 1, *Blitzkrieg*. London: Ian Allan,
    2002.
Fox, Robert, and Anna Guagnini, eds. *Education, Technology, and Industrial
    Performance in Europe, 1850–1939*. London: Cambridge University Press, 1993.
Fozard, John W., ed. *Sydney Camm and the Hurricane*. Washington, DC: Smithsonian
    Institution Press, 1991.
"France." In *Encyclopedia Britannica* 9 (1968): 685–776, esp. 766.
France. Ètat-major. *Exercise de combat de la courtine* 1, 2, 3 August 1933 (English
    section only.
————. Service Historique. *Les armées françaises dans la grande guerre*, 92 vols. Paris:
    Imprimerie Nationale, 1922–1938.
————. *Témoignes et documents recueillés par la commision de'enquière
    parlementerie . . .* 9 vols. Paris, 1947–1950.
"France's Noble Exasperating Icon." Review of Jonathan Fenby's *The General: Charles
    de Gaulle and the France He Saved* [New York: Simon and Schuster, 2010], in
    The Economist (17 June 2010): 85–86.
Frankenstein, Robert. *Le prix du réarmement français, 1935–1939*. Paris: Sorbonne,
    1982.
Franks, Norman. *Valiant Wings: Battle and Blenheim Squadrons Over France, 1940*.
    London: William Kimber, 1994; Crécy Books, 1998, 182.
Franks, Norman, and Mike O'Connor. *Number One in War and Peace: The History of
    No. 1 Squadron [RAF], 1912–2000*. London: Grub Street, 2000.
Fraser, David. *Alanbrooke*. New York: Athenaeum, 1982.
Fredette, Raymond. *The Sky on Fire: The First Battle of Britain 1917–1918, and the Birth
    of the Royal Air Force*. New York: Holt, Rinehart & Winston, 1966; Washington,
    DC: Smithsonian Institution Press, 1991.
Freeman, Kirrily. *Bronze to Bullets: Vichy and the Destruction of French Public Statuary,
    1941–1944*. Palo Alto, CA: Stanford University Press, 2009.
French, David. "'Perfidious Albion' Faces the Powers." *Canadian Journal of History* 28,
    no. 2 (Aug. 1993): 177–187.
French History 16, no. 4 (2002): 41–468; 21, no. 2 (June 2007): 231. [*French History* is
    the publication of the (British) Society for the Study of French History and has
    been supported since its inception in 1985–1986 by the Embassy of France in
    London.]
Fridenson, Patrick. "Automobile Workers in France and Their Work, 1914–1983." In
    Work in France: Representation, Meaning, Organization, and Practice, edited by
    Steven L. Kaplan and Cynthia J. Koepp. Ithaca, NY: Cornell University Press,
    1986, 514–547.
————, ed. *The French Home Front, 1914–1918*. Oxford: Berg, 1992.
Fridenson, Patrick, and Jean Lecuir. *La France et la Grande-Bretagne face aux
    problèmes aériens, 1935–Mai 1940*. Vincennes: SHAA. (1976). [On the Franco-
    British Staff talks.]

Friedmann. Georges. *Industrial Society: The Emergence of the Human Problems of Automation*. Edited with an introduction by Harold L. Sheppard. New York: Free Press of Glencoe, 1955, 1964.

Frieser, Karl-Heinz, with John T. Greenwood. *The Blitzkrieg Legend: The 1940 Campaign in the West*. Annapolis, MD: Naval Institute Press, 2005.

Furse, Anthony. *Wilfrid Freeman: The Genius Behind Allied Survival and Air Supremacy, 1939–1945*. Staplehurst, UK: Spellmount, 2000.

Fussell, Paul. *The Great War and Modern Memory*. New York: Oxford University Press, 1975, 2000.

Gallagher, Gary W., ed. *Lee, the Soldier*. Lincoln: University of Nebraska Press, 1996.

Galland, Adolph. *The First and the Last*. New York: Holt, 1934.

Gallie, Duncan. *Social Inequality and Class Radicalism in France and Britain*. Cambridge: Cambridge University Press, 1984.

Gamelin, Gen. Maurice. *Servir: Le prologue du drame (1930–août 1939)*. 3 vols. Paris: Librairie Plan, 1946–1947.

Gates, Eleanor, M. *End of the Affair: The Collapse of the Anglo-French Alliance, 1939–40*. Berkeley: University of California Press, 1981.

Gauché, Gen. Maurice-Henri. *Le deuxième bureau au travail (1935–1940)*. Paris: Amiot-Dumont, 1953.

Gaxie, Daniel. "Morphologie de l'armée de l'air: Les officiers (1924–1974)." In *Service Historique de l'Armée de l'Air. Recueil d'Articles et d'Études*. Vincennes: SHAA. (1975): 37–86.

Geer, Louise, and Anthony Harold. *Flying Clothing: The Story of its Development*. Shrewsbury, UK: Airlife, 1979.

Gibbs, Norman Henry. *Grand Strategy*. Vol. 1, *Rearmament Policy*. London: HMSO, 1976.

Gibson, Irving M. "Maginot and Liddell Hart: The Doctrine of Defence." In *Makers of Modern Strategy: Military Thought from Machiavelli to Hitler*, edited by E. M. Earle. Princeton, NJ: Princeton University Press, 1943.

Gilbert, André. "Robert Bouby." *Aero Journal* 34 (Dec. 2003–Jan. 2004): 45–46.

Gilbert, Martin. *Winston S. Churchill*. Vol. 4 and Vol. 6. London: Heinemann, 1983–1985.

Gildea, Robert. *Children of the Revolution: The French, 1799–1914*. London, Allen Lane, 2008. [The third volume in the Penguin trilogy replacing Albert Cobban's classic volumes, *History of Modern France*, which cover 1715–1962.]

———. *Marianne in Chains: Daily Life in the Heart of France During the German Occupation*. New York: Metropolitan Books, 2002.

Gille, Henri. "Mai–juin 1940—a un contre cinq au groupe de chasse, II/10." *Icare* 145, no. 2 (1993): 74–81.

Glass, Charles. *Americans in Paris: Life and Death Under Nazi Occupation*. New York: Penguin, 2010.

Glucksmann, Miriam. *Women Assemble: Women Workers and the New Industries in Interwar Britain*. London: Routledge, 1990.

Godfrey, John F. *Capitalism at War: Industrial Policy and Bureaucracy in France, 1914–1919*. Lexington Spa, UK: Berg, 1987.

Gonon, Bernard. "Les moteurs d'avion et leur evolution de l'armée aérienne, 1914–1940." *Proceedings, Colloque International*, Paris, École Militaire (4–7 Sept. 1984): 251–255.

Gooch, J. "The War Office and the Curragh Incident." *Bulletin of the Institute of Historical Research* 13, no. 114 (Nov. 1973): 202–207.

Gordon, G. A. H. *British Sea Power and Procurement Between the Wars: A Reappraisal of Rearmament*. Basingstoke, UK: Macmillan, 1988.

Goutard, Colonel A. *The Battle of France 1940*. New York: Ives Washburn, 1952.

Granick, David. *The European Executive*. New York: Doubleday, 1962.

Greasley, David, and Les Oxley. "Discontinuties in Competitiveness: The Impact of the First World War on British Industry." *Economic History Review*, new series 49, no. 1 (Feb. 1996): 82–100.

Great Britain. *See* United Kingdom.

Green, Constance M., Harry C. Thomson, and Peter C. Roots. "The Ordnance Department: Planning Munitions for War," in *The United States Army in World War II. The Technical Services*. Washington, DC: U.S. Army Center for Military History, 1955; reprint 1990.

Green, William. *Warplanes of the Third Reich*. New York: Doubleday, 1970.

Greene, Nathaniel. *From Versailles to Vichy: The Third French Republic, 1919–1940*. New York: Crowell, 1970.

Greenhalgh, Elizabeth. "Myth and Memory: Sir Douglas Haig and the Imposition of the Allied Unified Command in March 1918." *Journal of Military History* 68 (July 2004): 771–820.

———. "'Parade Ground Soldiers': French Army Assessments of the British on the Somme in 1916." *Journal of Military History* 83 (Apr. 1999): 283–312.

———. *Victory Through Coalition: Britain and France During the First World War*. New York: Cambridge University Press, 2005.

Gregory, Adrian. *The Last Great War: British Society and the First World War*. New York: Cambridge University Press, 2008.

Griffin, Emma. *Blood Sport: Hunting in Britain Since 1066*. New Haven, CT: Yale University Press, 2007.

Griffiths, Richard. *Pétain*. Garden City, NY: Doubleday, 1972.

Grimal, Henri. *Decolonization: The British, French, Dutch and Belgian Empires, 1919–1963*. Translated into French by Stephen de Vos. Boulder: Westview Press, 1965 (in French), 1978.

Gropman, A. L. "The Battle of Britain and the Principles of War." *Aerospace Historian* (Sept. 1971): 138–144.

Guerin, Général. "Les transmissions de 1919 à 1939." *Revue Historique de l'Armée* 23, no. 1 (1967): 51–56.

Guillen, Pierre. "Franco-Italian Relations in Flux, 1918–1940." In *French Foreign and Defence Policy, 1918–1940: The Decline and Fall of a Great Power*, edited by Robert Boyce. London: LSE/Routledge, 1998.

Gundelach, Karl. "Commentary." *The Conduct of the Air War in the Second World War: An International Comparison* [1988 Conference, The Conduct of the Air War in the Second World War]. Edited by Horst Boog. Oxford: Berg, 1992, 496–507.

Gunsberg, Jeffrey A. "Armée de l'Air vs. the Luftwaffe—1940." *Defense Update International* (Cologne) 45 (1984): 44–53.

———. *Divided and Conquered: The French High Command and the Defeat of the West, 1940.* Westport, CT: Greenwood Press, 1979.

Gunston, Bill. *By Jupiter: The Life of Sir Roy Fedden.* London: Royal Aeronautical Society, 1978.

Haight, John McVicar. *American Aid to France 1938–1940.* New York: Atheneum, 1970.

Hall, Catherine, and Sonya A. Rose. *At Home with the Empire: Metropolitan Culture and the Imperial World.* New York: Cambridge University Press, 2007.

Hall, David Ian. "From Khaki and Light Blue to Purple: The Long and Troubled Development of Army/Air Co-operation in Britain, 1914–1945." *Journal of the Royal United Services Institute for Defence and Security Studies* 147, no. 5 (Oct. 2002): 78–83.

Hall, H. Duncan. *North American Supply.* 2 vols. London: HMSO, 1955.

Hall, Hines H., III. "British Air Defence and Anglo-French Relations, 1921–1924." *Journal of Strategic Studies* 4, no. 1 (1981): 271–284.

———. "The Foreign Policy-Making Process in Britain, 1934–1935, and the Origins of the Anglo-German Naval Agreement." *The Historical Journal* 19, no. 2 (June 1976): 477–499.

Halpenney, Bruce Barrymore. *Military Airfields of Greater London.* Action Stations Series. Wellingborough, UK: Patrick Stephens, 1984, 1993.

———. *Military Airfields of Lincolnshire and the East Midlands.* Action Stations Series. Wellingborough, UK: Patrick Stephens, 1981.

———. *Military Airfields of Yorkshire.* Action Stations Series. Wellingborough, UK: Patrick Stephens, 1982.

Hamilton, Richard. *Affluence and the French Workers in the Fourth Republic.* Princeton, NJ: Princeton University Press, 1967.

Hardach, Gerd. "Industrial Mobilization in 1914–1918: Production, Planning, and Ideology." In *The French Home Front 1914–1918*, edited by Patrick Friedenson. Oxford: Berg, 1992, 57–88.

Harris, MRAF Sir Arthur. *Bomber Offensive.* London: Greenhill Books, 1997.

Harris, Stephen J. "RAF Bomber Command as Phoenix." In *Why Air Forces Fail: The Anatomy of Defeat*, 2nd ed., edited by Robin Higham and Stephen J. Harris. Lexington: University Press of Kentucky, 2012.

Harrison, Mark, ed. *The Economics of World War II: Six Great Powers in International Comparison.* Cambridge, UK: Cambridge University Press, 1998.

———. "Resource Mobilization for World War II: The U.S.A., U.K., U.S.S.R., and Germany, 1938–1945." *Economic History Review*, New Series 41, no. 2 (May 1988): 171–192.

Hart, Peter. *The Somme: The Darkest Hour on the Western Front.* New York: Pegasus Books, 2008.

Harvey, David A. *Constructing Class and Nationality in Alsace, 1830–1945.* DeKalb: Northern Illinois University Press, 2001.

Harvey-Bailey, Alec. *The Merlin in Perspective—The Combat Years.* Derby, UK: Rolls-Royce Heritage Trust, 1981, 1995.

Haslam, G/Cpt. E. B. "The French Aircraft Industry before 1939." Unpublished paper
(Air Historical Branch, 1972). Copy in National Archives, Kew (Public Record
Office).

———. *The History of Royal Air Force Cranwell*. London: HMSO, 1982.

———. "How Lord Dowding Came to Leave Fighter Command." *Journal of Strategic
Studies* 4, no. 2 (1981): 175–186.

———. "La préparation à la guerre: Étude de quelques éléments de l'efficacíté
opérationalle des forces aériennes sur le front du nord-est (de septembre 1939 à
mai 1940)." Comité d'histoire de la 2e Guerre Mondiale. *Français et Britannique
dans la drôle de guerre, actes du colloque franco-britannique tenu à Paris du
8 au 12 décembre 1975*. Paris: Editions de Centre National de la Recherche
Scientifique, 1979; *Colloque International* (Paris, 1975): 517–553.

Hatch, Fred. *The Aerodrome of Democracy: Canada and the British Commonwealth
Air Training Plan, 1939–1945*. Ottawa, Can.: Department of National Defence,
1994.

Hattersley, Roy. *Borrowed Time: The Story of Britain Between the Wars*. London: Little
Brown, 2007.

Haynes, John Earl, and Harvey Klehr. *Venona: Decoding Soviet Espionage in America*.
New Haven: Yale University Press, 1999.

Heffernan, John B. "The Blockade of the Southern Confederacy, 1861–1865."
Smithsonian Journal of History 12, no. 4 (Winter 1967–1968): 23–44.

Heggoy, Alf Andrew, and John M. Haar. *The Military in Imperial History: The French
Connection*. New York: Garland, 1984.

Henshaw, Alex. *Sigh for a Merlin: Testing the Spitfire*. London: John Murray Publishers;
Manchester, UK: Crécy Publishing, 1979.

Heron, S. D. "Development of Aircraft Fuels." In *The Development of Aircraft Engines
and Fuels: Two Studies of Relations Between Government and Industry*, edited
by Robert Schlaiffer and S. D. Heron. Boston: Harvard Graduate School of
Business Administration, 1950.

Hicks, James E. *French Military Weapons, 1717–1938*. New Milford, CT: N. Fraydeman,
1964.

———. *Notes on French Ordnance, 1717–1936*. Mt. Vernon, NY: Private Printing, 1938.

Higham, Robin. *The Air Battles of 1940: A Re-examination* [ms. in process, 2010].

———. "Air Operations as Guerrilla War." *Defence Analysis* 15, no. 2 (Aug. 1999):
215–222.

———. *Armed Forces in Peacetime: Britain 1918–1939*. London: G. T. Foulis, 1962.

———. *The Bases of Air Strategy: Building Airfields for the RAF, 1915–1945*.
Shrewsbury, UK: Airlife, 1998.

———. *Britain's Imperial Air Routes: 1918–1939*. London: G. T. Foulis, 1960.

———. "British Air Exercises of the 1930s." *Proceedings, National Aerospace Conference*
(Dayton, OH, 1998): 303–312.

———. *The British Rigid Airship, 1908–1931: A Study in Weapons Policy*. London: G. T.
Foulis, 1961.

———. *Diary of a Disaster: British Aid to Greece, 1940–1941*. Lexington: University
Press of Kentucky, 1986.

———. "Governments, Companies and National Defence: British Aeronautical Experience, 1918–1945 as the Basis of a Broad Hypothesis." *Business History Review* 39, no. 3 (Fall 1963): 325–344.

———. *A Handbook on Air Ministry Organization*. Manhattan, KS: MA/AH Publishing–Sunflower University Press, 1998.

———. *The Military Intellectuals in Britain, 1918–1939*. New Brunswick, NJ: Rutgers University Press, 1966.

———. *Official Histories*. Manhattan: Kansas State University Library, 1970.

———. *100 Years of Air Power and Aviation*. College Station: Texas A&M University Press, 2003.

———. "The Perils of Patriotism" [article, in process].

———. "Pipeline Purdah." *Defence Analysis* 15, no. 1 (Aug. 1999): 81.

———. "Quantity vs. Quality: The Impact of Changing Demand on the British Aircraft Industry 1900–1960." *Business History Review* 42, no. 4 (Winter 1968): 443–466.

———. "The RAF and the Battle of Britain." In *Case Studies in the Achievement of Air Superiority*, edited by B. F. Cooling. Washington, DC: Center for Air Force History, 1994, 115–178.

———. "Royal Air Force Spares Forecasting in World War II." *[U.S.] Air Force Journal of Logistics* (Spring 1996): 23–26.

———. "The Selection, Education, and Training of British Officers, 1740–1920." In *War and Society in East Central Europe 24*, edited by Bela K. Kiraly and Walter Scott Dillard (1988): 39–56.

———. "The Worst Possible Cases." *Australian Defence Journal* 100 (May–June 1993): 63–65.

Higham, Robin, and Charles D. Bright. "Failure of Defensive Imagination." *Australian Defence Force Journal* 117 (Mar./Apr. 1996): 49–55.

Higham, Robin, John T. Greenwood, and Von Hardesty. *Russian Aviation and Air Power in the Twentieth Century*. London: Frank Cass, 1998.

Higham, Robin, and Stephen J. Harris, eds. *Why Air Forces Fail: The Anatomy of Defeat*. Lexington: University of Kentucky Press, 2006; 2nd ed., 2012.

Higham, Robin, ed., with Dennis E. Showalter. *Researching World War I: A Handbook*. Westport, CT: Greenwood Press, 2003.

Hilbert, Lothar. "Les attachés militaries françaises: Leur statut de l'entre-deux-guerres." Transcript of paper presented to the International Commission of Military History (ICMH), Bucharest, Aug. 1980, reprinted in *ACTA* (1981).

Hinsley, F. H., E. E. Thomas, C. F. G. Ransom, and R. C. Knight. *British Intelligence in the Second World War: Its Influence on Strategy and Operations*. Vol. 1. London: HMSO, 1979.

"Histoire de l'armament française." Special issue of *La Revue Historique de l'Armée* (1984).

Histoire de le France Industrielle. Under the Direction of Maurice Lévy-Lebover. Paris: Larousse, 1996.

Hodeir, Marcellin. "La chambre bleu horizon et la commission de l'armée face aux problèmes de l'aviation militaire." *Colloque International*. Paris: Ecole Militaire, 4–7 Sept. 1984: 341–352.

Hoffmann, Stanley. "Paradoxes of the French Political Community." In *In Search of France: The Economy, Society, and Political System in the Twentieth Century*, edited by Stanley Hoffmann, Charles P. Kindleberger, Laurence Wylie, Jesse R. Pitts, Jean-Baptiste Duroselle, and François Goguel. New York: Harper & Row, 1965, 1–117.

Hoffmann, Stanley, Charles P. Kindleberger, Laurence Wylie, Jesse R. Pitts, Jean-Baptiste Duroselle, and François Goguel. *In Search of France: The Economy, Society, and Political System in the Twentieth Century*. Cambridge, MA: Harvard University Press, 1963; New York: Harper & Row, 1965.

Hogg, Ian V. *Anti-Aircraft Artillery*. Ramsbury, UK: Crowood Press, 2002.

Hogg, O. F. G. *The Royal Arsenal [Woolwich]*. Vol. 2, *The Background Origin and Subsequent History*. London: Oxford University Press, 1963.

Holley, Irving B., Jr. *Buying Aircraft: Matériel Procurement for the Army Air Forces*. Washington, DC: Office of the Chief of Military History, 1964.

———. *Ideas and Weapons*. New Haven, CT: Yale University Press, 1953.

Hollinshead, Byron, and Theodore K. Rabb, eds. *I Wish I Had Been There*. Vol. 2, *European History*. London: Doubleday, 2008.

Holman, Valerie, and Debra Kelly, eds. *France at War in the Twentieth Century: Propaganda, Myth, and Metaphor*. New York: Berghan, 2000.

Homze, Edward L., ed. *Arming the Luftwaffe: The Reich Air Ministry and the German Aircraft Industry 1919–1939*. Lincoln: University of Nebraska Press, 1976.

Honigsbaum, Mark. *Living with Enza: The Forgotten Story of Britain and the Great Flu Pandemic of 1918*. London: Macmillan, 2008.

Hood, Chalmers. "The French Navy and Parliament Between the Wars." *International History Review* 6 (Aug. 1984): 386–403.

Hooten, E. R. *Luftwaffe at War*. Vol. 1, *The Gathering Storm, 1933–1939*. Horsham, Surrey, UK: Classic, 2007.

Horn, Martin, and Talbot Imlay. "Money in Wartime: France's Financial Preparations for the Two World Wars." *International History Review* 27, no. 4 (Dec. 2005): 709–753.

Hornby, William. *Factories and Plant*. London: HMSO, 1958.

Horne, Alistair. *The French Army and Politics, 1870–1970*. New York: Peter Bedrick Books/Harper & Row, 1984.

———. *To Lose a Battle: France 1940*. Boston: Little Brown, 1969.

Horne, John. "The Comité d'Action (CGT-Parti Socialists) and the Origins of Wartime Labor Reformism (1914–1916)." In *The French Home Front, 1914–1918*, edited by Patrick Fridenson. Oxford: Berg, 1992.

———. "'L'import de sang': Republican Rhetoric and Industrial Warfare in France, 1914–1918." *Social History* 14, no. 2 (May 1989): 201–223.

Howard, Michael. *The Continental Commitment: The Dilemma of British Defence Policy in the Era of the Two World Wars*. London: Temple Smith, 1972.

Hucker, Daniel. "French Public Attitudes Towards the Prospect of War in 1938–1939: 'Pacificism' or 'War Anxiety'?" *Journal of French History* 21, no. 4 (Dec. 2007): 431–449. [Hucker argues that pacificism was but one element which brought on war after Munich. More powerful was that "war anxiety" that demanded France prepare for war.]

Huddleston, Sisley. *France and the French*. New York: Charles Scribner's, 1925.

———. *France—The Tragic Years, 1939-1947: An Eyewitness Account of War, Occupation, and Liberation*. New York: Devin-Adair, 1955.

Hughes, Judith M. *To the Maginot Line: The Politics of French Military Preparation in the 1920s*. Cambridge, MA: Harvard University Press, 1971.

Hume, John, ed. *State, Society, and Mobilization in Europe During the First World War*. New York: Cambridge University Press, 1997.

Hunt, Leslie. *Twenty-One Squadrons: The History of the Royal Auxiliary Air Force, 1925-1957*. London: Garnstone Press, 1972.

Huntington, Samuel P. *The Soldier and the State: The Theory and Politics of Civil-Military Relations*. Cambridge, MA: Harvard University Press, 1957, 33–58.

Hyam, Ronald. *Britain's Declining Empire: The Road to Decolonization, 1918-1968*. New York: Cambridge University Press, 2006.

Hyde, H. Montgomery. *British Air Policy Between the Wars, 1918-1939*. London: Heinemann, 1976.

Icare [France]. Nos. 53–55, 57, 59, 61, 74, 76, 79–80, 87, 91–92, 94, 97, 112, 115–116, 121, 123, 128, 131, 143, 145, 150, 156, 159, 183, 189 (1971–2004).

Imlay, Talbot C. *Facing the Second World War: Strategy, Politics, and Economics in Britain and France, 1938-1940*. London: Oxford University Press, 2003.

———. "France and the Phoney War, 1939-1940." In *French Foreign and Defence Policy, 1918-1940: The Decline and Fall of a Great Power*, edited by Robert Boyce. London: LSE/Routledge, 1998, 261–282.

———. "Strategic and Military Planning, 1919-1939." In *The Fog of Peace and War Planning: Military and Strategic Planning Under Uncertainty*, edited by Talbot C. Imlay and Monica Duffy Toft. London: Routledge, 2006, 139–158.

Imlay, Talbot C., and Monica Duffy Toft, eds. "Conclusion: Seven Lessons About the Fog of Peace." In *The Fog of Peace and War Planning: Military and Strategic Planning Under Uncertainty*, edited by Talbot C. Imlay and Monica Duffy Toft. London: Routledge, 2006, 249–260.

———. *The Fog of Peace and War Planning: Military and Strategic Planning Under Uncertainty*. London: Routledge, 2006.

"The Indomitable de Gaulle." *The Economist* (29 June 2010): 52.

Ingénieur militaire en chef des fabrications des armements Joyau. "La defénse contre avions." *Revue Historique de l'Armée* 12, no. 4 (1950): 141–154.

Inman, Peggy. *Labour in the Munitions Industries*. History of the Second World War: United Kingdom Civil Series, War Production Series. London: HMSO, 1957.

Irvine, William D. "Domestic Politics and the Fall of France in 1940." In *The French Defeat of 1940: Reassessments*, edited by Joel Blatt. Providence, RI: Berghahn, 1998, 85–99.

Irving, David. *Göring—A Biography*. New York: Morrow, 1989.

———. *The Rise and Fall of the Luftwaffe: The Life of Field Marshal Erhard Milch*. Boston: Little Brown, 1974.

Jackson, A. J. *De Havilland Aircraft Since 1904*. London: Putnam, 1962.

Jackson, Julian. *The Fall of France: The Nazi Invasion of 1940*. New York: Oxford University Press, 2003.

———. *France: The Dark Years, 1940–1944*. London: Oxford University Press, 2001.

———. *The Popular Front in France: Defending Democracy 1934–38*. New York: Cambridge University Press, 1988.

Jackson, Peter. *France and the Nazi Menace: Intelligence and Policy Making, 1933–1939*. New York: Oxford University Press, 2000.

———. "La perception de la puissance aérienne allemande et son influence sur la politique extérieure de la France pendant les crises internationales de 1938 à 1939." *Revue Historique des Armées* 4 (1994): 76–87.

Jackson, Robert. *The Air War Over France, May 1939–June 1940*. London: Ian Allan, 1974.

Jackson, [Gen. Sir] William, and Field Marshal Lord Bramall. *The Chiefs: The Story of the United Kingdom Chiefs of Staff*. London: Brassey's, 1992.

Jacob, Sir Ian. "Principles of British Military Thought." *Foreign Affairs* 29, no. 2 (Jan. 1951): 219–229.

Jacobson, Jon. "The Conduct of Locarno Diplomacy." *Review of Politics* 34, no. 1 (Jan. 1972): 67–81.

Jacomet, Robert. *L'armement de la France 1936–1939*. Paris: Les Editions La Jeunesse, 1945.

James, Derek N. *Gloster Aircraft Since 1917*. London: Putnam, 1971.

———. *Schneider Trophy Aircraft, 1913–1931*. London: Putnam, 1981.

James, Lawrence. *The Savage Wars: British Campaigns in Africa, 1870–1920*. London: R. Hale, 1985.

James, T. C. G. *Air Defence of Great Britain*. Vol. 1, *The Growth of Fighter Command, 1936–1940*. Edited with an introduction by Sebastian Cox. London: Frank Cass, 2002.

———. *Air Defence of Great Britain*. Vol. 2, *The Battle of Britain*. Edited with an introduction by Sebastian Cox. London: Frank Cass, 2000.

Jane's. *All the World's Aircraft*. London: Jane's, annual.

Jarrett, Philip, ed. *Biplane to Monoplane: Aircraft Development, 1919–1939*. London: Putnam; Herndon, VA: Brassey's, 1997.

Jauneaud, Jean-Henri. *De Verdun à Dien-Bien-Phu*. Paris: Collections Alternance; Editions de Scorpion, 1960.

Jeffery, Keith. "The British Army and Internal Security, 1919–1939." *The Historical Journal* 24, no. 2 (June 1987): 377–397.

Jefford, W/Cdr. C. G. *Observers and Navigators and Other Non-Pilot Aircrew in the RFC, RNAS, and RAF*. Shrewsbury, UK: Airlife, 2001.

———. *RAF Squadrons: A Comprehensive Record of the Movement and Equipment of All RAF Squadrons and Their Antecedents Since 1912*. Shrewsbury, UK: Airlife, 1988.

Jenkins, Brian. "Historiographical Essay: The *Six Fevrier* 1934 and the 'Survival' of the French Republic." *French History* 20, no. 3 (Sept. 2006): 333–351. [This essay points to the standard of 6 February as being deeply flawed. Jenkins sees the intentions of the actors as being judged by the outcomes, and not momentarily but as steps along the road to radicalization on the French Right.]

Jenkins, E. H. *A History of the French Navy from the Beginnings to the Present Day*. London: Macdonald and Jane's, 1973.

Jenkins, Roy. *Churchill*. New York: Farrar, Strauss & Giroux, 2001.

Johnson, Brian. *The Secret War*. London: BBC, 1978.

Johnson, D. W. J. "Britain and France in 1940." *Transactions of the Royal Historical Society* 11 (1972): 141–157.

Johnson, Franklyn Arthur. *Defence by Committee: The British Committee of Imperial Defence, 1885-1959*. London: Oxford University Press, 1960.

Jones, Neville. *The Origins of Strategic Bombing*. London: Kimber, 1973.

Jones, Thomas. *A Diary with Letters, 1931-1950*. London: Cambridge University Press, 1954.

Jordan, Nicole. "Strategy and Scapegoatism: Reflections on the French National Catastrophe, 1940." *Historical Reflections [Reflexions Historique]* 22, no. 1 (Winter 1996): 11–32.

Kaiser, David E. *Economic Diplomacy and the Origins of the Second World War: Germany, Britain, France, and Eastern Europe, 1930-1939*. Princeton, NJ: Princeton University Press, 1980.

Kaplan, Steven Laurence, and Cynthia J. Koepp. *Work in France: Representations, Meaning, Organization, and Practice*. Ithaca, NY: Cornell University Press, 1986.

Kaufmann, J. E., and H. W. Kaufmann. *Fortress France: The Maginot Line and French Defenses in World War II*. Westport, CT: Praeger/Greenwood Publishing Group, 2005.

Kedward, Rod. *France and the French: A Modern History*. New York: Overlook Press, 2006.

———. "Patriots and Patriotism in Vichy France." *Transactions of the Royal Historical Society* (1981): 175–192.

Keiger, J. F. V. "'Perfidious Albion?' French Perception of Britain as an Ally After the First World War." In *Knowing Your Friends: Intelligence Inside Alliances and Coalitions from 1914 to the Cold War*, edited by Martin S. Alexander. London: Frank Cass, 1998, 37–52.

Keith, C. H. *I Hold My Aim: The Story of How the Royal Air Force Was Armed for War*. London: Allen & Unwin, 1946.

Kemp, Tom. *The French Economy, 1913-1939: The History of a Decline*. New York: St. Martin's Press, 1972.

Kennedy, Paul M. "The Logic of Appeasement." *The Times Literary Supplement*, 28 May 1982, 585–586.

———. "Strategy vs. Finance in Twentieth Century Great Britain." *International History Review* 3 (Jan. 1981): 44–61.

Kerisel, Jean. *Albert Caquot, 1881-1976: Createur et precurseur*. Paris: Editions Eyrolles, 1978.

Kershaw, Alex. *The Few—The American "Knights of the Air" Who Risked Everything in the Battle of Britain*. Audio Book CD. Read by Scott Brick. Grand Haven, MI: Brilliance Audio, 2006.

Kesselring, Field Marshal Albert. *The Memoirs of Field Marshal Kesselring*. London: Greenhill, 2007.

Keynes, John Maynard. *General Theory of Employment, Interest and Money*. London: Macmillan; New York: St. Martin's Press, 1936.

Kier, Elizabeth. *Imagining War: French and British Military Doctrine Between the Wars*. Princeton, NJ: Princeton University Press, 1997.

Kiesling, Eugenia C. *Arming Against Hitler: France and the Limits of Military Planning*. Lawrence: University Press of Kansas, 1996.

——. "'If It Ain't Broke, Don't Fix It': French Military Doctrine Between the World Wars." *War in History* 3, no. 2 (1996): 208–223.

——. "Illuminating *Strange Defeat* and *Pyrrhic Victory*: The Historian Robert A. Doughty." *Journal of Military History* 71 (July 2007): 875–888.

——. "Resting Uncomfortably on Its Laurels: The Army of Interwar France." In *The Challenge of Change: Military Institutions and the New Realities, 1918–1941*, edited by Harold R. Winton and David Mets. Lincoln: University of Nebraska Press, 2000, 1–34.

Kindleberger, Charles P. *Economic Growth in France and Britain, 1851–1950*. Cambridge: Harvard University Press, 1964.

——. "Technical Education and the French Entrepreneur." In *Enterprise and Entrepreneurs in Nineteenth and Twentieth Century France*, edited by Edward C. Carter II, Robert Forster, and Joseph N. Moody. Baltimore: Johns Hopkins University Press, 1976, 3–39.

King, H. F. *The Armament of British Aircraft, 1909–1939*. London: Putnam, 1971.

King, Jere Clemens. *Generals and Politicians: Conflict Between France's High Command, Parliament and the Government, 1914–1918*. Berkeley: University of California Press, 1951.

Kinsey, Gordon. *Martlesham Heath*. Lavenham, UK: Terence Dalton, 1975.

Kirby, M., and R. Capey. "The Air Defence of Great Britain, 1920–1940: An Operational Research Perspective." *Journal of the Operational Research Society* 48 (May 1997): 555–568.

Kirkland, Faris R. "Anti-military Group-Fantasies and the Destruction of the French Air Force, 1928–1940." *Journal of Psychohistory* 14, no. 1 (Summer 1986): 25–42.

——. "The Aristocratic Tradition and Adaptation to Change in the French Cavalry, 1920–1940." *European Studies Journal* 4, no. 2 (Fall 1987): 1–17.

——. "The French Air Force in 1940: Was It Defeated by the Luftwaffe or by Politics?" *Air University Review* 36, no. 6 (Sept.–Oct. 1985): 101–118.

——. "French Air Strength in May 1940." *Air Power History* 40, no. 1 (Spring 1993): 22–34.

——. "The French Military Collapse in 1940: A Psycho-Historical Interpretation." *Journal of Psychohistory* 12, no. 3 (Winter 1985): 313–337.

——. "Military Technology in Republican France: The Evolution of the French Armored Force 1917–1940." Ph.D. Dissertation, Duke University, Durham, NC, 1968.

————. "Planes, Pilots and Politics: French Military Aviation, 1919–1940." *Proceedings of the 1998 National Aerospace Conference*. Dayton, OH: Wright State University, 1999, 285–293.

Klehr, Harvey, John Earl Hynes, and Fridrikh Igorevich Firsov. *The Secret World of American Communism*. New Haven: Yale University Press, 1995.

Knapp, Andrew, and Vincent Wright. *The Government and Politics of France*. 5th ed. London: Routledge, 2006.

Korda, Michael. *With Wings Like Eagles: A History of the Battle of Britain*. New York: Harper Collins, 2009.

Krauskopf, Robert W. "French Air Power Policy, 1919–1939." Ph.D. Dissertation, Georgetown University, Washington, DC, 1965.

Krepinevich, Andrew F., Jr. "Transforming to Victory: The U.S. Navy, Carrier Aviation, and Preparing for War in the Pacific." In *The Fog of Peace and War Planning: Military and Strategic Planning Under Uncertainty*, edited by Talbot C. Imlay and Monica Duffy Toft. London: Routledge, 2006, 179–204.

Kriegel, Anne. "The French Communist Party and the Problems of Power, 1920–1933." In *Contemporary France: Illusion, Conflict, and Regeneration*, edited by John C. Cairns. New York: New Viewpoint, 1978.

Kuisel, Richard F. *Capitalism and the State in Modern France: Renovation and Economic Management in the Twentieth Century*. London: Cambridge University Press, 1981.

"L'aviation française en août–septembre 1914." *Icare* 2, no. 193 (2005).

"La *chasse* française 1939–1945 (33) Le GC II/8." *Aero Journal* 35 (Feb.–Mar. 2004).

"La *coupe* Schneider, 1913–1931." *Icare* 189 (2004) [whole issue].

Lacaze, Yvon. "Daladier, Bonnet, and the Decision-Making Process During the Munich Crisis, 1938." In *French Foreign and Defence Policy, 1918–1940: The Decline and Fall of a Great Power*, edited by Robert Boyce. London: LSE/Routledge, 1998, 215–233.

Lammers, Donald N. "The Nyon Arrangements of 1937: A Success Sui Generis." *Albion* 3, no. 4 (1971): 163–176.

Langer, Rulka. *The Mermaid and the Messerschmitt: War Through a Mermaid's Eyes, 1939–1940*. 2nd ed. Los Angeles: Aquila Polonica, [1942] 2009.

Langer, William L., ed. *An Encyclopedia of World History*. 5th rev. ed. Boston: Houghton Mifflin, 1972, 1138.

Larnder, Harold, "The Origin of Operational Research." *Operations Research* 32, no. 2 (Mar.–Apr. 1984): 471.

Laux, James M. "Gnome et Rhône: Une firme de moteurs d'avions durant la Grande Guerre." In *1914–1918: L'autre front*, edited by Patrick Fridenson and Jean Jacques Becker. Paris: Les Editions Ouvrieres, 1977; English version in Patrick Fridenson, *The French Home Front, 1914–1918*. Oxford: Berg, 1992, 135–182.

Lawrence, Paul. "Un flot d'agitateurs politiques, de fauteurs de désordre et de criminels: Adverse Perceptions of Immigrants in France Between the Wars." *French History* 14, no. 2 (June 2000): 201–221. [Even in the 1990s the French saw immigrants as a threat to their "Frenchness," raising yet again the specter of racism. The French still see immigrants as a potent threat to French national identity, yet this is a centuries-old pattern, which reached a peak in 1931, not to be exceeded until 1996. It has been a historically neglected subject. French perceptions were largely adverse, suspicious, and full of stereotypes. In 1931 immigrants were 7.5 percent of the workforce, cheap and malleable.]

Le Clerc, Rémy. "Les ailes françaises en Tunisie." *Review Historique de l'Armée* 11, no. 1 (1955): 97–110.

Le Hénot, M. *Le rôle militaire des chemins de fer*. Paris: Burger-Levrault, 1923.

Le Hénot, M., and Henri Bornesque. *Les chemins de fer françaises et la guerre*. Paris: Chapelet, 1922; available in English from the U.S. Army Military History Institute, Carlisle Barracks, PA.

Lebovic, Herman H. *True France: The Wars Over Cultural Identity, 1900–1945*. Ithaca, NY: Cornell University Press, 1992.

Lecreox, Capitaine de Frégale C. R. "Leçons Méconnues, 1918 and 1940." *Revue Historique de l'Armée* (1961): 65–74.

Lee, Christopher. "Evolution of the Nation." *BBC History* (Dec. 2007): 33–35.

Léon Blum, Chef de governement 1936–1937. Colloquia held at the National Political Science Foundation, 17–26 Mar. 1965. Paris: Presses de la Foundation Nationale des Sciences Politiques, 1967.

Lettice, Curtis. *The Forgotten Pilots*. Henley-on-Thames, UK: Foulis & Co., 1971.

Levy, James P. *Appeasement and Rearmament: Britain 1936–1939*. Boulder, CO: Rowman & Littlefield, 2006.

Levy-Leboyer, Maurice. *Histoire de la France industrielle*. Paris: Larousse, 1996.

———. "Innovation and Business Strategies in Nineteenth and Twentieth Century France." In *Enterprise and Entrepreneurs in Nineteenth and Twentieth Century France*, edited by Edward C. Carter II, Robert Forster, and Joseph N. Moody. Baltimore: Johns Hopkins University Press, 1976, 87–135.

———. "Le patronat français, 1912–1973: Charles P. Kindleberger, Laurence Wylie, Jesse R. Pitts, Jean-Baptiste Duroselle, and François Goguel." In *Le Patronat de la seconde industrialisation*, edited by Maurice Levy-Leboyer. Paris: Editions Ouvrieres, 1979.

Lewis, David Levering. *The Race to Fashoda: European Colonialism and African Resistance in the Scramble for Africa*. New York: Weidenfeld and Nicolson, 1987.

Liddell Hart, Basil H. *The German Generals Talk: Startling Revelations from Hitler's High Command*. New York: William Morrow and Company, 1948.

Liddle, Peter H., ed. *Home Fires and Foreign Fields: British Social and Military Experience in the First World War*. London: Brassey's, 1985.

Liflander, Pamela. *Measurements and Conversions*. London: Running Press, 2002, 61.

Liskutin, M. A. *Challenge in the Air: A Spitfire Pilot Remembers*. London: Kimber, 1988.

Listermann, Philippe. "Le Brewster Buffalo." *Aero Journal* 7 (May 2004): 1–39. [On exports to Finland for the war there.]

Lloyd, Ian. *Rolls-Royce*. 3 vols. London: Macmillan, 1978, including *Rolls-Royce*: vol. 1, *The Growth of a Firm;* vol. 2, *Rolls-Royce: The Merlin Years;* and vol. 3, *Rolls-Royce: The Merlin at War*.

Locke, Robert R. *The End of the Practical Man: Entrepreneurship and Higher Education in Germany, France and Great Britain, 1880–1940.* London: JAI Press, 1984.

Lottman, Herbert R. *The Fall of Paris: June 1940.* New York: HarperCollins, 1992.

Lucereau, Hervé. *L'armée nouvelle issue de l'armistice, 1940–1942: Mémoire de maîtrise.* Paris: Institut Catholique de Paris, Oct. 1995.

Ludlow, P. "Le débat sur les buts de paix." In *Français et Britannique dans la drôle de guerre, actes du colloque franco-britannique tenu à Paris du 8 au 12 décembre 1975.* Comité de la 2e Guerre Mondiale. Paris: Editions de Centre National de la Recherche Scientifique, 1979, 93–122.

Lukacs, John. "The Coming of the Second World War." *Foreign Affairs* (Fall 1989): 167. [Lukacs states, "Although Britain and France declared war, they stopped short of waging war, except slightly in the air and more at sea."]

———. *Five Days in May.* New Haven: Yale University Press, 1999.

Lund, Eric. "The Industrial History of Strategy: Reevaluating the Wartime Record of the British Aviation Industry in Comparative Perspective, 1919–1945." *Journal of Military History* 62, no. 1 (Jan. 1998): 75–99.

Lyet, Pierre [Col.]. *La bataille de France (mai–juin 1940).* Paris: Payot, 1947.

———. "La Campagne de France 1939–1940." *Revue Historique de l'Armée* 1, no. 4 (1946): 37–70.

Macksey, Kenneth. *Kesselring: The Making of the Luftwaffe.* New York: David McKay Company, 1978.

———. *Technology in War: The Impact of Science on Weapon Development and Modern Battle.* London: Arms and Armour Press, 1986.

MacLean, W/Cdr. L. L. "Air Exercises 1935." *Journal of the Royal United Service Institution* (Jan. 1936): 50 ff.

MacLennan, Malcolm, Murray Forsyth, and Geoffrey Denton. *Economic Planning and Policies in Britain, France, and Germany.* New York: Praeger, 1968.

Macleod, Col. R., and Dennis Kelly, eds. *Time Unguarded: The Ironside Diaries.* London: Constable, 1962.

MacMillan, Margaret. *Paris 1919: Six Months That Changed the World.* New York: Random House, 2002.

———. "Tunnels, Territory, and Broken Promises: France Betrayed by the Anglo-Saxons?" In *I Wish I Had Been There.* Vol. 2, *European History,* edited by Byron Hollinshead and Theodore K. Rabb. London: Doubleday, 2008.

Magraw, Roger. *A History of the French Working Class.* Vol. 1, *The Age of Artisan Revolution, 1815–1871.* Vol. 2, *Workers and the Bourgeois Republic, 1871–1939.* Oxford: Blackwell, 1992.

Maier, Charles S. "Consigning the Twentieth Century to History: Alternative Narratives for the Modern Era." *American Historical Review* 105, no. 3 (2000): 807–831.

———. *Recasting Bourgeois Europe: Stabilization in France, Germany, and Italy in the Decade After the World War.* Princeton, NJ: Princeton University Press, 1975.

Maiolo, Joseph. *Cry Havoc: How the Arms Race Drove the World to War, 1931–1941.* New York: Basic Books, 2010.

Mandler, Peter. T*he English Character: The History in Idea from Edmund Burke to Tony Blair*. New Haven, CT: Yale University Press, 2006.

"Manifesto Takes Air Out of Racism in France." *USA Today,* 11 Nov. 2008.

Mann, Gregory. *Native Sons: West African Veterans and France in the Twentieth Century.* Durham, NC: Duke University Press, 2006.

Marshall-Cornwall, General Sir James. *Foch as Military Commander.* New York: Crane, Russak, 1972.

———. *War and Rumors of War.* London: Leo Cooper, 1984.

Martel, René. *French Strategic and Tactical Bombardment Forces of World War I.* Lanham, MD: Scarecrow Press, 2007.

Martin, Benjamin F. *France 1938.* Baton Rouge: Louisiana State University Press, 2005.

Martin, Paul. *Invisibles vainqueurs: Exploits et sacrifices de l'armée de l'air en 1939–1940.* Paris: Yves Michelet, 1990.

Mary, Jean-Yves, and Alain Hohnadel, with Jacques Sicard. *Hommes et ouvrages de la ligne Maginot.* 5 vols. Paris: Histoire et Collections, 2000–2009.

Masefield, Sir Peter. "La royal air force et la production d'avions de guerre en Grand-Bretagne, 1934–1940." *Colloque International* (1975–1979): 410–452; Comité d'histoire de la 2e Guerre Mondiale. *Français et Britannique dans la drôle de guerre, actes du colloque franco-britannique tenu à Paris du 8 au 12 décembre 1975.* Paris: Editions de Centre National de la Recherche Scientifique, 1979: 411–456, discussion 457.

Mason, Francis K. *Battle Over Britain: A History of German Air Assaults on Great Britain, 1917–18 and July–December 1940, and of the Development of Britain's Air Defences Between the World Wars.* London: McWhirter Twins; New York, Doubleday, 1969.

———. *Hawker Aircraft Since 1920.* London: Putnam, 1961.

———. *The Hawker Hurricane.* London: Macdonald, 1962.

Masson, Philippe. *Historie de la Marine.* Vol. 1, *L'ère de la voile.* Vol. 2, *De la vapeur à l'atome.* Paris: Lavauzelle, 1981, 1983.

May, Ernest R. *Strange Victory: Hitler's Conquest of France.* New York: Hill and Wang, 2000.

McDonough, Frank. *The Origins of the First and Second World Wars.* London: Cambridge University Press, 1997.

McKercher, B. J. C. "No External Friends of Enemies: British Defence Policy and the Problem of the United States, 1919–1939." *Canadian Journal of History* 28 (Aug. 1993): 257–293.

———. "Old Diplomacy and New: The Foreign Office and Foreign Policy, 1919–1939." In *Diplomacy and World Power: Studies in British Foreign Policy, 1890-1951,* edited by Michael Dockrill and Brian McKercher. London: Cambridge University Press, 1996, 79–114.

McKercher, B. J. C., and Roch Legault, eds. *Military Planning and the Origins of the Second World War in Europe.* Westport, CT: Praeger, 2000.

McKinstry, Leo. "How the Spitfire Nearly Missed Its Finest Hour." *BBC History* 8, no. 11 (Nov. 2007): 16–20.

McPhail, Helen. *The Long Silence: Civilian Life Under the German Occupation of Northern France, 1914–1918.* London: I. B. Tauris & Co., 1999, 2001.

Mecozzi, Amadeo. *Scritti Scelti sul potere aereo e l'aviazione d'assalto (1920–1970).* Vol. 1, *Il periodo tra le due guerre e la seconda guerra mondiale (1920–1943);* Vol. 2, *Il Dopoguerra e la guerra fredda (1945–1970).* Rome: Aeronautica Militarie Ufficio Storica, 2006.

Meilinger, Phillip S. *Airmen and Air Theory.* Maxwell AFB, AL: Air University Press, 2001.

———. "Clipping the Bomber's Wings: The Geneva Disarmament Conference and the Royal Air Force, 1932–1934." *War in History* 6 (1999): 306–330.

Meyer, Corky. "The Best World War II Fighter." *Flight Journal* (Aug. 2003): 30.

Michel, Henri. *La défaite de la France: Septembre 1939–juin 1940.* Paris: Presses Universitaires de France, 1980.

———. *Le procès de Riom.* Paris: Albin Michel, 1979.

Middlemas, Keith, and John Barnes. *Baldwin: A Biography.* London: Weidenfeld and Nicolson, 1969.

Mierzejewski, Alfred C. *The Most Valuable Asset of the Reich: A History of the German National Railway.* Vol. 2, *1933–1945.* Chapel Hill: University of North Carolina Press, 2000, 82–83.

Mignon, A. *Le service de santé rendu la guerre 1914–1918.* 4 vols. Paris: Masson, 1926–1927.

Miller, Donald L. *Masters of the Air.* New York: Simon and Schuster, 2006, 68.

Miller, Joyce Laverty. "The Syrian Revolt of 1925." *International Journal of Middle East Studies* 8, no. 4 (Oct. 1977): 545–565.

Miller, M., and R. A. Church. "Motor Manufacturing." In *British Industry Between the Wars: Instability and Industrial Development, 1919–1939,* edited by Neil K. Buxton and Derek H. Aldcroft. London: Scota Press, 1979, 179–215.

Miller, Ronald, and David Sawyers. *The Technical Development of Modern Aviation.* New York: Praeger, 1970.

Millet, Jerome. "Un exemple de lutte pour la superiorité aérienne: La Bataille de France." *Colloque Internationale—Histoire de la Guerre Aérienne* (Paris, 10–11 Sept. 1987): 93–113.

Millett, Allan R., and Williamson Murray. *Military Effectiveness.* Vol. 2, *The Interwar Period.* Winchester, MA: Allen & Unwin, 1988.

Millett, Allan R., Williamson Murray, and Kenneth H. Watman. "The Effectiveness of Military Organization." *International Security* 11, no. 1 (Summer 1986): 37–71.

Mitchell, Allan. "A Dangerous Game: The Crisis of Locomotive Manufacturing in France Before 1914." *Technology and Culture* (1995): 29–45.

Morewood, Steven. *The British Defence of Egypt 1935–1940: Conflict and Crisis in the Eastern Mediterranean.* Abingdon, UK: Frank Cass, 2005.

Morpurgo, J. E. *Barnes Wallis: A Biography.* London: Longman, 1972; New York: St. Martin's, 1972.

Morrow, John H. *The Great War: An Imperial History.* New York: Routledge, 2003.

———. *The Great War in the Air: Military Aviation from 1909 to 1921.* Washington, DC: Smithsonian Institution Press, 1993.

———. "Review Article: Refighting the First World War." *International History Review* 28, no. 3 (Sept. 2006): 560–566.

Moulton, J. L. *A Study of Warfare in Three Dimensions: The Norwegian Campaigns of 1940.* Athens, OH: Ohio University Press, 1967.

Mouré, Kenneth. "'Une eventualité absolument excluée': French Reluctance to Devaluation, 1933–1936." *French Historical Studies* 15, no. 3 (Spring 1988): 479–505.

Moy, Timothy. "Structure Ascendant: I. B. Holley, *Ideas and Weapons.*" *Technology and Culture* (Oct. 2005): 797–804.

Murray, Williamson. "Armored Warfare: The British, French, and German Experiences." In Williamson Murray and Allan R. Millett, eds., *Military Innovation in the Interwar Period.* New York: Cambridge University Press, 1996, 6–49.

———. "The Influences of Pre-War Anglo-American Doctrine on the Air Campaigns of the Second World War." In *The Conduct of the Air War in the Second World War: An International Comparison,* edited by Horst Boog. Oxford: Berg, 1988, 235–253.

———. "The Luftwaffe Experience, 1939–1941." In *Case Studies in the Development of Close Air Support,* edited by Benjamin Franklin Cooling. Washington, DC: Office of Air Force History, 1990.

———. *Strategy for Defeat: The Luftwaffe 1933–1945.* Maxwell AFB, AL: Air University Press, 1983; Baltimore: The Nautical and Aeronautical Publishing Co., 1986.

Murray, Williamson, and Allan R. Millett, eds. *Military Innovation in the Interwar Period.* New York: Cambridge University Press, 1996.

———. "The Strategy of the Phony War." *Military Affairs* (1981): 13–17.

Murray, Williamson, and Richard Hart Sinnreich. *The Past Is Prologue: The Impact of History to the Military Profession.* New York: Cambridge University Press, 2006.

Mysyrowicz, Ladislas. *Autopsie d'une défaite: Origins de l'effondrement militaire français de 1940.* Lausanne, Switzerland: L'Age d'Homme, 1973.

Neave-Hill, Col. W. B. R. "L'évolution de la stratégie franco-anglaise (1939–1940)." Comité d'histoire de la 2e Guerre Mondiale. *Français et Britannique dans la drôle de guerre, actes du colloque franco-britannique tenu à Paris du 8 au 12 décembre 1975.* Paris: Editions de Centre National de la Recherche Scientifique, 1979; *Colloque International* (Paris, 1975): 333–358.

Neiberg, Michael S. *Foch: Supreme Allied Commander in the Great War.* Dulles, VA: Potomac Books, 2003.

———. *The Second Battle of the Marne.* Bloomington: Indiana University Press, 2008.

Neilson, Keith. "Review of Joseph Moretz: *The Royal Navy and the Capitol Ship in the Interwar Period: An Operational Perspective.* London: Frank Cass, 2002." *International History Review* 25, no. 1 (Mar. 2003): 180–182.

Neville, Peter. *Hitler and Appeasement: The British Attempt to Prevent the Second World War.* London/New York: Hambledon Continuum, 2006.

Nicolson, Juliet. *The Great Silence, 1918–1920: Living in the Shadow of the Great War.*
    London: BBC History Books, 2009.
No. 1 Technical Training School, Halton. Halton, Buckinghamshire, UK: RAF Halton,
    ca. 1984.
Nogueres, Henri. *Munich: Peace for Our Time.* New York: McGraw Hill, 1965.
Nora, Pierre, ed. *Rethinking France: Les Lieux de Memoire.* Vol. 1, *The State.* Vol. 2,
    Space. Chicago: University of Chicago Press, 1999, 2006.
Northedge, F. S. *The Troubled Giant: Britain Among the Great Powers, 1916–1939.* New
    York: Frederick A. Praeger, 1966.
Nowarra, Heinz. *Heinkel He 111: A Documentary History.* London: Jane's, 1980.
Omissi, David E. *Air Power and Colonial Control: The Royal Air Force 1919–1939.*
    Manchester, UK: Manchester University Press, 1990.
Onderwater, Hans. *Second to None: The History of No. II (AC) Squadron, Royal Air
    Force, 1912–1992.* Shrewsbury, UK: Airlife, 1992, 35–76.
Orange, Vincent. *Dowding of Fighter Command: Victor of the Battle of Britain.* London:
    Grub Street, 2008.
———. *Sir Keith Park.* London: Methuen, 1984.
———. *Tedder.* London: Frank Cass, 2004.
Orde, Anne. *Great Britain and International Security, 1920–1926.* London: Royal
    Historical Society, 1978.
O'Riordan, Elspeth Y. *Britain and the Ruhr Crisis.* New York: Palgrave, 2001.
Osgood, Samuel M. *The Fall of France 1940: Causes and Responsibilities.* Boston: Heath,
    1965.
Overy, Richard J. *The Air War, 1939–1945.* New York: Stein and Day, 1980.
———. *The Battle of Britain: The Myth and the Reality.* London: Penguin, 2000; New
    York: W. W. Norton, 2000.
———. *Bomber Command, 1939–45.* London: Harper Collins, 1997.
———. *1939: Countdown to War.* New York, Viking, 2010.
———. "The German Prewar Aircraft Production Plans, November 1936–April 1939."
    English Historical Review 90, no. 357 (Oct. 1975): 778–797.
———. *The Inter-War Crisis, 1919–1939.* London: Pearson/Longman, 1994; 2nd ed.,
    2007.
———. *The Twilight Years: The Paradox of Britain Between the Wars.* New York: Viking,
    2009.
Paillole, Colonel Paul. *Fighting the Nazis: French Intelligence and Counter-Intelligence,
    1935–1945.* New York: Enigma Books, 2003.
Pakenham-Walsh, Major General R.[idley] P. *The History of the Corps of Royal
    Engineers.* Vol. 8, *1938–1945, Campaigns in France and Belgium, 1939–40,
    Norway, Middle East, East Africa, Western Desert, North West Africa, and
    Activities in the U.K.* Chatham, UK: Institution of Royal Engineers, 1958.
Pallud, Jean Paul. *Blitzkrieg in the West, Then and Now.* London: After the Battle, 1991.
Pannebecker, John. Review of Bruno Belhoste, *La formation d'une technocratie: L'école
    polytechnique et ses élèves de la révolution au deuxieme empire.* Paris: Belin,

2003, in *Technology and Culture* 46, no. 3 (July 2005): 618–622. [Pannebecker's review provides a useful introduction to the French *écoles*.]

Paoli, Col. François-André. *L'armée française de 1919 à 1939: La reconversion*. Vincennes: SHAA. (n.d.).

Papet, Philippe. L'armée de l'air et les accords de Munich: Étude de la presse parisienne de l'automne 1938. *Revue Historique des Armées* 2 (1980):141–170. Also published in *Recueil d'Articles et Études 1979-1981*. Vincennes: SHAA. (1986): 81–115.

Parker, H.[enry] M.[ichael] D.[enne]. *Manpower: A Study of Wartime Policy and Administration*. London: HMSO, 1957.

Parry, Matt. "Unemployment Revolutionizes the Working Class." *French History* 16, no. 4 (2002): 441–468.

Parton, Air Cdre. Neville. "The Development of Early RAF Doctrine." *Journal of Military History* 72, no. 4 (Oct. 2008): 1153–1177.

———. "Historic Book Review: *Victory Through Air Power*, by Maj. Alexandre P. de Seversky (1942)." *Royal Air Force Air Power Review* 11, no. 3 (Winter 2008): 88–94.

Passmore, Richard. *Blenheim Boy*. London: T. Harmsworth, 1981.

Patterson, Ian. *Guernica and Total War*. Cambridge, MA: Harvard University Press, 2007.

Paxton, Robert O. *Parades and Politics at Vichy: The French Officer Corps Under Marshal Pétain*. Princeton, NJ: Princeton University Press, 1966.

Payne, Stanley G. *France and Hitler: Spain, Germany, and World War II*. New Haven, CT: Yale University Press, 2008.

Peach, Stuart W. "A Neglected Turning Point in Air Power History: Air Power and the Fall of France." In *Air Power History: Turning Points from Kitty Hawk to Kosovo*, edited by Sebastian Cox and Peter Gray. London: Frank Cass, 2002, 142–172.

Peccia, Lt. Col. James D., III. "Defense Budgeting Challenges: Uncertainty and Unpredictability." *[U.S.] Air Force Journal of Logistics* 32, no. 3 (Fall 2008): 34–46.

Pedroncini, Guy. *Pétain, general en chef, 1917-1918*. Paris: Presses Universitaires de France, 1974.

Peer, Shanny. *France on Display: Peasants, Provincials, and Folklore in the 1937 Paris World's Fair*. Albany: State University Press of New York, 1998.

Pernot, François. "L'armée de l'air face aux crises des années trente: une étude du moral." *Revue Historique des Armées* 4 (1990): 116–127.

———. "Les missions aéronautiques françaises en Amérique du Sud dans les années vingt." *Revue Historiques des Armées* 4 (1991): 97–107.

Perry, Matt. "Unemployment Revolutionizes the Working Class: Le cri des chômeurs, French Communists and the Birth of the Movement of the Unemployed in France, 1931-1932." *French History* 16, no. 4 (Dec. 2002): 441–468. [French historians have long neglected the unemployed movement of the early 1930s though the archives have been open now for at least a decade (since 1992). At the time of the Great Depression, the French were behind in organizing the unemployed, an opportunity finally seized by the Communist Party, but it was unable to sustain a genuine national unemployment movement in France.]

Peyton-Smith, D. J. *Oil: A Study of Wartime Policy and Administration*. London: HMSO, 1971.

Philpott, William, and Martin S. Alexander. "The French and the British Field-Force: Moral Support or Material Contribution?" *Journal of Military History* 71, no. 3 (July 2007): 743–772.

Pile, Gen. Sir Frederick A.[rthur]. *Ack-Ack: Britain's Defence Against Air Attack During the Second World War*. London: Harrap, 1949; Panther, 1956.

Pollard, Sidney. *The Development of the British Economy, 1914–1967*, 2nd ed. London: Edward Arnold, 1969.

Porch, Douglas. "The Marne and After: A Reappraisal of French Strategy in the First World War." *Journal of Military History* 53, no. 4 (Oct. 1989): 363–386.

Porret, Daniel, and Franck Thevenet. *Les as de la guerre, 1939–1945*. 2 vols. Vincennes: SHAA. (1991).

Possony, Stefan T. "May 1940: The Pattern of Bad Generalship." *Military Affairs* 8, no. 1 (Spring 1944): 33–41.

Post, Gaines Jr. "Mad Dogs and Englishmen: British Rearmament, Deterrence, and Appeasement, 1934–35." *Armed Forces and Society* 14, no. 3 (Spring 1988): 329–357.

Postan, M. M., D. Hay, and J. D. Scott. *The Design and Development of Weapons: Studies in Government and Industrial Organization*. London: HMSO, 1964.

Powers, Barry P. *Strategy Without Slide Rule*. London: Croom Helm, 1976.

Prioux, Maj. René. [Articles on armored warfare, 1900–1924; unable to locate source.]

Probert, Air Cdre. H. A. *"Bomber" Harris: His Life and Times*. London: Greenhill Books, 2001.

Pugh, Peter. *The Magic of a Name: The Rolls-Royce Story*. 3 vols. Duxford, UK: Icon Books, 2000.

Purcell, Jennifer. *Domestic Soldiers: Six Women's Lives in the Second World War*. London: Constable and Robinson, 2010.

Quarrie, Bruce. *Action Stations: Supplement and Index*. Action Stations Series. Wellingborough, UK: Patrick Stephens, 1987.

R. L. [sic]. "Le service des essences jusqua au en 1942." *Revue Historique de l'Armée* 12, no. 1 (1956): 123–130.

RAF Historical Society Journal. (1982–)

Railston, David B. *The Army of the Republic: The Place of the Military in the Political Evolution of France, 1821–1914*. Cambridge, MA: The MIT Press, 1967.

Rainer-Horn, Gerd. *European Socialists Respond to Fascism: Ideology, Activism, and Contingency in the 1930s*. New York: Oxford University Press, 1996.

Raleigh, Sir Walter, and H. A. Jones. *The War in the Air*. 6 vols. London: HMSO, 1922–1937.

Ramsey, Winston G., ed. *The Battle of Britain Then and Now*. London: Battle of Britain Prints International, 1982.

Rasmussen, Jorgen S. "Party Discipline in Wartime: The Downfall of the Chamberlain Government." *Journal of Politics* 32, no. 2 (May 1970): 379–406.

Rawling, Gerald. "Lord Kitchener." *British Heritage* (Aug./Sept.1982): 30–33.

Ray, John. *The Battle of Britain: Dowding and the First Victory, 1940*. London: Cassell, 1994, 2002.

———. *The Battle of Britain: New Perspective—Behind the Scenes of the Great Air War*. London: Arms and Armour Press, 1994.

Reader, W. J. *Architect of Air Power: The Life of the First Viscount Weir*. London: Collins, 1968.

Record, Jeffrey. *The Specter of Munich: Reconsidering the Lessons of Appeasing Hitler*. Washington, DC: Potomac Books, 2007.

Renouvin, Pierre, and René Rénaud. *Léon Blum—chef de government, 1936–1937*. Paris: Presses de la Foundation Nationale des Sciences Politiques, 1981.

Review of the 2010 film *La rafle*. *The Economist* (20 Mar. 2010): 58.

Revue d'histoire de la seconde guerre mondiale, January 1969.

Revue Historique de l'Armée: Tables analytiques 1941–1988. Supplement au Numero IV (1963). [These are annual, not consolidated, indexes/tables of contents.]

Rexford-Welch, S/Ldr S. C. *Royal Air Force Medical Services.*Vol. 2, *Commands;* Vol. 3, *Campaigns.* History of the Second World War Series. London: HMSO, 1955.

Reynaud, Paul. *In the Thick of the Fight, 1930–1945*. Translated by James P. Lambert. New York: Simon and Schuster, 1955.

Reynolds, David. "1940: Fulcrum of the Twentieth Century?" *International Affairs* 66, no. 2 (Apr. 1990): 325–350.

Reynolds, Francis J., Allen L. Churchill, and Francis Trevelyan Miller, eds. *The Story of the Great War: History of the European War from Official Sources*. 15 vols. New York: P. F. Collier & Son, 1916; Holmes, PA: Weider History Group, [1916–1920], 2009– .

Reynolds, Sian. *France Between the Wars: Gender and Politics*. New York: Routledge, 1996.

Richard, Ivor. *We, the British: An Inside Look at Foibles, Customs, and Institutions*. New York: Doubleday, 1983.

Richardson, Charles O. "French Plans for Allied Attacks on the Caucasus Oil-Fields, January–April 1940." *French Historical Studies* 8, no. 1 (Spring 1973): 130–156.

Richardson, G/Capt. F. C. "Dickie." *Man Is Not Lost: The Log of a Pioneer RAF Pilot/Navigator, 1933–1946*. Shrewsbury, UK: Airlife, 1997.

Ritchie, Sebastian. "Aircraft Production Between the Wars." In *Biplane to Monoplane: Aircraft Development, 1919–1939*, edited by Philip Jarrett. London: Putnam; Herndon, VA: Brassey's, 1997.

———. *Industry and Air Power: The Expansion of British Aircraft Production, 1935–1941*. London: Frank Cass, 1997.

———. "A New Audit of War." *War and Society* 12 (May 1994): 125–147.

———. "The Price of Air Power: Technological Change, Industrial Policy, and Military Aircraft Contracts in the Era of British Rearmament, 1935–39." *Business History Review* 71, no. 1 (Spring 1997): 82–111.

Robb, Graham. *The Discovery of France: A Historical Geography from the Revolution to the First World War*. New York: W. W. Norton, 2007.

Robertson, A. J. "The British Airframe Industry and the State, 1918–1935: A Comment." *Economic History Review*. Also published in *Recueil d'Articles et*

Études 1981–1983. Vincennes: SHAA. (1987): 171–195; 28, no. 4 (Nov. 1975): 650–658.

Robertson, Bruce. *Aviation Archaeology,* 2nd ed. Cambridge: Patrick Stephens, 1983.

Robertson, F. A. de V. "Air Exercises, 1932." *Journal of the Royal United Service Institution* 77 (Nov. 1932): 808–814.

Robertson, Paul L. "Technical Education in the British Shipbuilding and Marine Engineering Industries, 1863–1914." *Economic History Review,* 2nd series, 26, no. 2 (May 1974): 236–251.

Robertson, Scot. *The Development of RAF Strategic Bombing Doctrine, 1919–1939.* Westport, CT: Praeger, 1995.

Robineau, Gen. Lucien. "French Air Policy in the Inter-war Period and the Conduct of the Air War Against Germany from September 1939 to June 1940." In *The Conduct of the Air War in the Second World War: An International Comparison,* edited by Horst Boog. New York: Berg, 1992, 627–657.

———. "L'armée de l'air dans la bataille de France." *Recueil d'Articles et Études, 1984–1985.* Vincennes: SHAA. (1991): 183–200.

———. *Letters of the Air and Space Academy* (June 2008): 2–3.

Robinson, Derek. *Piece of Cake.* London: H. Hamilton; New York: Knopf, 1984. [See also the video with Spitfires for the no-longer-available Hurricanes. New York: Knopf, 1984; on life in a fictional RAF fighter squadron in France, 1939–1940.]

Robinson, Frank, comp. *The British Flight Battalion at Pensacola and Afterwards.* Manhattan, KS: Sunflower University Press, 1984.

Rochat, Giorgio. "Douhet and the Italian Military Thought, 1919–1930." *Colloque International.* Paris: École Militaire du 4 au 7 Sept. 1984: 19–30.

Rogers, James Harvey. *The Process of Information in France, 1914–1927.* New York: Columbia University Press, 1929.

Romerstein, Herbert, and Eric Breindel. *The Venona Secrets: Exposing Soviet Espionage and America's Traitors.* Washington, DC: Regnery, 2000.

Roos, Joseph [Ingénieur général de l'air]. "La bataille de la production aérienne." *Icare* 59 (1971): 44–53.

Rosen, Barry R. *The Sources of Military Doctrine: France, Britain, and Germany Between the World Wars.* Ithaca, NY: Cornell, 1984.

Roskill, Stephen W. *Admiral of the Fleet Earl Beatty.* New York: Athenaeum, 1981.

———. *Hankey: Man of Secrets.* Vol. 1, *1919–1931.* London: Collins 1972.

———. *Naval Policy Between the Wars.* Vol. 1. *The Period of Anglo-Saxon Antagonism 1919–1929.* London: Collins, 1968.

———. "The Ten-Year Rule." *Journal of the Royal United Services Institute for Defence and Security Studies* 665 (Mar. 1972): 64–68.

Rossignol, Dominique. *Histoire de la propagande en France du 1940 à 1944: L'utopie de Pétain.* Paris: Presses Universitaires de France, 1991.

Rossi-Landi, Guy. "Le pacifism en France (1939–1940)." Comité de la 2e Guerre Mondiale, *Français et Britannique dans la drôle de guerre, actes du colloque franco-britannique tenu à Paris du 8 au 12 décembre 1975.* Paris: Editions de Centre National de la Recherche Scientifique, 1979; *Colloque International* (Paris, 1975): 123–153 (includes panel discussion).

Rossino, Alexander B. *Hitler Strikes Poland: Blitzkrieg, Ideology, and Atrocity.* Lawrence: University Press of Kansas, 2003.

Rousso, Henri. *The Vichy Syndrome: History and Memory in France Since 1944.* Cambridge, MA: Harvard University Press, 1987.

Rowe, Vivian. *The Great Wall of France: The Triumph of Her Maginot Line.* London: Putnam, 1959.

The Royal Air Force Builds for War: A History of Design and Construction in the RAF 1935–1945. Originally AP 3236 *Works,* Air Ministry (Air Historical Branch), 1956. London: HMSO, 1997.

Royal Air Force Historical Society. *Royal Air Force Reserve and Auxiliary Air Forces.* (Author, 2003); various authors.

———. *Royal Air Force Volunteer Reserve Memories* (RAF Historical Society, 1997); various authors.

Rubinstein, W. D. "British Millionaires, 1809–1949." *Bulletin of the Institute of Historical Research* (Nov. 1974): 202–223.

Sandbrook, Dominic. "Opinion: Chamberlain Deserves Our Admiration, Not Our Ridicule." *BBC History* 9, no. 6 (June 2008): 21.

Saunders, Hilary St. George. *Per Ardua: The Rise of British Air Power, 1911–1939.* London: Oxford University Press, 1944.

Saunders, Hillary St. George, and Dennis Richards. *The Royal Air Force: 1939–1945.* Vol. 1. London: HMSO, 1954.

Sauvy, Alfred. *Histoire économique de la France entre les deux guerres, 1939–1939.* Vol. 1, *De l'amistice à la dévaluation de la livre;* Vol. 2, *De Pierre Laval à Paul Reynaud.* Paris: Fayard, 1965, 1967.

Savage, C. I. *Inland Transport.* London: HMSO, 1957.

Schlaifer, Robert, and S. D. Heron. *The Development of Aircraft Engines and Aviation Fuels: Two Studies of Relations Between Government and Industry.* Boston: Harvard University, Graduate School of Business Administration, 1950.

Schuker, Stephen A. "France and the Penetration of the Rhineland." *French Historical Review* 14, no. 3 (Spring 1980): 299–338.

Scott, J. D., and Richard Hughes. *The Administration of War Production.* London: HMSO, 1955.

Seely, J. E. B. *Fear, and Be Slain: Adventures by Land, Sea, and Air.* London: Hodder and Stoughton, 1931.

Selsam, John Paul. *The Attempts to Form an Anglo-French Alliance 1919–1924.* Philadelphia: University of Pennsylvania Press, 1936.

Shambrook, Peter A. *French Imperialism in Syria, 1927–1936.* Reading, UK: Ithaca Press, 1998.

Shamod, Peter A. *French Imperialism in Syria, 1927–1936.* Reading, PA: Ithaca Press, 1998, 149–168.

Shapiro, Stanley. "The Celebrity of Charles Lindbergh." *Air Power History* 56, no. 1 (Spring 2009): 20–33.

Sharp, C. Martin. *DH: A History of De Havilland.* London: Faber and Faber, 1960; rev. ed., Shrewsbury, UK: Airlife, 1982.

Shay, Robert Paul. *British Rearmament in the Thirties: Politics and Profits*. Princeton, NJ: Princeton University Press, 1977.

Sheahan, John. *Promotion and Control of Industry in Postwar France*. Cambridge, MA: Harvard University Press, 1963.

Sheffield, G. D. *Leadership in the Trenches: Officer-Man Relations, Morale, and Discipline in the British Army in the Era of the First World War*. New York: Palgrave, 2000.

Sherman, Daniel J. *The Construction of Memory in Interwar France*. Chicago: University of Chicago Press, 1999.

Shipman, John. *One of the Few—The Memoirs of Wing Commander Ted "Shippy" Shipman*. Barnsley, UK: Pen and Sword Aviation, 2008.

Shirer, William L. *The Collapse of the Third Republic: An Inquiry into the Fall of France in 1940*. New York: Simon and Schuster, 1969.

Shlaim, Avi. "The British Offer of Union to France, June 1940." *Journal of Contemporary History* 9, no. 3 (July 1974): 27–63.

Shorter, Edward, and Charles Tilly. *Strikes in France, 1830–1968*. London: Cambridge University Press, 1974.

Showalter, Dennis E. *Hitler's Panzers: The Lightning Attacks That Revolutionized Warfare*. New York: Berkley Caliber, 2009.

———. "Military Innovations and the Whig Perspective of History." In *The Challenge of Change: Military Institutions and the New Realities, 1918–1941*, edited by Harold R. Winton and David Mets. Lincoln: University of Nebraska Press, 2000, 220–236.

Shuster, Richard J. *German Disarmament After World War I: The Diplomacy of International Arms Inspection, 1920–1931*. New York: Routledge, 2006.

Siegel, Mona L. *The Moral Disarmament of France: Education, Pacifism, and Patriotism, 1914–1940*. London: Cambridge University Press, 2006.

Silbey, David. *The British Working Class and Enthusiasm for War, 1914–1916*. London: Frank Cass, 2005.

Simon, Viscount [John Allsebrook]. *Retrospect: The Memoirs of the Rt. Hon. Viscount Simon, GCSI, GCVO*. London: Hutchinson, 1952.

Simpson, Diana. "France: Air Power, 1919–1945, Selected References at Air University Library." Accessed at www.au.af.mil/au/aul/bibs/france/france.htm.

Singer, Barnett. *Maxime Weygand: A Bibliography of the French General in Two World Wars*. Jefferson, NC: McFarland, 2008.

Sinnott, Colin. *The Royal Air Force and Aircraft Design, 1923–1939: Air Staff Operational Requirements*. London: Frank Cass, 2001.

Sixsmith, E. K. G. *British Generalship in the Twentieth Century*. London: Arms and Armour Press, 1969.

Slessor, W/Cdr. John C. *Air Power and Armies*. London: Oxford, 1936.

———. [MRAF Sir John]. *The Central Blue*. London: Cassell, 1956.

Smart, Nick. *British Strategy and Politics During the Phoney War: Before the Balloon Went Up*. Westport, CT: Praeger, 2003.

Smith, David J. *Britain's Military Airfields, 1939–1945*. Wellingborough, UK: Patrick Stephens, 1989.

———. *Military Airfields of Scotland, the North-East, and Northern Ireland.* Action Stations Series. Wellingborough, UK: Patrick Stephens, 1983, 1939.

———. *Military Airfields of Wales and the North-West.* Action Stations Series. Wellingborough, UK: Patrick Stephens, 1981.

Smith, Frederick Winston Furneaux [Earl of Birkenhead]. *The Prof in Two Worlds: The Official Life of Professor F. A. Lindemann, Viscount Cherwell.* London: Collins, 1961; U.S. title, *The Professor and the Prime Minister: The Official Life of Professor F. A. Lindemann, Viscount Cherwell.* Boston: Houghton Mifflin, 1962.

Smith, Herschel. *A History of Aircraft Piston Engines.* Manhattan, KS: Sunflower University Press, 1986.

Smith, J. R., and Antony Kay. *German Aircraft of the Second World War.* New York: Putnam, 1972.

Smith, Leonard V. *The Embattled Self: French Soldiers' Testimony of the Great War.* Ithaca, NY: Cornell University Press, 2007.

Smith, Leonard V., Stéphanie Audon-Rouzeau, and Annette Becker. *France and the Great War, 1914–1918.* New York: Cambridge University Press, 2003.

Smith, Malcolm. *British Air Strategy Between the Wars.* Oxford: Clarendon Press, 1984.

———. "The RAF and Counter-Force Strategy Before World War II." *Journal of the Royal United Services Institute for Defence and Security Studies* 121, no. 2 (1976): 68–77.

Smith, Michael Stephen. *The Emergence of Modern Business Enterprise in France, 1800–1930.* Cambridge, MA: Harvard University Press, 2006.

Smith, Richard K. "The Intercontinental Airliner and the Essence of Airplane Performance, 1929–1939." *Technology and Culture* 24, no. 3 (July 1983): 428–449.

Smith, W. H. B., and Joseph E. Smith. *Small Arms of the World.* Harrisburg, PA: Stackpole, 1962.

Snow, C. P. *Science and Government.* London: Oxford, 1961; Cambridge, MA: Harvard University Press, 1961; rev. 1962.

Spears, Edward [Major General Sir]. *Assignment to Catastrophe.* Vol. 2, *The Fall of France: June 1940.* London: William Heinemann, 1954.

———. *Prelude to Victory.* London: Jonathan Cape, 1939.

———. *Two Men Who Saved France: Pétain and de Gaulle.* New York: Stein & Day, 1966.

Spivak, Marcel. "Les problèmes posées à l'armée de l'air, et les perspectives d'independence de l'armée de l'air (1918–1934)." *Colloque International* (Paris, 4–7 Sept. 1984): 177–189.

Spotts, Frederick. *The Shameful Peace: How French Artists and Intellectuals Survived the Nazi Occupation.* New Haven, CT: Yale University Press, 2009.

"Squadron Leader" [pseud.]. *Basic Principles of Air Warfare: The Influence of Air Power on Sea and Land Strategy.* Aldershot, UK: Gale & Polden, 1927.

Steiner, James. *Hitler's Wehrmacht: German Armed Forces Support of the Fuhrer.* Jefferson, NC: McFarland, 2008.

Steiner, Rolf. "Hans Ulrich Rudel: Tueur de Chars." *Aero Journal* 37 (June–July 2004): 6–27.

Stewart, Mary Lynn. *Women, Work, and the French State: Labour Protection and Social Patriarchy, 1879–1919*. Kingston, Can.: McGill-Queen's University Press, 1989.

Stilton, Darrel. "The Structural Revolution." In *Biplane to Monoplane: Aircraft Development, 1919–1939*, edited by Philip Jarrett. London: Putnam; Herndon, VA: Brassey's, 1997.

Strachan, Hew. *European Armies and the Conduct of War*. London: George Allen & Unwin, 1983.

———. *The First World War*. 3 vols. New York: Oxford University Press, 2001– .

———. *The Politics of the British Army*. New York: Oxford University Press, 1997.

Suleiman, Ezra N. *Élites in French Society: The Politics of Survival*. Princeton, NJ: Princeton University Press, 1978.

———. *Politics, Power and Bureaucracy in France: The Administrative Elite*. Princeton, NJ: Princeton University Press, 1974.

Sullivan, Brian R. "Downfall of the Regia Aeronautica, 1933–1943." In *Why Air Forces Fail: The Anatomy of Defeat*, edited by Robin Higham and Stephen J. Harris. Lexington: University Press of Kentucky, 2006, 135–176.

Sumida, Jon T. "The Clausewitz Problem." *Army History* (Fall 2009): 17–21.

Sundbrook, Domnic. "Opinion: Chamberlain Deserves Our Admiration, Not Our Ridicule." *BBC History* (June 2008).

Sutherland, John, and Diane Canwell. *Images of War: Blitzkrieg Poland—Rare Photographs from Wartime Archives*. Barnsley, UK: Pen and Sword, 2010.

Swift, Will. *The Kennedys Amidst the Gathering Storm: A Thousand Days in London, 1938–1940*. Washington, DC: Smithsonian Institution Press, 2008.

Sykes, Sir Frederick. *From Many Angles*. London: Harrap, 1942.

Taylor, A. J. P. *English History, 1914–1945*. Vol. 15 of *The Oxford History of England*. London: Oxford University Press, 1965.

Taylor, Bill. *Halton and the Apprentice Scheme*. London: Midland Publishing, n.d. [ca. 1995].

Taylor, Douglas R. *Boxkite to Jet: The Remarkable Career of Frank B. Halford*. Derby, UK: Rolls-Royce Heritage Trust, 1999.

Taylor, H. A. *Fairey Aircraft Since 1915*. London: Putnam, 1974.

Taylor, J. W. R. *C.F.S.: Birthplace of Air Power*. London: Putnam, 1958.

Taylor, Telford. *The March of Conquest: The German Victories in Western Europe, 1940*. New York: Simon and Schuster, 1958.

Tedder, MRAF Lord. *With Prejudice*. London: Cassell, 1968.

Terraine, John. "The Theory and Practice of the Air War: The Royal Air Force." In *The Conduct of the Air War in the Second World War: An International Comparison*, edited by Horst Boog [1988]. Oxford: Berg, 1992, 467–495.

———. *To Win a War: 1918, The Year of Victory*. New York: Doubleday, 1981.

Teyssier, Arnaud. "L'appui aux forces de surface: L'armée de l'air à la réchèrche d'une doctrine (1933–1939)." *Colloque International—Histoire de la Guerre Aérienne, Hommage au Capitaine Guynemer*. (Paris: ENSTA, SHAA, IHCC, CEAS, 10–11 Sept. 1987), *Actes*. Vincennes: SHAA. (1988): 247–277.

———. "L'armée de l'air et l'aviation d'assaut, 1933–1939: Histoire de l'un malentendu." *Revue Historique des Armées* 1 (1989): 98–109.

———. "La crise en pied de l'armée de l'air . . . Dec. 1940." *Colloque de FEDN and IHCC.* (Paris, 1985): 323–337.

———. "Le général Vuillemin: Un haut responsible militaire face du danger allemande (1938–1939)." *Revue Historique des Armées* 2 (1987): 104–113.

Thetford, Owen. *Aircraft of the Royal Air Force.* London: Putnam, 1957; 8th ed., 1988.

———. *British Naval Aircraft Since 1912.* London: Putnam, 1977.

Thomas, Martin. "At the Heart of Things? French Imperial Defense Planning in the Late 1930s." *French Historical Studies* 21, no. 2 (Spring 1998): 325–361.

———. "European Crisis, Colonial Crisis? Signs of Fracture in the French Empire from Munich to the Outbreak of War." *International History Review* 32, no. 3 (September 2010): 389–413.

———. "France in British Signals Intelligence, 1939–1945." *French History* 14, no. 1 (Mar. 2000): 41–66.

Thompson, Mark. *The White War: Life and Death on the Italian Front 1915–1919.* London: Faber and Faber, 2008.

Thomson, Harry C., and Lida A. Mayo. *The Ordnance Department: Procurement and Supply.* In *The United States Army in World War II. The Technical Services.* Washington, DC: Office of the Chief of Military History, 1960.

Till, Geoffrey. "The Strategic Interface: The Navy and the Air Force in the Defence of Britain." *Journal of Strategic Studies* 1, no. 2 (1978): 179–193.

TIME. 26 Sept. 1969, 34–35.

The Times. London. 1934–1939; 5, 7 Sept. 1935; 8 Sept. 1936; 14, 18 Sept. 1937; 20 June 1938, 22; 20 July 1938, 22.

Toft, Monica Duffy, and Talbot C. Imlay. "Strategic and Military Planning Under the Fog of Peace." In *The Fog of Peace and War Planning: Military and Strategic Planning Under Uncertainty*, edited by Talbot C. Imlay and Monica Duffy Toft. London: Routledge, 2006, 1–10.

Tombs, Robert, and Isabelle Tombs. *That Sweet Enemy: The French and the British from the Sun King to the Present.* New York: Alfred A. Knopf, 2006.

Torigian, Michael. *Every Factory a Fortress: The French Labor Movement in the Age of Ford and Hitler.* Athens, OH: Ohio University Press, 1999.

Toubert, Joseph. *Étude statistical que des pertres subier par les français pendant la guerre 1914–18: Progrés accomplis dans le functionment de service de santé pendant la guerre.* Paris: Charles-Lavauzelle, 1920.

———. *Le service de santé militaire au grand quartier générale français (1918–1919).* Paris: Charles-Lavanzelle, 1934.

Toutain, J. C. "La population de la France de 1700 à 1959." *Cahiers de l'Institut de Science Economique Appliquée (ISEA)* 133 (Jan. 1963): 3–45.

Travers, T. H. E. [Tim]. *How the War Was Won.* London: Routledge, 1992.

———. *The Killing Ground: The British Army, the Western Front and Emergence of Modern Warfare 1900–1918.* London: Allen & Unwin, 1987.

Trenchard, Air Marshal Sir Hugh M. *Clausewitz* [See "Squadron Leader"].

———. Permanent Organisation of the Royal Air Force—Note by the Secretary of State for Air on a Scheme Outlined by the Chief of the Air Staff (Dec. 1919) [*Cmd. 467*. United Kingdom, AHB].

Trythall, Anthony. "Hitler and His Generals: The German General Staff and Blitzkrieg Reappraised." Review of Mathew Cooper, *The German Army 1933–1945: Its Political and Military Failure*. New York: Stein and Day, 1978, in *Journal of the Royal United Services Institute for Defence and Security Studies* (Dec. 1978): 74–75.

Turner, Arthur. *The Cost of War: British Policy on French War Debts, 1918–1932*. Brighton, UK: Sussex Academic Press, 1998.

Turner, C. C. [Major]. "The Aerial Defense of Cities: Some Lessons from the Air Exercises, 1928." *Journal of the Royal United Service Institution* 73 (Nov. 1928): 697–699.

Turner, E. S. *The Phoney War*. New York: St. Martin's, 1961.

Turner, John, ed. *Britain and the First World War*. London: Unwin Hyman, 1988.

———. "Cabinets, Committees, and Secretariats: The Higher Direction of War." In *War and the State: The Transformation of British Government, 1914–1919*, edited by Kathleen Burk. London: George Allen & Unwin, 1982, 57–79.

United Kingdom. Air Historical Branch (AHB). *Command Paper 467*, "An Outline of the Scheme for the Permanent Organisation of the Royal Air Force." Memorandum, Chief of the Air Staff Hugh Trenchard, 25 Nov. 1919.

———. *The Second World War, 1939–45*, Royal Air Force *Bases*, Royal Air Force *Works* (AP.3236), in Public Record Office [PRO] AIR 10/5559, 1956.

———. Air Ministry. *Abteilung* [Department] VI, [Intelligence] CAB [Cabinet] 106/262.

———. *The Luftwaffe in Poland* (11 July 1944), Air Historical Branch translation of the 8th *Abteilung*, history in CAB 106/282.

———. *Rise and Fall of the German Air Force, 1933–1945*. London: HMSO, 1948; Leeds, UK: Arms and Armour, 1983.

———. Great Britain Home Office. *Air Raid Precautions*. London: HMSO, 1938; Stroud, UK: Tempus, 2007.

———. National Archives [formerly Public Record Office (PRO)]. Air Historical Branch (AHB), AIR 5/299, Air Publication (AP) 882, *CD 22 [Confidential Document], Operations Manual for the Royal Air Force* (July 1922).

———. National Archives [formerly Public Record Office]. Aircraft Daily State Lists, Sept. 1939, Apr./May 1945; AIR 2/5246; AIR 5/564, 17 January 1921; AIR 9/78; AIR 9/105, AFC 14, *Anglo-French Staff Conversations: Preparations of Joint Plans for Action for Franco-British Air Force*, and AFC 30, *Anglo-French Staff Conversations, 1939: Summarized History of the Conversations*; AIR 10/906, "Schedule of Fittings and Accessories for Aircraft Engines" (1923) and "Airframes" (1917–); AIR 10/1442 (1928), 1445 (1928), 1447, 1448 (1929), 1458 (1929), 1459 (1930), 1470 (1930), 1471 (1931), 1479 (1931), 1480 (1932), 1492 (1932), 1493 (1933), 1560 (1934), 1561 (1934), 1573 (1932, 1933), 1574, 1586 (1934), 1587 (1935), 1588 (1936), 1589 (1936), 1590 (1937), 1591 (1937), 1592 (1938), 1593 (1938); AIR 10/1594, 1934 edition of Air Staff Memorandum No.

50, *Data for the Calculation of Wastage and Consumption in War;* AIR 10/1595, *SD98, Air Staff Memorandum No. 50* (3rd ed., Sept. 1936), *Data for Calculating Consumption and Wastage in War,* tables 1, 8, 16, 17; AIR 10/1644, *SD* [Secret Document] *128,* July 1939, *Air Ministry Handbook on the German Air Force,* 56; AIR 10/1648, *SD132, Handbook of the French Air Forces.* London: Air Ministry, Jan. 1939; *SD139, Handbook on the French Air Force;* AIR 10/1659, *SD98;* AIR 10/3916, 4th edition (1941–1943) of *SD98;* AIR 10/5351, *Flying Training, Policy and Planning* (1937), 529–561; AIR 10/5520, *The Second World War, 1939–1945,* Royal Air Force, *Signals,* Vol. 5, *Fighter Control and Interception* (*CD116,* 1952), 42–48; AIR10/5551, AP3233, *Flying Training.* Vol. 1, *Policy and Planning.* London: Air Ministry, AHB, 1952, 48–107, 272–273; AIR 10/5552, *CD1131, Maintenance.* London: Air Ministry, AHB, 1951, 6–54; AIR 10/5559, *CD1131, Maintenance* (1954) and AP [Air Publication] 3236 *Works* (1956); AIR 16/942; AIR 16/943; AIR 16/944; AIR 16/945; AIR 19/572; AIR 16/983; AIR 20/32, *Review of Air Defence Policy, 1923–1935;* AIR 20/1835 of June 11, 1945; AIR 20/4174; AIR 20/5246, Report by AOC, No. 11 Group, 7 Nov. 1940; AIR 27/703, ORB of No. 85 Squadron, ORB of No. 1 Savage and Repair Unit; AIR 29/802; AIR 33, Reports of the Inspector General; AIR 40/2032, Minutes of a meeting at the Air Ministry, London, to discuss the establishment of the AASF in France; AIR 41/14; AIR 41/21, First Draft of the Air Historical Branch (AM), *The War in France-Flanders* (n.d.), The Air Historical Branch Narrative of the Battle of France [*The Campaign in France 10 May–18 June 1940; The Campaign in France and the Low Countries,* Sept. 1939–June 1940, especially pp. 1–32, 273–285, 425]; AIR 41/22, 12–28, Appendices 13–14; AIR 41/65, RAF monograph, *Manning: Plans and Policy,* n.d.; AIR 44/27, 129; AIR 50/1564, *20th Report on Flying Accidents During July–December 1933*(*SD90 [2]*) (Apr. 1934); AP [Air Publication], *History of Flying Training in the RAF* (1952); AP113, *Vocabulary of Stores for the Royal Air Force* (*prices*); AP1086 and 1086A; CAB 3/3, CID, *Note on the Comparative Cost of the British and French Air Services,* CID 106-A, July 1922.

———. Public Record Office. Ministry of Aircraft Production [PRO AVIA] 46/228, "Aircraft: The Spares Problem—Narrative."

———. Public Record Office. Ministry of Munitions [MUN] 5/187/137011. MUN 5/360/1000, *The History of the Ministry of Munitions,* 12 vols. London: HMSO, 1918–1922.

———. War Office [WO]. *Notes on the French Army. Prepared by the General Staff of the War Office.* July 1936, as amended November 1937. (PRO WO 287/17).

United States. Air Force. *Tooling for War: Military Transformation in the Industrial Age,* USAF Academy Library, Special Bibliographical Series No. 87. Colorado Springs, CO, Sept. 1994.

———. Army General Staff. *Combat Estimate: France* (rev. 1 Oct. 1939 and 6 Apr. 1940), 236-D-France. National Archives and Records Administration.

———. War Department. *The German Campaigns in Norway and Sweden 1940—Operation Weserübung.* Derbyshire, UK: Military Library Research Service [MLRS], reprint 2005.

Urquhart, Diana. *The Ladies of Londonderry: Women and Political Patronage*. London: J. B. Taurus, 2007.

Vaisse, Maurice. "Le procès de l'aviation de bombardement." *Revue Historique des Armées* 2 (1977): 41–61.

Vajda, Ferenc A., and Peter Dancey. *German Aircraft Industry and Production, 1933–1945*. Shrewsbury, UK: Airlife, 1998.

van Creveld, Martin. *Supplying War: Logistics from Wallenstein to Patton*. London: Cambridge University Press, 1977.

———. *The Training of Officers*. New York: The Free Press, 1990.

Van Haute, André. *Pictorial History of the French Air Force*. Vol. 1, *1909–1940*. London: Ian Allan, 1974.

Vann, Frank. *Willy Messerschmitt. First Full Biography of an Aeronautical Genius*. Sparkford, UK: Patrick Stephens, 1993.

Varley, Karine. "Under the Shadow of Defeat: The State and the Commemoration of the Franco-Prussian War, 1871–1914." *French History* 16, no. 3 (Sept. 2002): 323–344.

Vennesson, Pascal. "Institution and Air Power: The Making of the French Air Force." *Journal of Strategic Studies* 18 (1995): 36–67.

Verry, Vital. *L'aviation populaire*. Paris: Editions du Genfaut, 2007.

Vincent, K. Steven, and Alison Klairmont-Lingo, eds. *The Human Tradition in Modern France*. Wilmington, DE: SR Books, 2000.

Vinen, Richard. *The Politics of French Business 1936–1945*. New York: Cambridge University Press, 1991.

———. *The Unfree French: Life Under the Occupation*. New Haven, CT: Yale University Press, 2006.

Vivier, Thierry. "La commission G entre la défaite et l'armée de l'air de future (1941–1942)." *Revue Historique de l'Armée* 3, no. 176 (1989): 113–121.

———. *La politique aéronautique militaire de France: Janvier 1933–septembre 1939*. Paris: Editions Harmattan, 1997.

———. "Le général Denain, bâtisseur de l'Armée de l'Air." *Revue Historique des Armées* 4 (1990): 108–115; also in *Revue Historique des Armées* 3 (1993): 21–31.

———. "Pierre Cot et la naissance de l'armée de l'air (1933–1934)." *Revue Historique des Armées* 4 (1990): 108–115.

Wagstaff, Peter. *War and Society in Twentieth Century France*. Oxford: Berg, 1991.

Wallace, G. F. *The Guns of the Royal Air Force 1939–1945*. London: Kimber, 1972.

Wandycz, Piotr S. *The Twilight of French Eastern Alliances, 1926–1936: French-Czechoslovak-Polish Relations from Locarno to the Remilitarization of the Rhineland*. Princeton, NJ: Princeton University Press, 1988.

Wark, Wesley K. "The Air Defence Gap: British Air Doctrine and Intelligence Warnings in the 1930s." In *The Conduct of the Air War in the Second World War: An International Comparison, 1988*, edited by Horst Boog. Oxford: Berg, 1992, 511–526.

———. "British Military and Economic Intelligence: Assessments of Nazi Germany Before the Second World War." In *The Missing Dimension: Governments and*

Intelligence Communities in the Twentieth Century, edited by Christopher Andrew and David Dilks. London: Macmillan, 1984.

——. *The Ultimate Enemy: British Intelligence and Nazi Germany, 1933–1939*. Ithaca, NY: Cornell University Press, 1985.

Warner, Philip. *The Battle of France: 10 May–22 June 1940: Six Weeks That Changed the World*. New York: Simon and Schuster, 1990.

Watkins, Geoff. "Review Article: Recent Work on France and the Second World War." *Journal of Contemporary History* (2002): 637–647.

Watson, Alexander. *Enduring the Great War: Combat, Morale, and Collapse in the German and British Armies, 1914–1918*. London: Cambridge University Press, 2008.

Watson, Janet S. K. *Fighting Different Wars: Experience, Memory, and the First World War in Britain*. New York: Cambridge University Press, 2003.

Watson, Mark S. *Chief of Staff: Prewar Plans and Preparations*. Washington, DC: Historical Division, Department of the Army, 1950.

Watt, D. C. "The Anglo-German Naval Agreement of 1935: An Interim Judgment." *Journal of Modern History* 28, no. 2 (June 1956): 155–175.

Watts, Barry, and Williamson Murray. "Military Innovation in Peacetime." In *Military Innovation in the Interwar Period*, edited by Williamson Murray and Allan R. Millett. New York: Cambridge University Press, 1996, 369–415.

Weber, Eugen J. *The Hollow Years: France in the 1930s*. New York: W. W. Norton, 1994.

Webster, Sir Charles, and Noble Frankland. *The Strategic Air Offensive Against Germany, 1939–45*. 4 vols. London: HMSO, 1961.

Weinberg, Gerhard L. "Hitler and England, 1933–1945: Pretense and Reality." *German Studies Review* 8, no. 2 (May 1985): 299–309.

Weinberger, Barbara. *Keeping the Peace? Policing Strikes in Britain, 1906–1926*. Oxford: Berg, 1990.

Werth, Alexander. *The Twilight of France, 1933–1940*. New York: Harper, 1942, 1966.

Westermann, Edward B. "Fighting for the Heavens from the Ground: German Ground-Based Air Defenses in the Great War, 1914–1918." *Journal of Military History* 65 (Apr. 2001): 641–670.

——. *Flak: German Anti-Aircraft Defenses, 1914–1945*. Lawrence: University Press of Kansas, 2001.

Weygand, Gen. Maxime. *Recalled to Service: The Memoirs of General Maxime Weygand of the Academie Français*. Translated by E. W. Dickes. 3 vols. Paris: 1950–1951.

Wheeler, Air Cdre. Allen Henry. *"That Nothing Failed Them."* London: G. T. Foulis, 1963.

Whittell, Giles. "When Women Flew Spitfires." *BBC History* 8, no. 11 (Nov. 2007): 26–27.

Williams, Anthony G. *Rapid Fire: The Development of Automatic Cannon, Heavy Machine Guns and Their Ammunition for Armies, Navies, and Air Forces*. Shrewsbury, UK: Airlife, 2000.

Williams, Anthony G., and Emmanuel Gustin. *Flying Guns: World War I and Its Aftermath, 1914–1932*. Shrewsbury, UK: Airlife [Crowood Press], 2003.

Williams, Charles. *Pétain: How the Hero of France Became a Convicted Traitor and Changed the Course of History*. New York: Macmillan, 2005.

Williams, George Kent. *Biplanes and Bombsights: British Bombing in World War I*. Maxwell AFB, AL: Air University Press, 1999.

Williams, John. *The Ides of May*. London: Constable, 1968.

Williams, W. T. S. "Air Exercises 1927." *Journal of the Royal United Service Institution* 72 (Nov. 1927): 739–745.

Williamson, Gordon. *The Luftwaffe Handbook, 1939–1945*. Stroud, UK: Sutton, 2006.

Wilson, C. M., and W. J. Reader. *Men & Machines: D. Napier & Son, 1808–1958*. London: Weidenfeld and Nicolson, 1958.

Windrow, Martin C. *Aircraft in Profile*, 1.2. London: Profile, 1965. [Includes the Heinkel He 111H.]

Winter, J. M. [Jay Murray]. *The Experience of World War I*. London: Oxford University Press, 1989.

———. *Remembering War: The Great War and Historical Memory in the Twentieth Century*. New Haven, CT: Yale University Press, 2006.

Winter, Jay, ed. *The Legacy of the Great War: Ninety Years On*. Columbia: University of Missouri Press, 2009.

Winter, Jay, Geoffrey Parker, and Mary Habeck, eds. *The Great War and the Twentieth Century*. New Haven: Yale University Press, 2000.

Winterbotham, F. W. *Secret and Personal* [U.S. title, *The Nazi Connection*]. London: Kimber, 1969; Harper Collins, 1978.

———. *The ULTRA Secret*. London: Weidenfeld and Nicolson, 1974.

Winton, Harold R., and David R. Mets, eds. *The Challenge of Change: Military Institutions and the New Realities, 1918–1941*. Lincoln: University of Nebraska Press, 2000.

Wise, Sydney F. *The Official History of the Royal Canadian Air Force*. Vol. 1, *Canadian Airmen and the First World War*. Toronto, Can.: University of Toronto Press, 1980.

Wiser, William. *The Twilight Years: Paris in the 1930s*. London: Robson Books, 2001.

Wood, Anthony Terry [Tony], and Bill Gunston. *Hitler's Luftwaffe: A Pictorial and Technical Encyclopedia of Hitler's Air Power in World War II*. London: Salamander, 1977.

Wood, Chalmers. "The French Navy and Parliament Between the Wars." *International History Review* 6, no. 3 (Aug. 1983): 386–403.

Wood, Derek. *Attack Warning Red: The Royal Observer Corps and the Defence of Britain, 1925–1975*. London: Macdonald and Jane's, 1976.

Wormser, Georges. *La république de Clemenceau*. Paris: Presses Universitaires de France, 1961.

Wragg, David. *"Sink the French!" At War with an Ally—1940*. South Yorkshire, UK: Pen and Sword Books, 2007.

Wright, Julian. "The State and the Left in Modern France." *French History* 21, no. 4 (Dec. 2007): 450–472. [A historiographical essay.]

Wright, Robert. *The Man Who Won the Battle of Britain*. New York: Scribner's, 1969.

Wrigley, Chris. "The Ministry of Munitions: An Innovative Department." In *War and the State: The Transformation of British Government, 1914–1919*, edited by Kathleen Burk. London: George Allen & Unwin, 1982.

Yool, M. W. "Air Exercises 1930." *Journal of the Royal United Service Institution* 75 (Nov. 1930): 755–762.

Young, Robert J. *France and the Origins of the Second World War*. London: Macmillan; New York: St. Martin's Press, 1996.

———. *In Command of France: French Foreign Policy and Military Planning, 1933–1940*. Cambridge: Harvard University Press, 1978.

———. "Preparation for Defeat: French War Doctrine in the Interwar Period." *Journal of European Studies* 2, no. 2 (June 1972): 155–172.

———. "The Strategic Dream: French Air Doctrine in the Inter-War Period, 1919–1939." *Journal of Contemporary History* 9, no. 4 (Oct. 1974): 57–76.

———. "The Use and Abuse of Fear: France and the Air Menace in the 1930s." *Intelligence and National Security* 4, no. 2 (Oct. 1987): 88–109.

Zdatny, Steven. *Fashion, Work, and Politics in Modern France*. New York: Palgrave Macmillan, 2006.

Zimmerman, David. *Britain's Shield: Radar and the Defeat of the Luftwaffe*. Stroud, UK: Sutton, 2001.

INDEX

About the Author

Robin Higham was born in the United Kingdom and educated there and in the United States. He served in the RAF as a pilot. He is the author of numerous books and articles in the field of aviation history. He was professor of military history at Kansas State University for thirty-five years.